ORDERS FROM THE TOP

I watched Ed Clark testify about the usual manner in which he and another FBI supervisor, Ed Quinn, conducted an interview with convicted Boston marijuana trafficker Joseph Murray in 1989. Murray was a longtime confederate of Whitey Bulger and Steve Flemmi, the FBI's prized informants, and was offering to implicate them in no less than three unsolved murders. Murray was also saying that two FBI agents, John Connolly and John Newton, had been selling information on government investigations to Bulger and Flemmi.

I was stunned to hear Clark testify under oath that he and Quinn didn't ask Murray a single question about the three killings. Nor was Murray's offer to cooperate ever followed up after the interview was over, he said. Finally, Clark admitted that Quinn's report of the meeting was placed in the FBI's highly sophisticated filing system in a manner that effectively hid it from other agents seeking information on the murders.

Clark's explanation: He had just been doing what his bosses at the FBI told him to do.

My God, I thought, *this was supposed to be one of the good guys.*

DEADLY ALLIANCE

THE FBI'S SECRET PARTNERSHIP WITH THE MOB

RALPH RANALLI

HarperTorch
An Imprint of HarperCollinsPublishers

DEADLY ALLIANCE is the journalistic account of the history of the FBI's Top Echelon Informant Program. The events recounted in this book are true. The scenes and dialogue have been reconstructed based on interviews, police department records, and published news stories. Quoted testimony has been taken verbatim from pre-trial transcripts and other sworn statements.

❦

HARPERTORCH
An Imprint of HarperCollins*Publishers*
10 East 53rd Street
New York, New York 10022-5299

Copyright © 2001 by Ralph Ranalli
ISBN: 0-380-81193-6

First HarperTorch paperback printing: July 2001

HarperCollins ®, HarperTorch™, and ❦ ™ are trademarks of HarperCollins Publishers Inc.

Printed in the United States of America

Visit HarperTorch on the World Wide Web at www.harpercollins.com

10 9 8 7 6 5 4 3 2 1

For my wife and the player to be named later

•••••••••••••••••••••••••••••••

Acknowledgments

•••••••••••••••••••••••••••••

A great many people were instrumental in helping with the writing of this book and are deserving of great praise and my everlasting gratitude. First, no one was more important to this project than the editors at the *Boston Globe,* particularly Patricia Nealon and Peter Canellos, whose offer of a flexible work schedule while writing for New England's premier news organization was a gift of immeasurable value. I am also indebted to my agent, Kristen Wainwright of Boston Literary Group, and my editor at Avon Books, Sarah Durand, for their unflagging enthusiasm for this project. I would also like to thank my former employer, the *Boston Herald,* for the opportunity to cover this incredible story and for granting permission for use of many of the photos in this book.

Many other people in the law enforcement and legal communities were extremely helpful, but five merit particular mention: former FBI Assistant Special Agent in Charge Robert Fitzpatrick, Tulsa Police Sgt. Michael Huff, former Tulsa Assistant District Attorney Jerry Truster, and Boston attorneys Anthony Cardinale and Kenneth Fishman. All five of these men were distinguished not only for their helpfulness but for their dogged determination in seeing that the truth behind the FBI's Top Echelon Informant Program would out. On that score, numerous members of the Massachusetts State Police and other federal agencies also merit outstanding mention, including Capt. Thomas Foley, Lt. Richard Fralick, Lt. Thomas Duffy, Sgt. Greg Foley and troopers John Tutungian and Steve Johnson, former State Police investigators Joseph Saccardo, Robert Long, and

Henry "Chip" Werner; IRS Criminal Investigation Division Special Agent David Lazarus; and DEA Special Agent Dan Doherty. Authorities in Connecticut and Miami were also invaluable in their assistance, especially Metro-Dade Police detectives Ram Nyberg and Greg Smith, and several current and former Connecticut State Police investigators, especially Dan Twoomey and Andrew Ocif. Several other attorneys contributed to this work, including John Mitchell, Robert George, and Richard Egbert. U.S. District Court Judge Mark L. Wolf is also to be commended for his courage in dealing with this case and making it open—albeit carefully at times—to the public and press. Also helpful were numerous relatives of the characters in this story, including Larry and David Wheeler, Carolyn Wood, and Emily and Chris McIntyre. There were also many people who were helpful to this work who did so only on the condition that their names not be mentioned, but they know who they are.

I would also like to thank the prosecutors at U.S. Attorney Donald K. Stern's office—although some were slower to come around than others, they all eventually recognized the problems in the FBI for what they were. Meriting particular mention are U.S. Attorney Stern and Assistant U.S. Attorneys James Herbert, Fred Wyshak, and Brian Kelly. While it was often difficult to get documents important to the case, several people were very helpful, including Suffolk County Clerk of Courts John Nucci; Wolf's courtroom clerk, Basil Cronin; Dayna Hansen of the U.S. Justice Department Press Office in Washington, D.C.; and Donald Stern's press liaison, Samantha Martin. Several other former FBI officials were also helpful, including Oliver "Buck" Revell and R. Wesley Swearingen.

Other reporters did considerable work on this story, and I would be remiss not to mention them here, particularly Ron Gollobin of WCVB-TV, Dan Rea of WBZ-TV, *Boston Herald* reporter Jon Wells and columnists Peter Gelzinis and Howie Carr, and *Boston Globe* reporters Kevin Cullen, Shelley Murphy, Dick Lehr, Gerard O'Neill, and Christine Chinlund. Also, of course, former reporters Paul Corsetti and Jim Southworth, who risked more than their reputations pursuing the story. I would also like to thank the various television and radio outlets that have asked me to provide expert commentary on this story, including Chris Lydon and Elizabeth First of WBUR-FM radio and NPR's "The Connection," Fred Rothenberg and "Dateline NBC," Chris Szechenyi and Bill Curtis of A&E's "Investigative Reports," Rick Segall of Fox Television's "America's Most Wanted," David Brudnoy and Lovell Dyett of WBZ-AM radio and the staff of New England Cable News.

Most of all I must thank my wonderful wife, Jill, my parents, my in-laws, my brothers and sisters and other family members, for their patience as I spent time in front of my computer instead of with them through countless late nights, early mornings, weekends, and missed birthdays and holidays. Many friends also offered invaluable support and encouragement, particularly Ted Doyle, Allison Hill, and *Globe* writers Brian McGrory and Matthew Brelis. Special thanks also go to my attorney and good friend David Herlihy, and to Warren Rogers for helping me see the honor and value of journalism as a profession.

Contents

....

Key Figures

....

James J. Bulger, aka "Whitey"—South Boston crime boss, multiple murderer and member of the FBI's Top Echelon Informant Program for as long as twenty years.

Dennis Condon—FBI agent who originally helped recruit Whitey Bulger in the early 1970s.

John Connolly—longtime FBI agent and South Boston native who became the Boston FBI office's chief recruiter of Top Echelon informants and the primary handler for James "Whitey" Bulger, Stephen J. Flemmi, Angelo "Sonny" Mercurio, and numerous others; later arrested on federal racketeering charges.

Robert Fitzpatrick—Boston FBI Assistant Special Agent in Charge who recommended that Bulger and Flemmi be discontinued as Top Echelon informants.

Stephen J. Flemmi, aka "The Rifleman"—Winter Hill Gang crime boss, multiple murderer, and survivor of Boston's infamous Irish gang wars of the 1960s who became a thirty-year Top Echelon informant and Whitey Bulger's partner in crime.

J. Edgar Hoover—longtime director and chief architect of the modern FBI; ordered the widespread recruiting of underworld killers as long-term secret sources of information.

John V. Martorano—prolific underworld hit man; later struck a plea deal to become a government witness and admitted to committing twenty murders, many allegedly on orders from Stephen Flemmi and Whitey Bulger.

Angelo Mercurio, aka "Sonny"—member of the Patriarca family of the Italian-American Mafia in New England and Top Echelon informant.

John Morris—Boston FBI Organized Crime Squad supervisor and handler of informants who admitted taking bribes from Stephen Flemmi and Whitey Bulger; later testified for the government after being granted immunity from prosecution.

Jeremiah T. O'Sullivan—New England Organized Crime Strike Force chief prosecutor who played a key role keeping Top Echelon informants out of jail and on the streets.

Larry Allen Potts—Boston FBI Assistant Special Agent in Charge, who was later nominated by FBI Director Louis Freeh as second-in-command for the entire Bureau but resigned in disgrace after allegations of misconduct and cover-up in the FBI's handling of the siege at Ruby Ridge.

Jackie Presser—mob-connected Teamsters Union president and longtime Top Echelon informant.

H. Paul Rico—prolific Boston FBI informant recruiter in the 1960s who later became chief of security for World Jai Alai, a Miami gaming company with alleged underworld ties.

Gregory Scarpa—top Columbo family Mafioso from New York, who committed numerous murders while working as a Top Echelon informant.

Kevin J. Weeks—South Boston native and longtime lieutenant of Whitey Bulger and Stephen Flemmi who later became a government witness.

William F. Weld—U.S. Attorney for Massachusetts who later became Chief of the Criminal Division for the U.S. Department of Justice.

Foreword

••••••••••••••••••••••••••••••

There is always a possibility that a secret police may become a menace to free governments and free institutions, because it carries with it the possibility of abuses of power that are not always quickly apprehended or understood.

> Attorney General Harlan Fiske Stone cautioning J. Edgar Hoover while naming him Director of the U.S. Bureau of Investigation (later renamed the FBI) in 1924

THIS BOOK WAS inspired by two eye-opening experiences I had during early court hearings in a federal racketeering case, *United States* v. *Francis P. Salemme et al.*, in Boston. The courageous U.S. District Court judge in the *Salemme* case, Mark L. Wolf, ordered the hearings in an effort to uncover criminal acts and unethical conduct by FBI agents and federal prosecutors who worked with high-level organized crime informants. I was the sole journalist to cover all 150 days of the historic early proceedings in Judge Wolf's courtroom, which exposed, to an unprecedented extent, the sordid machinations of the FBI's secret Top Echelon Informant Program.

The first was my rediscovery—after spending more than

1

an hour excavating dusty files in my twelfth floor office in
the aging granite J.W. McCormack Post Office and Courthouse in downtown Boston—of some papers I'd received a
few years earlier from FBI Headquarters in Washington.

They were copies of Section 137 of the FBI's *Manual of
Investigative and Operational Guidelines*, which I'd obtained through a federal Freedom of Information Act request. They hadn't panned out as a story for my
then-employer, the *Boston Herald*, but I had hung onto them
anyway being something of a compulsive filer. Section 137
covered the FBI's rules on handling confidential sources of
information, and I wanted to see if the manual said anything
about something called the "Top Echelon Informant Program," which the lawyers had been mentioning in court.

I was curious because two of Boston's most powerful organized crime figures and notorious killers, James J.
"Whitey" Bulger and Stephen "the Rifleman" Flemmi, had
been exposed as members of the Top Echelon program during the misconduct hearings, yet no one in Boston outside
the FBI seemed to know exactly what it was. I had asked
everyone I could think of about it, including four former
United States Attorneys, several top U.S. Drug Enforcement
Administration officials, agents from the U.S. Bureau of Alcohol, Tobacco and Firearms and of the DEA, as well as a
score of federal prosecutors and longtime organized crime
defense attorneys.

"Never heard of it," was the universal reply.

As I flipped through the pages, I finally found two sections headed TOP ECHELON CRIMINAL INFORMANT PROGRAM.
Some FBI press officer, however, had taken a black Magic
Marker and blotted out all the other text. There was virtually
nothing left to indicate whatsoever who Top Echelon informants were supposed to be or why they were recruited.

Curious, I called the FBI press office in Boston.

"You'll have to call Washington," the reply came back.

I did.

"FBI Press Office," a male voice answered.

"Hi. I'm a reporter calling from Boston, my name is Ralph Ranalli and I work for the *Herald.*"

"What can I do for you?"

"I was hoping to get some information on something called the Top Echelon Informant Program. It's come up as an issue during some hearings up here in Boston."

"Sorry. We don't talk about our informant programs. Ever."

"But I just—"

"Ever." He cut me off.

"You mean you can't answer even one question about informants?"

"No."

"Okay, then what's your name?"

"Why?"

"I just want to quote you saying you can't say anything."

"You can't quote me," he said, a note of panic creeping into his voice.

"Why not?"

"I'd get in trouble. I thought we were off-the-record. And I'm certainly not telling you my name."

I was stunned. "Nobody said anything about being off-the-record," I said. "You mean you can't even be quoted saying you can't say anything about the FBI's informant programs?"

"Yes. This phone call is over. Good-bye." The line went dead.

I was beginning to realize that the FBI didn't like to talk about how it handled informants during its forty-year war on the Mafia.

As the hearings unfolded I learned more about the Top Echelon program and how high-level informants committed larceny, extortion, assault, and scores of murders—all while being protected and even abetted by FBI agents who treated them more like close friends than dangerous criminals. The more I learned, the more I became troubled by the Bureau's stubborn insistence on keeping details of the program a secret.

I had never encountered a situation quite like this before—
a federal agency was insisting that it could keep a matter of
purely domestic government policy a secret from an American citizen, namely me. Even as a journalist and longtime
advocate of First Amendment rights, I have no problem with
the FBI or other law enforcement agencies keeping secret
the *details* of a particular investigation or operation. Such
secrecy is a common and often-necessary tool used to protect the safety of law enforcement officers, the integrity of
the probe, and the privacy rights of persons under investigation. I firmly believe, however, that it is both morally offen-
sive and fundamentally antidemocratic for a government
agency not to tell its citizens the rules by which it is enforcing the law.

As I began to do more research, it became clear to me that
the secrecy enveloping the Top Echelon program had much
more to do with catering to the FBI's desire to avoid embarrassment than serving any legitimate public good. Explod-
ing that secrecy became a fundamental motivation for
writing this work.

I am not, however, claiming to be the program's discov-
erer, like Howard Carter digging up some Egyptian
pharaoh's tomb. Indeed, T.E. informants have been mentioned in several prior books. I was particularly impressed
by James Neff's *Mobbed Up: Jackie Presser's High-Wire
Life in the Teamsters, the Mafia and the FBI,* about the former Teamsters union president and longtime Top Echelon
informant. Unlike Neff's excellent book, though, most of
the other works were either written by former FBI agents or
by journalists who received the FBI's official cooperation
and stamp of approval. No book I could find had ever taken
a critical look at the Top Echelon Informant Program as a
whole, its origins, its fundamental assumptions, its imple-
mentation, and its effects.

Nor is this work intended as the all-encompassing last
word on the Top Echelon program. Top former FBI officials
have told me that several hundred T.E. informants were re-

cruited beginning in the early 1960s, but at most a few dozen have been publicly identified. The identities of the majority may never be known. The FBI, citing understandable concern about the safety of the informants' families—but also obsessed with its own public image—keeps their names a closely held secret even long after they are dead. Also, even at this writing, most of my queries to the FBI's Freedom of Information Act office are still mired in a giant backlog of similar requests.

This book will largely be a case study on how the Top Echelon program was used and terribly abused in Boston, for several reasons. First, the relationships between the FBI's Boston field office and T.E. informants Stephen Flemmi and Whitey Bulger endured for decades, virtually the entire life span of the T.E. program, and are therefore useful for tracing its history and development. Second, the complex legal issues involved in *U.S.* v. *Salemme* case made necessary a thorough and unprecedented legal examination of the program and broke much new ground. And third, it is the story I know best, having covered it as a reporter for more than half a decade. Rather than the final word, I hope this book will instead become a starting point for critical discussion of the Top Echelon program, the FBI and its policies, and of the misuse of informants in general.

The second experience that prompted me to write this work happened inside Judge Wolf's courtroom when former FBI supervisor Edward Clark took the witness stand.

I had been to Clark's retirement party at Joe Tecce's restaurant two years earlier. It had been a particularly unctuous affair, full of interminable testimonials by fellow FBI agents clapping Clark—and by extension themselves—on the back for being the protectors of motherhood, apple pie, and all things sacred and American. The sanctimonious monotony was broken only by a Boston Police detective named Charlie Clifford, who made a joke that fugitive Whitey Bulger was "living in Johnny Connolly's basement in Lynnfield." It was widely suspected that FBI Special Agent

Connolly had been Bulger's handler, and the joke got a big nervous laugh from the two hundred or so assembled agents.

I couldn't shake the mental image of that party as I watched Clark testify about the unusual manner in which he and another FBI supervisor, Ed Quinn, conducted an interview with convicted Boston marijuana trafficker Joseph Murray in 1989. Murray was a longtime confederate of Whitey Bulger and Steve Flemmi, the FBI's prized informants, and was offering to implicate them in no less than four unsolved murders. Murray was also saying that two FBI agents, John Connolly and John Newton, had been selling information on government investigations to Bulger and Flemmi.

I was stunned to hear the agent testify, under oath, that he and Quinn didn't ask Murray a single question about the three murders. Nor was Murray's offer to cooperate ever followed up after the interview was over, Clark said. Finally, he admitted that Quinn's report of the meeting was placed in the FBI's highly sophisticated filing system in a way that effectively hid it from other agents who might be seeking information on the murders.

Clark's excuse: He had just been doing what his bosses at the FBI told him to do.

My God, I thought, he blows off evidence of four unsolved murders and then says "I was just following orders"—and this was supposed to be one of the good guys. I followed Clark into the marble-tiled hallway after he left the stand.

"Ed, wait," I said.

"What's up?"

"I have to ask you this, Ed. What happened with the Murray thing? How do you explain that?"

"You know I can't talk to you about that."

"C'mon, Ed. Jesus, the guy was talking about murders and nobody followed up. I think someone's owed an explanation here."

"I did what I was told to do. You weren't there, you don't

know what it was like. You wouldn't understand," he told me.

He was right. I didn't understand.

I made a silent promise to myself to try. That promise became this book.

Author's Note

••••••••••••••••••••••••••••••••

A FEW POINTS about source materials and literary style:

All conversations between characters in this book are based on at least one participant's best memory of what was said, taken from interviews, transcripts, law enforcement reports, court documents, or witness testimony. They are not intended as a verbatim transcription of the conversation, but in the author's estimation they do faithfully represent the tenor and content of the exchange between the speakers.

A caution about FBI informant reports: Many contain information that is unsubstantiated, rank hearsay, and in some places simply wrong. Since they are written exclusively for an FBI audience, they can also be self-serving, misleading, and outright falsified, depending on the author. Only FBI reports containing information corroborated by other facts or sources have been relied on as factual material for this book.

No names in this book have been in any way altered, including those of informants. However, many former FBI agents, other law enforcement officials, prosecutors, defense attorneys, and other sources consented to be interviewed and quoted only if their names were not used. While such agreements are not preferred, many sources were fearful of reprisal, were subject to judicial gag orders, or had been called as grand jury witnesses. At all times during the writing of this work, various aspects of the Boston FBI scandal were being investigated by one or more federal grand juries.

CHAPTER ONE

With Impunity

••••••••••••••••••••••••••••••••

The FBI's favorite son gets away with murder

A BADLY RUSTED swing bridge connects the gleaming sky-scrapers of Boston's financial district to Northern Avenue, a windswept road that commands a panoramic view of Boston Harbor and runs from the northeastern tip of South Boston down to the shipyards and fish-processing plants of the Boston Marine Industrial Park. City planners proposed that Northern Avenue be the heart of a grand Seaport Development district in the late 1990s, complete with a contemporary art museum, luxury hotels, and a giant, high-tech convention center. The idea was to capitalize on the biggest and most expensive public works project in U.S. history, the $1.7 billion-per-mile "Big Dig," an ambitious plan to build a ten-lane underground expressway replacing the old Central Artery, an unsightly green steel elevated highway that for years had literally and symbolically cut off the waterfront from the rest of the city.

In the early 1980s, though, the South Boston waterfront was still an isolated, foreboding place. Motorists who ducked under the grimy artery and clattered across the Northern Avenue Bridge saw only water, old brick warehouses, and a desolate stretch of weed-infested parking lots until they reached the State Fish Pier and a cluster of bars and tourist-trap seafood restaurants with names like Anthony's Pier 4, Jimmy's Harborside, and the No Name.

Lee DuPre and Bob McCain were two hours into an evening shift on May 11, 1982, when their Boston Police cruiser reached the steel bridge at about six P.M.—just in time to see a motorist frantically honking his horn and waving.

"There's been a shooting over by the Pier restaurant," the man shouted. "I heard a hell of a lot of shots—you better get over there."

It took just forty-five seconds for the cruiser to reach restaurant row, where the two officers spotted a blue Datsun F10 about a dozen feet from the curb in front of the Port Café. A big, slightly balding man in his early forties was lying facedown about ten feet from the open passenger door.

Blood was already forming pools around the body. The two cops saw bullet holes everywhere: Blood was seeping through the victim's blue shirt from holes in both arms, his left shoulder, and right wrist. There was also a gaping hole in the right thigh of his gray pants, and his white sneakers were soaked in red. The attack had obviously come at first from behind; every window of the Datsun was blown out except for the windshield, and there were shell casings on the ground behind it. Inside the car a second man, wearing a green MAGOO'S windbreaker, was slumped over the steering wheel. An ambulance siren's wail joined the cacophony of noise headed toward the scene, but the officers peering in the door could see it was too late for the driver. A high-velocity bullet had blown a huge hole in the back of his head.

McCain and DuPre tried to stanch the large man's wounds until Boston Emergency Medical Services paramedics took over. Other officers and detectives piled out of police cruisers that streamed in from all directions. One was Sergeant Bo Millane, a detective from South Boston.

Millane knew both men. The one on the ground was Brian Halloran, a violent, unpredictable thug with a cocaine habit and ties to the Winter Hill Gang, an opportunistic band of Irish and Italian criminals who survived the infamous gang wars of the 1960s to emerge as the only legitimate rival to the Patriarca family, the New England franchise of the Italian-American Mafia. The word on the street was that Halloran was "ratting"—working as a law enforcement informer—because he was on the hook for murdering a fringe underworld player in Chinatown. The other man in the car was Michael Donahue, a cop's boy, who Millane figured, poor bastard, had probably just been in the wrong place with the wrong company.

Halloran's ability to name his shooters was fast flowing crimson into the gutters as three paramedics fought a losing battle to stop the blood surging out of a multitude of entrance and exit wounds. Millane later testified in court that he stuck close as the paramedics lifted Halloran onto a gurney and it into the ambulance.

As he rode along on the way to the hospital, Millane asked the dying man: "Brian, who did this to you?"

"Jimmy Flynn . . . Weymouth."

That was it, Millane said. Halloran lost consciousness and never woke up again. An emergency room doctor at Boston City Hospital pronounced him dead less than an hour after the first shot was fired.

Back on the waterfront, other detectives and some FBI agents were interviewing witnesses. The consensus seemed to be that a green late 1970s-model Chevrolet Chevelle with three men inside had pulled up on the parked Datsun from behind. Two of the men in the Chevy opened fire, raking the smaller car and its occupants from behind and from the side. Halloran stumbled out of the Datsun, followed by one of the gunmen from the Chevelle, who shouted, "I'll show you!" and pumped more bullets into him. The Chevelle then sped off back into South Boston, cut through a viaduct and disappeared.

Another witness, an off-duty sergeant from the Boston suburbs, told the FBI that a half hour before the murder she had seen a new black sedan, maybe a Mercury Marquis, parked on Northern Avenue. A dark-haired, clean-shaven man in his forties, wearing a shirt, tie, and a business suit had been behind the wheel, watching the Port Café through binoculars. A second witness said the man in the business suit pulled his car into the street just as the shooters opened fire, to block anyone from following them.

Two and a half hours earlier Special Agent Leo Brunnick of the Federal Bureau of Investigation's Boston office had received a telephone message from his partner Jerry Montanari. Montanari told Brunnick that Halloran, who had been working with the two agents as a cooperating witness, had called him from a pay phone.

Brunnick dialed the number Montanari had scribbled down. A woman answered, but it was hard for Brunnick to hear her voice over the din of some sort of tavern.

"Hello, the . . ."

Brunnick couldn't make out the name of the bar. "Is Brian there?" he asked.

"Brian? Just a minute, let me check."

A gruff male voice came on the line. "What's up? I hear you've been looking for me."

"Nope."

"Fuck."

"Who told you that?"

"Now I'm not sure. I think it was Patty." Patty was Halloran's wife and the mother of his two young sons.

"I wasn't looking for you. And I didn't tell Patty anything."

"Jesus. What the fuck's going on? This is screwed up. Listen, I know that fucking Jimmy Flynn's looking all over town for me. He's blaming me for ratting for the warrant at his house and the one at Weasel Mantville's."

"Uh-huh."

"That was good fucking information. That ought to get me into the program."

"I don't know, Brian, we'll see."

Despite his words, Brunnick already knew there was little chance that Halloran would get into the federal Witness Protection Program. The chief of the New England office of the U.S. Organized Crime Strike Force, Jeremiah O'Sullivan, had already branded him a drunk and an unreliable witness and had refused to sign off on the request.

"How would Flynn know it was you?" Brunnick asked.

"I heard that a Boston cop told Weasel it was me when they were searching his house. I'm worried, man, I think Flynn's coming after me."

"Look, Brian, just take it easy, okay? One more thing— you have to be out of the house on the Cape by Saturday, the Bureau's not going to pay after that and it's not coming out of my wallet."

"No promises, Leo. I have to figure out my next move first. Rome wasn't built in a day, you know. That's why I came in, I need to hit up some of my old friends for some dough."

"Brian, listen to me. Stop running around the goddamn city like this. It's crazy. And dangerous. And stupid. Just get back to the Cape with your family and stop bouncing around—"

Halloran cut him off. "Gotta go. I'm double-parked." The line went dead.

Brunnick put the receiver back in its cradle, shaking his head. Frustration was nothing new to his six-month relationship with Halloran. The big hoodlum had great information, but his behavior was erratic, especially when he was drinking.

Halloran was also convinced that several people, including Jimmy Flynn, were out to get him. Not without reason. Thirteen months earlier he had stepped out the door of his condominium in Quincy, a city just to the south of Boston, when he heard the crack of a rifle shot. Unhit, he dove for cover and pulled his own gun, but it was too late to get a look at the fleeing assailant. A little more than a month after that, Halloran had been leaving a Teamsters Union hall when someone fired a shotgun at him. Again the gunman missed.

Halloran knew the word on the street was that he was co-operating. Even if it was only a guess by his friends in the underworld, it wasn't a bad one. For the last six months he had been out on $50,000 bail after being arrested for murdering a rival drug dealer, Georgie Pappas, during a four A.M. argument at an all-night Chinese restaurant. Among criminals it is widely presumed that anyone out on bail for murder may well be working with law enforcement—which in fact Halloran was.

He desperately wanted to avoid prison. Friends and relatives said he seemed to take his responsibilities as the father of a young family seriously. But Brian Halloran could never seem to get out of his own way. The Pappas murder, after all, occurred just five months after his second son was born.

Friends and family members all said there were really two Brians, each one at war with the other. One was gentle and jovial, especially with children, while the other—usually under the influence of alcohol, cocaine, or both—was brutish, violent, and exceptionally vulgar.

He was big: six feet two and a solid 260 pounds. On the streets and in the bars of Boston he wore long leather coats and a permanent aura of menace. "You were rarely afraid when you were out with Brian," said one of his friends. "It was never a question who was going to be the first one to wade into any fight." Two of Halloran's favorite running buddies were the McNeeley brothers, the uncles of the boxer "Hurricane" Peter McNeeley, who lost a heavyweight world title fight to Mike Tyson on a first-round knockout in 1995. "Halloran was a nasty fucking individual all on his own, but when those guys got together—look out," according to a Boston lawyer who knew them well.

One story that made the rounds concerned an argument

between Halloran and a married couple at Hurley's Log Cabin, a nightclub in Boston's Roxbury neighborhood. Halloran punched and kicked the husband to the ground. Halloran then unzipped his pants and in full view of the man's wife and the rest of the crowded nightclub, emptied his bladder on his bleeding adversary and walked out, laughing. Another friend told of a time when Halloran beckoned him out of a bar once to see a "surprise" in his car—the trunk was full of machine guns. "Are you out of your mind?" the friend asked, frantically looking around to see if anyone else was watching.

Most of Halloran's friends were members or associates of what police commonly called the "Winter Hill Gang" or the "Irish mob." Neither name really fit. The gang wasn't just Irish, but a powerful, loosely associated group of mixed-ethnic criminals—some Irish like Halloran and Whitey Bulger, some Italian like Steve Flemmi and the Martorano brothers, and some of mixed ethnic heritage. Though inaccurate, the "Irish" tag was generally used because it distinguished them from Boston's traditional Italian Mafia.

Truthfully, they weren't really the Winter Hill Gang anymore either. The group had started out in Winter Hill, a section of a working-class city called Somerville just northwest of Boston, but now its members were from all over the city. After boss and Somerville resident Howard "Howie" Winter had gone to prison three years earlier, members James "Whitey" Bulger and Stephen Flemmi had seized control and were moving the gang's power base to Bulger's native South Boston. Federal prosecutors eventually dubbed them the "the Bulger Group"—almost making them sound more like investment bankers than vicious killers.

Halloran's family knew about his wild side, but they mostly saw the gentle one. He had grown up near the Baker Chocolate Factory, in the Welles Avenue section of Dorchester, where luscious candy smells filled the air on summer afternoons. Edward Brian Halloran was the oldest of

"Big Ed" and Ann Halloran's five children. The divergent
paths taken by the children was typical of a Boston Irish
Catholic family of the era. The oldest girl, Brenda, became
a nun. One of the boys, Barry, became a cop. Ann, the next
sister, became a housewife. And Dennis, the youngest,
joined the Teamsters. Ann and Big Ed called their middle
child Brian to distinguish him from his father. He had a difficult time at St. Anne's School—family members believe he
may have been dyslexic—and adjusted poorly to his
mother's death when he was twelve years old. By nineteen
he had begun compiling a criminal record that included burglary, bank robbery, assault, and extortion. But at home he
was a different person, so gentle with his nieces and
nephews that his brothers and sisters never thought twice
about having him over for dinner or to babysit.

The dichotomy between the two Brians was the theme of
his brother Kenny's eulogy. Most of the 150 mourners were
family members from Dorchester and South Boston, but a
handful of Brian's hoodlum friends also showed up, skulk-
ing in the back of the church, in open shirts and shiny gold
chains. Kenny Halloran glared at them as he finished his
speech about his brother.

"He was a high-roller. When things were going good for
him in the sixties and seventies, he had a lot of hangers-on.
Those of you who went through that will know what I mean."

Two of the "hoodlums" in the back of the church were actually undercover Massachusetts State Police troopers. One of
them, Henry F. "Chip" Werner, was probably one of the last
friendly faces to see Halloran alive.

Halloran and Werner were made for each other, in a
doomed sort of way. When they stepped into each other's respective worlds, the crossover set forces in motion that
would destroy them both. Werner had been submerged undercover for nearly two years already, his only connection to
the State Police were intermittent secret meetings with a supervisor, and he had been consumed by the blur of drug

dealers, bookie joints, and dive bars that had become his life. Deepening alcoholism and the stress of working undercover ruined his marriage; his wife and five children had moved back to his native Cincinnati. Within a year he would be convicted of taking two pounds of cocaine out of a State Police evidence room and sent to prison.

Werner and Halloran became friends when another undercover trooper, Jack Towsey, invited them both out on his fishing boat. Throwing bait at striped bass off the thirty-foot Seacraft, the pair hit it off, talking about boxing and their kids. Werner offered Halloran a ride home, and was surprised to find that not only did they live just a few hundred yards away from each other, but Halloran was living in the same gray stone house Werner had rented the previous summer. The four-bedroom home was spacious, with a huge lawn, a private dock, and an expansive view of scenic Buzzard's Bay.

The two men began hanging out. Halloran fed tips to Werner about bookmakers (though never his close friends), and they started making evening forays into Boston together, driving ninety minutes from the Cape to hang out at bars and nightclubs like the Dockside near historic Faneuil Hall.

Halloran confided in Werner that he was also working for the FBI, and that the Bureau was paying the rent on the big house. He said he was frustrated. Brunnick and Montanari seemed to be stringing him along—one day assuring him that he, Patti, and the children would get into the federal Witness Protection Program, the next day saying it was still up in the air. They promised to support him financially too, but the money was coming only a few hundred dollars at a time—mostly when he threatened to quit.

Worse, he also couldn't figure out what the Bureau wanted. He'd offered to testify against Whitey Bulger and Steve Flemmi, the new chieftains of the Winter Hill Gang. It seemed like a win-win to Halloran: the FBI would get convictions on two major organized crime figures, and he would get some breathing room and maybe a break on the Pappas murder. Halloran believed Bulger and Flemmi had been the ones trying to kill him the previous year—he thought he had spotted them following him several times, including once in a van outside St. Margaret's Hospital, where his second son was born.

Why was the FBI jerking him around, he asked, when he was giving them a chance to be heroes and solve the murder of Oklahoma computer and communications tycoon Roger Wheeler? The case was big; it had made national headlines the year before.

The chairman of the Tulsa-based Telex Corporation and several other companies, Wheeler believed he had discovered a cash-skimming scheme in one of his subsidiaries, a Miami sports-betting company. John Callahan, an accountant and wiseguy wannabe with whom Halloran shared a condo in Florida, had helped set up the scheme and said Wheeler "had to go" before it was discovered. During a meeting at the accountant's Boston business office, Callahan, Whitey Bulger, and Stephen Flemmi had offered Halloran a contract to murder Wheeler. Callahan said that Johnny Martorano, a hit man sometimes referred to as "Johnny and his Bazooka," would also take part in the hit.

It was weird, Halloran told Werner, the FBI agents seemed obsessed with the Wheeler murder—maybe because a former agent was involved—but appeared totally disinterested in other hits he said he could pin on Bulger and Flemmi, like the 1980 killing of a South Boston bookie named Louis Litif. Werner could always tell when Halloran had spent a couple of days working with the Bureau; a darkness seemed to close in over him. His overall mood wasn't helped by the fact that he believed Bulger and Flemmi were trying to kill him because he knew too much about the Wheeler contract.[1] Halloran was also worried about Jimmy Flynn, having given Werner information for a search warrant for Flynn's home that led to the arrest of Jimmy and his wife on gun charges.

On the morning of May 11, though, Halloran seemed un-

---

[1] Members of Halloran's family believe he was also aware that Bulger and Flemmi were working for the FBI.

usually chipper, despite the fact that the FBI was about to evict him. Werner stopped by a Dunkin' Donuts for coffee and brought an extra cup over to the big house on the bluff. He pulled his big undercover Lincoln up the driveway and saw that Halloran was on the big lawn, throwing a ball to his young son. Werner watched for a minute and shook his head. It always blew him away that the big thug with the killer's reputation could be so sweet around kids. He brought the coffee over.

"Hey, Brian."

"Hey, Jerry," Halloran said, smiling. He always used Werner's undercover name.

"What's going on?"

"Good news, Jerry. Good news."

"What?"

"It's a big score, man, a big one."

"Listen, you want a ride into Boston? I'm going in this morning and I could drop you in Southie or something."

"Nah. I've got a ride already. I'm waiting for a phone call. Thanks anyway."

"Okay. That's great, congratulations. I guess I'll see you later."

"See ya," Halloran said.

Twelve hours later Werner got a call from Jack Towsey.

"It's Brian," Towsey said. Halloran and a guy who was driving him around had been ambushed. They were both dead.

Christ, Werner said to himself, that could have been me. Halloran's "big score" had been a setup, he thought. A fucking setup.

Bob Fitzpatrick and his wife Jane were having dinner at an Irish pub in Brookline Village when his pager started bleeping. Oh no, he thought. The Assistant Special Agent in Charge of the Boston FBI office threw his napkin on the table and strode over to a pay phone. The switchboard operators had gone home, but the night clerk at the FBI office told him that Brian Halloran, a cooperating witness, had been gunned down on the South Boston waterfront and wasn't expected to survive.

"Oh, shit, it's started," he muttered to himself. "Now we have a *real* problem on our hands."

Fitzpatrick dropped his wife at home and drove to the office, flashing back to a conversation about a week earlier with Bill Weld, the U.S. Attorney for Massachusetts. It had been pretty uncomfortable—he'd had to pull Weld out of an afternoon meeting.

"He's busy, is it important?" Weld's secretary had asked. It was, Fitzpatrick said. Weld emerged from a conference room a few moments later.

The two men had a good rapport, they were "Fitzy" and "Bill" to each other despite not having much in common. Weld was the scion of a Wasp family that, as he was fond of joking, "landed in America with nothing but the shirts on their backs and a couple million pounds of gold." Fitzpatrick was raised in a New York City orphanage, the Mission of the Immaculate Virgin. Weld went on to Harvard College, Harvard Law School, and a stint on the House Watergate Committee staff before joining the Justice Department. Fitzpatrick followed a stint in the Army with a diploma from Vermont's tiny St. Peter's College and graduate studies in psychiatric social work at Columbia University in New York.

The stocky FBI man wore a sheepish expression looking up at the tall, red-haired prosecutor. It was embarrassing, Fitzpatrick explained, but the FBI had a cooperating witness who was potentially in grave danger and he needed Weld's help.

Ordinarily, Fitzpatrick should have been dealing with Jeremiah O'Sullivan, chief of the New England Organized Crime Strike Force. The strike force, independent of Weld's office, had jurisdiction over any FBI organized crime prosecution in the six New England states. O'Sullivan, however, was refusing to sign off on Brian Halloran's application for the federal Witness Protection Program, even though there had already been one attempt on Halloran's life. Fitzpatrick was taking a political risk bypassing O'Sullivan, but he felt compelled to do something after Leo Brunnick had vouched for Halloran's value as a witness and insisted that he was in grave danger.

Not everyone in the FBI office was convinced of Halloran's value. The most vocal were two members of the Organized Crime Squad, Special Agent John Connolly and his boss, Supervisory Special Agent John Morris. When Halloran first went to the FBI early in 1982, Brunnick asked Morris for his opinion. It was overwhelmingly negative. Halloran was "unstable," Morris said, and would say anything to get out from under the Pappas murder. Plus, the rest of the Winter Hill Gang had stopped trusting Halloran years earlier, when his clumsy pressuring of a loanshark victim had resulted in several members of the gang getting indicted for extortion. Why, then, would Whitey Bulger and Steve Flemmi entrust him with a high-risk, high-profile crime like the Wheeler murder?

Fitzpatrick liked his Organized Crime Squad supervisor, but he also knew that Morris, John Connolly, and even Jerry O'Sullivan had serious conflicts of interest when it came to Flemmi and Bulger.

Ever since Fitzpatrick had arrived in Boston, the words "Bostar" and "Mandarin" had been whispered in hushed, reverent tones. They were the code names for the Boston FBI's mission impossible, a daring operation that had planted listening devices inside the Boston headquarters of the New England Italian-American Mafia underboss Gennaro "Jerry" Angiulo and a social club where family consigliere (head counselor or top adviser) Ilario "Larry" Zannino held court. The bugs had been spectacularly successful, capturing hundreds of hours of incriminating conversations. Morris and Connolly were working with O'Sullivan on a planned indictment that promised to be the biggest blow ever struck against the Mafia in Boston, possibly in the entire country.

Whitey Bulger and Steve Flemmi had helped make the triumph possible.

The two criminals had been recruited as members of a secret FBI initiative, set in motion almost twenty years earlier, called the "Top Echelon Criminal Informant Program." Connolly was their "handler," the agent responsible for taking their information and keeping it flowing. Connolly, Morris, and O'Sullivan had already gone to bat for Bulger and Flemmi more than once, to keep them on the street where they were most useful. Fitzpatrick, though, wasn't as convinced that their value outweighed their down side. He had met personally with Bulger, and came away with the feeling that Bulger should be targeted for prosecution, not embraced as part of the FBI's anti-Mafia crusade. But he had been overruled by his boss, Boston FBI Special Agent in Charge Larry Sarhatt, who had been lobbied hard by O'Sullivan.

Fitzpatrick was now in a bind. Without the approval of a prosecutor, the U.S. Marshals Service wouldn't relocate Halloran and his family. The hoodlum's behavior, meanwhile, had become increasingly squirrely; he was spending more time in Boston and less in the FBI's expensive safe house down on the Cape, even though word somehow had leaked out to the street that he was cooperating.

Fitzpatrick believed Halloran was probably telling the truth about Bulger and Flemmi's involvement in the Wheeler murder. Fitzpatrick had reviewed the FD-302s— the official FBI report forms—on the Wheeler murder, which referred to Halloran only as "source," to protect his identity. The Assistant Special Agent in Charge had found Halloran's story convincing and his promise to help sincere.

```
Source was asked why he was coming for-
ward with this information. He advised
that he is in fear of his life and at-
tempts have been made on his life. He ad-
vised that he is willing to testify in
```

open court to what he said, however, he
wants protection for him and his family
and immunity from prosecution. He said he
would "go all the way" and furnish other
information to "put these guys away."

Fitzpatrick knew that offering to "go all the way" against
Whitey Bulger and Stevie Flemmi was a very risky business.

"We always say there's a danger for this snitch or that
snitch; that they could get killed," he told Weld. "But this
one's for real."

How bad is it? Weld asked.

"Let's put it this way. I wouldn't want to be standing next
to the guy."

Weld said he would think about it and maybe speak to
O'Sullivan.

Before he could try, Halloran was dead.

A few weeks after Halloran was killed, John Morris placed
a call from a government training center in Glencoe, Georgia, to the Organized Crime Squad offices in the John F.
Kennedy Federal Building in Boston's Government Center
district. One of the agents in his squad, a tall and broad-
shouldered man wearing an expensive Italian suit, picked up
the line.

"John Connolly," the man answered.

"It's John," the supervisor said. "I'm down in Glencoe. Do
you think they could arrange an airline ticket for Debbie?"

"Sure," Connolly replied.

Loneliness and boredom had gotten the better of John
Morris. The slight, pale-skinned agent was going out of his
mind sitting through a boring Drug Enforcement Administration training seminar. But he thought that Glencoe, a
smudge on the map about seventy-five miles south of Sa-
vannah, might be tolerable if Debbie, his secretary, were
there. They had been having an affair for about three years,
since his wife insisted on going back to work. Morris re-

membered how, before he'd left, Connolly had approached him in the office.

"These guys really like you, you know," Connolly had said. "If you ever need anything, if you ever want anything, just let me know."

The "guys," Morris admitted under oath years later, were Connolly's informants, Whitey Bulger and Stephen Flemmi. Morris had an idea why they might be grateful, but he didn't like thinking about it. Earlier that spring, Morris had pulled Connolly aside and told him what Halloran was saying about Whitey Bulger and Steve Flemmi's ties to the Wheeler murder. Both men knew what that meant—big trouble for perhaps the biggest, most ambitious Mafia case the Boston FBI had ever attempted. Both had a lot to lose if Bulger and Flemmi went down for murder. Several years earlier, Morris had convinced Richard Bates, the SAC who promoted him, to approve the ambitious plan to bug Angiulo's headquarters in Boston's North End. Angiulo was notoriously adept at insulating himself from prosecution, and many in law enforcement believed bugging his headquarters was an impossible dream.

Yet the bugging effort did succeed, beyond the FBI's wildest fantasies, and a small army of agents was now transcribing the six months' worth of tapes and helping the strike force prepare a massive racketeering indictment against the Boston Mafia. The danger was that Morris and Connolly had already stepped in more than once to keep Bulger and Flemmi out of trouble, and if the Mafia's defense lawyers learned that the government had protected two killers in order to get the bug, the entire Angiulo case could be in jeopardy. Connolly, meanwhile, was earning accolades for having the biggest stable of organized crime informants in the Boston FBI office, maybe the entire Bureau. Bulger and Flemmi were his show horses.

Connolly told Morris that he didn't believe Bulger and Flemmi would be involved in a high-profile, out-of-state murder like Roger Wheeler's. They were "too smart" for that. Morris knew he had taken a risk by telling Connolly about Halloran. Connolly's bond with the two seemed to be much more of a friendship than a traditional informant-agent relationship. His fears were confirmed a short while later. Connolly admitted that he had leaked news of Halloran's cooperation to Bulger and Flemmi. After Halloran was killed, Morris had few doubts about who had done it.

Morris was faced with a choice. Speaking out might be the right thing to do, but it would also endanger the Angiulo case, expose Bulger and Flemmi as informants, and embarrass the FBI. Morris, like every agent who came on the job in the J. Edgar Hoover era, knew that the unwritten first rule of being an agent was "never embarrass the Bureau." By staying silent, he was keeping two murderers on the street, but he would be also adhering to the Justice Department's top priority—getting the Italian-American Mafia at all costs.

John Morris made a decision. He was about to take his first bribe.

Later that day, Connolly handed an envelope containing $1,000 in cash to Debbie Noseworthy.

It was from John, he explained, who wanted her to join him down in Georgia.

After she arrived, Morris lied to Debbie about where the money had come from, saying he had been saving it in his desk as a surprise for her.

Jimmy Flynn, the man Brian Halloran named as his killer, was acquitted of murder charges five years after the Northern Avenue shooting. The jury found that he had a near air-tight alibi.

The Wheeler murder, meanwhile, went unsolved for another eighteen years.

It was finally solved by Johnny Martorano, the Winter Hill Gang associate who Halloran had identified to Montanari and Brunnick. Martorano, drawing comparisons to Mafia hit man "Sammy the Bull" Gravano in New York, cut

a blockbuster three-state plea and confessed to murdering
Wheeler and nineteen other people. Whitey Bulger and Stevie Flemmi hired him to do the Wheeler hit, Martorano said,
because the businessman uncovered their skimming operation in one of his businesses.

Brian Halloran had been right.

The Boston FBI and the Organized Crime Strike Force
held the keys to the Wheeler and Halloran murders in their
hands, so why would they throw them away? Were Morris
and Connolly "rogue agents," as the Justice Department
would later brand them? Years later, Morris, under a grant of
immunity, admitted to taking bribes and testified that Connolly had tipped the mobsters off about Halloran's cooperation. Or was it something else?

An incident that occurred several years later, when the
FBI got a second chance to solve Brian Halloran's murder,
may help provide an answer.

By early 1988 the Halloran-Donahue murders had long
since been relegated to the bottom of the Boston Police
cold case files. To the FBI and the strike force, basking in
the glow of laudatory news reports and a book written
about the successful convictions in the Angiulo case, the
big hoodlum from Dorchester had become a blissfully distant memory.

Bill Weld's career arc, meanwhile, had continued upward. As Assistant Attorney General for the Criminal Division of the Justice Department, he was one of the top two
or three officials under Ronald Reagan's Attorney General,
Ed Meese. On January 6, Weld's confidential assistant,
Judith Woolley, took a call from a mysterious woman who
gave only a first name. Part of Woolley's job was to screen
the daily calls from people convinced that the Justice
Department was monitoring the fillings in their teeth, but
something told her this one wasn't one of the usual fruit-
cakes.

The woman said she could give Weld information about

corrupt law enforcement officials who were working with Whitey Bulger and Steve Flemmi. "Please, please, don't pass any of this information along to the authorities in Boston," the woman pleaded with Woolley. "You'll be surprised at the names of the people on the list."

Woolley typed up a short memo. Weld looked it over with some interest. He had thought since his days in the U.S. Attorney's Office that there was a problem inside the Boston FBI; he had heard the complaints about Connolly and the rumors that there was an unsavory aspect to his relationship with Whitey Bulger. Weld wasn't jumping to any conclusions on one phone call, but he told Woolley he wanted to hear more if the woman called again. "Okay, this checks out—maybe not a nut," he scribbled in the upper right-hand corner of the memo, and put it aside.

Two weeks later the mysterious woman called again and, true to her word, started dropping names. Weld got another memo from Woolley.

```
WW,

[Anonymous] called again to give you
names of law enforcement officers in-
volved in obtaining information on wire-
taps, etc.
  "Agent John Connolly—FBI"
  "Boston Police Deputy Ed Walsh"
  Both sell information to Whitey Bulger
and Stevie Flemmi—and that's how they
find wiretaps.
```

This time, Weld was intrigued. He scribbled a note on the second memo: "I knew all this! So this woman is on the up-and-up!" and shot off a copy to Jack Keeney, the Deputy Assistant Attorney General for the Organized Crime and Racketeering Section.

Exactly one week later the same woman called again.

I have information on the Brian Holloran
(sic) killing. It was done by Whitey Dul-
ger (sic) and Pat Nee. I may possibly
have an eyewitness [informant] who may
possibly come forward.

Again, the mysterious female caller said she would call
back the next week with more information.

WW,

[Anonymous] called at 3:04 P.M. on Feb.
3 and dictated the following:

Re: Whitey Bulger and Pat Nee, they also
kidnapped Arthur, nickname Bucky, Barrett looking for money from the Medford
Bank Depositor's Trust. They held him and
went to his house and took $300,000 and
then they killed him. They kidnapped him
between his restaurant and the Federal
Probation Office as he went to sign in.
    If you have any specific questions,
maybe she can get them answered for you.

That was it for Weld. The Medford Depositor's Trust robbery had been one of the biggest crimes during his tenure as
U.S. Attorney in Massachusetts. Several corrupt police officers had been involved in the $1.5 million heist.

He dictated his own memo, ordering that the notes of the
calls be sent back to Boston to U.S. Attorney Frank McNamara
and Organized Crime Strike Force Chief Jeremiah O'Sullivan.
The federal prosecutors in Boston were "well aware of the history" and the information, Weld wrote, "sounds good."

A week later the mysterious woman made her final call.
Bulger and Flemmi, she said, were "really worried" about a
marijuana smuggler named Frank LePere. "They did a lot of

work for LePere," she said. The word "work" or sometimes "wet work" was a euphemism for murder in Boston's underworld. It was said on the street that Bulger and Flemmi "always did their own work."

The female caller was also being more specific on the Halloran murder. She alluded to a potential breakthrough witness in the murder case named "John," who had talked to Bulger and Pat Nee as they sat in a car waiting on Northern Avenue for Brian Halloran. "He sits in a bar and talks about it," the caller said. "He saw the whole operation."

A month or two later Weld ran into Frank McNamara at a Justice Department conference and urged him to do something about the memos he had sent. "We need to talk about this," he told his successor. Within a few weeks after urging McNamara, Weld was gone, having resigned from the Justice Department in a political dispute with Meese.

The leads from the mysterious caller languished during McNamara's bizarre, brief tenure as U.S. Attorney. It was a commonly held belief in Boston's legal community that the prosecutor was a couple of lobsters shy of a clambake, and the U.S. Attorney's office was in constant turmoil during his administration. It finally ended when, after publicly accusing other government officials in Boston of drug use, he admitted that he had himself recently smoked marijuana. He resigned under pressure.

That left the mysterious female caller in the hands of Jeremiah O'Sullivan, who left the strike force to replace McNamara as interim U.S. Attorney. Despite her pleas not to give her information to the "Boston authorities," O'Sullivan took the sensitive case and handed it right back to the Boston FBI office, for reasons he later refused to explain.

The FBI eventually found the mysterious woman. It was Suzanne Murray, the wife of Joseph Murray, a hoodlum from Charlestown. Murray had once worked as a compositor at the *Boston Globe*, but he was also one of the biggest marijuana smugglers in New England history, and an avid supporter of the Irish Republican Army who had taken part in several gun-smuggling operations from the U.S. to Northern Ireland. When agents confronted Suzanne Murray, she admitted that she had been calling on behalf of her husband. Murray himself agreed to be interviewed by the FBI—but only in Boston, not at the federal prison in Danbury where he was being held. It was too dangerous for him to be seen talking to the feds, he said.

In June 1989, Murray was secretly transported to the U.S. Attorney's office in Boston. Boston FBI Assistant Special Agent in Charge Dennis O'Callaghan sent Supervisory Special Agent Ed Quinn, whose work as the Angiulo case agent had earned him a promotion. They also sent Ed Clark, a veteran agent who spent most of his career working bank robberies but who was then overseeing the Economic Crimes Squad.

The interview the two agents conducted with Murray may have been one of the most extraordinary in the history of the Boston FBI, both for what was said *and* the way it was conducted.

Clark later recalled that O'Callaghan specifically instructed him to get to the bottom of the allegations against FBI agents John Connolly and John Newton. He did not remember being told to ask Murray about anything else. Nor did he remember doing any research on Murray's criminal background before the interview, which would have been standard FBI procedure. Pretty much all he knew at the time of the interview was that Murray was a federal prisoner and that Bulger and Flemmi were Top Echelon informants.

Clark's five-page report of the interview, however, gives a good indication of what the FBI was hoping to accomplish.

According to the report, the meeting began on a cautious note. Clark asked Murray whether he was willing to furnish information on the matters that his wife had called about. Clark also wanted to know what Murray was expecting as a "quid pro quo."

FBI agents were generally more subtle with potential wit-

nesses and informants. Murray may have been taken aback
by the blunt approach, because he backed off any demands,
saying he wanted to begin providing information to the FBI
with no strings attached, but that he was fearful of being
trapped between two powerful forces. Whitey Bulger and
Steve Flemmi, he said, had one "machine." The FBI and the
Boston Police had another. "I can't survive against those
machines," he asserted.

At the time of the interview, Murray was aware that
Bulger might be working with the FBI. His wife had actually called Washington several more times after Weld left
the Justice Department, and during one of those calls she
said that Bulger and Flemmi were "very concerned" over
an article in the *Boston Globe* that had identified Bulger
as an informant. "The Italians feel they have been used as
chess pieces and were allowed to fall by Bulger and
Flemmi," she said. "This is a case of grave concern for
both parties."

Clark wrote down Murray's "quid pro quo."

```
He's willing to furnish information and
wants nothing in return. The information
he furnished will now help save the life
of a friend or a loved one in the future.
```

Murray then launched into the story of his friend, former
business partner and codefendant Arthur "Bucky" Barrett,
who had mysteriously disappeared. Bulger and Flemmi were
also silent partners in their marijuana smuggling operation.
At the time that he vanished, Barrett, whose ability to beat
burglar alarms and locks was renowned in Boston criminal
circles, was widely believed to have amassed a huge personal
fortune, Murray said. The rumors were his undoing.

On the night he vanished, Barrett called Murray and said
he needed $2 million, that very night. It was after eight
o'clock, Murray replied, and there was no way he could get
that kind of money. I need it, Barrett pleaded, "I have been

tied up all day." He then threatened Murray that he would "give him up."

Murray hung up on his friend, who was never heard from again. When Barrett said he was "tied up all day," he was being literal. There was a longstanding rumor that Barrett had been kidnapped and tortured—his teeth extracted one at a time—for his share of the Medford Depositor's Trust money. The next day, Murray said, he talked to Barrett's wife Elaine, who said she had been told to take their baby and leave the house in Quincy for the night. When she arrived home the next day, the house had been ransacked and a box where her husband sometimes kept money had been emptied.

```
The word on the street was that South
Boston people snatched Bucky Barrett,
tied him up, and had him make phone calls
to raise money, and then put him under.
Murray, a good friend of Barrett, feels
that Whitey Bulger and Stevie Flemmi are
responsible for the death of Bucky Bar-
rett.
```

Murray then outlined his suspicions about FBI agents John Connolly and John Newton being on the take. Murray said that he had once mentioned Connolly to Patrick Nee, a close Bulger confederate from South Boston, who nodded, "meaning that Connolly was no problem." Murray said Nee insinuated that Connolly was "close" to Bulger. A fellow hoodlum from his native Charlestown, meanwhile, had told Murray that Connolly and Bulger rented an apartment together and were seen socializing on Cape Cod.

Nee also once told Murray that he had received a tip from a law enforcement source who lived a few blocks behind his house in South Boston. Newton's apartment was just a few blocks behind Nee's residence, Murray said.

Murray also said Bulger and Flemmi murdered Eddie

Connors, a well-known gangster from Dorchester, gunning him down in a telephone booth because Connors had helped them set up another gangland hit "and became a liability." There was some talk on the street that Connors had become a rat, Murray said, "but that may have just been cover for justifying his murder," according to Clark's notes.

Finally, Murray told the two supervisors what he knew about Brian Halloran. The word on the street, he said, was that "Halloran had turned." Halloran knew that Jimmy Flynn and Weasel Mantville were out to get him, Murray said, but it was Whitey Bulger and Pat Nee who had "rolled to make the hit" after a confederate spotted Halloran on Northern Avenue in South Boston. The machine gun used in the shooting, Murray said, was "possibly an Uzi," and there had actually been two cars, the gun car and a backup, involved in the murder.

"Whitey's crew keeps cars ready to go at all times. They're equipped with guns and radios and are kept in a garage in South Boston."

At face value, the information Murray was offering—the possibility of corrupt agents and the identities of men who had committed four murders—was remarkable.

The way Clark and Quinn handled it was extraordinary.

Mostly, during the interview, they just let Murray talk, only occasionally breaking in with questions when there was a logical gap in the stories the marijuana smuggler was telling them. They never asked Murray about his bona fides as a criminal—standard procedure to help determine whether his information was real or just street talk—and they never offered to follow up, even though he said he was willing to provide more information.

Murray clearly had the potential to be an astoundingly productive source, particularly on murders. Yet the two agents never asked him to elaborate on the Barrett, Connors, Donahue, and Halloran murders, which were all unsolved. In particular, Murray could have been helpful in identifying "John," the mysterious eyewitness who had seen Whitey

Bulger and Pat Nee on Northern Avenue. Had the agents bothered to ask about the Eddie Connors murder, it might have helped explain why Bulger and Flemmi—who supposedly didn't like or trust Halloran—would have offered him a contract for the Wheeler hit. Like Connors, they may have been planning to have Halloran do their dirty work and then get rid of him. The agents also never asked Murray about the three other unsolved murders that Suzanne Murray mentioned in her calls to the Justice Department, or the undoubtedly murderous "work" Flemmi and Bulger had allegedly done for marijuana smuggler Frank LePere. Murray could have been a good source of information there—he had essentially taken over LePere's smuggling business when LePere went to prison.

Instead, Clark's five-page report, and a subsequent memo written to FBI Headquarters by his boss, O'Callaghan, make it clear that the FBI wasn't particularly interested in the six murders or anything else that Murray had to say—other than the allegations against Connolly and Newton.

Clark later said he reported back to O'Callaghan with the results of the meeting and told him that the bribery allegations against Connolly and Newton appeared to be based on Murray's conjecture and could easily be explained by Connolly's official contact with Bulger as an informant. They did not discuss the other matters Murray had brought up, and O'Callaghan never asked them to follow anything up, Clark said.

Two months after the Murray interview, O'Callaghan sent a copy of Clark's report and his own memo to FBI Headquarters, marked, "Attn: Office of Professional Responsibility"—OPR is the Bureau's internal affairs division. The contents, he wrote, were "self-explanatory."

> The allegations that SSA Connolly and SA
> Newton are disclosing information re-
> garding investigations being conducted
> by this division to criminal elements

are unsubstantiated by specific facts,
but are more properly described as rumor
and conjecture on the part of Murray and
others.

In view of the unsubstantial and un-
specific allegations, and the official
relationship between SSA Connolly in
sources, SAC Boston recommends that this
inquiry be closed, and no administrative
action taken.

A subsequent handwritten note on the memo bearing
O'Callaghan's initials indicates that the FBI's internal
watchdogs took his advice.

"Allegation unsubstantiated. Closed administratively by
OPR on 9/22/88."

The FBI appears to have done its best to bury Murray's allegations and limit the number of people who knew about
them. According to testimony in court years later, Clark's report was put in the FBI's "administrative inquiry" files,
which were not generally available to other agents. Such
files were segregated to protect the reputations of agents
who had been falsely accused of wrongdoing. Yet treating
Murray's bid to cooperate as simply a misconduct allegation
against Connolly and Newton had another effect—it kept
the murder allegations against two valuable Top Echelon informants out of the FBI's file indexing system, where other
agents would have access to it. Special Agent Jerry Montanari, meanwhile, who was still in Boston and still nominally
the case agent for the Halloran and Wheeler murders in
1989, was never informed about the Murray interview. Finally, in another departure from FBI procedure, Special
Agent John Newton was never even told that a misconduct
allegation had been made against him.

In fact, there is no evidence that FBI officials in both
Boston and Washington did anything other than hush the
Murray matter up and let it drop.

Joe Murray served out his prison term uneventfully. On September 16, 1992, two years after he was released, he and Suzanne got into a violent argument at their lakeside cabin in Maine. When police arrived, they found his lifeless body riddled with bullets from a .357 Magnum handgun. Maine State Police detectives interviewed several witnesses who all said it appeared to be self-defense—Murray was seen chasing his wife through their yard with a knife just prior to the shooting. No charges were ever filed.

By early January 2000, Joe Murray was largely forgotten. Until, that is, a close associate of Whitey Bulger and Steve Flemmi named Kevin J. Weeks led a group of Massachusetts State Police and Boston Police detectives and DEA agents to a mass grave, just off the southbound side of Route 93 in the Dorchester section of Boston. They dug up the bones of three people, two men and a woman. One of the male skulls was missing most of its teeth. That was Bucky Barrett, Weeks said, confirming the story that Flemmi and Bulger had tied Barrett up, tried to extract the location of his rumored treasure trove by pulling out his teeth, and then murdered him. Seven months later, in exchange for a promise that federal prosecutors would recommend that he serve as little as five years in prison, Weeks, who many had dubbed "Whitey Bulger's surrogate son," agreed to testify against Bulger and Flemmi and pled guilty in U.S. District Court to helping them commit five murders, by either kidnapping the victims beforehand or disposing of their bodies afterward. He also admitted helping Bulger and Flemmi shake down drug dealers and bookmakers, extort local business owners, and launder money.

"I did it all," the bull-necked forty-four-year-old criminal told Judge Richard G. Stearns.

The venue for Kevin Weeks's plea hearing was sadly appropriate. The brand new U.S. District Courthouse on the South Boston waterfront was just a few hundred feet up Northern Avenue from where Brian Halloran and Michael Donahue had been gunned down eighteen years earlier.

Weeks admitted acting as a lookout for the "Bulger group" car that carried Halloran and Donahue's killer. Bulger and Flemmi wanted Halloran dead, Weeks said, because he was planning to testify against them on the Roger Wheeler murder.

Joe Murray had been right.

In his landmark 661-page ruling on the Boston FBI office's misconduct in the handling of informants, U.S. District Court Judge Mark Wolf found that Joe Murray, like Brian Halloran, had been purposefully "eliminated as a threat to the symbiotic relationship between the FBI and Bulger and Flemmi." It wasn't that the Murray information wasn't potentially useful, Wolf decided, it was that FBI officials made a decision that keeping Bulger and Flemmi as Top Echelon informants was more important than prosecuting them for murder. Again, the timing of another major Mafia prosecution appears to have played a role—in the summer of 1989, Stevie Flemmi and Whitey Bulger were proving very useful to the Boston office of the FBI. A new bugging operation was under way, one equally as ambitious as the prior effort to infiltrate Jerry Angiulo's headquarters. The result—unprecedented tape recordings of the Mafia's arcane, ultrasecret induction ceremony, the Italian mob's holiest-of-holies—was later hailed nationwide as one of the greatest achievements in the FBI's war on organized crime.

Taken together, the Murray and Halloran cases form a disturbing pattern. If Bulger and Flemmi were murderers, the Bureau simply didn't want to know. While some FBI apologists have tried to dismiss the Bulger and Flemmi case as the work of a few "rogue" agents, the Bureau's own records make it clear that the information received from both Brian Halloran and Joe Murray made it all the way up to FBI Headquarters level. Those records show that when faced with either pursuing prosecutions of its own Top Echelon informants or protecting them, the FBI as an agency consistently chose to protect them.

In the late 1990s the Boston FBI office was the epicenter of what some government officials have called the worst public scandal in the Bureau's ninety-two-year history. The scandal exposed the relationships between the Boston FBI office and its Top Echelon informants, the misconduct of numerous agents, and the total cost of decades of protection of Bulger and Flemmi, and its proportions were shocking. Whitey Bulger and Steve Flemmi were ultimately believed by law enforcement officials to have been involved in more than twenty murders, including Halloran's, by doing the "work" themselves or ordering someone else, like John Martorano. In fully half of those cases, the FBI was told in one way or another that Bulger and Flemmi were involved— yet everything possible was done to keep them in the informant program rather than prosecuting them. In at least three cases there was strong evidence that FBI agents themselves had facilitated the killings by leaking the identities of other informants to the two killers. Aside from the murders, it was found that numerous FBI agents looked the other way when they came across evidence of other crimes by Flemmi and Bulger that, if prosecuted, would have prevented some of the killing. Instead, agents and FBI-friendly prosecutors in many cases did their best to undermine other law enforcement agencies that tried to investigate the crime bosses.

While the scandal in Boston may well have been a worst-case scenario, Whitey Bulger and Steve Flemmi were part of a program that was national in scope. The problems they caused were duplicated by other informants in other cities and can be traced directly back to two national FBI initiatives traceable all the way up to J. Edgar Hoover himself.

The first was the FBI's thirty-year-war on the Italian Mafia. There can be little argument that the Bureau was targeting a legitimate, nationwide criminal menace—mobster Meyer Lansky did, after all, once proudly boast that the Mafia was "bigger than U.S. Steel." Yet even some high-ranking former FBI officials acknowledge that the anti-Mafia crusade eventually grew into a publicity-driven obsession that crowded out other legitimate priorities and put too much power in the hands of the organized crime squad agents and their superiors.

The second key initiative was the FBI's secret weapon in the Mafia war. It was a patently immoral scheme, born out of FBI Director J. Edgar Hoover's hubris and his disdain for constitutional rights, that created strategic, often deadly alliances with killers like Bulger and Flemmi in a Faustian bargain to make the FBI the premier Mafia-fighting agency in America.

Hoover's plan was called Top Echelon.

CHAPTER TWO

Top Echelon

....

Dangerous secret weapon in the war on the Mafia

THE FUNNY THING about black bag jobs, Wesley Swearingen always thought, was that the bags mostly weren't black. They were canvas satchels or metal toolboxes or anything else that made it look like what was inside was something other than sophisticated FBI bugging and snooping equipment. The men who carried them often bought their clothes from Sears Roebuck—flannel shirts, painter pants, work boots—in an attempt to look like ordinary laborers and blend in with the urban scenery that provided cover for their true mission: breaking into the homes of suspected Communist sympathizers to plant listening devices and conduct illegal searches.

Federal Bureau of Investigation Director J. Edgar Hoover nursed a visceral hatred of the Soviet Union—for more than four decades he aimed the muscle of his agency against suspected Communists and subversives of various stripes. In one of his frequent appearances before Congress in the 1950s, the bulldog-faced director said: "Communism is not a political party. It is a way of life. It spreads like an infection akin to disease. It must be treated like a disease and eradicated like one." It is probably somewhat ironic, then, that Hoover was as adept a master at bureaucratic infighting and empire building as the most Machiavellian member of the Politburo. It is impossible to understand the modern FBI, a highly complex agency in both structure and organizational psychology, without understanding how Hoover transformed the Bureau from an obscure, almost powerless appendage of the Justice Department into the most famous and arguably the most powerful law enforcement agency in the world.

The modern FBI began in 1908 as the Bureau of Investigation, an investigative arm of the U.S. Department of Justice under Attorney General Charles Bonaparte and President Theodore Roosevelt. Both Progressives, they shared a vision of a group of federal agents dedicated to enforcing the law fairly without the prejudice and corruption that often plagued local law enforcement at the time. Bonaparte created his own investigative force by hiring a handful of ex-Secret Service agents, but his investigators were a far cry from the "G-men" later popularized in film and on television. They were forbidden to carry guns and were empowered to investigate only banking and antitrust violations, land fraud and white slavery.

World War I marked the first serious expansion of the Bureau of Investigation's ranks and powers, when it was given jurisdiction over espionage, draft dodging, sabotage, and, shortly after the war ended, the transportation of stolen vehicles over state lines. As trench warfare raged in Europe and the Bolsheviks revolted in Russia in late 1917, J. Edgar Hoover, a young lawyer and son of a government mapmaker, left a job in the stacks of the Library of Congress for a slightly higher salary in the Department of Justice mailroom.

The first Red Scare in 1919 launched the twenty-four-year-old's career as a bureaucrat. After a spate of domestic bombings blamed on Communist and anarchist agitators, Hoover was promoted to Special Assistant in charge of a project to gather information on "ultraradical groups." The ex-librarian's anal-retentive cataloging of information on those groups was the forerunner of the FBI's vaunted indexing system, which by the year 2000 contained an estimated eighty million names. Hoover's index was the first of numerous innovations the Bureau introduced over the years, including the scientific handling of evidence, a national fingerprint database, and a national academy to teach police officers modern investigative methods. The creation of the index was also a defining moment for the agency's soul. At its core, the FBI is a domestic intelligence-gathering agency. Some of that information is used to prosecute crimes, some to track foreign intelligence agents and spies, and some to keep tabs on potentially violent domestic groups ranging from the Ku Klux Klan to right-wing militias. Much of it is filed away in the FBI's massive indexed files and archives, waiting for a day when it might become useful.

The government's excesses during the first Red Scare, in which Hoover played a key role, actually led to his taking over the Bureau of Investigation. On January 2, 1919, nearly ten thousand suspected subversives were rounded up in twenty-three cities by federal agents and local police; many were detained for days on trumped-up or nonexistent charges and some were roughed up. Some 249 actual and suspected Communists were put on a ship in New York and deported to Russia in what newspapers dubbed the "Red Raids" or the "Palmer Raids," after then–Attorney General A. Mitchell Palmer.

"Every scrap of radical literature demands the overthrow of our existing government," Palmer wrote in a 1920 editorial defending the raids. "All of it demands obedience to the instincts of criminal minds, that is, to lower appetites, material and moral. The whole purpose of communism appears to be a mass formation of the criminals of the world to overthrow the decency of private life, to usurp property that they have not earned, to disrupt the present order of life regardless of health, sex or religious rights." Hoover, an ardent Palmer supporter, would repeat such rhetoric almost verbatim in hundreds of speeches over the next fifty years.

Yet many Americans—not a few of whom held seats in

Congress—believed that it was Palmer, not the Bolsheviks, who had done the trampling of rights. Investigations and congressional hearings followed, dragging on for several years even after Palmer left the office. Hoover quietly moved over from Main Justice to the Bureau of Investigation as an Assistant Director in 1921, during an era when Palmer's replacement, Harold Daugherty, was padding the Justice Department payrolls with political cronies. It wasn't until President Warren G. Harding died and Calvin Coolidge was sworn into office that a serious effort was made to clean up the mess at the Justice Department. Harlan Fiske Stone, the highly esteemed Dean of the Columbia University Law School, had orders from Coolidge to straighten things out.

Hoover was never held accountable for his role in the Red Raids. He claimed to have just been following Palmer's orders and insisted that he had no knowledge of the abuses, but his excuses were paper-thin. The unit he oversaw within the Justice Department, the General Intelligence Division, planned and directed the raids. In fact, Hoover personally boarded the New York deportation ship for a press conference, boasting to the newspapers that more "Soviet arks" would soon be helping rid America of the Bolshevik menace.

For reasons never fully explained, Stone promoted Hoover to director in 1924, setting another precedent in the process. Many former agents readily admit that the FBI, throughout its history, has been infamous for punishing screw-ups with promotions—a phenomenon known in agent-speak as "mess up, move up." Perhaps Stone, the old professor, thought it was enough to give the obviously well-organized young lawyer a civics lesson and written guidelines on how to conduct investigations without violating civil rights.

The Bureau, Stone admonished Hoover, should not be "concerned with political or other opinions of individuals. It is concerned only with their conduct and then only with such conduct as is forbidden by the laws of the United States."

Stone warned: "There is always a possibility that a secret police may become a menace to free governments and free institutions because it carries with it the possibility of abuses of power that are not always quickly apprehended or understood."

Hoover agreed to rid the Bureau of political hacks and promised to abide by Stone's written guidelines. Partially true to his word, Hoover fired dozens of agents, based promotions on merit instead of seniority, and began imposing draconian rules governing agents' personal conduct. Agents were forbidden, for example, from drinking addictive stimulants, that is, coffee, while on duty, and could be fired if caught sipping the forbidden brew. Yet Hoover had cleansed only the body, not the soul. The historical record shows that the director almost immediately began ignoring Stone's admonitions against turning the Bureau into a "secret police" that trampled civil rights and hid behind a cloak of expediency and necessity.

As director, Hoover set about increasing the FBI both in size and jurisdiction, displaying the political savvy of a D.C. native. To grow, the FBI needed two things from Congress: laws to enforce and the money to enforce them. Hoover knew that the two worked in tandem: As long as the public believed that the FBI was doing a good job enforcing existing laws, Congress felt comfortable granting the agency more authority. Along with that new authority came the inevitable request for more funding for more agents. Even Hoover's top lieutenant for years, Cartha "Deke" DeLoach, describes him as "a master bureaucrat."

Hoover's tools were public image and statistics, and his obsession with both was deeply ingrained in the agency long after his death. Each year at budget time Hoover would present Congress with bigger and better numbers to justify funding increases while he carefully crafted the agency's image—and his own—as America's premier crime-fighter. In 1935, to avoid confusion with Prohibition agents in the

U.S. Division of Investigation, Hoover changed the name of the agency to the Federal Bureau of Investigation and began simply using the initials FBI, which also loaned themselves to a nifty motto: "Fidelity, Bravery, and Integrity." The thrust of the publicity was to wrap the FBI and its director in near-papal infallibility. Mistakes were never the biggest sin at the FBI, admitting them was. (See "mess up, move up.") The chief rule-of-thumb, agents knew, was "never embarrass the Bureau."

Hoover's plan to increase the FBI's power and stature worked. In 1924 he assumed control of an agency employing 650 people, of which 440 were agents. By 1943, Hoover had approximately 4,000 agents at his command, and the total number of FBI employees swelled to over 13,000.

Prohibition, which lasted from 1919 until 1933, transformed the American criminal landscape. Organized criminal groups had access to nearly limitless profits, supplying speakeasies with illegal liquor, profits which they used to bribe police officials and politicians across the country.

In Chicago, just two years after legal liquor was banned, Chief of Police Charles Fitzsimmons was forced to admit that many of his own officers were "actively involved" in bootlegging and smuggling. In Boston, a variety of Irish, Italian, and Jewish gangs led by the likes of Frankie Wallace, Filippo "Phil" Buccola, and Charles "King" Solomon, all made big money smuggling liquor into various places along the New England coastline. In New York two young criminal masterminds, Charles "Lucky" Luciano and Meyer Lansky, made millions importing scotch whiskey at $26 per case, then selling it for $30 a bottle—a 1,285 percent profit.

The eye-popping profits were a direct contributor to the development of a centralized Italian-American Mafia. Before prohibition the Mafia in the U.S. consisted of gangs headed by either Sicilian immigrants or their first-generation progeny, who imported the codes of strict hierarchical obedience and *omerta* ("silence") within the organization. Struggles for power were common, and often bloody. Luciano and Lansky realized that infighting between Mafia groups—particularly the five powerful New York families—only hindered the ability of each to maximize profits. In 1931 four Jewish gunmen posing as IRS agents murdered Salvatore Maranzano, a Sicilian Mafia boss who, after a bloody war with rival Guiseppe "Joe the Boss" Masseria, had declared himself *tutti di tutti capi* ("boss of all bosses").

A few weeks later Luciano called a national meeting in Chicago and declared: "It's time we grew up. Let's use our brains instead of our guns." No boss of bosses, he said, would ever rule again. Instead, families would be ruled by a "Commission" that would divvy up territories and arbitrate disputes. *Pax Luciano* made the Italian-American Mafia rich. Even when the Twenty-first Amendment ended Prohibition in 1933, the Italian mob simply redirected its profits into a variety of both legal and illegal endeavors, including construction, garbage hauling, organized labor, gambling, loansharking, and drug trafficking.

Curiously, the FBI, whose institutional growth was proceeding apace with the Mafia's, remained on the sidelines. FBI historians have put forward numerous theories for why the Mafia was in full flower for three decades before Hoover would admit it even existed. They range from his supposed rivalry with Federal Bureau of Narcotics Director Harry Anslinger to Hoover's own sheer bullheadedness and arrogance. Hoover had decreed that the Mafia did not exist, therefore, by definition, it could not.

Most likely, though, investigating the Mafia was simply at odds with Hoover's passion for empire-building. Hoover wanted his agents pursuing bank robberies, interstate car theft, draft dodging, and other crimes solvable with an economy of manpower. Organized crime investigations made for bad statistics, eating up lots of man-hours while yielding comparatively few arrests. If Hoover could not go to Capitol Hill with his gaudy statistics, his funding increases would be at risk. Hoover also knew that mixing wealthy gangsters with underpaid agents—the FBI starting annual salary in the mid-1950s was a pitiful $5,500—carried a major potential for the corruption of his supposedly incorruptible agency.

So, while Eliot Ness and his agents from the U.S. Treasury's Prohibition Bureau went after Capone in the 1930s, and Anslinger's FBN[2] targeted the Mafia's Corsican Connection, which poured tons of cheap heroin into the inner cities in the forties and fifties, Hoover stayed out of the fight. Agents who would later take down entire Mafia families freely admit that, for an agency that billed itself as the nation's premier crime fighting force, the FBI was stunningly ignorant about the Mafia in the mid-1950s. In contrast, by 1957 the FBN under Anslinger had compiled extensive files on known Mafia members in dozens of cities. U.S. Senator John J. McClellan's Select Committee on Improper Activities in the Labor or Management Field (thankfully known as the McClellan Committee, for short) meanwhile had eight offices across the nation conducting fifteen separate investigations of Mafia infiltration into the Teamsters and other unions.

Two major events in the late 1950s and early 1960s, however, forced Hoover kicking and screaming into the war on the American Mafia. The first was a picnic in upstate New York.

Disturbed by a wave of internecine violence that culminated in the barbershop rub-out of New York "Murder Inc." mobster Albert Anastasia, the Commission convened a summit conference at the upstate New York farm of Joseph Barba, a senior captain in the Buffalo mob. More than a hundred mobsters from across the country assembled at Barba's bucolic estate in the town of Appalachin on the weekend of November 14, 1957. An alert New York State

---

[2]The Federal Bureau of Narcotics was the forerunner of today's U.S. Drug Enforcement Administration.

Police trooper, who saw that Barba had booked a suspiciously large number of rooms at a local motel, drove out to the estate. The pasture next to Barba's house looked like the VIP parking section from a Sinatra concert, with row upon row of Cadillacs and Lincolns, luxury sedans and limousines. When a squad of New York troopers descended on the farm, the guests scattered in all directions, many comically bumping across cornfields and cow pastures in their big, city cars. A few escaped, but many were rounded up and detained long enough for the locals to figure out who they were.

When the news hit newspaper front pages coast to coast, the Appalachin conference was a humiliating rebuff to Hoover's contention that there was no such thing as an American Mafia. The attendees had come from all over the U.S.—including Russell Bufalino from Philadelphia, James Colletti from Colorado, the Falcone brothers from New York City, Santos Trafficante from Florida, and Vito Genovese from New Jersey.

Robert Francis Kennedy, the young chief counsel for McClellan's committee, was incensed to learn that more than a third of the mafiosi at the Appalachin conference at least nominally held jobs in labor-management relations. For months the McClellan committee had been hunting for proof that American organized labor was riddled with mob influence, yet when Kennedy had gone to a top Hoover aide for the latest news on the Mafia, the aide replied that there wasn't any due to "a newspaper strike."

The Kennedy brothers, rising stars in Washington, began pressuring Hoover to get in the fight against the Italian mob. The campaign intensified when JFK was elected President and named his brother Attorney General.

The Kennedys hated the Mafia, particularly their hometown mob boss, Raymond L.S. Patriarca, who had taunted the brothers during the McClellan committee hearings, saying: "You two don't have the brains of your retarded sister." Bobby Kennedy told a friend that he and Jack were "going

after that pig on the hill," referring to the mob boss's Federal
Hill stronghold in Providence, Rhode Island. The brothers
mounted a pressure campaign on Hoover, calling him with
information requests at all hours and bursting into his office
unannounced—even during his sacred afternoon nap.
Hoover and his top aides sneered in private over informant
reports about the Kennedy brothers' extramarital sexual es-
capades, but the director was smart enough to know that
after Appalachin, and with another round of McClellan committee hearings approaching, his beloved FBI was in danger
of becoming a national laughingstock.

The result was a program dubbed "Top Hoodlum."
Hoover fired off a memo to all his field offices on November 27, 1957, ordering them to compile lists of the Top Ten
organized crime figures within their jurisdictions. The Top
Hoodlums[3] were supposed to receive priority for investigation and prosecution, and the order sent FBI agents in
Omaha scrambling to find anyone they could possibly clas-
sify as a "Top Hoodlum." In New York, where twenty-five
agents were assigned to a newly formed Organized Crime
Squad, the agents had a different worry. With virtually no information on the Mafia, they wondered how they could possibly choose ten "top" hoodlums out of the hundreds
available.

The dictates of the Top Hoodlum Program were so foolish that, given Hoover's previous position on the Mafia, few
agents were convinced that the FBI was in the organized
crime fight for good. In fact, Special Agent Anthony Villano
said that when he first tried to join the new organized crime
squad in New York, a supervisor warned him the whole exercise might turn out to be nothing but a publicity stunt.
"The administrative officer cautioned me that the squads
might very well be only a temporary operation designed to

---

[3]The term "hoodlum" was used because the word "Mafia" was still verboten.

satisfy criticism and would be disbanded after the heat died down," Villano wrote in his book, *Brick Agent*.

The new squads were not disbanded. However silly it was, the Top Hoodlum Program actually created an important legacy. The FBI was in the organized crime game for good.

Top Hoodlum was the public side of Hoover's drive to catch up in the fight against organized crime. The secret side consisted of Hoover's plan to help the Bureau leapfrog both the Federal Bureau of Narcotics and the McClellan committee in its knowledge of the Mafia. Information was the coin of Hoover's realm, and he was about to strike it rich using a tool long employed by the FBI's Intelligence Division: electronic surveillance, or "ELSUR" in FBI-speak. In the late 1950s and early 1960s, Hoover deployed an array of illegal tactics, including wiretapping, bugging, break-ins, and searches, against the Communist party of the United States, his central preoccupation. Used against Communists, electronic surveillance was relatively easy both to justify, on national security grounds, and to keep secret. Since the Bureau was mostly keeping tabs on the Communists and their suspected sympathizers, not building criminal cases against them, most of the information was kept safely tucked away in the FBI's files.

The new anti-Mafia squads—desperate to play catchup—borrowed people, tactics, and equipment from the anti-Communist squads.

"The FBI didn't really know what they were doing when it came to the Mafia. So essentially we said, 'Gee, why don't we do what we did against the Communist party,'" said Swearingen, a former agent from the so-called "Infiltration Squad" in Chicago that did illegal wiretaps and break-ins, better known as "black bag jobs." Swearingen wrote a book about his experiences in the Bureau called *FBI Secrets: An Agent's Expose*.

Inside the bags were burglary tools, ten-pound Army surplus Motorola walkie-talkies, and some specialized equipment developed at FBI Headquarters just for the infiltration squads. According to Swearingen, most of the bugging equipment was fairly primitive by today's standards. The FBI did have some small microphones equipped with wireless transmitters, but their range was extremely limited and the sound quality so poor that any background noise at all—a radio, a whistling teakettle—would render them useless. If the agents were lucky enough to be able to gain access to a room directly next door, they could insert a thin "pencil mike" into a hole drilled as far as possible into the adjoining wall without actually breaking through.

The tried and true surveillance weapon, however, was the telephone bug. Although it was installed in the lower part of the telephone handset, it could constantly monitor all the sounds in a room, not just telephone conversations. Since it used existing telephone lines, it solved numerous problems with the other bugs, like the need for a separate power source or a risky monitoring station in the next room. Once a "slave" line was added for the bug by the telephone company, it could be monitored from the comfort and safety of the local FBI office across town. In Chicago the telephone bugs were monitored in the Sound Room, a twenty-by-twenty-foot space where the walls were covered by more than two dozen listening stations, each outfitted with a reel-to-reel tape recorder and a pair of headphones hung from a peg on the wall. Access to the Sound Room was strictly limited to the surveillance technicians and their immediate supervisor, a senior agent.

One of the agents who moved from surveilling Communists to bugging Italian wiseguys was William F. Roemer, an ex-amateur boxer who later identified himself as the "coordinator" of the Top Echelon Informant Program in Chicago. Roemer was disenchanted with his work on the S-1 Security Squad bugging the Communists. Like a lot of agents who had actually observed the CP-USA close up, Roemer didn't share Hoover's view that it posed any legitimate threat to overthrow the government. "I felt we had beaten the Communist party. I did not now deem my work to be of great import. It had been, I thought, but now I perceived the threat to be greatly exaggerated. As a result, I had lost some of my zest for the job," Roemer wrote in one of several books he penned about his experiences in the FBI's Chicago office. The unhappy Roemer began making plans to join his family's law firm, taking long lunches to study for the bar exam at the Chicago Public Library. His slacking off prompted his supervisor to suggest, firmly, that he volunteer for the newly forming C-1 Organized Crime Squad. Roemer and two other Communist surveillance agents, Marshall Rutland and Ralph Hill, were transferred to the new squad in the mid-1950s.

"Bill came onto the Security Squad," Swearingen said. "I had already been on the Surveillance Squad before that, and we started doing bag jobs and bugs and wiretaps together. Later [on the Organized Crime Squad] he just followed the same general routine." According to Swearingen, when Roemer and his team began installing the illegal bugs around Chicago mob hangouts, they were monitored side by side with illegal bugs installed in the homes of suspected Communists. One technician might be listening to a discourse on Marx while another would be overhearing mob boss Sam "Mooney" Giancana ordering a contract murder.

The FBI Organized Crime Squad in Chicago had had little success going after the leadership of Chicago's Italian mob using traditional law enforcement methods. Bugging changed everything. The wiseguys were mostly unaware of the FBI's eavesdropping technology, which hitherto had been used exclusively against spies and suspected Communists. But because the police and the FBN regularly listened in on telephone conversations, the wiseguys had long ago learned to be cautious when talking on the phone. In the summer of 1959, Roemer and the other agents, using their Security Squad training, installed a more sophisticated, hardwired bug in a tailor's shop at 620 North Michigan, in the heart of Chicago's Magnificent Mile.

Celano's Custom Tailors was not only where Al Capone's successors bought their suits and overcoats, but also where big shots like Giancana and Tony "the Big Tuna" Accardo met to discuss their illicit business. The hidden microphone operated faithfully, while the wiseguys were blissfully unaware that the FBI was listening to their every move. In the first few months, the agents recorded the mafiosi discussing contract murders, extortion, and jury tampering—then sending underlings out to use pay phones so their orders to soldiers in the field wouldn't be intercepted.

Roemer dubbed the microphone "Little Al," a joking reference to Capone. For an amazing six years it gave the FBI priceless information on the mob, including proof of the existence of the Commission.

When the agents used the information, they did their best to conceal it, for two reasons: (1) they didn't want anything to interrupt the information of valuable intelligence on the Mafia, and (2) it was illegal. Actually, the bugging itself was a legal gray area (the FBI preferred the term "extralegal," according to former high-ranking FBI official Oliver "Buck" Revell), but the method used to install the bugs, breaking and entering, was clearly against the law. Agents on the bag job squads, in fact, were ordered to leave their credentials at home and warned that if they were caught by local police, the FBI would deny any knowledge of their activities.

In 1958, Hoover ordered hundreds of illegal wiretaps across the country, sometimes euphemistically referring to them in his own memos as "highly confidential sources." According to Buck Revell, in the years before bugging was legalized, the FBI had a standing order from the Attorney General that permitted bugging in cases of "national security." Hoover, however, stretched this authority well past the breaking point. Even arch-Hoover defender Deke DeLoach said as much in his memoir, *Hoover's FBI.*

"In the past," DeLoach wrote, "Hoover had sometimes found it necessary to work with less than full authority. The

FBI adhered rigidly to most of the restrictions placed on it; but occasions arose when Hoover believed the end justified the means, that regulations should give way to expediency."

The agents didn't have many moral qualms over the practice either, according to Swearingen: "We knew it was an invasion of privacy, but that was beside the point, if you are talking about the Mafia. We felt that they didn't deserve the privacy if they weren't paying millions in taxes so the heck with them. If you got approval from the AG, as far as we were concerned it was all right. Even if it was not authorized, we knew we wouldn't be able to use it in court, but we could still use it for intelligence information. An illegal bug or wiretap could lead to a search warrant if you faked it and said the information came from a source, if it ever came up."

The Top Hoodlum ELSUR program was eventually tripped up, interestingly enough, by its own success. In 1965 one of the bugs installed in a Washington, D.C., hotel room started picking up information on Robert Baker, a former top aide to President Lyndon Johnson when he had been in the U.S. Senate. Apparently counting on Johnson's friendship with the Bureau, FBI officials told the President, as a courtesy, that his former aide was the target of eavesdropping. Johnson's alarmed reaction shocked the FBI. Citing concerns about civil rights violations, the President ordered that *all* the Bureau's illegal bugs be not only turned off, but physically removed from their locations, according to Roemer.

On July 11, 1965, all the tape recorders were shut down. Despondent Organized Crime Squad agents broke back into the Mafia-controlled tailor shops, dry cleaners, restaurants, and social clubs and tore their eavesdropping equipment out.

"We had feasted at the table of plenty and we were about to go hungry," Roemer wrote. "July 11, 1965, was one of the worst days of my life."

Other than electronic surveillance, informants are the FBI's only other direct source of inside information. Because it is primarily an intelligence-gathering operation, the FBI has used informants since its creation. Informants were particularly important to the FBI because Hoover—again fearing that his incorruptible agency would be corrupted—generally frowned on agents working undercover.

Exactly how the FBI uses its informants is one of the Bureau's least-favorite topics of discussion. Much of that secrecy is arguably necessary. The underworld has many euphemisms for turncoats—"snitches," "squealers," "stoolies," and, most popularly, "rats." But an exposed informer by any other name would be just as dead. In the early 1960s the FBI learned that the Mafia required all its members, when they were initiated, to swear an oath to kill even their close relatives if they turned informer. The source of that information was a rat himself, Joseph M. Valachi, whose defection was the second major event that forced the FBI into the war on the Mafia for good.

Valachi, a heroin smuggler and lower-level associate of one of the five New York Mafia families, was arrested by the Federal Bureau of Narcotics and convicted on drug charges in the early 1960s. Stuck doing twenty years in the U.S. Penitentiary in Atlanta, the FBN agents who arrested him believed he could potentially be persuaded ("turned" or "flipped," in law enforcement parlance). Valachi was targeted by FBN agents as a potential cooperator. They used one of their favorite tricks: first putting his life in danger, then offering to save it. The FBN agents made a very public show of visiting the prison to speak with him, purposefully creating the appearance that he indeed had already turned. Valachi soon became so paranoid that he beat another inmate to death with a two-foot section of iron pipe. With a murder charge hanging over his head, Valachi had no choice but to cooperate.

When word of his predicament reached the Attorney General's office, Bobby Kennedy saw another opportunity to push Hoover. He ordered the FBI to take over the Valachi matter. FBI Special Agent James Flynn, who had studied the transcripts from Roemer's "Little Al" bug, used the inside information to eventually coax out the entire story of the Italian-American Mafia—*omerta*, the five ruling families, the initiation rites.[4]

Once Valachi had been successfully flipped, Kennedy moved to cut off any future attempt by Hoover to wiggle out of responsibility for taking on the Mafia. He thrust Valachi in front of the television lights and cameras as a witness before the McClellan committee, and on September 27, 1963, an entire spellbound nation watched the FBI's own Mafia insider outline a vast, national Italian-American criminal conspiracy. Hoover was beside himself. "I never saw so much skullduggery," he wrote in an angry memo about the affair.

If the Appalachin Conference six years earlier had raised the public possibility that a national Italian-American criminal conspiracy existed, Valachi removed any doubt. For the FBI, there would be no turning back in the fight against the Mafia.

The first references to something called the "Top Echelon Criminal Informant Program" in FBI memos began appearing during the period between Valachi's conversion in 1963 and Johnson's shutdown of the illegal bugs in 1965.

The exact origins of the program aren't documented—at least according to the FBI—but the reasoning behind it is fairly obvious. Valachi had proven that mafiosi, given the right motivation, could be coaxed into breaking *omerta*. After the illegal bugs were yanked out and the FBI was plunged from enlightenment back into darkness, high-level informants were the only potential source of the sort of in-

---

[4]Valachi also provided the FBI with a name for the American Mafia that stuck for the next thirty-seven years: "La Cosa Nostra" or "the LCN" to the acronym-happy Bureau. There was no doubt that America had its own Mafia; it was imported directly from Sicily with the same rules and methods, but Hoover had said the "Mafia" didn't exist and "La Cosa Nostra" kept the director from having to eat that particular piece of crow. The phrase means "this thing of ours" in Sicilian.

side information they had come to depend on. The idea to recruit high-level mafiosi as informers was classic Hoover: expediency begat by necessity and shrouded in secrecy.

Without a doubt, the 1995 racketeering case in Boston against New England Mafia boss Francis P. "Cadillac Frank" Salemme and Winter Hill Gang chieftains Whitey Bulger and Stephen Flemmi provided the most comprehensive look inside inside the Top Echelon program. Secret FBI reports made public in *U.S.* v. *Salemme* show that one of the first references to it appears in a memo circulated by Hoover to the various field offices in September 1963—the same month Valachi testified.

At the time, the FBI's guidelines for handling informants were contained in a large book called the *Manual of Instructions* (MOI). By December 1964 the MOI had been changed to include a new class of informant, called "Top Echelon," defined as:

> *Members of the underworld and those who closely associate with them, [including] Madams, prostitutes, pimps, fences, con men, hijackers, robbers, burglars, hoodlums and gangsters and those persons associated with such persons.*

A Top Echelon informant, the guidelines stated, should be chosen on the basis of:

> *. . . his position in the organized hoodlum element and upon circumstances indicating his possible vulnerability to development.*

The change in the MOI was a watershed. Under the guidelines of the new Top Echelon Informant Program, Hoover allowed his agents—indeed encouraged them—to recruit sources of information who were murderers, crime bosses, and, especially, men who had been sworn in as members of the Italian mob.

For the next thirty-five years, driven by the federal government's zeal to prosecute the Italian-American Mafia and the FBI's own unique institutional culture and salary structure, the Bureau created secret strategic alliances with mobsters across the United States. While the FBI refuses to release the total number of informants given "Top Echelon" status, two separate former high-ranking FBI officials interviewed by the author put the number as high as four hundred. Boston Special Agent John Connolly alone has said he had ten T.E. informants. William Roemer has admitted to at least three in Chicago, and Anthony Villano said he had five in New York's underworld. There can be little doubt that hundreds of T.E. informants committed thousands of crimes—building criminal empires, trafficking in drugs, embezzling union funds, committing murder, and destroying the lives of innocent civilians—all while their FBI handlers, following the dictates of Hoover's 1963 order, looked the other way and even helped.

To be fair, at the time the Top Echelon program was created, the FBI faced a nearly insurmountable task in going after the Mafia. It would be several years before Congress would pass crucial antiracketeering and antigambling laws. As yet, there was also no federal Witness Protection Program. The laws the FBI did have at its disposal carried prison terms too short to be an incentive to become an informant or a witness. Most criminals were content to do their time rather than risk getting "two in the hat" or turning a car ignition wired to four sticks of dynamite.

Over the years, however, the program became mostly a shortcut. Faced with an admittedly difficult task, the FBI simply changed the legal and moral rules under which law enforcement was supposed to operate, then did its best to keep the program a secret and cover up the consequences. FBI officials have long been loath to officially admit the existence of the Top Echelon program. When pressed, officials would say that T.E. was the designation for a very good or very productive informant. The truth was that T.E. informants were the Bureau's dirty little secret in the war on the Mafia—a clandestine program that was deeply troubled and fundamentally immoral.

In order to fully understand the problems inherent in the Top Echelon Informant Program, it is important to understand some definitions.

While the word "informant" is used by the media as a generic term for anyone who cooperates with authorities, it is actually a very specific FBI term of art. In FBI parlance, neither Joe Valachi nor "Sammy the Bull" Gravano, were informants. Rather, they were *cooperating witnesses,* or *C.W.'s.* A cooperating witness is a person who, generally after getting into some kind of trouble with the law, agrees to cooperate in return for a lighter sentence or even a free pass and sometimes witness protection. Cooperating witnesses may work undercover, even for extended periods of time, but eventually testify in court and serve time in prison and are relocated or given new identities.

Informants, in contrast, are true underworld spies. Their identities are never revealed to anyone outside the FBI, with the exception of a few prosecutors in emergency situations. While cooperating witnesses work undercover for finite periods of time, informants stay undercover indefinitely, providing information until either they or the FBI decide to break off the relationship.

Another key difference is that cooperating witnesses operate under the supervision of a prosecutor, so at least two agencies are involved in the relationship. There are no external checks and balances on the FBI's relationships with its informants, all supervision is handled in-house.

The level of supervision evolved over the years, as did the entire T.E. program. By 1971 the definition of a Top Echelon informant in the *Manual of Instructions* was clarified to actual "members of La Cosa Nostra" and those closely associated with them, but there were few written restrictions on what FBI agents could do to recruit and keep their sources of information. In 1976, however, the Justice Department imposed a new set of guidelines on the FBI, set forth by Attorney General Edward H. Levi. The Levi rules were a response to congressional pressure in the wake of a FBI sting called ABSCAM, in which FBI agents posing as middlemen for a wealthy Arab sheik snared U.S. Senator Harrison Williams of New Jersey on influence-peddling charges. The Bureau's undercover operations, not informants, were the major issue in the controversy following ABSCAM, but Congress, badly shaken by the arrest of one of its own, took the opportunity to examine virtually all of the FBI's covert policies. Four years later, the guidelines were fleshed out and modified somewhat by then-Attorney General Benjamin R. Civiletti.

The Levi/Civiletti guidelines specifically allowed the FBI to "authorize" some minor crimes committed by its informants and, in some cases, look the other way. In order to remain credible in the criminal world, the guidelines recognized that informants *had* to commit some crimes or else risk being exposed.

> *Informants who are in a position to have useful knowledge of criminal activities often are themselves involved in criminal livelihood. It is recognized that in the course of using an informant or confidential source, the FBI may receive limited information concerning a variety of criminal activities by the informant or confidential source, and that in regard to less serious participation in criminal activities unconnected to an FBI assignment, it may be necessary to forego any further investigative or enforcement action in order to retain the source of information.*

The concept of authorization, however, appeared to cause confusion even among high-ranking FBI officials. At the *Salemme* hearings, former top FBI official James Greenleaf, for example, was asked under oath whether "an individual acting as an informant for the FBI, at least as far as you understand the guidelines, could be authorized to conduct criminal activity."

"Yes, I believe that's correct," Greenleaf replied.

Yet, the man he replaced as Boston FBI Special Agent in Charge, Lawrence Sarhatt, testified to the exact opposite when he was asked if the supervisory special agents under his command had the authority to authorize "criminal activity."

"No," he replied.

"Who had that authority?" Sarhatt was asked.

"Nobody had that authority."

The guidelines also spelled out a series of mandatory actions that the FBI had to take if and when agents learned that their informants had been committing either unauthorized or "serious" crimes.

Whenever a Special Agent learns of the commission of a serious crime by an informant or confidential source, he shall notify a field office supervisor. The supervisor shall make the determination whether to notify appropriate state or local law enforcement or prosecutive authorities of any violation of law and shall make a determination whether the continued use of the informant or confidential source is justified.

Each FBI field office shall immediately notify FBI Headquarters when it learns of participation by an informant or a confidential source in a serious act of violence, even when the appropriate state or local law enforcement or prosecutive authorities have been notified. Detailed records shall be maintained at Headquarters regarding each instance of informant or confidential source participation in a serious act of violence, and these records shall be subject to periodic review by a designee of the Deputy Attorney General in a form suitable to protect the identity of the informants and confidential sources. A determination to continue use of the informant or confidential sources

*must be approved by the Director or a senior Head-
quarters official, after consultation with the Assistant
Attorney General in charge of the Criminal Division.*

On paper the Levi/Civiletti guidelines appeared to provide a safeguard against out-of-control informants. A closer
look, however, reveals ample wiggle room. According to
Section 137G(4) of the *Manual of Investigative and Operational Guidelines* (formerly the MOI), a determination
whether to keep the informant is supposed to be made using
six criteria:

1. Whether the crime has already occurred or is imminent
2. The potential for danger to life and property
3. Whether the crime is a felony or a misdemeanor
4. The *"degree of certainty"* of the information
5. Whether the appropriate state or local authorities
   already know about the criminal activity
6. The *"effect of notification on FBI investigative activity"*

Over the life of the T.E. program, criteria numbers 4 and 6
proved the most problematic. Time and again FBI informant
handlers and their supervisors on the Organized Crime
squads, hearing reports of serious crimes such as murder, extortion, and drug trafficking, even from fellow FBI agents on
other squads, pushed the definition of "degree of certainty"
to ridiculous extremes. One former Boston FBI supervisor
even went so far as to say that, in his estimation, "proof" consisted only of another law enforcement agency actually
bringing criminal charges against a Bureau informant. That
circular logic, of course, conveniently negated a primary purpose of the guidelines, which was to have *the FBI* tell other
law enforcement agencies when its informants went south.

Using their incredibly strict definitions of proof, the
agents and supervisors could then successfully argue that

the "effect on FBI investigative activity" would be too great, and thus they were able to maintain permission to continue using informants even after they went bad. In other words, there was virtually no situation contemplated under the guidelines—even in the case of informants committing murder—under which the FBI had no choice but to break off its relationship with a Top Echelon informant.

Indeed, the better the information, the more easily the FBI could justify the informant's continued use. Of course, the T.E. informants with the best information were the ones at the highest levels of the Mafia and other underworld groups. The worst informants, therefore, had the best chance of convincing the FBI not to go after them. It was, literally, a vicious circle.

The FBI's exclusive ability to decide for itself whether its informants should be prosecuted appears to be unique in law enforcement. Section D-3 of the DEA's informant guidelines, for example, states that: *"Whenever DEA has reason to believe that an informant or a defendant-informant has committed a serious criminal offense, an appropriate law enforcement agency **shall** be advised by DEA, and the appropriate United States attorney **shall** be notified."* The DEA guidelines do not allow agents to keep their informants' wrongdoing under wraps altogether.

An even more serious problem was that the mandates from Levi and Civiletti and the Top Echelon Informant Program fundamentally contradicted. Rather than changing FBI policy, the new guidelines were simply grafted onto the existing MOI, which was later renamed the *Manual of Investigative and Operational Guidelines* (MIOG). The result was a set of muddled rules that sent mixed messages to the agents who handled Top Echelon informants. On one hand, agents were supposed to target their own informants for prosecution when they were accused of committing "serious" crimes. On the other, T.E. informants were assumed to be committing "serious" crimes such as loansharking, extortion, assault, and even murder *all the time*, as several former

FBI officials testified under oath in the *U.S.* v. *Salemme* case.

John Morris, the Boston FBI supervisor who admitted taking bribes from T.E. informants Whitey Bulger and Stephen Flemmi, was questioned about the issue by Assistant U.S. Attorney Fred Wyshak, one of the *Salemme* prosecutors.

"The very definition of a Top Echelon informant is an informant who can provide information at the policy-making level of organized crime. There's absolutely no way that anybody can provide information at the policy-making level of organized crime unless they have some involvement in criminal activity," Morris testified.

"And is organized crime different from other kinds of crime?" Wyshak asked.

"Well, organized crime essentially is a way of life. I mean, that's essentially what they do day in, day out. That's their life."

From the beginning, the Top Echelon program was cloaked in secrecy. U.S. District Court Judge Mark L. Wolf, who ordered the unprecedented *Salemme* hearings, in fact opened his 661-page preliminary decision, a scathing assessment of FBI conduct in the case, by addressing the secrecy issue. "In 1861, Lord Acton wrote that, '[e]very thing secret degenerates, even the administration of justice,' " Wolf wrote. "This case demonstrates that he was right."

However questionable keeping the entire concept of T.E. informants a secret was, the need for extreme discretion within the program was undeniable. Once the FBI had committed to using high-level members of the Mafia and their associates as informers, any carelessness about their identities would almost certainly lead to their deaths. Plus, if word hit the streets that the FBI could not protect its organized crime informants, Bureau officials knew that all their informant programs could be in jeopardy.

The Bureau's solution was keeping informant information on a strictly "need-to-know" basis, where almost all direct contact between the informant was restricted to the "han-dler"—who was usually a line agent, the FBI's lowest rank—and that agent's direct supervisor. The guidelines also required that an "alternate contact agent" be named for each informant, to keep the informant relationship from getting too cozy. The best informant recruiters, however, said that T.E.'s preferred dealing with just one agent, and that the alternates were mostly there for show. "The alternate agent is really not a big deal," one longtime agent said. "It's to be there if the primary agent isn't around, and to meet him once a year. It's not a big obligation."

The practice of giving control to low level agents and supervisors codified in the Levi-T.E. guidelines, was effective in keeping a lid on the highly sensitive T.E. information. It had the unfortunate side effect, however, of crippling any effective supervision of the program up the chain of command. There seems to have been little oversight above the supervisor level. This was confirmed by the man who recruited Stephen Flemmi as a Top Echelon informant in the early 1960s, Special Agent H. Paul Rico. "I think that the intention . . . was to try to limit the knowledge of who was an informant, and that was part and parcel of the Bureau's policy at that time," Rico testified at the *Salemme* hearings.

There were other indications that oversight of the FBI's informant programs was significantly lacking. One is the fact that many informant decisions were made on a "UACB" basis, another bit of FBI-speak that stood for "Unless Advised to the Contrary by the Bureau." As one supervisor explained: "It means that I or some other supervisor or the agent in charge could have decided to take a position and . . . send it to Washington. And if they want to correct it or change it, they can come back and instruct us. And if they don't answer, then our proposal stands." In other words, Headquarters didn't actually have to *approve* many of the decisions made in the field about informants. As long as no negative answer came back—or no answer at all, for that matter—the decision stood.

Nominally, overall supervision at the local level was also supposed to include an "Informant Coordinator," but it wasn't a full-time job. The coordinator had other responsibilities, sometimes running an entire squad, and received only nominal training. James Blackburn, who served as Boston FBI informant program coordinator during part of the 1980s, said he received no formal training until ten months *after* being given the assignment, when he was flown down to the FBI Academy for three days of in-service training. Blackburn said he threw out the materials he received during the training sessions as soon as he returned to Boston. "There was nothing I needed in there," he said. Nicolas Gianturco, who also held the post, said it was his understanding that the Informant Coordinator's job was to make sure that the paperwork was up-to-date and that "unproductive" informants were dropped—not check for potential violations of the Attorney General's Guidelines.

FBI Headquarters, meanwhile, was supposed to review informant "suitability" determination rulings made by field supervisors. Larry Potts, who Director Louis Freeh would later nominate as the number two man at the Bureau, testified at the *Salemme* hearings that he could not remember one time, in his twenty-one-year career, that anyone at FBI Headquarters had ever reversed a supervisor's finding that an informant was suitable. "I'm not suggesting there hasn't been one; I'm just saying that I'm not aware of one," Potts said.

Section G-1 of the guidelines required FBI agents to send word up the Justice Department food chain if a decision had been made not to tell local law enforcement officials that one of their T.E. informants was involved in "acts of violence, corrupt action by high public officials, or severe financial loss to a victim." Yet several top former officials said they couldn't remember any such notification ever occurring. One was William Weld, who served as Chief of the Justice Department's Criminal Division during the Reagan administration.

The FBI does have a mechanism, at least in theory, for breaking off relationships with rogue informants, called "closing." Despite what the name seemingly implies, closing does not signify a complete breakup of the relationship between the FBI and a Top Echelon informant. Instead, under FBI rules, agents may continue to receive information from a closed informant, they just can't "task" that informant to get a particular piece of information. James Greenleaf, who was a former Assistant Director in Charge of Inspections for the Bureau before moving to the CIA, was asked during the *Salemme* hearings why it was not "inappropriate" for FBI agents to receive information from a closed informant. "If somebody is going to give us significant information, we'd be foolish not to accept it," Greenleaf replied.

Another aspect of the closing process casts even more doubt on its true purpose—informants were routinely not informed that they had been "closed." ASAC Larry A. Potts testified that one reason he recommended Whitey Bulger and Stephen Flemmi not be closed was "if suddenly there was no contact . . . then they could be suspicious that there was an investigation." In essence, the same reason for closing informants—that they were suspected of serious crimes—was used by Potts for *not* closing them. Obviously, closing wasn't a very meaningful process.

The more logical explanation for not telling informants they were closed, of course, was to keep the information pipeline flowing. As numerous experiences with T.E. informants would show, the FBI was too addicted to and too dependent on the information they were providing to turn around and investigate them in any meaningful way. Putting informants in "closed" status on paper, in short, seems to have been a pure ass-covering technique. What it really meant was that the FBI had a backup plan when there was a danger that one of its informants—particularly at the Top Echelon level—would get into serious trouble. If it was merely an internal FBI inquiry, line agents and supervisors could show the brass in Washington that they had done something. If the informant was arrested by another agency and somehow exposed as a rat, the FBI could truthfully say that the person wasn't officially an informant.

On the street, nothing changed. "Closed" informants weren't told of their status, and their precious inside information kept flowing into the Bureau's files. Informants often closed only until the storm passed. After it did, the handlers would begin shooting off memos back to headquarters requesting that their informants be returned to active status.

The entire career advancement structure at the Bureau not only exacerbated the already serious pressures to produce informants and significant Mafia cases, it provided every incentive for FBI agents *not* to do the right thing when one of their informants went off the reservation.

The heads of field offices were required by FBI rules to submit a yearly report on informant activity back to Headquarters. The report contained the symbol numbers of all informants—only the supervisors and handling agents knew the actual names—and a list of the help they had given the Bureau. Each instance of aid to the FBI was marked down as a "statistical accomplishment." The handler and supervisor would also be given a "stat" that would count toward their performance reviews and merit pay increases. "Stats" were the currency of the Bureau's promotions and evaluation program and a legacy of Hoover's desire to quantify and categorize.

The FBI also had a unique system of awarding cash bonuses to reward agents for their successful work on a particular case. Roemer, for example, wrote that he received a substantial sum from Hoover for installing the illegal "Little Al" bug, although he declined to say how much. "Mr. Hoover was very generous to me on that occasion and I have always appreciated that." Top former Hoover aide Cartha DeLoach speculated that the origin of the cash bonuses was personal to the socially awkward Hoover, who sometimes handed out the checks in person and took a souvenir photo with the agent. "Hoover was really a shy man who found some words difficult to say and could better communicate with cash," DeLoach wrote.

The awards ranged from a few hundred dollars to, on some occasions, several thousand. To an agent earning $225 a week before taxes in 1970, a few hundred dollars was not an insignificant sum. If an agent's informant did well—providing the Bureau with valuable intelligence that led to wiretaps and arrests—the agent also benefited. The cash incentive program is another aspect of its operations that the Bureau rarely talks about, probably with good reason. When witnesses, even FBI agents, are called to testify in a criminal case, prosecutors are required to turn over information they might have that could affect the witnesses' credibility, including "promises, rewards, or inducements." Some judges have held that a cash award for work on a particular case is clearly a "reward" and must be turned over.

Finally, Top Echelon informants often transformed their handlers into de facto power brokers within the offices where they worked. Other agents working cases who needed inside information on the Mafia had no choice but to depend on the T.E. handlers. "The guys who had the T.E.'s were the king shits in the office, they were the ones that had all the power," one Organized Crime Strike Force prosecutor said.

With so many incentives not to follow the Levi guidelines, many agents simply ignored them. Both Morris and James Ring, his successor running the Organized Crime Squad, testified that when they were running the Boston FBI's Organized Crime Squad in the 1970s and 1980s, they were forced to choose between following the T.E. program mandates and the contradictory Attorney General's Guidelines. Both men chose the T.E. guidelines.

An April 1, 1981, addendum to an internal Boston FBI memo helps explain why. Morris's comments were attached to a memo written by John Connolly, the handler of T.E. informant James Whitey Bulger, attempting to justify the continued use of Bulger as a T.E.:

> The stated national priority of the
> FBI's Organized Crime Program is to ad-
> dress La Cosa Nostra—related problems.
> Consistent with the national priority,
> the LCN is the primary target of the Or-
> ganized Crime Program in the Boston Di-
> vision.

By the early 1980s, attacking organized crime had become not only the FBI's, but also the Justice Department's, first priority. It was a far cry from "the Mafia doesn't exist" days under Hoover. The FBI's ardor for Mafia cases cooled again after JFK was assassinated in 1963 and Bobby Kennedy left the Attorney General's office. From the Kennedy assassination until Hoover's death in 1972, the FBI's organized crime effort limped along, with only the occasional success. Hoover, now into his seventies, turned his attention back to leftist subversives, only his definitions seemed to have expanded alarmingly. People ranging from members of the violent Weather Underground to American Indian Movement (AIM) activists to some members of the NAACP were lumped in the category of the so-called New Left. Swearingen said no one at the FBI ever defined what the New Left was except that it "was newer than the Old Left."

Hoover's attention to constitutional niceties reached a new low. The low was called COINTELPRO, FBI-speak for "Counter-Intelligence Program." It had all the elements of Hoover's previous efforts against suspected Communists and their sympathizers—black bag jobs, illegal wiretaps, unauthorized opening of mail, and infiltration of political groups—but added a new wrinkle: dirty tricks. "The FBI resorted to counterintelligence tactics in part because its chief officials believed that the existing laws could not control the activities of certain dissident groups, and that court decisions had tied the hands of the intelligence community. Whatever opinion one holds about the policies of the targeted groups, many of the tactics employed by the FBI were indisputably degrading to a free society," a congressional committee reported in 1975.

After Hoover's death in 1972, Clarence Kelley, a former agent who returned to the Bureau after serving as Chief of Police in Kansas City, was named director and received a full briefing on COINTELPRO. Appalled, Kelley ordered a drastic cut in domestic intelligence operations and renewed attention to the FBI's criminal responsibilities. He also ordered that the emphasis on silly statistics be shelved and that agents be encouraged to make "quality" criminal cases instead of just piling up the numbers. Former U.S. Appeals Court Judge William Webster, who replaced Kelley in 1978, continued the trend, ordering increased attention to white collar crime and organized crime cases. Under both Kelley and Webster, the FBI's anti-Mafia effort gradually picked up speed.

The new members of the FBI's Organized Crime Section at Headquarters and the OC squads in the field offices would go into battle better armed than their predecessors, thanks to three major developments in federal law enforcement. All three occurred during the down years of the FBI's organized crime effort, so they went largely unnoticed. Together, they were a quiet revolution in the way the war on organized crime would be fought.

The first was part of a grandiose-sounding bill signed into law by President Richard Nixon, which Congress called the Omnibus Crime Control and Safe Streets Act of 1968. Title III of the new law stated that, while unregulated bugs and wiretaps endangered the privacy rights of American citizens, electronic surveillance was a necessary and legitimate law enforcement tool because "organized criminals make extensive use of wire and oral communications in their criminal activities." Electronic surveillance would be permitted as long as FBI agents could show a federal judge that "probable cause" existed to believe that criminal conversations were likely to take place in a specified location. Title III put the FBI, legally this time, back in the electronic eavesdropping business. Now, not only could the tapes be made, but they were admissible as evidence in court.

A second law passed two years later, the Racketeer Influenced and Corrupt Organizations (RICO), was even more revolutionary. The law for the first time allowed the FBI and federal prosecutors to target entire Mafia organizations at the same time. Relatively minor crimes like extorting tribute from a bookmaker or collecting a loanshark debt, instead of being charged individually, could be aggregated as "racketeering acts" in a RICO case, which carried much heavier penalties.

Finally, the FBI had traditionally been loath to share information with Assistant U.S. Attorneys, who, unlike most FBI agents, considered government work to be a steppingstone to a career in the private sector. Why should an agent entrust an informant's identity or the secrets of a wiretap to a federal prosecutor who, the next week, might very well join a firm of defense lawyers offering twice his or her government salary? In 1967, however, the FBI was given what amounted to their own force of prosecutors by Attorney General Ramsey Clark. Recognizing that the Mafia didn't respect state lines, Clark established two dozen regional Organized Crime Strike Forces, groups of prosecutors based in large cities with the power to conduct long-term organized crime investigations that spread across the jurisdictions of the U.S. Attorney's offices in the various states. The FBI Organized Crime squads developed close working relationships with the strike force lawyers.

Title III would prove to be the cornerstone of the new RICO prosecutions, but the FBI was slow to realize the importance of the new law. In fact, the law languished unused for nearly a decade until Webster took over the Bureau, then finally a major effort was launched. Until the late 1970s the Bureau had also conducted relatively few Title IIIs—which some attribute to a lingering leeriness of the high amount of man-hours required to sit on a bug long-term.

Some former FBI officials have tried to downplay the importance of both wiretaps and informants. FBI Supervisor Ring, who oversaw the Boston FBI's Organized Crime Squad for most of the 1980s, said that "one good cooperating witness is worth twenty good informants." The assertion is patently ludicrous. As the Honorable Edward F. Harrington, a former chief of the New England Organized Crime Strike Force who became a federal judge, once said: "You can't cross-examine a tape." Unlike rat witnesses, tapes made from wiretaps or bugs have no criminal rap sheets. They have no shifty eyes or "dis, dem, deese, and dose" accents to put off a jury. Caught on a legally admissible tape, the gangsters ended up testifying against themselves.

Virtually the only way to get "probable cause" for a Title III was through the use of informants. When the Justice Department geared up its big anti-Mafia crusade in the late 1970s, it looked to the FBI to come up with the evidence for the Title IIIs. On the surface it appeared that, between the judicial approval required by Title III and the Levi guidelines dictating the handling of informants, all the proper constitutional safeguards were in place. Yet, few people, even inside the Justice Department, knew that one of the FBI's primary weapons against the Mafia was a badly flawed, morally bankrupt informant program left over from the era of J. Edgar Hoover's worst abuses against civil and constitutional rights.

CHAPTER THREE

Dark Alliance

••••••••••••••••••••••••••••••

*The FBI's courtship of Steve Flemmi
and the Winter Hill Gang*

WITHOUT AN APPOINTMENT, the Winter Hill boys rolled into the plush law offices of Crane, Inker & Oteri in downtown Boston at about eight A.M. The dozen or so hoodlums shed their coats, mostly leathers and furs, and shook out the unseasonably sharp cold of the December 1965 morning. For the next four hours they transformed the firm's oak-paneled offices into their personal clubhouse, sipping coffee, flipping through the waiting room copies of *Life* and the *Saturday Evening Post*. They also chatted and joked with the secretaries and the lawyers—in fact it seemed like they made a point of saying hello to each of the firm's twenty-six employees. A few used the firm's expensive new color Xerox machine to see who could come up with the most realistic-looking counterfeit twenty-dollar bill.

"Not this again," attorney Joseph S. Oteri muttered to himself.

Oteri, famous for getting off some of Boston's most notorious killers and for once being shot by a deranged husband in a divorce case, watched the invasion with amused bewilderment. The boys were welcome at the firm—they were mostly polite and several were clients who actually paid on time. In cash. But the odd little routine was starting to become as familiar as the faces: Joe "the Animal!" Barboza's heavy-browed, simian mug. Edward "Wimpy" Bennett's cherubic Irish visage, which looked like it belonged behind the bar in some Dublin pub. The moon-faced Jimmy Flemmi, who, except for being totally bald, resembled his nickname "the Bear." And the Bear's serious, dark-eyed brother Stevie.

By noon the boys would gather in the library conference room. Ten minutes later they would all leave. This time Oteri was determined to know what was going on. He stuck his head in the library just in time to see Stevie Flemmi turn on the radio.

" 'Topping the news at noon, Boston's bloody gang war has apparently claimed another victim. Just an hour ago, the bullet-riddled body of . . .' "

Oteri saw the boys seated around the big mahogany conference table, leaning their ears intently toward the broadcast. He understood.

"All right you guys, out. Now," he said.

"Aw c'mon, Joe, give us a break," Jimmy Flemmi said.

"I mean it. Get your sorry asses out of here."

"Okay, okay. No hard feelings."

"And don't let me catch you pulling this shit again," Oteri said as they doffed on their coats and hats.

The Winter Hill Gang boys sheepishly nodded good-bye to the lawyer as they passed through the double oak doors toward the street. They left the tranquillity of the law firm and stepped back into the madness of the great Irish Gang War, alibis for the morning firmly in place.

There were many such stories in the Boston media through the 1960s. The *Record*, the *American*, the *Herald,* and the *Globe* newspapers kept the unofficial tally—locals jokingly began referring to the obituaries as "the Irish sports page." The only things that changed were the victims, the methods, and the death toll. George Ash, stabbed fifty times in a parked car outside a Catholic church, victim No. 14. Edward

"Punchy" McLaughlin, hit in the heart, lungs, and spleen by six bullets from an assassin's .32 as he boarded a bus to his brother's murder trial, victim No. 22. John Locke, identified through fingerprints because his face had been shot off, victim No. 40. When the killing finally stopped a decade later, the mob war death toll had climbed past sixty, making it one of the bloodiest underworld feuds in the annals of American crime.

In 1914 no one could conceive that an obscure Austrian archduke's assassination by a nineteen-year-old Serbian student would drag all of Europe into the War to End All Wars. The Irish Gang War had similarly obscure beginnings. In fact it didn't even start in Boston, but in a tiny town up on the New Hampshire border where three couples had decided to go for a weekend of fun in the autumn of 1961. Salisbury Beach, Massachusetts, was still thriving in the early 1960s, a holdover from the heyday of New England coastal resorts, with boardwalks and amusement piers and seaside ballrooms big enough to host jitterbug contests for five thousand.

Two of the men were from Somerville, Massachusetts, a working-class city that bordered Boston to the north. The third man was Georgie McLaughlin, a well-known thirty-three-year-old hoodlum. Georgie's physical appearance was somewhat ridiculous: He was only five feet four inches tall and had a doughy face and a persistent cowlick that added to his comical-yet-maniacal look. His reputation, however, was fearsome. He and his brothers, Bernie and Punchy, ran the loansharking, gambling, and truck hijacking rackets in Charlestown, Boston's northernmost neighborhood. Georgie carried a revolver in one pocket and, in the other, a lead window sash weight wrapped in a sock, which he used to crush the elbows and knees of tardy debtors. He was also a known killer and a vicious drunk.

The weekend veered out of control at about six on Sunday morning. The couples had been up all night drinking highballs, and whiskey-soaked Georgie wouldn't stop leering at one of his companions' buxom girlfriend. When he finally reached out to touch her, her boyfriend punched him in the face. Knowing the McLaughlin brothers' taste for revenge, the two men panicked and beat Georgie to death. Or so they thought. They were on their way south to Boston to dump the body when he moaned his way out of unconsciousness and sat up briefly in the backseat, scaring them out of their minds. Without stopping the car, they tossed his body onto the lawn of the nearest hospital and sped away.

Punchy and Bernie McLaughlin swore revenge at their brother's bedside. But first they had to find the two men from Somerville. After a few weeks of frustration, they went up to the city's Winter Hill section to see a longshoreman named James McLean. They knew McLean, better known as "Buddy," was friendly with the two men, and the McLaughlins hoped he would agree to help lure them into an ambush.

"I want you to help me set up these guys who beat up Georgie," Bernie McLaughlin said as they sat in McLean's living room.

"Listen, I'm friends with you and I'm friends with them and I don't set up my friends," McLean replied.

"You're still friends with these guys after what they did to Georgie?"

"From what I hear, Georgie was way out of line. I don't want to get involved."

"I'm making you involved. You're either with them or with us."

"You don't scare me. I'm not helping you set up my friends."

A few nights later McLean was awakened by his dog's barking and looked out the window to see two men lying on the ground, their arms up underneath his car. He barged out the door with a pistol, still in his boxer shorts, and opened fire. One of the men turned to fire back. McLean saw his face. It was Bernie McLaughlin. McLean walked back to his car and found five sticks of dynamite wired to the ignition.

Nine days later Bernie McLaughlin was back in

Charlestown at the Morning Glory, a bar underneath the enormous Tobin Bridge. At just past midnight he said good-bye to his friends and took the short walk to his car. Two men stepped out from behind one of the concrete bridge supports; one was carrying a revolver and pumped four bullets into McLaughlin, who fell to the sidewalk clutching his chest and rolled into the gutter, dead. Police arrested Buddy McLean in Somerville a few hours later in a black sedan matching the description of the getaway car from the McLaughlin shooting. Two witnesses picked him out of a lineup as the shooter and he was charged with murder.

The Irish Gang War had begun.

Before the war started, Boston's criminal rackets were divided between the Italian-American Mafia and a large number of independent Irish and mixed-ethnic gangs comprised of hoodlums of Irish, Italians, Jews, Lebanese, and Portuguese descent. The Boston Mafia was based in the city's historic North End (Paul Revere's house is still there) and had tight control of East Boston and a half-dozen cities in the northern suburbs. No one used the word "Mafia," though. The Italian wiseguys were usually referred to as "the Office."

Unlike the New York families, the Office never achieved total dominance over its own turf. The reason was simple arithmetic: the Italians were better organized, but they were simply outnumbered. A century earlier, the Great Potato Famine had forced two million to emigrate from Ireland. Boston was a favored destination, with 37,000 Irish immigrants entering the city in the year 1847 alone. Italians generally found New York and even New Orleans more hospitable. In 1880, Boston residents born in Ireland outnumbered those born in Italy by fifty to one. Several bad agricultural years in Sicily, followed by the collapse of the important sulfur-mining industry and out-of-control labor unrest in the 1890s, tipped the scales the other way somewhat, but the dominant Irish would control politics and culture in Boston for most of the twentieth century. For sixty-three years beginning in 1930, every single mayor of Boston was of Irish descent.

The New England Mafia didn't even bother establishing its headquarters in Boston, but instead opted for Providence, Rhode Island, where the ratio of Italians to other ethnic groups was more favorable. The Boston Mafia, smack in the center of New England's political and economic heart, was just a branch office. The Irish and independent gangs controlled other Boston neighborhoods and surrounding towns. The McLaughlins ran Charlestown. Buddy McLean and his longshoremen friends operated in Somerville. Joe "the Animal" Barboza's crew was based in East Boston. The Bennett brothers' gang controlled Roxbury, the South End, and Jamaica Plain.

The mob war changed everything. The McLaughlin brothers declared that anyone in the underworld who wasn't with them was against them. They made an example out of Frank Benjamin, an ex-con who loudly and drunkenly declared his loyalty to McLean one night in a Roxbury tavern. A rival who supported the McLaughlin side grabbed Benjamin and dragged him into the bar's storeroom, where Punchy McLaughlin sawed off his head. Tommy Ballou, one of McLean's closest associates (widely regarded as the last victim of the gang war, No. 61 or 62) found Benjamin's head on his doorstep the next morning.

The other gangs saw the McLaughlin power play for what it was. Their close association with the Italian Mafia was well known—the word was that they took murder-for-hire contracts considered too dangerous for the Italians to risk one of their own gunmen. Choosing the McLean side became a matter of survival. If the McLaughlins won, members of the other crews would end up as their flunkies or dead. It also didn't hurt McLean's cause that he was actually well-liked. Compared to the McLaughlins—who were widely considered a pack of treacherous, bullying midgets—the former longshoreman McLean had a reputa-

tion as a violent, tough, but essentially honorable hoodlum.
And they knew that if Buddy fell, they were next.

Steve Flemmi wasn't thinking much about the big picture in
1964. He was just trying to stay alive. Flemmi was aligned
with the Bennett brothers, Walter, William, and Edward, aka
"Wimpy." Wimpy Bennett was the loyalist involved with the
shooting and decapitation of Frank Benjamin, but the brothers later switched sides and threw their support behind
Buddy McLean. Furious, the McLaughlins came after the
Bennett crew with a vengeance, and Flemmi was a prime
target.
   Flemmi's life was pretty miserable. He'd moved out of his
wife Jeannette's house and was shuffling from cheap apartment to cheap apartment to avoid being ambushed. His
Army paratrooper days during the Korean War had taught
him how to avoid enemy fire, but the need for constant mo-
bility was cutting uncomfortably into his gambling and
loansharking profits. He was tired and strung out. The bodies piled up around him, and, if anything, the war was getting more brutal and insane.
   In mid-August a McLaughlin loyalist, Harold Hannon,
and a friend were kidnapped by Buddy McLean. McLean
had Hannon stripped naked and tied to a chair. The sicken-
ing smell of burning human hair and flesh permeated the
room as McLean held an industrial torch to Hannon's testi-
cles, demanding that he talk. A screaming Hannon admitted
that he had been hunting McLean, driving a car with a trunk
equipped with a peephole and a latch that would open it
from the inside. Georgie McLaughlin was hiding in the
trunk as Hannon drove around, ready to pop up and open fire
with a submachine gun if they spotted McLean. Hannon was
tortured some more and finally garroted. McLean was
kinder to Hannon's friend, Wilfred Delaney, who had nothing to do with the gang war and was just in the wrong car at
the wrong time. "It's not personal," he said, "I just can't
have any witnesses." McLean let Delaney drink and drug

himself unconscious with Seconals and whiskey. Both bodies were dumped in Boston Harbor. An autopsy by the Suffolk County Medical Examiner found that Delaney had drowned.

Flemmi feared the same carloads of McLaughlin assassins. Gunmen had twice shot at him already, and lately the Hughes brothers—top lieutenants to the McLaughlins—were seen driving slowly past Flemmi's hangouts in Roxbury's Dearborn Square.

The Hughes brothers weren't the only ones who had targeted Flemmi. FBI Special Agent H. Paul Rico was hearing stories too. The cigar-chomping Rico made it his business to know about the mob war and its participants, even if few federal crimes were involved. Flemmi was making a name for himself, like the time he was challenged in a Roxbury tavern by a local truck driver. The guy was huge, the story went, a half foot taller than the five-eight, 150-pound Flemmi and at least sixty pounds heavier.

"Hey, Flemmi, I hear you're a real fucking tough guy. Why don't we find out how—"

Crack. He never finished the sentence. Flemmi whirled on a heel and landed a fist flush to the trucker's jaw. His knees buckled and he began to wobble like a drunken sailor on the deck of a pitching battleship. *Crack, crack, crack, crack, crack. Boom.* Witnesses at the bar swore Flemmi hit the guy five more times before he hit the floor, the fastest hands they had ever seen.

Such stories made their way to Rico's eager ears. Rico was born in the Boston suburb of Belmont in the 1920s, the son of an Irish mother and Spanish father who worked for New England Telephone. He graduated from Boston College in 1950 with a history degree, then joined the FBI. His Spanish roots gave him a Mediterranean look often mistaken for Italian—an impression Rico sometimes used to his advantage when schmoozing wiseguys. "He was always a very knowledgeable, streetwise guy who had an incredible stable of informants," one longtime Boston lawyer who knew Rico said. "He was always the lead guy in everything he did—very forceful, very smart." The FBI first posted him to the Chicago office, but he soon transferred back to the Boston office when his father fell terminally ill.

That was when the young agent worked on the first of his big cases—and when he may have learned the value of informants. The $2.7 million "Brink's Job" on January 17, 1950, was—and perhaps still is—one of the most famous stickups of all time. But by late 1955 the case was still unsolved and the end of the six-year state statute was looming. The FBI was saved from failure by one of the robbers, Joseph "Specs" O'Keefe. Angry that his share of the loot had been stolen, O'Keefe began cooperating with FBI agent John F. "Jack" Kehoe. O'Keefe's cooperation broke the case and made Kehoe famous. Sources said Kehoe worked with both H. Paul Rico and Dennis Condon.

Rico and Condon became a team, but it was Rico who had the gift of gab that allowed him to recruit informants. Part of his patter was that he was "close friends" with FBI Director J. Edgar Hoover. The claim was patently ludicrous—even top FBI officials who worked with the director for decades describe Hoover as a fastidious, even priggish loner with few friends save his mother, Annie Hoover, and longtime top lieutenant Clyde Tolson. Rico later admitted that it was a lie he used to impress potential sources. "I told them a lot of things," he said with a smirk.

Rico first met Flemmi investigating a bank robbery on State Street. Flemmi was tough, smart, scared, and connected, exactly the kind of guy the Bureau needed to fulfill the latest edict handed down by Hoover. The previous autumn, the FBI director had been humiliated by his archrival, Attorney General Robert F. Kennedy, and Mafia turncoat Joseph Valachi. On September 10, 1963, the director fired off a memo to all regional offices, demanding the recruitment of high-level informants from within the ranks of organized crime for his new Top Echelon Informant Program.

Rico figured recruiting Flemmi might be possible. They

already knew each other; Rico made it a point to introduce himself to every known hoodlum in Boston. It was kind of fun, actually, the way it rattled their cages; their eyes would dart nervously back and forth to see if anyone could see them talking to the agent as Rico prattled on about the unseasonably cool weather or Yaz and the Red Sox. Yet his wide-ranging, constant contacts with the criminal element also had a strategic purpose: If he talked to everyone, then no one could draw any definite conclusions even if he were spotted talking to one of his actual snitches. Rico had plenty of those, and they kept telling him things about Steve Flemmi that further convinced him that he would be the perfect Top Echelon informant.

First, Stevie was a hundred percent Italian (his parents both spoke only broken English), which made him eligible for membership in the Mafia. He had also grown up in the South End and Lower Roxbury, as had the Boston Mafia's most-feared hit man, Ilario "Larry" Zannino. The Flemmi and Baione families were friends in the neighborhood. Flemmi's brother, Jimmy the Bear, was also best friends with Joe "the Animal" Barboza, a notorious contract killer who had taken jobs from the Mafia.

But best of all, Flemmi was vulnerable. Rico knew about the attempts on his life, and he knew that as much as the gangsters were fond of flashing their big wads of $100 bills, information was the real currency of the mob war. The right tip at the right time could keep you alive. The wrong whisper in the wrong ear meant they might find your bloated body, two bullets in the back of the head, washed up with the flotsam on one of the Boston Harbor beaches. Or they might not find you at all; the rumor was that one side had bribed a local gravedigger who, the night before a funeral, would excavate a hole ten feet deep, dump in a gangland victim, then cover it over to the customary six. The next day the grieving family had no idea that they were, in effect, interring their loved one in a duplex.

Rico was sure to tell his informants that he could trade in

both kinds of information. It kept them loyal. He had a certain reputation in the underworld, evidenced by the advice Raymond Patriarca gave to Frank Salemme on learning that Salemme had been approached by the FBI agent. "Stay away from Rico," Patriarca hissed. "He's a treacherous motherfucker." It was a telling statement. Presumably, Patriarca knew a little about treachery himself.

In November 1965 the agent sent a memo to J. Edgar Hoover saying Flemmi might make a great Top Echelon informant.

```
STEPHEN JOSEPH FLEMMI is being desig-
nated as a target in this program.
    This individual appears to be emotion-
ally stable, and if he survives the gang
war he would be a very influential indi-
vidual in the Boston criminal element.
```

Given the way the mob war was going, Flemmi's survival was a very big if. Remarkably, the tide of the war began to change. Critics of the FBI would later charge that Rico played a role in turning the tide to help his valuable source. Flemmi was no use to him dead. "Rico was giving Flemmi information that helped him eliminate his enemies," one lawyer close to the case said. "The FBI didn't have jurisdicton over murders, so they dealt with their problems vigilante-style to take care of anyone who was going to be a problem to them." Years later Justice Department and FBI investigators launched a grand jury investigation of those allegations, trying to determine exactly what role Rico played in Flemmi's activities during the gang war.

What the agent's memos at the time suggest, however, is that he must have had little doubt that Flemmi was rubbing out his enemies.

```
Informant advised on 6/1/66 that COR-
NELIUS HUGHES, who was murdered on 5/25/66
in Revere, Mass., had previously been around
```

```
Dearborn Square in Roxbury, Mass., obvi-
ously in an effort to try and set him
(informant) up for a "hit" and that the
fact that CONNIE is now deceased is not
displeasing to him.
    Informant was asked if he had an idea who
committed the murder, and he advised that
"he had an excellent idea who committed
the murder" but it would be better if he
did not say anything about the murder.
```

You can virtually see the wink in Flemmi's eye, but there
is no discernible note of concern from Rico, the memo's author, about whether his potential informant had blood on his
hands. Since the memo was written to FBI Director J. Edgar
Hoover, it is likely that officials in Washington also knew
what their potential source was up to—up to and including
even Hoover himself, although he didn't necessarily read
every memo addressed to him.

The same 1965 memo also outlined a potential problem.

```
Informant did say, however, that LARRY
[Zannino] allegedly gave $5,000 to STE-
VIE HUGHES, CONNIE's brother, to be
given to CONNIE's wife.
    Informant advised that [Zannino] has
definitely "got to go." The only thing
is that suspicion has to be thrown on
some other group. Informant advised that
it is for that reason that a story was
being manufactured now that is practi-
cally based on fact that the MARTORANO
brothers are very disturbed over LARRY
[Zannino] and over the way one of
ZANNINO's associates slapped their fa-
ther around in Basin Street South.
    Informant advised that he is hopeful
```

```
that if [Zannino] is killed that suspi-
cion will go to one of the MARTORANOs.
```

It is interesting to note that Rico's memo still describes Flemmi as a "target" of the Top Echelon program, even though he was clearly providing the FBI with information. The problem may well have been not that Flemmi wasn't cooperating, but that he was on the wrong side. The FBI wanted sources *inside* the Mafia or at least closely allied with it—the Italians weren't about to share their deepest secrets across the trenches of a shooting war. From the FBI's standpoint, murdering Zannino, who was Flemmi's best chance for a Mafia mentor, simply would not do. In fact, it was most likely a death sentence. The Italians in Boston, Providence, and even New York would certainly hit back with all they had in response to the murder of a made guy.

No, the only way Flemmi would be saved as a potential Top Echelon informant was if he switched allegiances. Whether by design or whether it was just some happy accident for the FBI, he did, going to his old friend Zannino and pledging to betray the Bennett brothers. Flemmi certainly had his own good reasons to dispose of the Bennetts, not even counting the fact that he could take over their territory after they were gone. Success had gone to their heads, and the brothers had also become dangerously ambitious. Taking out Zannino, the Office's top killer, Wimpy Bennett reasoned, would leave the McLean forces as the top criminal group in Boston. Everyone else, of course, thought the idea was certifiably nuts. There was no winning an all-out war with the Mafia. It was suicide.

The Bennett murders increased Flemmi's value as an informant. And there is little doubt from other Rico memos that, after the fact at least, he knew Flemmi was involved. In a February 8, 1967, memo Rico wrote:

```
Through informants of this office, it
has been established that this individ-
```

ual enjoys a reputation of being a very
capable individual and that he will now
be the leader of the group formerly
headed by EDWARD "WIMPY" BENNETT, who,
according to informants, had been murdered and buried around 1/19/67.

Informant also has been engaged in
bookmaking, shylocking, robberies and is
suspect of possibly being involved in
gangland slayings.

The memo went on to describe the new, close relationship
between Flemmi and the Mafia, and how he and Zannino
had agreed to settle all Mafia–Winter Hill disputes "peacefully."

The informant originally was furnishing
information on LCN members whom he considered as his enemies. Since the death
of EDWARD "WIMPY" BENNETT, RAYMOND PA-
TRIARCA has indicated a friendship to-
wards the informant, and LARRY BAIONE
[Zannino] has met with the informant and
he has now been accepted as an ally of
theirs.

In view of the informant's excellent
reputation with the hierarchy of the LCN
in his area, he eventually could be
brought in as a member of this organization.

There was a jocular, even cocky tone to another Rico
memo, dated April 14, 1967, about the disappearance of
Walter Bennett.

Informant advised that the FBI should
not waste any time looking for WALTER

> BENNETT in Florida or any place else because BENNETT is not going to be found.
>
> Informant was asked what actually happened to WALTER. Informant advised that he could not see any point in going into what happened to WALTER but that WALTER's "going" is all for the best and he was beginning to think aggressively and could have caused additional problems in the city. Informant advised that the Italian element is aware of the fact that he is gone and is not coming back and they are pleased.

It may seem remarkable that an FBI agent would write down that an informant had—in a joking tone no less—refused to talk about his involvement in a murder without apparent consequence. There were probably two reasons. The first was that Rico was filling out a FD-209, a form so secret that few outside the employment of the Justice Department knew they existed. A generation of agents grew up fully expecting that they would live long contented lives and die without ever seeing their informant files go public. Plus, the only four people who had access to the file were the informant's "handler," his direct supervisor, the Assistant Special Agent in Charge, and the Special Agent in Charge.

The second reason was that Rico was, after all, following Hoover's secret orders to recruit informants inside the Mafia, or at least close to it. Post-Valachi, everyone knew that a Mafia soldier had to "make his bones" (commit a murder) before being eligible for membership. In suggesting Flemmi was a murderer, Rico was doing nothing more than establishing his credentials as a Top Echelon informant.

According to Barboza, Flemmi and Salemme shot Wimpy Bennett in the face then buried him under a corpse-dissolving layer of lime. They strangled Walter (who had been watching Zannino's house in preparation for avenging his brother) and buried him next to Wimpy. The burial site was never found. One story on the street was that the telltale heads and hands of the bodies were removed with a length of piano wire strung between two sections of a broom handle. Looped around a body part and yanked by a strong man on either side, the wire sliced through flesh and bone like a knife through ripe melon.

The killers could have avoided a lot of hassle later on if they had taken the same care with Billy. For some reason—perhaps they thought they were being followed and panicked—they dumped Billy Bennett's body onto a snowbank in front of an elementary school. It was a shabby job compared to the disposal of the other brothers.

Flemmi fed regular updates to Rico about the activities of Larry Zannino, Boston underboss Jerry Angiulo, and boss Raymond Patriarca in Providence in 1966 and 1967. Information, however, only went so far.

There was no such thing as a legal wiretap in those days, so the tapes could not be admitted as evidence. The FBI needed a witness willing to testify in court. Flemmi was out. Not only was he too valuable on the inside, but Rico had already made his standard informant promises—that Flemmi's identity would be kept secret, that he would be protected from prosecution and would never be expected to testify—a part of their deal. Besides, Flemmi, the quintessential survivor, had already proven that he wasn't stupid enough to take on the Mafia out in the open.

Rico had his eye instead on the undisputed Wild Thing of the gang war, Joseph "the Animal" Barboza. Absolutely fearless, Barboza stomped through the underworld like a silverback gorilla, growling and dominating, smashing down rivals. He looked as if he had been created by some Warner Bros. animator: a massive brow over a huge chin, ridiculously large shoulders, abnormally long and heavily muscled arms—but his legs were almost comically short. Almost. Comedy was not usually on the minds of those looking at the Animal. His first impressions generally inspired thoughts along the lines of: "Please don't kill me."

Born to Portuguese parents in the old whaling city of New Bedford, Barboza would never be inducted into the Mafia. It was widely believed, however, that he had performed contract killings for Raymond Patriarca. He also single-handedly turned the tide of the gang war. In his 1975 autobiography he admitted murdering at least seven men, although he bragged to friends that the total was closer to twenty-nine. The victims included Punchy McLaughlin and both Hughes brothers, who Barboza hunted down in a fit of rage when his best friend, Jimmy the Bear Flemmi, was badly wounded in a 1967 shootout. Barboza chose the Winter Hill side in the gang war in part because Buddy McLean was tight with the Bear. Barboza trusted the Flemmis, and as early as 1965, Rico was using that trust to drive the Animal into captivity.

In the summer of 1965, Flemmi telephoned Barboza and said he urgently needed to see him. When they met at Bennett's Bar in Dorchester, Flemmi told Barboza that both the authorities and the Winter Hill Gang had tapped Boston Mafia underboss Jerry Angiulo's telephones. Angiulo was planning to have Barboza killed, Flemmi said.

"I heard the tapes myself. I heard Jerry say he was going to have you killed no matter what the cost. We also found out that Jerry met with the Hughes brothers down in Haymarket Square."

"What else did you hear?" Barboza asked.

"Joe, everything points to the fact that he is going to have you killed. I got in touch with you as quick as I could."

The FBI *had* illegally bugged Angiulo's tavern, Jay's Lounge, as part of Hoover's desperate attempt to close the Bureau's Mafia information gap after Valachi. Yet, in hindsight, Flemmi's story seems utterly implausible—that by some monumental coincidence the law and the Winter Hill Gang had tapped Angiulo's phone at exactly the same time. Why would Barboza buy Flemmi's story? There are several possibilities. For one thing, the gang was extremely fond of gadgets. Police called Barboza's blue and gold 1965 Oldsmobile "the James Bond car" because it had a sophisticated alarm system and a device for making thick black smoke come out of the tailpipe. Technologically, a wiretap was doable.

It was also quite plausible that Angiulo wanted the big Portuguese dead. Barboza knew the eventual fate of all the Mafia's hired killers. Albert Anastasia, head of the New York Mafia's infamous assassination squad, Murder Incorporated, supervised the murders of more than a hundred men before he was done in by Boston hit man Jack "Mad Dog" Nazarian in 1963. Nazarian was fond of boasting that he had killed twenty-six men for New England Mafia boss Raymond Patriarca Sr., who had loaned him to New York for the Anastasia hit. Nazarian himself was murdered less than a year later. Still, Barboza felt betrayed and angry. He confronted Henry Tameleo, one of Patriarca's captains, with what he had "learned." Tameleo denied there was any contract, but Barboza left without being reassured. Now both sides were worried. Patriarca knew Barboza's capacity for violence all too well. If the Animal rallied the Winter Hill Gang behind him, the result would be Gang War II.

Before any hostilities could break out, Barboza was arrested on a gun-possession charge. Prosecutors said police pulled him over after a "reliable informant" tipped them that he was armed. Because it was a third offense, and because of his fearsome reputation, a state judge set a high bail of $100,000. Two of Barboza's friends began scouring the underworld for "donations," but the Mafia was determined to keep Barboza off the streets. Barboza's pals made it as far as the Nite Lite Bar & Grill in the North End, where they were robbed of the $72,000 they had already collected and viciously stomped to death by a dozen Mafia soldiers.

Paul Rico had Joe Barboza exactly where he wanted him. The agent sent Flemmi into the jail with a few more rumors of Mafia murder plots before he made his move. At first Barboza refused to be a witness, but said he would consider becoming an informant. Rico said no dice. "He thought that he could become an informant and that we would reward him by helping him because he was an informant. And we told him that we didn't need him as an informant. What he knew, we knew," the agent said later. Barboza had nowhere to go.

The Animal agreed to become a cooperating witness if the FBI promised to protect his wife and children. His defection was a seismic event in the underworld. BARBOZA CALLED SONGBIRD screamed a headline in the *Boston Record*. Predictions were made about an unprecedented law enforcement assault on the Boston underworld. Special Agent Paul Rico and his partner, Dennis Condon, meanwhile, were credited in the newspaper stories as the intrepid G-men who had tamed the Animal.

Flemmi's role in flipping Barboza never made it into the newspapers, of course, or even any FBI reports. By the fall of 1968 taking credit for anything was the last thing Flemmi wanted. His attempts to curry favor with Larry Zannino and protect his brother Jimmy had landed him in muck so deep that not even Paul Rico could wade in and get him out.

Things had been going fairly well, especially from the FBI's standpoint. Their dream for Flemmi—having him become a "made" member of the Mafia—actually had a chance of coming to fruition. The previous summer, Flemmi and Salemme—thanks to their dispatching of the Bennetts—were being embraced, literally, by the Italian wiseguys in the North End.

The two friends went up to the North End for dinner and ended up heading over to Zannino's bar near the Boston Garden, the Bat Cove, for drinks with the wiseguy and another mafioso, Peter Limone. Flemmi, ever distrustful, was taking small sips of his drink, being careful not to get too loaded. Limone, drunk, put his arms around Flemmi and Salemme and let them in on a secret.

"I shouldn't tell you this, but I'm sponsoring you for

membership in our organization," Limone slurred. "Ordinarily, before you were made a member, you would have to make a hit and I would have to be with you as your sponsor to verify that you made the hit and report on how you handled yourself. But with the reputations you two guys have, that may not be necessary."

Flemmi reported the meeting back to the FBI. It was exactly what Rico and the Bureau higher-ups had been hoping for—they had a chance to get their guy on the inside. Flemmi appears to have been somewhat less enthusiastic.

```
Informant advised that he does not look
up to the people in "the organization";
he does not like the individuals as men
but it is possible that he will join it
as Salemme is impressed with these peo-
ple and Salemme, after all, is his part-
ner.
```

At the same time, the FBI's success with witness Joe Barboza was proving to be a problem for Steve Flemmi and his brother Jimmy the Bear. Jimmy Flemmi and Barboza had once been close friends; the Bear was one of the few people that even the Animal was physically intimidated by. The three of them had all been on the same team during the gang war, but now that Flemmi was allying himself with the North End, Barboza was the enemy and Stevie's new friends were expecting him to come through.

Barboza's cooperation resulted in three cases that by far were the biggest assault to date against the New England Mafia. Raymond L.S. Patriarca and one of his top associates, Henry Tameleo, were charged in federal court in Rhode Island with interstate transportation of hoodlums to murder a mob associate named Willie Marfeo. Back in Boston, underboss Jerry Angiulo and three of his henchmen were charged in state court with conspiring to murder one of Barboza's friends, Rocco DeSeglio, who allegedly had the temerity to rob a Mafia-protected high-stakes poker game. In the third case, six men, including Tameleo, Peter Limone, and four other men were charged with helping Barboza murder a small-time crook named Edward "Teddy" Deegan. Virtually the entire leadership of the New England Mafia had been indicted based on the word of one man.

The Office had to do something to stop him. Zannino reached out for Flemmi.

"Go see your brother in prison," Zannino said. "Ask him on behalf of Jerry to see if he can do anything to hurt that rat bastard Barboza."

What Zannino didn't know was that Paul Rico had gotten to Jimmy Flemmi first. Three years earlier, the Bear had been one of the agent's FBI informants, just like his brother, for five months, until he went to jail and was no longer useful. As the keeper of that secret, Rico had Jimmy Flemmi well under control. Actually, Rico had another secret that was even more potentially damaging. Two days before the murder, Rico was told that the Deegan murder had been approved by Raymond Patriarca and that it would be carried out by Barboza and Flemmi. He apparently did nothing to stop it. On March 13, 1965, the day after Deegan was gunned down in an alley in the gritty, working class city of Chelsea, Flemmi confessed that he, Barboza, and two associates—Roy French and Ronald Casseso—had committed the crime.

Apparently not realizing Rico's hold on Jimmy Flemmi, Barboza put some of his own pressure on his old friend the Bear, according to one of Rico's informant reports.

On September 14, 1967, informant advised
that Attorney John Fitzgerald had been
up to see Jimmy Flemmi and Nick Femia at
the Massachusetts Correctional Institution, Walpole, Massachusetts, on Saturday,
September 9, 1967, and that Fitzgerald
told Flemmi that Joe [Barboza] does not

appreciate Jimmy Flemmi's brother associating with Peter Limone and Larry [Zan-
nino] and that if he [Barboza], learns
that Jimmy is going to be used by the defense, in any of the upcoming trials
against "the organization," he will furnish enough information to indict Jimmy
Flemmi.

Informant advised that Fitzgerald then
attempted to obtain from Jimmy information concerning crimes in which he,
Jimmy, was involved in that Joe [Bar-
boza] can testify on. Jimmy Flemmi told
[informant] that he did not tell
Fitzgerald of any crime that he was involved in but he definitely feels that
Fitzgerald is trying to cause trouble
between he and Joe [Barboza] and he is
acting more like a cop than an attorney.

John Fitzgerald, the attorney who helped Barboza defect to
the government side, was playing a dangerous game. Like a
cornered animal, the Mafia was getting more desperate by the
day with the approach of the three trials. They couldn't touch
Barboza, who was under heavy U.S. Marshals Service guard
on barren Thatcher Island off the town of Rockport, Massachusetts, which was inhabited only by seagulls and a care-
taker who tended the island's distinctive twin lighthouses.

The results of Barboza's testimony were almost as spectacular as his decision to cooperate. A jury found Raymond
Patriarca and Henry Tameleo guilty, and they were each sentenced to five years in prison and a $10,000 fine.

Without any interference from the Bear, Barboza was free
to spin his tale that the Deegan murder was a Mafia contract
killing. Six men, Tameleo, Limone, mob-connected bookmaker Louis Greco, and an underworld hanger-on named
Joe "The Horse" Salvati were convicted of the execution-

style murder along with actual killers French and Casseso. Tameleo, Limone, Greco and Casseso were sentenced to die in the electric chair.[5] Only Jerry Angiulo was acquitted.

By so aggressively representing Barboza's interests, Fitzgerald was making himself an inviting substitute target. He was even driving Barboza's old "James Bond car." The last straw may have been the news that the Animal planned to sell his life story as a book, which Fitzgerald was working with Rico and Condon to set up. The Mafia told Flemmi in late 1967 that Fitzgerald had to go. Flemmi relayed the news to Paul Rico.

> Informant further advised that Attorney
> John Fitzgerald, who is Joseph Barboza's
> attorney, is still definitely "on the
> hit parade" and will get "whacked out"
> if he leaves the slightest door open.

What Flemmi didn't say—or at least what Rico didn't write down—was that Flemmi was planning the murder himself. He had a powerful motive: Fitzgerald was threatening his brother Jimmy. Flemmi, Cadillac Frank Salemme, and another gangster, Robert Daddieco, were later charged with wiring dynamite to Fitzgerald's car. Only Fitzgerald's habit of leaving the door open when he turned the key—which allowed some of the explosive force to dissipate—saved his life, though both his legs had to be amputated.

The brazen attack on a civilian caused a public uproar. Bostonians had been willing to tolerate the gang war be-

---

[5]The death sentences were commuted to life after the U.S. Supreme Court overturned the death penalty in 1972 and doubts about the veracity of Barboza's testimony led to Salvati's sentence being commuted in 1997. Reports discovered at FBI headquarters in December 2000 showed that Salvati, Limone, Tameleo, and Greco had been framed and that the FBI knew that Barboza, Jimmy Flemmi, French, and Casseso were the real killers. Discovery of the documents—which should have been turned over to the defense—led to Limone's and Salvati's convictions being overturned, but Tameleo and Greco had long since died in prison.

cause the victims were all gangsters, but the Fitzgerald bombing hit too close to home. Politicians and clergymen joined in, decrying the violence in the streets and putting state prosecutors under tremendous pressure. The wily Rico came to the rescue, announcing that he had landed Daddieco as a cooperating witness in both the Fitzgerald bombing and the William Bennett murder. Indictments were imminent, but Rico wasn't about to forget his prize Top Echelon informant.

Flemmi's phone rang at about seven A.M. one morning in the winter of 1969.

"You and your friend need to get out of town. The indictment's coming in a week," the voice said. It was Rico.

Flemmi and Salemme hit the road. They stayed in New York for a while, guests of the bosses of the major families, who hated Barboza and were grateful for what they had done to Fitzgerald. After a few months Flemmi relocated to Montreal, where he rented an apartment in a fashionable part of the city and found legitimate work in a printmaking shop. The job plus a monthly cut of the old loanshark business he had turned over to a friend gave him a comfortable living with few risks. In Canada, Flemmi felt like a drowning man who'd been pulled to the surface—he was free from the suffocating fear of the gang war and of his relationship with the FBI being unmasked.

After the Bennett murders, Flemmi and Salemme's friendship began to erode. Flemmi had gladly betrayed the Bennetts to head off a disastrous war with the Mafia, but that didn't mean he was ready to enlist as one of Raymond Patriarca's soldiers.

For one thing, Flemmi couldn't forget the time he and Salemme had driven down to Federal Hill in 1967 to talk to Raymond Patriarca about a used-car scam they were running with their buddy Georgie Kaufman. The three friends owned a repair garage and enlisted some shady dealers to sell them damaged cars that had been declared "totaled" but in truth were only slightly damaged. The Brink's Job it wasn't, but the scam was steady money and the risks were low because everyone except the insurance company walked away happy. The owner got a big insurance check, the dealer got to sell him a new car, while Flemmi, Salemme, and Kaufman fixed the relatively minor damage and resold the car at a nice profit. Flemmi and Salemme were hoping that Patriarca would use his connections to help them improve the scheme.

The meeting went smoothly enough. They met the boss at NuBrite Cleaners, an unassuming dry cleaning shop on Atwells Avenue that also served as Patriarca's headquarters. The boss sent for his brother Joe and the four men went to lunch. By the time they finished, Flemmi and Salemme had a commitment that Joe Patriarca, who had connections in the auto business, would send more cars their way.

After they made their way back to the dry cleaning shop, the hawk-nosed mob boss fixed his steely gaze on Flemmi.

"Frankie, could you step outside for a minute? I have some business I need to discuss with Stevie alone."

"Sure, Raymond," Salemme said.

When they were alone, the boss said he wanted to talk to Stevie about his brother, Jimmy the Bear, who was still in prison. Patriarca had been unsuccessfully pushing the Bear to testify in a way that would discredit Joe Barboza, who countered by threatening to testify against Jimmy Flemmi unless he resisted the pressure from Providence.

"Stevie, I don't want you talking any business with Jimmy that involves us. Jimmy can't keep his mouth shut."

The boss then changed the subject, giving Flemmi $5,000 to tide the car business over until the cars from Rhode Island started to arrive in Boston. He made some small talk, asking Flemmi where in Italy his parents came from. But Patriarca's words about his brother no doubt sent a chill down Flemmi's spine. It was clear that Raymond Patriarca didn't think his brother would be a stand-up guy, and when a Mafia boss fingered someone as a squealer, his life expectancy was shortened by a considerable margin.

Patriarca's attempt to drive a wedge between the two

brothers failed. Eventually, he went off to prison to serve his time. Paul Rico was asked years later if he ever feared that the Bear would become a defense witness against Barboza. "I wasn't real concerned," he replied. Rico, the "treacherous" agent, had outmaneuvered Patriarca, the Mafia boss.

For the next thirty years, Steve Flemmi cast his loyalty to the FBI and became arguably the most important single weapon against the Italian mob in New England.

Flemmi periodically kept tabs on what was going on back in Boston as his Canadian exile stretched from a few months to one year, then three. He would call Rico occasionally using their code name, "Jack from South Boston," and leave a number where he could be reached. For a long time there was no reply. Then one day in 1974, Rico did call back. The furor over the Fitzgerald bombing had blown over, Flemmi would get bail and the charges would go away, he said. He told Flemmi to get in touch with Condon, his former partner, because he had transferred to the FBI's Miami office in 1970.

J. Edgar Hoover was dead. His successors had declared an end to domestic political spying and dirty tricks and began a new focus on actual crime. The Bureau was about to launch an all-new assault on the Mafia.

"It's time to come home," Rico said.

CHAPTER FOUR

The Bulger Connection

••••••••••••••••••••••••••••••

*Two brothers rise in the worlds of politics and crime—
with some help from the FBI*

THE SEEDS OF what might be called the South Boston Irish consciousness may well have been sown by the banks of the sleepy River Boyne north of Dublin during a military engagement fought in 1690. An English army led by Protestant King William of Orange routed an inferior force of Irish rebels who had rallied behind James II, the deposed Catholic Stuart monarch. The Battle of the Boyne effectively ended, for hundreds of years, the dream of an independent Catholic Ireland and ushered in an era of harsh English dominion.

Within a year all property belonging to Catholics was transferred to English and Scottish Protestants. It was an extraordinary upheaval for the Irish, who were transformed from a static, largely agrarian people to one essentially without roots, who could be easily blown far and wide by the winds of calamity and fate. The harsh Penal Laws followed in 1691, preventing Irish Catholics from attending universities, voting, or holding jobs in the government. The uprooting sparked waves of emigration that were followed by Irish hoping to escape famine, economic hardship, and oppression. The problem for the emigrating Irish, however, was that the English Protestants already had the upper hand in the New World as well as the old, particularly in the young colony of Massachusetts. It was all very hypocritical—the original Plymouth Colony was, after all, settled by Puritans fleeing religious intolerance—but ships bearing Irish immigrants in the early 1700s were often met by rioting townspeople determined not to let them land. Irish Protestants eventually began receiving some grudging acceptance, but their Catholic countrymen were the subjects of harsh discrimination up until the American Revolution, possibly the worst manifestation of which was the annual "Pope's Night" in the autumn. Pope's Night would have made the Ku Klux Klan proud: Wagons and carts bearing anti-papal themes were paraded through the streets, climaxing in a mass demonstration where the pope was burned in effigy and riots ensued, as Catholics cowered in their homes

Historians like James Carroll believe it was General George Washington, horrified at the Bostonians' insult to the religion practiced by the struggling country's French Catholic allies, who essentially ordered an end to the demonstrations. The new bill of rights in the Massachusetts Constitution (which became a model for the U.S. version) also gave the Catholics some legal protections. Legislation never could change attitudes, however, and "No Irish Need Apply" signs greeted new immigrants looking for work well into the nineteenth century. In 1834 a convent in Charlestown was burned to the ground by a mob of Protestant workmen.

The fear and oppression of the Anglo-Saxon Bostonians largely prevented the new immigrants from moving inland, compressing them into waterfront sections of the city. The largest Irish enclave was South Boston, a peninsula that formed Boston Harbor's southern boundary. There, Irish were the overwhelming majority, with a Catholic church every few blocks or so. Though technically still part of Boston, residents lovingly referred to "Southie" as their "town" and passed down an oral tradition and identity that made liberal use of the indignities and oppression the Irish had suffered at the hands of their Brahmin neighbors to the north. Southie was loyal, clannish, distrustful of outsiders—an attitude that persisted long after the Irish had supplanted the hated Brahmins in both city and state politics.

In the last thirty years of the twentieth century, the Bulger brothers became the central figures in the South Boston story. Their tales, in fact, are so enmeshed in the neighborhood mythology that it is often difficult to separate fact from fable.

Among what is known for certain about James Joseph "Whitey" Bulger Jr. is that he wasn't originally from Southie at all. He was born on September 3, 1929, in Dorchester, a working class section of the city even farther south. One of the few published sources of information about Whitey Bulger is his brother's highly partisan account of their childhood in his autobiography, *While the Music Lasts: My Life in Politics*.

According to Billy's memoir, James was the second child of James J. Bulger, a laborer who had lost one arm in a railyard accident, and his much younger wife, the former Jane V. McCarthy, whom everyone called Jean. James Bulger Sr. was originally from Boston's north end, which would later become almost exclusively Italian. His wife was from Charlestown, Boston's other famous Irish enclave. The young couple lived simply, James Sr.'s lack of formal schooling and physical handicap keeping him from lucrative or steady work, although he always managed to eke out a living doing odd jobs. They had three children in Dorchester: a girl named after the mother, James Jr., and William.

In 1938 the couple made a decision that would change Boston history forever. They moved from the relatively ethnically diverse Dorchester to an apartment at 41 Logan Way in the Old Harbor housing development project in South Boston, one of three publicly funded projects in the neighborhood. Family friends started calling the oldest boy, a towhead, "Whitey," because of his hair, and the nickname stuck. The brothers, who were five years apart, took different paths as teens. If Jimmy Bulger (he disliked the name Whitey) had grown up in the 1990s instead of the 1940s, he would probably been diagnosed with a behavior-related learning disability, maybe even Attention Deficit Disorder, despite his high IQ. Boston school officials of the time did what they did with most restless boys who had problems with authority. When he wasn't confronting police officers and teachers at Brandeis High, he was vanishing for weeks at a time.

One of his disappearances suspiciously coincided with the departure of the Ringling Brothers Circus. His family's fears were confirmed when he returned weeks later and laughingly recounted helping the elephants construct the Big Top as the show pulled into each new town. But he bored of that too. Whitey also kept a pet ocelot (named Lancelot) as a teenager and dated a much older burlesque dancer from notorious Scolley Square whose nickname was "Tiger Lil," according to his brother's memoir.

Aside from the whimsical anecdotes, though, the younger brother's remembrances do contain some insights into the mind of the man who arguably became Boston's most notorious criminal. As his brother grew into adulthood, William Bulger wrote, he changed from "a blithe spirit to a rebel whose cause I could never discern."

> *He was in a constant state of revolt against . . . I'm not sure what. He was as restless as a claustrophobic in a dark closet.*
>
> *"Where's Jim?" my mother was always asking. "I turn my back for a second and he's out the door. He's always out the door. Where does he go?"*
>
> *I couldn't answer. I didn't know. I don't think Jim knew where he was going most of the time—just out.*

Constant motion and a hatred of any authority but his own were themes running throughout Whitey Bulger's life and criminal career. In his teens he ran with a gang of toughs called the Shamrocks, but he never joined the gang as a member. In the 1950s he joined the Air Force, but his service record is spotted with trouble—including repeated citations for being absent without leave. He was arrested in 1950 on a charge of being AWOL in Oklahoma City and released back to the military. The next year, he was arrested for rape in Montana, but the charge was eventually dropped and he was discharged in 1952. Many people join a branch of the service to avoid trouble, to get themselves straightened out. The military seemed to have the opposite effect on Whitey; when he returned to Boston, his rebellion blossomed into full-fledged law-breaking.

In the spring of 1955, Bulger and two friends, Ronnie Dermady of Cambridge and Carl Smith Jr. of Somerville, drove a few miles across the southern Massachusetts border and walked into the Darlington, Rhode Island, branch of the Industrial National Bank. The three men pulled guns and ordered about twenty customers to hit the floor, then cleaned out three teller cages of more than $42,000 in cash. That autumn, Bulger and another confederate, William L. O'Brien, hit a bank branch in the Boston suburb of Melrose, but got away with just $5,000.

After the Melrose robbery, Bulger and Dermady took off cross-country driving a four-year-old blue Oldsmobile sedan and landed in Hammond, Indiana, a week later. Hammond, just a few miles over the state border from Chicago, was where Carl Smith had moved after the Rhode Island heist. They stole a car and donned identical crude disguises: hunting caps with the earflaps pulled down, but no masks. As two girlfriends watched from the getaway car for signs of the police, the two men walked into the Hoosier State Bank, pulled out automatic pistols, and calmly demanded money. Police said Bulger had graduated from one pistol to one in each hand. They escaped with more than $12,000. They switched cars in a nearby supermarket parking lot and got away.

Ten days later employees of a Bar Harbor, Florida, bank saw the twenty-six-year-old Bulger and his "beautiful, model-type" blond girlfriend from Southie, Jacqueline McAuliff, put a pouch containing jewels in a safe deposit box, only to come back and quickly remove it. Suspicious, they called local police, who learned from authorities in Boston that Bulger was suspected of a recent jewelry heist. The couple was soon pulled over in Miami Beach, the police searched the couple's car, and found $360 in cash, a .22 caliber pistol, and a couple of suitcases—but no jewelry. They were released the next day.

A month later the FBI in Boston broadcast a thirteen-state bulletin that Bulger was wanted for bank robbery, adding that he should be considered "armed and dangerous" and listing his two nicknames as "Whitey" and "Sonny" (his mother's pet name for him). Bulger may have been betrayed by Carl Smith, who was arrested in Tennessee and held for questioning shortly after the Hammond robbery, the proceeds of which authorities believed that Bulger used for spending money out on the road. His cross-country jaunt apparently ended back where it had started, because agents from the Boston FBI Bank Robbery Squad heard rumors that Bulger might be back in town, hiding in the city's fashionable Back Bay section. They came up empty, but Bulger's pal Ronnie Dermady wasn't so lucky. He was arrested and charged with both the Rhode Island and Indiana robberies. Already on parole for an armed robbery, Dermady was facing serious time.

A dozen agents finally cornered Whitey Bulger outside a nightclub on the North Shore about four weeks after Dermady's arrest. At his arraignment, the federal prosecutor in the case called him a "vicious person, known to carry guns" who, by his own admission, harbored "an intense dislike for police and law enforcement officials." The prosecutor, Daniel Needham, argued for high bail, saying the FBI had information that Bulger traveled the country extensively while on the run. Needham said Bulger had also tried to disguise himself by dying his hair jet-black, smoking cigars, and "changing his style of hat." The cocksure Bulger boasted to police that he had done the dye job himself.

A federal judge ordered him held on $50,000 bail, which his family was too poor to raise. Bill Bulger was serving a two-year hitch in the Army at the time of his brother's arrest, and later said that his family kept the news of his brother's arrest from him. Whitey decided to plead guilty. Needham recommended twenty-five years. U.S. District Court Judge George Sweeney went a little easier, sentencing Bulger to twenty years in the federal penitentiary at Atlanta, Georgia.

It was almost certainly during the bank robbery case that at least laid the groundwork for Whitey Bulger's informant relationship with the FBI. H. Paul Rico, the same agent who recruited Steve Flemmi and helped flip Joe "the Animal" Barboza, was a star member of the Bank Robbery Squad that arrested Bulger, as was his partner, Dennis Condon. The two agents were a team. They started work together in Boston on the same day in 1952 and were both considered extremely adept at cajoling informants during the FBI's efforts to solve the infamous 1950 Brink's armored car depot robbery, which at $2.7 million was the largest heist of its kind in U.S. history. Their mentor, John "Jack" Kehoe, broke the case—and became an FBI legend in the process—by flipping one of the robbers, Joseph "Specs" O'Keefe.

Condon, and especially Rico, were solicitous of the Bulger family while Whitey was away. Both Rico and Billy Bulger attended Boston College and saw each other at university functions. Instead of vilifying the Bulger family, Rico asked after Whitey and the family's well-being. Word of Rico's attitude reached Bulger in prison and it made an impression. During a 1980 meeting with the head of the Boston FBI office, Lawrence Sarhatt, Bulger said that his motivation to help the FBI could be traced directly back to "the favorable treatment received by his family from Special

Agent Paul Rico after Special Agent Rico was responsible for his incarceration."

The treatment Whitey Bulger was getting inside prison, however, was anything but favorable. Like most true predators, Bulger adapted poorly to being caged, and if anything, his antiauthoritarian streak got worse. There are consequences for rebellion in federal penitentiaries, though, and Bulger was destroying his chances for parole by getting into repeated altercations with the guards, whom he considered inferior and stupid. He was transferred to Lewisburg, Pennsylvania, and began making plans to escape, but the tools for his plan were discovered during a search of his room. Prison officials had had enough. They shipped him off to Alcatraz, the maximum-security island prison in San Francisco Bay.

Everything about Alcatraz was designed to break defiant inmates like the thirty-year-old tough guy from South Boston. His test of wills with the guards continued, leading to lengthy stretches in "the hole," solitary confinement—a punishment so cruelly perfected at Alcatraz that it was eventually deemed unconstitutional and led to the prison's closure.

Unruly inmates were thrown into the unheated steel boxes in just their underwear. The San Francisco Bay's perpetually damp, nasty climate—which once provoked Mark Twain to remark, "The coldest winter I ever spent was a summer in San Francisco"—did the rest. The bone-gnawing cold, just above the level that would cause hypothermia, resulted in a constant, uncontrollable shivering that prevented sleep and, combined with the lack of light and sense of time, quite literally drove some inmates insane. Bulger, a frequent visitor, later bragged that he developed a technique where he would crouch for hours on the metal floor, with his entire body weight resting on his elbows, knees, and toes—putting the smallest skin area possible in contact with the frigid, body-heat-sapping steel.

At Alcatraz, Bulger found a friend and mentor in Clarence

Carnes, an inmate known as the "Choctaw Kid." Carnes was apparently a good influence, because there were signs that Bulger was tactfully modifying his behavior. "He uses no profanity and dislikes to hear it. He dislikes hearing disparaging remarks about religion, country, and women," an assistant warden wrote in a prison log book about Bulger. He also took to reading books on war and battles, and it was said he liked to read about the same battle from different perspectives, to get a better sense of strategy. The Rock was finally closed for good in 1963—although his experience there would color the rest of his life—and Bulger was transferred out of Alcatraz to Leavenworth. As disciplined as his mind was, he became desperate for a way to reduce his sentence and get out. He volunteered as a guinea pig in MK-Ultra, a CIA-sponsored experiment with d-lysergic acid diethylamide, better known as LSD, ignoring the pleas in letters from his brother that it was too dangerous. At least Bulger took the drug voluntarily; in Canada it was tested on mental patients without their consent.

Bulger was finally paroled from federal prison in 1965.

The Whitey Bulger who got out of prison had changed. He was harder, more calculating, quicker to anger. He tried working as a courthouse custodian, in a job arranged by his brother Bill, who was on his way to becoming president of the State Senate. He soon quit. "I can't stand it, Bill, I'm bored sick," he reportedly told his brother. His new, highly disciplined attitudes and habits, vestiges of his life in prison, shaped him as a criminal. He lifted weights several hours a day, never drank more than a glass of wine, and eschewed drugs, both legal and illegal. He interpreted the hard-drinking habits of other criminals as signs of weakness, and Bulger despised weakness in any form, particularly what he perceived as a lack of intelligence.

The way Southie functioned as a neighborhood had much in common with the Irish Catholic families who lived there—everyone knew each other's business, but it was deemed unforgivably disloyal to talk about dirty laundry with outsiders. Whitey Bulger used the Southie way to his full advantage, carefully crafting an image that capitalized on the neighborhood's insular, "us versus them" quality, that of the benevolent yet iron-fisted neighborhood boss.

Stories that became part of the neighborhood lore burnished that image. A local man in his early twenties, for example, was supposedly double-parked on one of Southie's narrower streets, a common-enough sight in the neighborhood. Bulger, unable to pass, laid on the horn. A hand with the middle digit extended emerged from the other car's driver-side window. Bulger jumped out of his car and with an iron pipe smashed the young man's face, knocking out several teeth. Then, legend had it, Bulger paid for the youth's dental work. Another group of boys unintentionally scraped Bulger's car during a joyride, and word spread through the neighborhood that retribution would be swift. The boys heard Bulger was looking for them and came clean, fully expecting a beating. Instead, Bulger magnanimously forgave them because of their honesty.

As far as true friends go, Bulger is believed to have had few, if any, outside the members of his immediate family. Acquaintances describe him as being more like the neighborhood's alpha dog—the people around him were either tolerated or overpowered. One friend of longtime Bulger paramour Theresa Stanley said Bulger had a compulsive need to be the smartest person in any room, and anyone who appeared more intelligent than he was—particularly a woman—did so at great peril. "If you were ever talking on a subject you knew more about than he did, you got the *look*. The one that said in a minute, you were dead," she said. "Women were simply incapable of knowing anything."

Yet Bulger also had a great need and affection for women—to the point where he actually kept up two simultaneous long-term relationships: one with Stanley and another with Catherine Greig, a blond dental hygienist twenty years his junior. As a surrogate husband and father to Stanley and her four children, Bulger was by turns kind and abusive. Believing her mother was about to be assaulted during one of his tirades, one of Stanley's teenage daughters jumped on Bulger's back. He threw her across the room. The next morning, according to a friend, the girl discovered his apology in the driveway—a new car. Bulger's LSD experiment exacerbated his normally hyperactive behavior and sometimes prompted him to complain about nightmares and an inability to sleep. Yet insomnia actually enhanced his ability to lead multiple lives—he could see Stanley during the day, Greig in the evening, and prowl the streets conducting his illegal business into the dawn.

His minimal sleep habits also afforded time for obsessive planning, his true advantage over any adversary.

"Whitey was always thinking," said a longtime Massachusetts State Police detective. "He never stopped. Ever. That was his edge. He was always five steps ahead of everybody else."

His chief plan appears to have been staying out of prison. He habitually wore an Alcatraz belt buckle as a memento and frequently spoke about his experiences behind bars. The one thing he said most often was that he was never going back. Authorities discovered the true extent of his planning after he skipped town in early 1995, just ahead of a federal racketeering indictment. Investigators tracing his movements found that, during the early 1990s, he had taken his long trips around the country to hide stashes of cash and false papers, clearly planning for an extended life as a fugitive. In fact, all major aspects of his life after prison—the alliance with the FBI that protected him from prosecution, the murder of anyone who could testify against him, his obsessive preparations for life on the run—point to one inescapable conclusion.

No one was ever going to put Whitey Bulger in a cage again.

John Connolly claims that he convinced Whitey Bulger to join the Top Echelon Informant Program by offering Bulger a chance to eliminate his Mafia rivals. A close examination both of Bulger's life and of FBI documents, however, indicates that it is more likely that Paul Rico and Dennis Condon recruited him by offering to do what they had already done for Steve Flemmi—give him a chance to stay out of prison. Rico later denied recruiting Bulger as an informant, but the denial is less than plausible. Rico had contact with Bulger from his work on the Bank Robbery Squad, and the FBI's own documents indicate that the agent laid the groundwork for wooing Whitey by being kind to the Bulger family. Rico also recruited Bulger's bank-robbing cohort, Ronald Dermady, as a source. It is only logical, then, to believe that he would have at least made a pass at Bulger.

Condon, trapped by FBI documents that show his early attempts to recruit Bulger, simply claimed not to remember developing Bulger as an informant. He did not deny it, however.

Documents from Whitey Bulger's own informant file show that Condon apparently followed up on the groundwork laid by Rico with Bulger's family at a time when Billy was trying to keep his brother on the straight and narrow, having arranged a janitor's job for him at the South Boston courthouse. Whitey had returned to tense times in South Boston, times that did not bode well for any attempt to go straight even if he had even been inclined to. Donald Killeen's gang, which had controlled the neighborhood for years, was feuding with the Mullins Gang, an up-and-coming group of toughs. The Killeen brothers controlled the illegal numbers racket in Southie, and operated out of a bar called the Transit Café on West Broadway.

Just like Flemmi, Bulger was recruited when his life was in danger and he needed all the allies he could get in order to survive. In mid-May of 1971, Condon wrote a memo to J. Edgar Hoover, with the name "James J. Bulger" in the caption.

Captioned individual born 9/3/29, white
male, brown hair, blue eyes, 5 feet 10
inches tall, 165 pounds, FBI No.
169486A, address: 252 O'Callahan Way,
South Boston, Mass. employed by Suffolk
County, Mass. in maintenance department.
Bureau is advised over that because of
current gang war in South Boston, his
life may be in jeopardy.

The memo also assigned Bulger a number as a "potential
criminal informant" or "PCI." Twelve days later Condon wrote
another memo to Hoover about his protégé, saying his first
contact with Bulger had been very productive and that Bulger
had "furnished extensive information as to the identities of individuals on both sides in a gang war which is currently being
waged in South Boston, Mass. and is closely associated with
major hoodlums and bookmakers in South Boston area."

It is believed that with further contact
he could be a very valuable source of information relative to the organized
criminal activities in South Boston,
Mass. Details of information furnished
by him will be furnished in subsequent
communications. Information furnished by
him has been corroborated through other
informants and sources of this office.
Arrangements will be made at an appropriate time to meet with an alternate
agent. He has displayed signs of emotional stability and a check of his background fails to indicate any emotional
instability.

FBI Headquarters, perhaps even Hoover himself, appeared very interested in developing Bulger. A one-sentence

memo in the director's name was fired back to Boston a week later.

```
To: SAC, Boston
From: Director, FBI

Promptly advise results of your contacts
with captioned source.
```

The interest apparently spurred Condon to action. He met with Bulger again on the same day that the memo from the director was logged into the FBI's files. At least according to the 209 Condon wrote about the meeting, the Bureau's relationship with its new source of information appeared to be off to a rousing start. Bulger told Condon that the recent murder of William O'Sullivan, a "tough guy" who was a close associate of both Bulger and his boss in the South Boston rackets, Donald Killeen, was a major problem. O'Sullivan, powerfully-built and good with a gun, was one of Killeen's security blankets.

Much of Killeen's bravado died with him, but O'Sullivan's demise also dampened the Irish boss's hope for a strategic alliance as well. O'Sullivan had been a close ally of both Frank Salemme and Steve Flemmi, who he knew were working with Larry Zannino and the Italian mob after they had double-crossed the Bennett brothers in the late 1960s. The Italians had been making noises about moving to control the South Boston rackets, and the muscle for the operation was supposed to be Flemmi and Salemme. When they fled the state to avoid the Bennett murder and Fitzgerald bombing indictments, the Mafia's plan to move on Killeen stalled. O'Sullivan had been Killeen's insurance policy. If Flemmi and Salemme did come back, Killeen and Bulger hoped that O'Sullivan might convince them to help forge an alliance and avert a hostile takeover.

O'Sullivan was the victim of a new rising criminal force in South Boston, a group of brash young "holdup and B&E

men" known as the Mullins Gang. Unlike the Killeen brothers, who made most of their income from bookmaking and running the illegal policy number, the Mullins Gang were mostly thieves who stole from the ships that brought goods into Boston Harbor and from the warehouses where they were stored. The harbor had always provided a rich source of income for South Boston's underworld, creating ample opportunity for smuggling—first liquor during Prohibition, then drugs starting in the 1960s—as well as theft, truck hijacking, and labor racketeering. The Mullins crew was particularly talented and opportunistic, as likely to steal a truckload of Easter hams as one of televisions. They also had strength in numbers—Boston Police at one time estimated that there were as many as sixty members.

The Killeen-Mullins rivalry was bitter. A plastic surgeon had to replace the tip of Mullins Gang member Mickey Maguire's nose after Donald Killeen bit it off during a fight. The Mullins boys were also eager to taste blood, especially leader Paul McGonagle, whose look-alike older brother, Donnie, a local Teamster who had little to do with the South Boston rackets, had been gunned down while driving Paulie's car. Paulie McGonagle believed the bullets had been meant for him and that Whitey Bulger had a hand in the shooting. Another top gang member, Patrick Nee, had sworn revenge on Killeen after they shot his brother Peter.

Things finally came to a head in early 1971. One of Paul McGonagle's associates, Dennis "Buddy" Roache, asked for a meeting with Bulger and O'Sullivan at the Colonial Lounge on West Broadway, a second floor barroom that was a Mullins stronghold.

"Killeen's day is over. I'm going to take him out," Roache said. "If you guys stand in the way, you'll get yours too."

"Fuck you," O'Sullivan shot back.

A fight ensued, and Roache went for his gun. O'Sullivan was faster and shot first, severing Roache's spinal cord. Bulger and O'Sullivan ran out the back of the bar. Paul McGonagle and the Mullins Gang swore revenge.

Bulger kept on the move, showing an extremely low profile and expecting retribution. Billy O'Sullivan's comparative brashness was his undoing. Late one night a few weeks after the Buddy Roache shooting, he drove away, quite drunk, from Billy Wallace's Sportlight bar on Old Colony Avenue toward his home in the nearby Savin Hill section of Dorchester. At least three carloads of armed men, who had been tipped off that he was inside the bar, silently picked up his tail. O'Sullivan parked near his house, got out of the car, and looked up to see a dozen members of the Mullins Gang striding toward him. He ran, but they caught him in a nearby vacant lot, where his broken and bullet-riddled corpse was found the next morning among the weeds.

What happened next is again remarkably similar to what happened to Steve Flemmi in Roxbury. Donald Killeen had no love for the Italian Mafia in the North End and no wish to make peace with them. Once the "organization" felt you needed their help, Killeen said, they would take you over. Killeen didn't want to reach out to the old Winter Hill Gang in Somerville, now being led by Howie Winter, fearing that the Mullins Gang had already beaten him to it. Killeen, like Wimpy Bennett, foolishly decided to remain independent and take on the Italian mob.

The handwriting on the wall for Whitey Bulger was getting clearer, according to Condon's report of a June 6, 1971, meeting with his prospective informant.

```
Bulger had been extremely careful since
the murder of O'Sullivan and feels that
he will be murdered if he lets his guard
down.
```

A strange thing happened, though, later in the summer. Like Flemmi had with Rico, Bulger seemed to be telegraphing to Condon his intentions to commit murder. Yet, at a time when Whitey Bulger should have needed the FBI most, the agent's report creates the impression that he was pulling back from the relationship.

Informant advised that there has been no
change in South Boston gang war situation since his last contact. He said that
the young group under the direction of
Paul McGonagle and Pat Nee are still attempting to "eliminate" Donald Killeen
and his associate James Whitey Bulger.
He said he did not know whether Killeen
and Bulger were planning any sort of of-
fensive action but was convinced if they
did not make a move, they would be eliminated. (Emphasis added.)

Contact with this informant on this occasion was not overly productive and it
is felt that he still has some inhibi-
tions about furnishing information.

Additional contacts will be had with
him, and if his productivity does not increase, consideration will be given to
closing him out.

Two months later, Condon wrote a two-sentence memo to
Hoover, saying:

Contacts with captioned individual have
been unproductive. Accordingly, this matter is being closed.

The FBI has insisted that Bulger was dropped from the informant rolls shortly after and was not rerecruited until four
years later, in 1975, by John Connolly. Some observers,
however, believe that he actually may have been in contact
with the FBI the entire time, and that Condon was simply
more circumspect in his handling of Bulger than Rico was
in handling Flemmi. Condon's report does not mention his
informant's lack of "productivity" until after Bulger suggests that he may have to resort to murder to protect himself.

Top former FBI officials admit that some Top Echelon informants were so hot to the touch that they had to be kept "off the books"—that is, without the agents taking direct credit for their accomplishments. Circumstantial evidence, at least, indicates that Bulger may have been one such informant.

The most compelling indication comes from Bulger and Flemmi's longtime friend and Winter Hill Gang colleague Johnny Martorano, who was arrested and charged with racketeering alongside them in the *Salemme* case. After sitting in court for months listening to stories of how they betrayed him and the rest of their friends in the underworld to the FBI, Martorano decided it was time to make his own sweetheart deal. His plea deal and confession shocked a nation. In exchange for a twelve-year sentence, he confessed to committing twenty murders—at least half of them committed at the behest of Flemmi and Bulger. The lenient deal immediately drew criticism and comparisons to the one given Sammy "the Bull" Gravano in New York, for his testimony against Gambino family boss "Teflon Don" John Gotti, who agreed to serve just five years for nineteen murders. Republican House Majority Leader Richard Armey of Texas even fired off an angry letter to Attorney General Janet Reno, demanding that she review the deal struck by federal and state prosecutors in Massachusetts, Oklahoma, and Florida. "What signal does this administration send when it allows dangerous predators like Mr. Martorano to receive a token slap on the wrist after a life of crime?" Armey wrote.

In the furor over Martorano's spectacular revelations and cushy deal, little notice was taken that ten of Johnny's twenty murders were committed during the time when Bulger, Flemmi, Martorano, and the Winter Hill Gang were making a violent bid to force bookmakers on their primary turf—Somerville and South Boston—to pay them protection money. Conveniently, they also occurred during the time when Bulger disappeared off the FBI's official radar screen.

Early in the morning of March 8, 1973, a group of friends
were getting into a maroon Mercedes-Benz, heading home
from a bar called Mother's in Boston's Brighton section.
Suddenly, bullets crashed through the car's windows. One
passenger, Louis Lapaina, had his spine severed. Another, a
thirty-year-old bartender named Michael Milano, was
killed.[6] Bulger participated in the Milano murder and was either involved in or ordered seven others during the same
time period, according to Martorano's plea agreement.

Later in the year, meanwhile, Condon filed an odd little
report about information that supposedly came from one of
his informants.

```
Informant advised that JAMES WHITEY BUL-
GER has been moving around the city pres-
suring   bookmakers   and   shylocks   for
payments of money. BULGER was told that
he was coming on too strong and is going
to curtail these activities in the fu-
ture.
```

The memo does not say *who* is telling Bulger to curtail his
activities, whether it is Condon or the informant. What
seems clear is that Condon had a good idea of what Bulger
was up to—all he had to do was read the obituaries to
glimpse the results of Whitey Bulger's "pressuring" of
bookmakers and loansharks. The memo certainly raises
questions about what the FBI knew in 1975, when Bulger
was allegedly "recruited" by John Connolly. By then, predictably, the killing had mostly stopped, police weren't even
close to solving any of the murders, and Bulger had consol-
idated his position as a rising force in the Boston underworld—and was exactly the sort of criminal the FBI wanted
for the Top Echelon program.

---

[6]Milano was the wrong man. Martorano later admitted that he and Bulger
had been looking to kill a bookmaker who drove a nearly identical maroon
Mercedes.

*   *   *

The Condon reports appear to call into question Connolly's story of recruiting Bulger during a clandestine moonlit meeting in an empty beach parking lot in 1975. In fact, it is difficult to know what is true in the carefully crafted mythology of the relationship between John Connolly and Whitey Bulger.

Connolly had a basic schtick of anecdotes that he told repeatedly about Bulger's background in South Boston, including the few times that they ran into one another as boys. One story has an awestruck Connolly being hoisted up on a seat in a soda fountain shop and treated to an ice cream cone by the much older Whitey. Connolly told that one around the office so often, it became known around the FBI office simply as "The Ice Cream Cone Story." As the tale goes, Bulger won over the shy eight-year-old by talking about their shared heritage.

"Hey kid, I'm no stranger. Your mother and father are from Ireland. My mother and father are from Ireland. What kind of ice cream do you want?" Bulger said, according to Connolly.

Another had the nineteen-year-old Bulger rescuing an eight-year-old Connolly from a gang of older boys who were beating him up after a playground argument. Connolly would also recount how Bulger, as an adult, would help women with their groceries and bring turkeys to poor families in the South Boston housing projects at Thanksgiving. Taken at face value, the stories are fairly cheesy. They work better as myth, depicting the Whitey Bulger that Connolly wanted people to see. Whitey, the gangster with the heart of gold. Whitey, the protector of the weak.

Another story some people believe to be apocryphal is the tale of Bulger's supposed recruitment by Connolly from a car parked near a beach in Quincy. As the tale goes, Connolly set up a meeting with Bulger on a moonlit night overlooking the water and the Boston skyline. Then Whitey, appearing wraithlike out of nowhere, opened the car door and climbed inside. "Just hear me out," the agent has said he said to the gangster. Connolly's pitch: the Boston Mafia had corrupt police contacts that could help them, so why not use the FBI in the same way? In exchange for information, the FBI could eliminate his rivals in the North End while shielding him from bookmaking and loansharking charges. Bulger was "intrigued" by the idea, Connolly said, and agreed.

On one hand it is certainly a plausible story. On the other, it is difficult to accept his self-serving moonlight Bulger serenade story at face value. A deeper look at the whole Bulger-Condon-Connolly relationship reveals a number of coincidences that raise doubts about the FBI's official version of events—that Connolly somehow succeeded in his effort to recruit Bulger in 1975 where Condon had failed four years earlier.

First of all, Condon admits that he was introduced to Connolly in 1968 by Boston Police Detective Ed Walsh, (the same Boston Police detective later named by Joe Murray as being on the take) even before he began working for the FBI. At the time, Connolly, who had attended Boston College at Billy Bulger's suggestion, was teaching school but had been accepted into the Bureau.

"He [Walsh] thought that it would be nice if a local fellow from the area—if we met," Condon said later. Condon denied ever becoming a mentor for Connolly in the FBI, but he admitted talking to him on the telephone when the young agent was being shuffled to his first assignments in Baltimore, San Francisco, and New York. Condon even admitted bringing Connolly along once when he had to fly to San Francisco to conduct an interview in an organized crime case. Condon was also instrumental in getting the young agent back to Boston in 1973, just a few years after he joined the Bureau.

While many agents waited decades to be transferred back to their hometown, Connolly's road back to Massachusetts was smoothed considerably by his remarkable arrest of a top fugitive, Cadillac Frank Salemme, in New York, with Condon's help. The way Condon handled the fugitive case strongly suggests that in pursuing Salemme he was helping both Connolly and T.E. informant Flemmi at the same time. Condon later testified that he called Connolly in New York because he was frustrated that Salemme and Flemmi had been on the run for the better part of four years. The New York office hadn't been doing much to find them, Condon said, despite the fact that Salemme was believed to be in the midtown Manhattan area with another fugitive wiseguy from Rhode Island. Condon said he sent Connolly some photos to use in locating Salemme and told him, "See if you can spark them up down there."

Condon was right, Salemme *was* in New York, living under the name "Jules Daniel Selig" of Philadelphia. The odd thing was, Condon wasn't assigned to the Flemmi-Salemme fugitive case. Arguably, it was a personal matter, since Fitzgerald had been the lawyer for Barboza, Condon's witness. Yet Condon's own reports reveal another irregularity. It appears that while he was hot after Salemme, he was much less concerned with Flemmi.

In a report dated December 22, 1972—a month after Salemme's arrest—Condon wrote that one of his informants said Flemmi was "laying low" and waiting to see what happened to Frank Salemme and the Fitzgerald case. The report doesn't say whether the informant knew where Flemmi was or if Condon even asked. This was a departure from the previous two dozen or so reports written by Condon on the subject over two years, beginning in February 1970. In report after report, averaging about once a month, Condon asks his unidentified informant if he has any information on both Salemme and Flemmi's whereabouts. In December of that year, the informant told Condon that Flemmi and Salemme were in New York, but there appears to be no record in the FBI's files of any action being taken on the tip.

It wasn't until Flemmi and Salemme had split up, eleven months later, that the FBI made its move—and Condon took a personal interest in the case. On October 26, 1971, Con-

don's informant said Flemmi and Salemme had parted ways.
A month later John Connolly "bumped into" Salemme on
the street and arrested him, while Flemmi escaped to Montreal. Over the next few years, Condon's reports mention
Flemmi repeatedly, but unlike the prior two dozen reports,
which also mention Cadillac Frank—there is no indication
after Salemme's arrest that Condon is asking his informants
for Flemmi's whereabouts.

According to sworn testimony by Connolly at Salemme's
trial on the Fitzgerald bombing, the December 1972 arrest
went like this:

Salemme made the Boston Police Department's "Six
Most Wanted List" in 1970 for the Billy Bennett murder and
the Fitzgerald bombing. Connolly began carrying a picture
of Salemme in his wallet, after learning that he might be in
New York. He was with two other FBI agents when he spotted Salemme on the Upper East Side, walking on Third Avenue somewhere in the Eighties. He let Salemme walk past
so he could get a good look, then the three agents turned
around and followed the Boston gangster for three blocks.

"Frankie," the young agent finally called out. Salemme
snapped his head around, made a move like he was about to
run, then relaxed.

You got the wrong guy, Salemme said, pulling a draft card
out of his wallet that identified him as Selig. Salemme said
he had been living in Philadelphia for six years at 2466
Seventy-second Avenue. Connolly looked at the draft card.
The address on it was Seventy-sixth Avenue, not Seventy-
second.

In Boston, Connolly's story of the Salemme arrest always
scored high on the bullshit meter. Morris also said he had his
doubts about whether it really happened that way. Connolly
would stick to it, possibly because it made him look like the
kind of super-sharp young G-man that Hoover's FBI was
supposed to be about. Another possibility is that any back-
tracking on it would have opened him up to perjury charges.

Connolly did admit later that the Salemme arrest was a key

part of his getting transferred from New York back to Boston. Spotting one wanted fugitive on a sidewalk in a city of millions was just a remarkable coincidence. Another one was the fact that Connolly appeared in Boston just as Condon, the FBI's first link to Bulger, was getting ready to retire. Top Echelon informants were routinely passed from retiring agents to younger ones in other cities like New York, Cleveland, and Chicago, but FBI officials denied that any such thing took place in Boston. The chain of events that brought John Connolly together with Whitey Bulger, according to the Bureau, was simply a run of good luck.

Some people believe it was. Others do not.

John Connolly never made a secret of his respect and admiration for Billy Bulger. It was quite the opposite in fact. Agents said he talked of the politician Bulger often in an adoring tone, and took many of the SACs and ASACs who were new in town to meet Bulger in his imposing Senate president's office under the gold-leaf dome of the Massachusetts State House on Beacon Hill. Billy, after all, had encouraged the young Connolly to read, to attend Boston College, and even wrote a letter that helped Connolly be admitted to Harvard University's prestigious Kennedy School of Government. Connolly had also worked on Bulger's re-election campaigns, standing out on the street at rush hour with other volunteers waving a BULGER sign at morning commuters.

Connolly insists that there was little nexus—beyond himself—between the respective worlds of Billy and Whitey Bulger. "There was no connection. Billy didn't know what Whitey was doing, and Whitey wanted it that way," Connolly said. In fact, most of those involved in the Bulger and Flemmi affair on any side will agree that no one has ever made a credible, fact-based allegation that Billy Bulger was involved in his brother's relationship with the FBI.

Whether he may have benefited from it, however, is another matter. That question has been the subject of much conjecture, thanks to a run of good career fortune for Billy that was almost as impressive as his brother's—and also involved the FBI.[7]

Billy first ran for political office in 1960. His opponents in the State House of Representatives race derided him as "Same Suit Bulger" because one good outfit was all he could afford, and he wore it everywhere during the campaign. The jibes only made Bill Bulger seem more of a common man of the people, though, and probably helped him win votes in working-class Southie. His brother's reputation surfaced several times during his political career, and probably thwarted any hopes Billy Bulger might have had for running for election anywhere outside South Boston. As he was fond of pointing out, though, the sins of the brother weren't held against the entire family in Southie. Many families had one son in the rackets and another in the priesthood, or on the police force. Buddy Roache's brother Mickey was a cop, who later became the Boston Police commissioner and then a City Councilor. Even Steve Flemmi had a brother Michael who was a Boston cop.

In 1963, Bulger was part of an insurgent group of young Democrats who united behind Michael Paul Feeney, a rep from Boston's Hyde Park section, in his bid to unseat unpopular Speaker John "Iron Duke" Thompson, whose hold on the House was as tenuous as his grip on sobriety. Through an exhausting marathon session, Bulger voted five times for Feeney, but at the last minute changed his vote to back Thompson. Bulger said he was urged to switch sides by the Speaker of the U.S. House of Representatives, John McCormack, whose home was in Bulger's South Boston district. McCormack said that Thompson had vowed to change his ways, and he urged Bulger to give him a chance.

Another legislator, however, tells the story differently, saying Bulger came back from McCormack's call ashen-

---

[7]William Bulger has consistently refused interview requests since his brother Whitey's racketeering indictment in January 1995.

faced and said: "I got a call from John McCormack. He got my brother out of Alcatraz, so I have to go with Thompson."

In his memoir, Billy Bulger was less specific, saying only that he "owed much" to Thompson. "He had tried to keep us abreast of my brother's situation in prison, and he had been our only source of information about Jim through many years of worry," Bulger wrote. "I remember him saying: 'James made a mistake and is paying for it, but he can change if they give him a chance.' "

After ten years in the State House of Representatives, Bulger moved to the Massachusetts Senate, where, after his brother had agreed to become an informant, he became the beneficiary of the Federal Bureau of Investigation in the late 1970s.

The Democratic majority whip in the Senate, Joseph Di-Carlo, and Ways and Means Committee chairman James A. Kelly Jr., were indicted for extorting money from a New York construction firm bidding on state contracts. The scandal forced Senate President Kevin Harrington from his leadership post, and Harrington named Billy Bulger as his heir apparent. The case, known as the MBM scandal after the name of the construction company, McKee, Berger & Mansueto, was investigated by the FBI. Bulger held the Senate presidency for the next two decades and became one of the most powerful politicians in Massachusetts.

Bill Bulger dodged another bullet in the 1980s. The first involved a high-living real estate developer named Jack Collins, who drove a big Lincoln, lived in the exclusive Charles River Park luxury apartments, and courted politicians on behalf of the East Bay Development Corporation. The company was supposedly planning a retail and restaurant complex in Somerville and needed two new liquor licenses.

In reality, "Jack Collins" was Jack Callahan, an FBI agent who had grown up in Dorchester and graduated from Boston College before joining the FBI and moving to Detroit. Callahan started in Somerville and worked his way up the ladder,

first snaring Alderman Timothy Creedon on tape offering
city approval for the two licenses in exchange for an $8,500
bribe. Creedon was confronted and agreed to cooperate. Because there was a freeze on new liquor licenses in the city,
anyone who could not wait to buy an existing one had to go
through the state legislature. On the House side that meant
Vincent "Vinny" Piro, the local Somerville rep who was also
the Assistant House Majority Leader, and Speaker Thomas
McGee, a Billy Bulger ally. Piro had plans to run for the
State Senate, where he also presumably would have become
a Bulger supporter. When it became clear that Creedon
wasn't lying about being able to broker a deal with Piro, the
U.S. Attorney's office, which was overseeing the probe,
started thinking big. If they could turn Piro, he might take
them to the very top: McGee in the House and Bulger in the
Senate.

Piro, a glad-handing, perpetually suntanned former
schoolteacher turned real estate investor, agreed to help push
the East Bay liquor license bill through the legislature for
$25,000, federal indictment prosecutors later charged. The
exchange was recorded by Callahan's hidden body wire.

"So here's the deal. It will be a total of twenty-five. Five
will come up front. The first five has got to be a little walking
around money. Got to do some things. Grease a few guys."

Piro took an envelope from Callahan containing a hundred marked fifty-dollar bills.

"I've got to consider other people, especially the speaker,"
Piro said, in what prosecutors said was a reference to
McGee. Piro also told the agent how he and "the speaker"
were left "holding the bag" when a racetrack owner from the
Berkshires welshed on a large bribe payment after they had
pushed through a bill extending the racing calendar.

The agents and prosecutors were ecstatic. It didn't last.
Three weeks later Callahan took a call from Piro, who asked
him to come to his office on Beacon Hill. Something was
definitely wrong. All the bravado had disappeared from
Piro's voice, he sounded almost sheepish. Piro was sitting at

his desk when Callahan walked in. He was looking down at his lap as he was talking.

"I'm glad you called, because I'm really distressed. Okay, the last time you were in, you know I was going to give you a call. The last time you were in, you came in and did something for me," Piro said.

"Yeah, yeah," Callahan said.

"Gave me that envelope. And Jesus Christ, like I told you then, I don't do things like that."

"Yeah," Callahan said, wondering what the hell Piro was looking down at.

"And I've been thinking about it, it's been bothering me. I've never done this before in the fifteen years that I've been here. I don't want to start now."

Callahan craned his neck to see what Piro was looking down at as he continued droning through his apology. Were they cue cards?

"The main thing is, I didn't want to offend you 'cause you're a decent guy. And I know you didn't want to offend me. And you did it in the spirit of good faith."

The liquor license bill, Piro said, would still have his support.

"That's gonna be done under no obligations for anybody," he said.

"Super," Callahan replied. "Thank you."

"And, ah, hey listen, I want you as my friend."

Callahan left Piro's office feeling like he wanted to throw up. The agents and prosecutors on the probe agreed there was no way that Piro's apology was genuine. Someone had dropped a dime and killed the investigation. It would stop with Piro, and now even that prosecution was in jeopardy, thanks to his carefully scripted and highly exculpatory change of heart.

The search began for suspects. One story, which many adopted as fact, was that Callahan and Connolly both attended a Boston Bruins hockey game together and were spotted by one of Piro's friends. That story never washed with Callahan. He *had* been at a Bruins game that Connolly

also attended, but he was smart enough to know that half of
Somerville was probably there, and he wasn't dumb enough
to let himself be seen with one of Boston's better-known
FBI agents.

Some FBI agents who knew of Whitey Bulger's relationship with the Bureau immediately suspected Connolly as the
leak. Connolly knew Callahan, whose father had been a
coach at South Boston High School, and it was no mystery
that he was close to Billy Bulger. Connolly vehemently denied being the leak, however, when a television station suggested that he had told Whitey Bulger the information. The
other theory probed by the agents and prosecutors was that
the leak had gone to Dennis Condon, the former FBI agent,
who worked as a private investigator for Piro's attorney,
Robert Popeo. Both Condon and Popeo denied it. The leak
probe never went anywhere.

However Piro came by his change of heart, Popeo, who
was making a name as both tough and politically connected, took the ball and ran with it. He derisively dubbed
the undercover sting "Operation Gotcha" and filed motions
saying that the FBI had offered Piro prostitutes and opportunities to participate in drug deals in order to entrap him—
a charge that Weld's office angrily denied. The
counterattack worked. An unapologetic Piro won the 1984
Democratic primary for his representative's seat six days
before the start of his trial.

"He could be tempted but not corrupted. If Vinny Piro *had*
attempted extortion, he would have succeeded," Popeo said
in his opening statement. "He stands before you as the only
man in America ever indicted for *not* taking a bribe." There
was evidence, though, that Piro had suffered something
other than pangs of conscience. Some of the bills he gave
back to Callahan had serial numbers that didn't match the
ones on the bribe money the agent had given him.

Piro testified for five hours at his first trial. Taking the
money, he said, was "the stupidest thing" he had ever done.
He tried to pass off the story about the Berkshires racetrack

bribe as a false and "ridiculous war story" told in an attempt to convince Callahan that he was "the one to deal with" so he could keep "Collins" from going to other legislators and offering them the same temptations.

"I was afraid he would start doing the same thing to others," Piro said. "I wanted to give him the impression I was in control so he wouldn't bribe anyone else."

The jury deliberated for twenty-two hours before pronouncing itself hopelessly deadlocked. U.S. District Court Judge Walter Jay Skinner declared a mistrial. Piro was acquitted at a second trial.

There is other circumstantial evidence that the third leg of the Billy-Whitey-FBI triangle existed, like the fact that Steve Flemmi moved his aging parents next door to Bill Bulger's house at 832 East Third Street in South Boston. By that time Billy Bulger was considered by many to be the most powerful politician in the state, and it is hard to imagine the house next to his being sold to relatives of a known gangster over his objection. Billy, for his part, never disavowed or condemned his brother, preferring instead in his few public statements to vilify the media for making up stories about him, and railing against the government witnesses who testified against him as mercenary turncoats. Those statements, many of which are enshrined in his memoir, provide some no doubt unintentional comic relief when juxtaposed against his brother's thick FBI informant file. "We loathed informers," Billy Bulger wrote of his childhood days in South Boston.

When Billy became a senator and began hosting his famous St. Patrick's Day breakfasts in 1972, Whitey was prudent enough to stay away from the politician-infested public affair that was usually carried live on television. It featured a roast of the state's top politicians—Weld later became a favorite speaker and target of Bulger barbs—and in some years a ceremonial call from the White House, which served to bolster Billy's image as a South Boston politician with clout far beyond the neighborhood. Friends said Whitey was a regular at the private party for close friends and family later at the house.

Shortly after the Massachusetts State Police failed in a 1980 wiretap scheme targeting Whitey Bulger, an ominous line item appeared in the Senate budget. The anonymous amendment, which eliminated the salaries of the State Police's top brass, was dropped after a bitter protest, but to some the message was clear: Don't fuck with Whitey.

CHAPTER FIVE

The New Untouchables

••••••••••••••••••••••••••••••

Ambitious FBI agents create a class of supercriminals

MANY FBI AGENTS still firmly believe in the underlying necessity of the Top Echelon program. One veteran agent from a major Midwest field office insists that the insidious nature and national scope of the Italian-American Mafia forced the Bureau to recruit inside sources.

"We are only as good as the information we get. Sometimes you have to deal with the Whitey Bulgers of this world. Is it an uncomfortable situation to be in? Sure. Your foot is poised to step on the third rail all the time. But you have to take your chances and roll the dice—until you get specific information that they were doing things that they really weren't supposed to be doing. Like murder. If allegations like that were true, they should go to jail. How could you ever justify that? Or if they are burning down churches. There is a limit to everything."

The FBI has never said exactly how many Top Echelon informants it recruited over the years. One former FBI Headquarters official estimates that the number could be as high as four hundred, while another said it is "in the hundreds." John Connolly says he had as many as ten Top Echelon informants. Anthony Villano, the New York agent, claimed to have recruited half a dozen "made" members of the Mafia while he was working organized crime cases. Villano said he paid little attention to the written rules while pursuing and protecting his sources.

"As an agent, I had to break almost every rule in the book to do my job," Villano wrote. "The Bureau never wanted to know about such transgressions, so, in the reports we filed, they were either not mentioned or covered up by lies. We also spent a good part of our time distorting the truth in the administrative accounts our supervisors received. The system, with all of its cumbersome record-keeping, forces a premium to be put on fakery."

And, apparently, on looking the other way. Villano wrote that one of his T.E.'s, identified only by the pesudonym "Jackie Gucci," was given the go-ahead to murder a rival loanshark by his bosses in the Gambino family. "Gucci" told Villano that once, while he was waiting in ambush outside an East Harlem tavern, the gun he kept tucked in his waistband clattered to the ground just as a police officer was about to walk by. Instead of trying to deter him, Villano wrote that he bought "Gucci" a holster as a present from the FBI.

The loanshark was later found murdered, and Villano did nothing to follow up.

"Jackie Gucci never volunteered, and I never asked about it," Villano wrote.

Villano's tales aren't unique. The Top Echelon Informant Program wasn't confined to New York, or to Boston. Time and again FBI agents, supervisors around the country, and their bosses in Washington tried to protect their valuable underworld allies from both fellow colleagues in law enforcement and their enemies in the mob, sometimes having to break the law themselves to do it. The Top Echelon program was a national initiative, so it is not surprising that similarly disturbing themes emerge from stories of T.E. informants across the country.

New York: Greg Scarpa

Hearing a "not guilty" verdict in her husband's December 1994 murder case, Marguerite Cutolo, a yellow ribbon pinned to her bosom, threw her hands together in a gesture of prayer and thanks directed in part to the jury in the U.S. District Courthouse in Brooklyn but mostly heavenward.

"Thank you, Jesus! Oh, St. Jude. Thank Jude!" she cried, invoking the Catholic patron saint of hopeless causes. She might have also thanked Colombo crime family captain Gregory Scarpa Sr. Six months after his death, he was still giving hope to numerous mobsters accused of taking part in a bloody war for control of one of New York's famous five Mafia families.

William Cutolo, like Scarpa, was a captain in the Colombo family, although they were members of opposing rival factions in the fractured family. Cutolo and six henchmen had just been acquitted on murder and murder conspiracy charges. "Merry Christmas to the world," the forty-five-year-old wiseguy, now a free man, exclaimed on the chilly sidewalk outside the courthouse a short time later. "I've got the best lawyer. This is the best present ever."

It took Cutolo's attorney, James LaRossa, to put the credit where it was due. Although Greg Scarpa would have happily gunned down Cutolo as soon as look at him, the dead wiseguy's double life as an ambitious underworld killer and Top Echelon informant for the FBI had given Cutolo a fighting chance to beat the charges. LaRossa said, "I think the greatest reason for this verdict was the jury's realization that the government was permitting Gregory Scarpa to be the main agitator in this war while keeping him as their informant."

Cutolo wasn't alone. In all, sixteen New York wiseguys in four separate trials were acquitted on the same shocking rationale: The juries essentially found that a dominant faction of one of New York's five great Mafia families had legitimately armed itself in self-defense against the FBI.

In terms of sheer FBI malfeasance, the stories of New York Top Echelon informant Gregory Scarpa and his son Greg Jr. come closest to Bulger and Flemmi in the length of the relationship and the depths to which the FBI was willing to stoop for their mob sources.

The elder Scarpa was a captain in the Colombo family and a T.E. informant for more than thirty years, according to formerly secret FBI documents. Testimony at various trials portrayed Scarpa as especially bloodthirsty—one witness said that after the wiseguy killed and buried rival Lawrence Mazza, he told three associates: "Dig him up. I want to shoot him again."

There can be no doubt that the FBI knew of Scarpa's reputation as a killer—even of other informants. An attorney who once worked for him, Martin Light, was asked by a federal crime commission in early 1986 how Scarpa and his associates would deal with any potential problems. "They'd get rid of them," Light replied. Scarpa was also publicly tied to the 1987 gang-style execution of Joseph De Domenico, a suspect in the murder of Scarpa's brother, Salvatore. Police and the newspaper accounts also linked five other revenge slayings to Scarpa's brother's killing.

Scarpa's crew operated out of the Wimpy Boys Social Club in the Dyker Heights section of Brooklyn, running mostly gambling, extortion, and credit card scams, authorities said. His crew was assigned to Colombo lieutenant Anthony Scarpati, but after Scarpati and Colombo family boss Carmine Persico were convicted and sent to prison in 1986, Scarpa and others started entertaining thoughts about moving up. Persico's unwillingness to let go of power, despite the fact that he had received a life sentence, helped spark the war. Persico's top underling, Victor Orena, responded to being named only "acting boss" by attempting to forcefully wrest control of the family. He was confident that he possessed an overwhelming advantage—one estimate had roughly two hundred soldiers loyal to his side versus the mere thirty loyal to the imprisoned Persico. What Orena didn't know was that the other side had Gregory Scarpa, and that Scarpa had the FBI.

Police believe that Scarpa was involved in as many as thirteen of the fifteen killings attributed to the Persico side in the Persico-Orena war. His gleeful pursuit of the shooting war, and the enthusiasm of Scarpa handler, Special Agent Lindley DeVecchio, may have been their undoing. As usual, a shooting war proved to be a fertile ground for recruiting informants. DeVecchio's fellow agents started hearing from their new sources that key pieces of FBI intelligence were being leaked into the Mafia's hands, and the beneficiary was invariably Gregory Scarpa. Other agents later alleged that DeVecchio fed Scarpa information on the whereabouts of his rivals. He was so obvious about it that a fellow agent who overheard him leaking information about another mobster threatened to "burn" Scarpa's identity if the other wiseguy came to any harm.

Donald North, DeVecchio's supervisor, testified that he ordered the agent to stop contacting Scarpa after learning that the T.E. informant was suspected of committing murder while working as an informant. Some said DeVecchio continued to keep in touch with the mobster via his girlfriend. North also said Scarpa was reopened as an informant without his approval. DeVecchio eventually became so partisan that one inside FBI account had him slapping his desk with satisfaction at the news that two of Scarpa's rivals had been killed, exclaiming: "We're going to win this thing."

Worst of all was the allegation that—like John Connolly's alleged leak about Brian Halloran in Boston—DeVecchio told Scarpa the identities of three former associates who were planning to become witnesses against him. DeVecchio has denied ever leaking any information to Scarpa and called the allegations "total nonsense." He continued to make the claim even after being given a grant of immunity by the Justice Department. DeVecchio was never charged with any crime.

Scarpa, dying of AIDS and having nothing to lose, even-

tually admitted to committing two murders. He died in a
prison hospital in June 1994.

One interesting parallel between the Scarpa case and the
Whitey Bulger case in Boston was that they were both protected not just by their FBI handlers, but by the basic immoral premise of the Top Echelon program itself. Whitey
Bulger was once asked by the head of the Boston FBI office
whether he feared for his safety since rumors of his informant status were being spread by other law enforcement
agencies. "No one would ever believe it," Bulger replied.

Onetime Colombo family acting boss—and Scarpa
friend—Carmine Sessa testified in the Orena appeal hearings that he always wondered about Scarpa's ability to walk
between the judicial raindrops, never getting convicted or at
least serving much time. Joe Tomasello, who Persico had
tabbed as acting boss during the war, once suggested that
Scarpa "go out and kill somebody on the Orena faction to
settle everybody's mind."

Scarpa promptly did, and the killing went on.

There is another tale about Greg Scarpa that would be almost too fantastic if it weren't true—and if it weren't dis-
turbingly similar to one told about Whitey Bulger.

Scarpa played a key role in one of the FBI's biggest cases
ever, the murder of three civil rights workers in Mississippi
during a tense period following passage of the landmark
Civil Rights Act of 1964. The case became known in FBI-
speak as "MIBURN," for "Mississippi Burning," because it
began with a series of KKK arson attacks on churches where
white civil rights workers from the North were suspected of
meeting with local African Americans.

Two young Jewish men from New York—a veteran civil
rights marcher named Michael Schwerner and Queens College anthropology student Andrew Goodman—and a young
local black man, James Chaney, disappeared on Sunday,
June 21, after interviewing several families about a church
burning in the tiny hamlet of Philadelphia, Mississippi.

Local police acknowledged that they had pulled over their Ford station wagon for speeding and then detained them, on the unlikely story that the civil rights workers were suspected of burning the church themselves. They were held until nightfall then released unharmed, the police said. Mississippi politicians, including U.S. Senator James Eastland, said their disappearance was probably just a "publicity stunt," staged by the three young men to call attention to their cause.

The case quickly developed into a national media event test of wills between the FBI and the locals, the federal government and rural southerners who saw their way of life being threatened. Hoover, who was being pressured by President Lyndon Johnson, was determined to break the case. He flew down to Mississippi just before the first anniversary of the disappearance, which was officially regarded as a kidnapping to justify the FBI's involvement. By the time Hoover arrived, there were more that four hundred agents in the state, and hundreds of U.S. Navy reservists had been shanghaied to drag a swamp where the burned-out station wagon had been found. Hoover touched down in his official FBI plane, a Lockheed Jetstar (the same model jet as the President's Air Force One), and threw down the federal gauntlet to local law enforcement officials.

"There will be attempted resistance, some possibly very violent. But this must be met by the united will, the united strength, of the Congress, the courts, the President, and the law of the land. The key to law and order in Mississippi remains the extent to which local authorities recognize their responsibilities and discharge them," Hoover said to an assemblage of national media. The FBI, the pugnacious director vowed, would be in Mississippi in force "until the three missing civil rights workers are found and those responsible for their disappearance brought to justice."

The import of Hoover's words was not lost on his agents. Hoover had thrown his beloved FBI's credibility—if not the credibility of the entire federal government—on breaking the MIBURN case. Solving it became imperative. What happened next is a matter of some debate.

The official FBI version of events, put forth by longtime top Hoover aide Cartha "Deke" DeLoach and others, is that the Bureau paid for its first big break in the case—the location of the bodies. DeLoach, in his memoir *Hoover's FBI,* describes the two cooperative men only as "a minister and a member of the highway patrol." DeLoach does not say how the two men knew that the three civil rights workers had been buried under twelve feet of dirt in an earthen dam on a large farm located a few miles outside of Philadelphia, but said the FBI paid $30,000 for the information.

The Hollywood version of the story, which starred Gene Hackman as a roguish FBI agent and Willem Dafoe as his button-downed partner, depicted the information being pried loose by a group of thuggish FBI operatives loyal to Hackman's character, Special Agent Anderson. The movie G-men bullied potential suspects and witnesses, including the local mayor, who in one memorable scene was threatened with castration by a black agent holding a double-edged razor blade.

"Don't drag me down into your gutter, Mr. Anderson," Dafoe's Special Agent Ward says at one point.

"These people crawled out of a sewer, Mr. Ward. Maybe the gutter is where we oughta be," Hackman's character replies.

In part due to its portrayal of southern blacks as passive victims, and the mostly white FBI agents as heroes, and in part due to the film's departure from the FBI's official story, *Mississippi Burning* was excoriated by many critics. One *Time* reviewer wrote that the film's alleged distortions amounted to a "cinematic lynching" of history. Ironically, the cinematic version may have come closer to the truth than the official FBI story out of Washington. At least that's according to Scarpa's son Greg Jr., whose tale has been backed up in several news accounts by unnamed FBI agents purported to have worked on the MIBURN case.

The younger Scarpa said his father offered his services in the case to his FBI handler, Tony Villano. He made a three-day trip to Mississippi, where, possibly posing as a member of the national Ku Klux Klan himself, he and an FBI helper kidnapped a local appliance salesman and KKK member who was viewed by the FBI as a potential weak link in the case. They took the man to a remote location, tied him to a chair, and interrogated him. The first two times he told the story, the agent and Scarpa believed that the man was lying. On the third try, Scarpa pulled his gun on the suspect.

"He said he took a gun and put it in the guy's mouth and said, 'For the last time, where are the bodies or I'll blow your head off,' " the son testified. The KKK member finally confessed to the location of the bodies, the son said.

Both the Justice Department and the FBI have officially declined to comment on any role Scarpa may have played in the MIBURN case. Yet there is evidence beyond the younger Scarpa's testimony and quotes from unnamed agents that the story is true, including the informant's own FD-209 reports released and made public after his death. One such report, written in January 1966, states that Scarpa was used as a "special" —the FBI term for a nonagent working for the Bureau—in the murder of Vernon Dahmer, the head of the NAACP office in Hattiesburg, Mississippi. Dahmer's house was torched by the Ku Klux Klan, and the memo states that Scarpa was sent to Hattiesburg to work on the case.

Also, although DeLoach's account of the MIBURN case does not mention Scarpa, it does state that a squad of COIN-TELPRO agents were sent to interview members of the Klan, and that "many of them were big, bruising men, highly trained in the tactics of interrogation."

Cleveland: Jackie Presser

Properly handled, the FBI's relationship with Teamsters Union President Jackie Presser could have been an example of how the Top Echelon Informant Program might have been both successful *and* relatively ethical.

Instead, it showed the lengths agents were apparently willing to go to protect their Top Echelon informants.

Jack Presser was literally born to the con. His father—a hatmaker who would later become president of a powerful union council in Cleveland—and his mother, a bootlegger's daughter, registered under false names at a maternity hospital in Cleveland and skipped out on the bill after young Jackie was born.

He learned how to co-opt law enforcement at his father's knee. Bill Presser was a friend of both Teamsters President Jimmy Hoffa and the Milano brothers, the bosses of the big Midwest Mafia family. When Jackie was in his mid-twenties and just starting his career as a labor racketeer, he watched his father woo Pat Foley, an influential detective who ran the Cleveland Police Department's labor bureau. Bill Presser and Louis "Babe" Triscaro, a Milano crime family associate, took Foley on a junket to California where they had poolside cocktails with movie stars like Bob Hope—all while Foley was signed in at police headquarters as being on duty back in Cleveland. Returning the favor, Foley helped convince reluctant merchants not to resist Bill Presser's strongarm labor tactics.

The Presser family business, the International Brotherhood of Teamsters, was at the heart of the tug-of-war between Attorney General Robert Kennedy and J. Edgar Hoover. Kennedy positively loathed the corrupt Hoffa—they openly screamed at each other during the 1957 hearings of the Senate Select Committee on Improper Activities in the Labor or Management Field. The thirty-one-year-old Attorney General was severely frustrated by Hoover's obtuse insistence on chasing suspected Communists while ignoring the Mafia's influence in organized labor and other industries.

Presser was recruited by William McCann, a supervisor of the Cleveland FBI office's Organized Crime Squad. Like his counterpart H. Paul Rico in Boston, McCann had a reputation for hard drinking, hanging out with criminals and politicians, and generally ignoring Hoover's proscriptions about the monastic life FBI agents were supposed to lead.[8]

And just like Flemmi, Presser was recruited during the tumult of a mob shooting war, which pitted his father's old allies in the Milano family against a younger, more aggressive gang. McCann actually first recruited Tony Hughes, Presser's ex-boxer bodyguard, as a Top Echelon informant. According to James Neff's excellent 1989 biography of Presser, *Mobbed Up,* law enforcement officials say Hughes was easy to recruit after his close friend, a Mafia-connected loanshark named Peter DiGravio, was killed on a golf course by three bullets from a sniper's rifle in 1969. McCann used Hughes to get an introduction to Presser. Just like in other cases, one T.E. informant was used to help recruit another—Hughes told McCann just which buttons to push when he met Presser.

The agent listened to Presser rail against the Communists he believed were still trying to make inroads into the American labor movement. McCann convinced the up-and-coming Teamster leader that the FBI would be a valuable ally fighting subversives. Over a period of several months, McCann continued cajoling, and Presser finally agreed to help the FBI make organized crime cases.

Most T.E. informants were documented, although a few, according to longtime agents, were so potentially controversial that they were kept "off the books." Presser was unique in that he was *officially* kept off the books, a concession to the danger he put himself in by agreeing to secretly help the FBI. When McCann retired in 1977, Presser negotiated a deal unprecedented even for a Top Echelon informant. FBI Director Clarence Kelley himself approved a plan by which Presser's new contact agent, Pat Foran, would type Presser's information on a sheet of plain white paper instead of a stan-

[8]Neff, James, *Mobbed Up* (Atlantic Monthly Press, 1989).

dard form FD-209 and would either hand-carry the information himself to Washington or have it couriered in a plain envelope. Presser was also given a code instead of an informant number, which was the usual procedure (Tony Hughes, for example, was CV 3963 TE—CV stood for Cleveland, 3963 was his number, and TE was for his designation, Top Echelon). Presser was simply known as ALPRO, a tribute to the quality and value of his information.

In a deposition taken during the U.S. Justice Department's civil racketeering case brought against the Teamsters, former top FBI official Oliver "Buck" Revell called Presser "highly productive" and the "number one labor racketeering source" for the FBI. Presser helped the government prosecute his rival and predecessor as president, Roy L. Williams, for trying to bribe a U.S. senator, Revell said. He also helped the government bring a case against several members of the Kansas City Mafia who had used Teamster pension money to buy into Las Vegas casinos and then skim cash out of them. In all, Presser provided information about wiseguys and corrupt union officials in half a dozen states, including New York and California.

Presser also helped himself—to his members' funds, that is. In one particular scheme he put four friends on the Teamsters payroll in no-show jobs that cost the union members more than $700,000 in dues that should have gone to services for them. The FBI either didn't know or didn't want to know what Presser was up to, as long as the information was flowing. Unfortunately for Presser, the U.S. Labor Department had its own investigators, who uncovered the no-show job scam.

A tug of war ensued at the Justice Department between the FBI and the Department of Labor over whether Presser would be indicted. The situation was incredibly ticklish; Presser was one of the few leaders in traditionally Democratic big labor to support President Ronald Reagan. Going off half cocked against a major presidential supporter with an iffy indictment could be disastrous—but even that might not be as bad as a public impression that the Reagan administration had helped a political ally escape indictment.

Buck Revell wrote a memo to Director William Webster, suggesting that the FBI ask Stephen Trott, head of the Justice Department's Criminal Division, to squash the case in return for everything Presser had done for the Bureau. All Webster had to do was say yes—Revell reportedly had already spoken with Trott and received assurances that the FBI would have its way. Webster may have simply believed that Presser deserved to be indicted or he may have feared the political repercussions if the indictment—which was widely anticipated in the press—were quashed, but for whatever reason, he ultimately declined to intercede with Main Justice.

Presser's FBI handlers were livid. Many saw the decision as an outright betrayal; Presser had risked his life for them. It was also embarrassing because they had been assuring the union leader that the Labor Department case would quietly go away.

"Because of the fact that he had stuck with us, had been an informant for ten years and provided some pretty significant information, I just didn't feel like the case that they had against him even compared to what he had done for us," FBI handler Robert S. Friedrick later testified. "I know it was a couple hundred thousand dollars, but I think within the scheme of things he's probably saved the government, you know, much more than that."

In June 1984 the high wire snapped from beneath Jackie Presser's carefully balanced life. In short order, a *Los Angeles Times* article identified him as a Bureau informant (sending his Mafia friends into a tizzy) and he was hospitalized for worsening heart disease.

The federal prosecutors who had been working the Labor Department investigation were given his FBI informant files to review. They found no documented evidence that Presser's no-show jobs scam had been authorized by the FBI. An indictment of the Teamsters boss was now virtually certain, although the behind-the-scenes wrangling continued for nearly another year.

The FBI faced a moment of truth. Just weeks before Presser was to be indicted, Friedrick, then the chief of the Cleveland FBI's Organized Crime Squad, took matters into his own hands. Friedrick became one of Presser's handlers after McCann left the Bureau, and quickly became quite attached to the gregarious, overweight Jackie. He couldn't believe the FBI was turning its back on a promise. First meeting with Presser's lawyer, then the retired McCann, then with Pat Foran, Friedrick concocted a story that they *had* authorized each of the no-show employees because they were all important contacts of Presser's through whom he learned information about the Mafia.

The three agents dropped the bomb on the prosecutors in the Department of Labor case. In an instant their carefully constructed case against Presser had blown up in their faces. Given the testimony of three well-respected senior agents, there was no way they could charge Presser if the FBI, as the Attorney General's Guidelines permitted, had authorized him to embezzle. Reluctantly, they announced on June 23, 1985, that the investigation of Presser was over.

Predictably, a furor erupted in the media and on Capitol Hill. Who had let Presser off the hook? The FBI? The Reagan administration? Inside the Justice Department, the three Top Echelon informant handlers quickly became targets of an internal probe. One of their problems was that a top Justice Department lawyer, Paul Coffey, had already questioned the agents about Presser's authorization the previous year, and they had said nothing about approving a no-show jobs scam. The FBI's Office of Professional Responsibility questioned Friedrick under oath. He lied, again telling his original story. Then he called the OPR interviewers back and, while still insisting the authorization story was true, admitted that the three agents had met to discuss their testimony. Several months later, facing increasing pressure, he failed a polygraph, broke down and admitted his lies. He gave a detailed confession to two Justice Department lawyers.

The confession resurrected the Department of Labor case. Only this time, the Justice Department named Presser, fellow informant Tony Hughes, another union accomplice, and Special Agent Robert Friedrick as codefendants. The charges against Friedrick were eventually thrown out of court by a federal judge, who said he had not been properly informed of his legal rights before his confession to the Justice Department attorneys. Presser died before the case went to trial.

Many FBI officials see Presser as the epitome of what a Top Echelon informant could be, particularly because he was never accused of being involved in murders or other violent acts. "That is exactly the kind of nonviolent criminal activity in furtherance of the collection of intelligence that we want," Buck Revell said.

Presser was invaluable to the FBI in fighting the mob. Yet during his tenure, the union itself got no less corrupt. After his death, the federal government filed a massive civil racketeering case against the Teamsters, forcing the union to settle and agree to be run by a federal administrator.

New York: Willie Boy Johnson

The turbulent life and violent death of Top Echelon informant Wilfred "Willie Boy" Johnson confirmed the FBI's worst fears about prosecutors—that they couldn't be trusted with the identities of informants. The FBI put the blame for Johnson's murder squarely on an "out of control" prosecutor in New York who refused to play along with the Top Echelon Informant Program. Johnson's name would later become synonymous with the need for keeping T.E.'s secret inside the FBI family.

Willie Boy, aka "Wahoo," because his father was a Cherokee Indian, grew up in a section of Brooklyn called East

New York with John Gotti, the man who rose to become the infamous "Teflon Don" of the Gambino family.

Johnson made his bones as a young hoodlum—reportedly teaming with Gotti to hit two bookies stupid enough to have been skimming from the mob—but his mixed heritage precluded him from being inducted as a full member of the Mafia. His intimidating six-foot, 275-pound frame and his violent nature, however, made him an effective enforcer, and he became one of Gotti's closest associates in a crew headquartered in a grimy storefront incongruously named the Bergen Hunt and Fish Social Club.

He was also close to the FBI. Gotti's predecessor, Carmine Fatico, had committed a breach of mob protocol in the late 1960s, failing to provide financial support to the wife and children of a loyal underling in prison, namely Willie Boy Johnson. Johnson was stung by the slight and ripe for recruitment as a Top Echelon Potential Criminal Informant when he was busted on gaming charges by the FBI in 1972. Capitalizing on Johnson's feelings of betrayal, members of New York FBI's C-16 Gambino family squad agreed to let Johnson go on with his bookmaking and loansharking operations unmolested, in return for inside information.

Fatico eventually retired and Gotti took over as head of the crew at the "Bergen," but he gave his childhood friend little incentive to stop helping the Bureau, ragging him mercilessly as a "half-breed" who would never be a made guy. Willie Boy's payback was giving the FBI a wealth of information on Gotti, including his participation in the murder of an Irish gangster who had kidnapped Carlo Gambino's nephew, the date that Gotti and his brother Gene were formally inducted into the Mafia, and the fact that Gotti's crew was getting deeper and deeper into cocaine and heroin trafficking.

Johnson's undoing was a tug-of-war between the FBI and a hard-driving Assistant U.S. Attorney from Brooklyn, Diane Giacalone, who had successfully prosecuted a truck hijacking ring that had been paying tribute to Gotti's Bergen crew. Giacalone began a grand jury probe of Gotti, his crew, and his immediate superior, Gambino family underboss Neil Dellocroce, using investigators from the NYPD and the DEA. When the FBI heard about Giacalone's probe, they tried to kill it. Exactly why is disputed.

Some called it simple jealousy—the FBI was also trying to build a case against Dellocroce and Gotti, and wasn't about to let its rivals in the police department or the DEA steal the glory. Another potential reason was that indicting Johnson for gambling and loansharking was a breach of their agreement.

The official explanation out of the FBI, however, was that Giacalone's evidence was dangerously inadequate. If her racketeering charges didn't stick, Gambino squad chief Bruce Mouw argued, the specific acts alleged as part of the racketeering conspiracy could not be brought again under double jeopardy rules—Gotti would effectively be "immunized."

The FBI made several runs at Giacalone herself, first trying to sweet-talk her and then adopting a more heavy-handed approach. They did not tell her they had an informant sitting right next to Gotti.

"If you were a man, I'd hit you in the face," one agent is said to have told her in a particularly heated exchange.

"Take your best shot," Giacalone snapped back.

Mouw then tried official channels. Edward McDonald, chief of the FBI-friendly New York Eastern District Organized Crime Strike Force, wrote two memos to Justice Department higher-ups in Washington calling the case, among other things, "exceptionally weak." Finally, the FBI cut off all cooperation with the Brooklyn prosecutor. Giacalone, however, plowed ahead, backed by her bosses in the U.S. Attorney's Office, and in late March 1985 a grand jury handed up a sealed racketeering, murder, loansharking, truck-hijacking indictment against Dellocroce, John and Gene Gotti, Wilfred Johnson, and five other alleged hoodlums.

Three days after the indictment, NYPD detectives and DEA agents fanned out to make arrests. They found the Gotti brothers and Johnson at the Bergen at four A.M., still playing cards. Johnson, who believed he had a free pass for gambling and loansharking, made a fatal blunder. After he was out of Gotti's earshot, he blurted out his cooperation with the FBI to the cops and the DEA, who, of course, could not have cared less—Johnson had no agreement with *them*.

Johnson would obviously be a dynamite witness against Gotti. When word of Johnson's informant status was relayed to Giacalone, she met with him privately on the day of the arraignment in the case, but he refused to testify, fearing Gotti's vengeance. His T.E. status, however, provided Giacalone with a wonderful—and extremely dangerous—opportunity. If she "outed" Johnson as an informant, he would have little choice but to cooperate and accept witness protection. Of course, on the slim chance that he didn't, he was a dead man.

Giacalone rolled the dice. And lost.

At the arraignment, she told the judge that Johnson had been a paid informant for the FBI from 1966 until 1974, when he had been closed due to an armed robbery arrest and conviction. He was reopened again in 1978, but was not paid, she said. Giacalone asked that Johnson be held in a special unit of the Metropolitan Correctional Center for his own safety.

"He said that he and his family would be slaughtered if his identity were revealed," the prosecutor said. "He would face certain death at the hands of the individuals against whom he provided information."

Gotti fixed a laser stare on Johnson, who was shaking and staring straight ahead. Did you inform on Mr. Gotti? the judge asked. No, Johnson replied. The judge asked the question again. Well, Johnson said, the *agents* may have mentioned him.

After the hearing, the two men ended up in the maximum-security wing of the MCC together, separated by a wall of

Plexiglas, where Gotti blew Johnson kisses. It was a vision that made every FBI agent cringe. Giacalone's gambit backfired. Johnson refused to cooperate, instead sticking to his lame denial that: "I've talked to agents and everything but I am not an informant." Sammy "the Bull" Gravano later said that, in the end, Gotti proved more persuasive than the prosecutors and convinced Johnson not to testify. "You did a bad thing for all them years. But I'll forgive you," Gotti said. "It's not the first time it happened. You can never be with us after this case. But nothing will happen to you."

Johnson asked Gotti to swear on the name of his twelve-year-old son Frank, who had been killed in a motorbike accident.

"I swear," Gotti said.

The pretrial wrangling in the case lasted almost two years. After hearing 106 witnesses over seven months and deliberating for seven days, the jury came back. Not guilty on all counts. "I told you we would win!" a gleeful Gotti yelled at the assembled throng of media covering the case. The Gotti brothers, Johnson, and the other defendants tried to give a standing ovation as the jurors filed out of the courtroom, but the judge ordered them to stop. Gotti straightened out his expensive, double-breasted black suit and strode out of the courtroom to a big gray limo, leaving Willie Boy Johnson in his wake.

It was later revealed that while the case was in progress, a female informant told the FBI that the Mafia had paid a $60,000 bribe to the jury foreman. Following the Attorney General's guidelines, they notified Giacalone's boss, New York Eastern District U.S. Attorney Maloney, about the bribery allegation.

Making the allegations public might have salvaged Giacalone's case, but the FBI eventually convinced Maloney to let the trial go on. Giacalone had already burned one Top Echelon informant and they wouldn't risk another—the woman informant was told about the bribe by a top Gotti associate who shared her bed. Others said spite also may have played a role—the FBI was perfectly happy to see the DEA-NYPD case go down in flames because they had lost the bureaucratic battle to stop it.

Gotti seemed true to his word after the case was over. Johnson was ostracized, but he resumed a seminormal life, working in construction and seemingly secure in the Dapper Don's pledge on the name of his beloved son. After all, word on the street was that Willie Boy had helped kidnap and dismember John Favara, the Howard Beach factory worker who had accidentally run down young Frank Gotti.

He and his wife, Teresa, and their two children settled into a house in Brooklyn's Bergen Beach section, just five miles or so from Gotti, who, according to turncoat Gravano, was really just biding his time, waiting for Johnson to let his guard down.

At 6:05 on a muggy summer morning, sixteen months after the acquittals in the Giacalone case, two gunmen armed with .380 semiautomatic pistols ambushed Johnson as he left his Brooklyn house. It was a thoroughly professional job. The gunmen fired nineteen bullets. Johnson was hit fourteen times, six in the head. Before speeding off in a brown sedan without license plates, the gunmen threw down sharp jacklike metal spikes to burst the tires of any would-be pursuers. A Gambino family hitman, Thomas "Tommy Karate" Pitera, was eventually blamed for Johnson's murder.

Johnson's death became a rallying cry for FBI agents when it came to protecting their Top Echelon sources. In fact, ten years later in Boston, an FBI lawyer invoked Johnson's name with Judge Mark Wolf as an example of what could happen if Wolf ordered the FBI to turn over any informant identities.

Chicago: Dick Cain

Richard Scully Cain was just one of numerous T.E. sources developed by legendary Chicago FBI Special Agent

William F. Roemer. Cain also went by the name Ricardo Scalzitti, and he was quite literally a double agent for the FBI and the mob.

Cain, who made a good spy because he didn't look Sicilian, was inducted into the Chicago mob and sent to join the Chicago Police Department in 1953. His job was to be both spy and bagman for the Chicago family, warning the Mafia about impending busts and delivering cash to cops on the take. He eventually became one of the most successful corrupt law enforcement figures in U.S. history. He rose quickly in police ranks while feeding inside information to the Chicago Mafia and shaking down thieves and whorehouses to augment his salary. He went on to become chief of investigations for the Cook County Sheriff's office in the early 1960s, and became a media darling, frequently tipping reporters and photographers off to busts of illegal casinos and drug dens.

In 1964, Cain used his Sheriff's department contacts to arrange a lie detector test for several gunmen suspected of robbing the Franklin Park Savings and Loan. Another Chicago mafioso, Willie "Potatoes" Daddano, reached out for Cain, saying he wanted to know whether one of the bank robbers was an FBI informant. Cain had one of his crooked sheriff's deputies administer polygraphs to the robbers in a Chicago motel, and shortly afterward one of them, Guy Mendola, was murdered.

Cain, meanwhile, had made one of his most impressive-looking busts in the case of a major theft of drugs from a pharmaceutical company in suburban Chicago. The newspapers and television stations were tipped to meet Cain at a hotel in Rosemont. The sheriff's men burst through the door and found a large portion of the stolen drugs, resulting in more favorable stories about Cain. Unfortunately, the drugs were found in a room registered to one of Cain's deputies—a fact that Roemer pointed out to Cain's boss, Sheriff Richard Ogilvie.

During the resulting scandal, Cain and a couple of

deputies were indicted on numerous charges, convicted, and fired. Shortly afterward other agents in the Chicago FBI flipped the crooked deputy who had given the lie detector test to Mendola, and Cain and Daddano were indicted on federal charges, including the Mendola murder, and convicted. Daddano got fifteen years, Cain got four. It is not known whether Mendola actually *was* cooperating, but regardless, Cain was convicted of facilitating the murder of a man he *believed* was working for the Bureau. That fact alone might have given Special Agent Roemer cause to despise Cain, but apparently whatever personal feelings he had were outweighed by the dictates of the Top Echelon program and the war on the Mafia—much in the same way the Boston FBI office continued to use Steve Flemmi and Whitey Bulger after they were suspected of murdering FBI cooperating witness Brian Halloran.[9]

When Cain was released from prison and returned to Chicago, Roemer said, he offered his services as an informant to the FBI on the condition that he be guaranteed "the salary of an FBI agent . . . and the status of an FBI agent." The offer was tempting. At the time, Roemer's "Little Al" illegal bug had been silent for several years, thanks to Lyndon Johnson's executive order. The agent also knew that Cain was still a confidant of Chicago mob chieftain Sam Giancana, and that he would soon be heading south to the big oceanview compound in Cuernavaca, Mexico, where Giancana had been living for several years. Roemer told his old friend, Marshall Rutland, who had been named chief of organized crime investigations for the FBI in Chicago, what Cain wanted. Since agents were paid so poorly—about $23,000 in those days—the money was no problem, Rutland said.

Cain's request to be accorded agent status, however, was

---

[9]The author made several unsuccessful attempts to interview Roemer. This account of his relationship with Cain is based on news reports and the first-person narrative in his books, including *Roemer: Man Against the Mob.*

a nonstarter. Even before the Levi guidelines went into effect, scandal-conscious J. Edgar Hoover had made it *verboten* to tell informants—even ones who were paid for information—that they were FBI employees. In fact, agents were required to file memos assuring their supervisors that they were periodically reminding their snitches that they did *not* work for the Bureau.

Even Paul Rico in Boston paid lip service to the mandate. Rico, for example, filed a 209 report in 1967 stating that he "instructed" Steve Flemmi that he "was not to consider himself an employee of the FBI; that he was to provide information only to this Bureau; and that any payments of money made to him for services rendered must be reported as income on his federal income tax return." Predictably, Flemmi later said he had been told no such thing.

Roemer simply ignored the rule.

"I told him I would consider him a special agent of the FBI. I said so would Rutland back in Washington," Roemer wrote. "But I added that it would be so confidential that the two of us would be the only ones to know of his cooperation."

Cain met with Roemer and another agent for a two-day debriefing before Cain was supposed to fly down to Mexico and meet Giancana. Predictably, he was a font of information, giving the two agents a historical perspective on the Chicago mob over the previous two decades, the names of crooked cops, politicians, judges, and lawyers he had delivered bribes to when he had been the Mafia's bagman, and information about the Mafia's growing influence in Las Vegas.

During his time with Giancana in Mexico and even afterward, after the two gangsters had returned to Chicago, Cain was a regular source for Roemer. He moved into an apartment building that was connected by an underground pedestrian tunnel to an office building across the street, so the FBI agent would never be seen in the lobby. They met regularly and discussed the mob over beer, sandwiches, and potato chips. Sometimes, for fun, Cain would call a corrupt judge or another mobster in front of Roemer and let the agent listen in.

Once their relationship was established, Cain proposed a strategic alliance that turned out to be very much like the one John Connolly has admitted offering to Whitey Bulger.

Cain, with the FBI's help, wanted to take over all the illegal gambling operations in the Chicago area. He would feed information on his rivals to the FBI, who in turn would leave him free to operate as he pleased. Roemer said he believed the idea had merit, but insisted that the FBI made Cain no promises, except to say that if he didn't tell them himself what he was doing, then they obviously couldn't investigate what they didn't know about. The FBI didn't grant Cain immunity or even agree not to investigate him, Roemer insists.

Less than a month into the arrangement, Charles Carroll, a low-level associate of a mob boss on the city's South Side, was murdered. Cain, the FBI-sanctioned up-and-coming gambling kingpin of Chicago, was a prime suspect.

Unlike Connolly and Morris in the Wheeler and Halloran murders, however, Roemer didn't simply take Cain's word that he wasn't involved in the murder. "We decided to tell Cain that, friend or no friend, we were going to initiate an investigation into his gambling activities," Roemer wrote. "When it came to homicide, he was no different than any other hoodlum. If he was in any way involved in the Carroll murder, we would come down on him with both feet." The conversation resulted in a fistfight, but Roemer, a former amateur boxing champion at Notre Dame, managed to subdue Cain and calm him down.

From then on, the agent said, the informant knew if he was breaking the law, "he was fair game." The FBI's apparent surprise and stronger stance on Cain after the Carroll murder is somewhat puzzling—what did the Bureau *think* would happen when they gave Cain the go-ahead to take over the entire gambling rackets in Chicago, one of the most mobbed-up cities in the country? In any event, Cain was never prosecuted again after he became a Top Echelon informant, either for illegal gambling or the Carroll murder, which was never solved. The two resumed their agent-informant relationship.

The week before Christmas of 1973, Cain called Roemer in a panic. He had been leaving a mob-related meeting inside Rose's Sandwich Shop on Chicago's Grand Avenue when he heard car tires squealing and he ran for cover. "Somebody was after me. Was it you guys?" he asked the agent. Roemer said he doubted it. Three days later, Dick Cain was in the same sandwich shop when two shotgun-toting men burst in and announced that it was a holdup. They lined all the patrons up facing the wall, then walked over to Cain, put one of the weapons under his chin, and blew his head off.

Roemer said he was in his basement working out when he heard a news bulletin about Cain's murder come over the radio. He said he felt as if an unseen opponent had landed a body shot to his stomach. He sat down on the floor, feeling devastated.

According to Roemer, although no one was ever prosecuted for Cain's murder, another FBI informant eventually told the Bureau what happened. Cain had been killed by Joey "the Clown" Lombardo on orders from another Chicago Mafia boss. Another Chicago mob figure, Harry "the Hook" Aleman, was also later suspected of participating in Cain's murder. The informant said Chicago Police had ambushed a mob-connected burglary crew the previous week, and Cain had been suspected of tipping off the cops who made the arrest.

At a minimum, the Roemer-Cain story illustrates the type of activity agents were willing to tolerate—Cain was convicted of aiding the murder of a suspected FBI informant and suspected of committing another murder himself—and how grateful they were to receive inside information on the Mafia. As Roemer himself put it: "Dick Cain was a friend. There were few people I felt closer to."

CHAPTER SIX

Justifiable Homicide

....

Top Echelon informants get away with murder

THE DRUM TELECOPIER whirred constantly in Roger Wheeler's house on the island of Nantucket during 1978 as proposals and counterproposals zipped back and forth between the Tulsa oil tycoon, a Boston bank, and a Miami-based gaming company. Set on a bluff, the 4,500-square-foot beach house in the exclusive Siasconset section of the island had been specially designed to allow the flow of gentle summer ocean breezes off Nantucket Sound. Wheeler built the house as a trophy retreat, but the ever-restless deal maker was never too far from work.

The brash chairman of the $187 million Telex Corp. wasn't much in tune at all with the restrained, Waspy spirit of the island and his neighbors. The big Wheeler house was the first new one built on the bluff in a decade, and the clannish Nantucket crowd didn't exactly welcome the new neighbors from Oklahoma with open arms. When the Wheelers wanted to cut the trees that had grown up to block the view from the front of the house, the neighbors objected. In typical impatient fashion, Roger Wheeler hired a local laborer and the trees disappeared in the middle of a winter night while most of his neighbors were off-island. The establishment took its revenge in whispers and disdain. Soon, a tour trolley guide who took tourists through Siasconset—whose microphone was loud enough to be heard by the Wheeler family inside the house—started referring to Wheeler as "the rich Okie."

The trolley driver and Wheeler's neighbors might have been surprised to learn that the "Okie" had grown up not much more than a ferry ride away. Wheeler's father had been a typesetter for a Boston newspaper and lived in Reading, a quiet suburb northwest of the city. As teenagers, both Roger and his brother Alfred spent summers on Cape Cod working in tourist restaurants. Roger never took the three-hour ferry ride to Nantucket, but the stories he heard about the idyllic, genteel life on the island stuck with him. Wheeler lettered in cross-country at Reading High School and landed a track scholarship to Notre Dame, but in the waning years of World War II, he left South Bend for Texas and an ROTC scholarship to Rice University. By the time he earned his electrical engineering degree, though, the war was over. The military, in the process of discharging personnel by the hundreds of thousands, said thanks, but no thanks, to his compulsory service.

Free but jobless, Wheeler traveled to Venezuela, where he stumbled on an industry that changed his life and made him a millionaire. In the postwar era, soldiers were coming home, moving to newly constructed suburbs, and buying more and more automobiles to take them to and from work. With gas rationing over, oil production soared, feeding the demand for drilling around the world. The oil was often transported through pipelines built under the ground, including in Venezuela's rich fields, where Wheeler went to work for a large construction company. With a good salary, and Venezuela's cheap cost of living, Wheeler thought the job was too good to be true. He was right. The country's ditch diggers went on strike shortly after he moved to South America.

Where a lesser man might have seen a problem, Roger Wheeler saw opportunity. The country's railroad workers were also on strike, and many of them, desperate to feed their families, agreed to cross the ditch diggers' picket lines to work for a new company Wheeler was putting together himself. He soon had a thriving business specializing in attaching and burying magnesium anodes, a key part of the pipeline installation and maintenance process. Anodes were a simple, clever solution to the constant rusting that was the major maintenance problem with oil pipelines. The anodes consisted of a ring of copper wire, onto which magnesium was poured. Attached by the copper wire to the metal pipeline at regular intervals, the anodes channeled the oxidation from the pipeline to the magnesium. Anodes were much cheaper to replace than metal pipe and could be swapped without cutting the flow of oil.

The transformation from Roger Wheeler the businessman to Roger Wheeler the tycoon began when he noticed something else about the business. He was buying prefabricated anodes from suppliers at about four dollars a pound, but a postwar glut of raw magnesium had driven the price way down. At sixty cents a pound, Wheeler decided the real money was in making anodes, not maintaining them. He and his wife Pamela moved to Oklahoma, the epicenter of the domestic postwar oil boom. He found a mothballed smelting plant in West Tulsa and began buying surplus WWII magnesium aircraft wheels, melting them down and pouring his own anodes.

Wheeler's Standard Magnesium and Chemical Corp. was so successful that giant Kaiser Aluminum paid $9.8 million for it in 1964. Wheeler, who started in the oil business at $300 a month, walked away from the transaction a certified millionaire. Kaiser gave him an executive's job in Oakland, and Wheeler moved his growing family to nearby Marin County, just over the Golden Gate Bridge from San Francisco.

Wheeler soon chafed at the country-club corporate life. He far preferred being a deal maker to being an executive, and it wasn't long before he spotted an opportunity to reestablish himself as an entrepreneur. The Telex Corp., a computer and communications company, was on the block, and Wheeler and several partners jumped at the opportunity, buying up a majority of public shares in an established company with two thriving divisions. The well-known communications group was the backbone of international business communication in the era before cheap long distance, video-conferencing, and the Internet. The manufacturing division made tape drives for the giant mainframe business computers of the 1970s.

Just as he had in the magnesium business, Wheeler spotted an opportunity in Telex that would drastically increase the company's profitability. He hired away several IBM engineers to develop an interface that allowed Telex tape drives to be hooked up to existing IBM computers as stand-alone components. For users at the time, data storage was the most expensive part of owning and maintaining their computers. Wheeler started selling his drives for half of what it was costing companies to buy direct from IBM. Business for Telex tape drives exploded and the stock price shot up from $2.50 per share to a high of $64. Roger Wheeler's personal stake in the company rose to more than $60 million.

Oklahoma was still the U.S. oil capital in the 1970s, and Wheeler went about acquiring the trappings of the Tulsa elite. He built a big house in the city's Forest Hills section, a sprawling, red-brick contemporary mansion off Forty-first Street on a big lot full of hundred-year-old oak trees. The big house had square pillars and a Spanish tile porch in the front, and a stone patio out back with a swimming pool. While his childhood home in Reading, Massachusetts, could have fit comfortably on the back patio, the new mansion was dwarfed by the homes of the nearby oil tycoons, who built huge Tudor mansions and Italianate palazzos with ballrooms, indoor swimming pools, and private bowling alleys. Wheeler really didn't want the biggest house on the block, he had other uses for his money. He bought an 11,000-acre horse and cattle ranch in Wyoming, which he dubbed the

WW. He shopped around for a boat, looking at a variety of hundred-plus-foot yachts. He eventually decided it would be cheaper to build a house on Nantucket instead of paying $120,000 a year in crew salaries and upkeep. He bought a Learjet to shuttle between the ranch, the Nantucket house, and his various businesses.

He used the boat-shopping experience to explain his business philosophy to his son Larry. "Always pay cash, Larry. Plan your life so that if you want to, you can quit the next day. You can walk away from it. That way you can make clearer decisions."

For a time Wheeler's decisions were so clear, they were practically visionary. Almost everything he touched seemed to turn a profit. He bought a successful home appliance distributorship, expanded his magnesium business, and acquired Franklin Supply, a troubled equipment supplier for oil and gas drilling companies, for about $1 million. He turned Franklin around and a few years later sold it for $11 million in cash. It was 1975, Roger Wheeler was on a roll, and the $10 million profit from the Franklin Supply sale was burning a hole in his pocket. He used the money to buy World Jai Alai, a Miami-based gaming company.

It was the worst investment he ever made.

Native to the Basque region of Spain, jai alai is played sort of like racquetball or squash, except instead of a nylon-strung racquet and rubber ball, the players use banana-shaped wicker baskets to hurl a potentially lethal, rock-hard goatskin pelota at speeds in excess of a hundred miles per hour. In the 1920s a group of New England businessmen got a glimpse of the fast-paced sport during a visit to Havana and saw an opportunity. The game had a crossover appeal to both American and Latin bettors, so it was perfect for South Florida with its large Hispanic population and gaming-friendly political climate.

Spectators loved the game's rapid-fire action. Gaming regulators, however, were never as enamored of jai alai. For one thing, it was far too easy to fix; in fact, until sports book was legalized in Nevada, Florida's jai alai stadiums ("frontons" in Spanish) were the only place in America where it was legal to bet on human beings, and the players were entirely beholden to the fronton owners for their livelihood. The game was also notorious for being connected to the underworld.

Larry Wheeler said his father went into the deal with his eyes open. Unfortunately, Roger Wheeler's gaze was fixed on the huge cash-flow numbers the business generated, not its unsavory reputation. "It was the deal that was too good to be true," the son said.

The chain of events that led to Wheeler's purchase of World Jai Alai began in 1972, when the Connecticut state legislature voted to legalize jai alai gambling. A short time later a rogue faction of WJA's board of directors who wanted to grow the company forced out president L. Stanley Berenson. One of their first moves was to hire John B. Callahan, a former accountant who left the Arthur Anderson firm to open his own business consulting firm. Callahan had a reputation as a brilliant "turnaround man"—someone who would take a struggling company, restore it to profitability, and then move on to his next project. Callahan installed himself as president of WJA in December 1974 and brought along a former Arthur Anderson colleague, Richard Donovan. A short time later he hired former FBI agent H. Paul Rico as the company's new chief of security. Callahan continued WJA's expansion plans, applying for permission to build a fronton in Hartford. Connecticut gaming regulators turned out to be quite a different breed from their laid-back Florida counterparts. On direct orders from a suspicious Governor Ella Grasso, the Connecticut State Police began a thorough background check on World Jai Alai's executives.

In early 1976 a State Police detective and a high-ranking state corruption prosecutor met with Callahan at the Sonesta Hotel in downtown Hartford. Callahan begged out midway through the meeting, saying he had to get to nearby Bradley

Field for a "shuttle back to Miami." The only problem was
that there *was* no afternoon shuttle from Hartford to Miami.
Connecticut State Police detectives followed Callahan, who,
instead of flying south, drove north, up Interstate 84 to the
Massachusetts Turnpike and into Boston, where local police
joined the surveillance.

The police watched as Callahan strolled into the Playboy
Club in Park Square. Bosomy Bunnies brought drinks over
to the men at Callahan's table, who included Jimmy Martorano, a reputed Winter Hill Gang associate; Tom Mc-
Neely; and former television reporter Jack "TV" Kelly. The
night became the beginning of an intense surveillance of
Callahan and his cronies. He was seen ten times in the space
of a month, meeting repeatedly with Martorano at the Playboy Club or several other bars and restaurants, including
Chandler's in the South End, which was owned by Winter
Hill Gang boss Howie Winter.

On March 18, 1976, for example, police saw Callahan,
Martorano, Kelly, and another reputed Winter Hill associate,
Vincent Solomonte, meet with three women at the Playboy
Club for dinner and drinks. At twelve-thirty A.M., Martorano
and Callahan and two of the women adjourned to the Colesium restaurant, a famous after-hours joint favored by gangsters, businessmen, and politicians. The bleary-eyed
detectives sat on the Colesium until five-forty A.M., when
they watched the married Callahan and one of the women—
who police were able to identify only as "Debbie"—stumble
out onto the street. They broke off the surveillance just before six, after watching the giggling couple check into a
room at a Howard Johnson's.

Armed with the surveillance information, Connecticut officials got ready to ambush Callahan with it at a public hearing on the proposed Hartford license. He never showed.
Instead, Paul Rico—who investigators still believe was
tipped off by sources inside the Boston Police Department—announced that Callahan had resigned to pursue
"other business interests."

The Connecticut license in jeopardy, World Jai Alai directors, who were now led by Alan Trustman, had no choice but to sell the company to a "clean" owner. Someone, however, was apparently unhappy with Berenson's ouster and the directors' plans to take the company public. Trustman, a part-time screenwriter who wrote two famous Steve McQueen films, *Bullitt* and *The Thomas Crown Affair,* was badly spooked to find a dead cod on the bank of his backyard pond in Concord, Massachusetts. The fish was a long way from home. Concord is nearly twenty miles from the nearest saltwater. One of Trustman's allies on the board found a bullet on his front doorstep.

Rico had a hand in the first clumsy attempt to sell the business. Jack B. Cooper wasn't exactly the "clean" owner the directors were looking for. True, the Florida courts had deemed him technically licensable as a gaming operator under state laws, but an organized crime task force had also determined that he was a business associate of Meyer Lansky's. After the Cooper sale blew up in an explosion of bad press, the Bally Corp. stepped up to the plate, but also struck out due to its alleged ties to organized crime. In desperation, the WJA directors turned to their banker, Dave McKown of the First National Bank of Boston, for help.

McKown heard that the chairman of the Telex Corp. was looking for new investments and approached him with WJA. Negotiations began in early 1978 and continued even as the Wheelers were opening the Nantucket house for the season.

At about the same time Roger Wheeler was contemplating entering the jai alai gaming business in Florida, a cooperating witness was telling FBI Agent Thomas Daly that something was terribly wrong with the horse-racing industry on virtually the entire East Coast.

A few years earlier Winter Hill Gang boss Howie Winter and one of his gang's toughest enforcers, Billy Barnowski, cornered jockey Eddie Donnally in a Somerville restaurant and beat him silly. A month before, Barnowski had put another rider in a hospital in Pennsylvania. Donnally didn't know how lucky he was. Joe McDonald, a seasoned killer who was also a member of the gang, had an alternate suggestion—shooting Donnally and dumping his body on the backstretch at Suffolk Downs, a thoroughbred track in East Boston, as a "warning" to his brethren. Donnally's offense was being stupid enough earlier that day to win the third race at Suffolk, after Anthony "Big Tony" Ciulla had paid him to finish out of the money.

After law enforcement officials in New Jersey uncovered the scheme, Big Tony flipped. Now he was laying out the whole scheme for Tom Daly, who worked out of the FBI's satellite office in Lowell, Massachusetts. A professional gambler, Ciulla approached Winter and his gang with the plan in late 1973. They didn't need much convincing, it was a beaut. Ciulla would use his connections at racetracks up and down the East Coast to bribe jockeys in various races to rein in the favorites, allowing Winter's gang to get bets down on horses with longer, more lucrative odds. The Winter Hill Gang would bankroll the operation, betting races both at racetracks and with unwitting bookmakers.

Millions poured in—they even bought their own horse, Spread the Word, and won more than $450,000 by rigging races. The scheme also expanded the gang's criminal empire—the bookies suckered by the gang into taking their bets, meanwhile, found themselves forced to borrow money at exorbitant loanshark rates to cover their losses. Everyone had their own job: Ciulla fixed the races; Winter, McDonald, and Barnowski provided the cash and the muscle; Whitey Bulger and Stevie Flemmi rounded up bookmakers to take bets; Johnny Martorano kept the books, and his brother Jimmy laundered the money through legitimate business investments. They brought several Las Vegas casino executives into the scheme and fixed races at Suffolk, Garden State Park, and Atlantic City Raceway in New Jersey; Lincoln Downs in Rhode Island; Rockingham Park in New Hampshire; and Pocono Downs in Wilkes-Barre, Pennsylvania.

Daly talked about Ciulla's testimony with Jerry O'Sullivan, the New England Organized Crime Strike Force chief, who agreed that it would be a major case. Morris and Connolly, though, panicked when word about the case spread through to the Boston FBI office. Concerned about Flemmi and Bulger, they ran to Jerry O'Sullivan too. It was a major gamble. The FBI was only supposed to divulge the names of informants to prosecutors in the most dire of circumstances. They were also supposed to seek permission from Bureau headquarters before doing so. They took the risk, without authorization, according to Morris.

Bulger and Flemmi were among the informants who had provided probable cause for an ambitious plan to bug the Boston Mafia's key stronghold on Prince Street in the North End, Connolly and Morris told O'Sullivan.

Bulger and Flemmi, the pair said, had "maintained their innocence" in the face of Ciulla's allegations and insisted that they weren't involved. In fact, they said it was a scheme the other members of the gang had come up with despite their disapproval, and that "they recommended against the others participating in it because they didn't trust this guy Ciulla," Morris later testified. What it essentially came down to, the two agents told the prosecutor, was Ciulla's word against Bulger and Flemmi's, with little information to corroborate the story. Then Morris added the kicker.

"These guys were in a position to help us in what was our number-one priority, the Mafia," he later testified. "We asked O'Sullivan to consider these facts and consider not indicting them—based on that information or whatever information that he had—because he was in a position to make a judgment."

O'Sullivan's reply (according to Morris) was, "I'll think about it, I have to talk to the case agent first."

Soon, word came back to Morris that Bulger and Flemmi had been spared indictment in the horse-race case. There appears to have been little basis for doing so other than keeping them on the street as informants. Morris admitted later that he never even tried to talk to Ciulla to confirm or debunk the allegations against Bulger and Flemmi, so when he approached O'Sullivan, Morris had little more than Bulger and Flemmi's word. For the prosecutor it was an easy choice—a couple of defendants out of a gambling case or the biggest Mafia prosecution in the district at a time when the Mafia was becoming the Justice Department's highest priority.

O'Sullivan has steadfastly refused any comment on his conduct as strike force chief, saying he doesn't care to be "second-guessed" by the media. Others say there is no doubt that he gave Bulger and Flemmi a break on the case.

"It was a battle and the Bureau won. Jerry felt that the main goal [prosecuting the Mafia] was most important," said Richard Gregorie, the coprosecutor in the race-fixing case, who eventually transferred to the U.S. Attorney's office in Miami. Gregorie said he would have done the same thing himself in his colleague's shoes: "You can't reach the high level of criminal activity without sources." Instead of being among the twenty-one defendants charged, their names showed up instead next to Ciulla's on a list of sixty-four "unindicted coconspirators"—a law enforcement term of art used for three kinds of people: little fish who weren't worth indicting, those who prosecutors believed were involved but didn't have enough evidence to charge, and informants.

The race-fixing case was a watershed for the FBI-Bulger-Flemmi relationship. The two killers learned that when the chips were really down, the Bureau would stand by its Top Echelon informants. Over the next five years, secure in the relationship with the FBI and the strike force, investigators from other law enforcement agencies believe the two informants were responsible for the murders of at least eight people.

Jay's Lounge, a tavern opened by Boston Mafia underboss Gennaro Angiulo, was one of the targets of the illegal bugging effort in the early 1960s. The tapes from the bug of Angiulo's office in the bar were intriguing but useless in court, and didn't bring the Bureau any closer to putting Angiulo in prison. After Angiulo beat the rap that Joe "the Animal" Barboza put on him for allegedly ordering the Rocco DeSeglio murder in early 1968, it would be nearly a decade before the Bureau made another serious attempt to pursue him.

That effort began in 1977, when John Morris took over the C-3 Organized Crime Squad. Morris had taken an interest in Angiulo while working with Dennis Condon on the OC squad in 1975, but he had gotten sidetracked with other cases. When he took over the squad, he walked over from the JFK Federal Building to the J.W. McCormack Post Office and Courthouse, where Jerry McDowell, O'Sullivan's predecessor as the chief of the strike force, had his offices. At the time, the Justice Department and the FBI were both just waking up to the possibilities of both Title III and the RICO act, which had both been on the books for years. McDowell assigned an aggressive young prosecutor, Wendy Collins, to work with Morris and his team.

The plan was to bug the garrulous Angiulo inside the 98 Prince Street headquarters and place an additional listening device inside a social club on nearby North Margin Street where Zannino was known to hold court. The FBI dubbed the Prince Street operation "Bostar" and the Zannino bug "Mandarin." Much ado would be made later in the press about the difficulties of the surveillance effort that preceded the bug. The surveillance *was* undeniably difficult. Angiulo—who some called wily, others borderline paranoid—managed to sniff out two videocameras pointed at his headquarters before the FBI hit on a system that didn't attract suspicion. The agents used a brace of cars equipped with videocameras and kept rotating them so as not to let one car stay on the street too long and attract attention.

Surveillance information, however, was really only included in a Title III application for the purposes of corroborating information from informants. After all, the agents had to show there was "probable cause" to believe criminal conversations were happening inside a particular location. There was no way to know, based on surveillance alone, whether a group of mafiosi in a windowless social club were plotting a murder or playing bridge. No informants, no wiretaps.

"Informants were everything, the surveillance was just corroboration, window dressing essentially," one government lawyer who worked on the case later said.

John Connolly by definition became one of the most important members of Morris's team, which also included Ed Quinn, Michael Buckley, and Jack Cloherty. While Quinn, Buckley, and others were worrying about the surveillance, both Connolly and Morris were working their informants for information. Bulger and Flemmi came through.

Bulger told Connolly about negotiations that the "outfit" [Angiulo] had tightened the Boston area betting line. Flemmi told Connolly about a meeting at 98 Prince Street with Angiulo's three brothers, Mike, Frank, and Danny, along with Frank Salemme's brother Jack and Peter Limone, talking about how football cards—a popular form of illegal sports betting—would be distributed.

Morris wanted more. To help with the installation of the bugs, the FBI needed to know as much as it could about the interior layout of 98 Prince Street. He and Connolly asked Bulger and Flemmi to go inside and gather intelligence. "It would have dealt with looking at the premises, determining if there were alarms, looking at the doors, how many doors, what type of locks," Morris said. "I believe it was a lot of information dealing with the technical part of the [bug] installation." Reluctantly, the two informants obliged there too, even though the claustrophobic and wary Bulger was always uncomfortable going into Angiulo's lair for fear of an ambush.

Morris later downplayed Bulger and Flemmi's contribution to the Angiulo and Zannino wires, saying they could have been done anyway without their help. A former Special Agent in Charge of the Boston office, however, chalked up Morris's difference of opinion to "sour grapes." Morris, the

SAC said, was jealous that Bulger and Flemmi received so much of the credit inside the FBI while his own informant, Sammy Berkowitz, received relatively little, even though Berkowitz was a regular visitor to 98 Prince and had provided loads of information on Angiulo.

How far was the FBI willing to go to reward Top Echelon informants? All the way to the White House.

In the 1980s it was no exaggeration to say that bookmaker Sammy Berkowitz ran the small city of Chelsea, Massachusetts. The city is known mostly as landfall for the state's poorest immigrants and the massive green steel Tobin Bridge, which connects downtown Boston with the North Shore suburbs over the Mystic River. Hundreds of thousands of motorists drive to Chelsea every day, but few give the grubby little city much thought.

That neglect helped bookmaking become one of Chelsea's biggest industries. Loanshark Michael London, known as "Banker to the Bookies," laundered hundreds of thousands of dollars a week out of Heller's Café, while Berkowitz, the town's biggest bookie, kept things safe by corrupting four of the city's mayors and the police vice squad. Berkowitz obviously didn't rely on luck to keep him out of trouble, but he did carry a talisman of sorts in his pocket. It read:

Executive Grant of Clemency

After reviewing the applications for Executive clemency of the following named persons and giving consideration to a letter from the Associate Attorney General recommending Executive clemency in each case, I hereby grant full and unconditional pardons to the following named persons for those offenses against the United States described in each such recommendation:

> Samuel Berkowitz
> Bernard Fineman
> John Ralph Gallo

> *Allen Richard Holcomb*
> *Everett Sutton Moore*
> *Courtney Clifford Smith*
> *I hereby designate, direct and empower the Associate Attorney General, as my representative, to sign each grant of clemency to the persons named herein. The Associate Attorney General shall declare that his action is the act of the President, being performed at my direction.*
>
> *IN TESTIMONY WHEREOF I have hereunto signed my name and caused the seal of the Department of Justice to be affixed.*
>
> > *DONE at the City of Washington this 13th day of February in the Year of Our Lord One Thousand Nine Hundred and Eighty-four and the Independence of the United States the Two Hundred and Eighth.*
> >
> > > *(signed)*
> > > *Ronald Reagan*
> > > *President*

Law enforcement sources have confirmed for the author that Berkowitz was one of the informants used by John Morris and the FBI for the Angiulo bug at 98 Prince Street. Investigative sources say Berkowitz ran the Italian mob's numbers racket in Chelsea for Jerry Angiulo and would have been in a position to know inside information.

The pardon, for bookmaking and theft convictions in the late 1960s and early 1970s, was apparently part of Berkowitz's reward. U.S. Pardon Board officials refused to say who helped apply for the pardon, but one of the people who reportedly helped was New England Organized Crime Strike Force Chief Jeremiah O'Sullivan. O'Sullivan would not comment on whether he helped Berkowitz get his presidential pardon. Berkowitz refused to talk at all.

Perhaps the most troubling aspect of the pardon is that Berkowitz applied for it just months after the successful eavesdropping effort was complete in 1982, but when

Berkowitz later pleaded guilty to federal bribery charges in the 1990s, he admitted paying bribes to one of the mayors in 1983—after the pardon had been applied for but before Reagan signed it. In fact, a 1993 FBI affidavit alleged that the bribes dated as far back as 1976. Particularly puzzling was how he passed muster after six Boston FBI agents reportedly spent two months in 1982 investigating his background. State Police officials, who were investigating Berkowitz for gaming while the ink from Reagan's pen was still wet, said no one ever asked them for any information about Berkowitz.

"Other than murder and drug dealing, the only thing that the FBI shouldn't tolerate is corrupting police and public officials," one former law enforcement official said. "But it looks like they went for the trifecta."

While Morris tried his best to coddle Sammy Berkowitz, Connolly did the same for Bulger and Flemmi, playing up the accomplishments in his reports and memos. In a 1984 memo he said Bulger had given information of "superior value," resulting in "an enhancement of the overall TECIP[10] and the general objectives of the FBI."

Morris later qualified his statement about Bulger and Flemmi's contribution to the Title III, saying it was a quirk of fate, not necessarily their performance as informants, which ultimately diminished their contribution to the bugging effort. While the affidavit was being compiled, the RICO statute was being challenged in the U.S. Court of Appeals. If it were struck down, their whole bugging effort could be declared illegal, Morris said. So instead, saying they were looking for evidence of a racketeering enterprise—which, as virtual partners of Angiulo in crime, Bulger and Flemmi had much information on—the FBI applied for a bug looking for violations of federal laws against gambling

---

[10] Top Echelon Criminal Informant Program.

and loansharking, which bookmakers like Sammy Berkowitz would have a better handle on.

"This was a very unusual affidavit for us at the time. Ordinarily, we would have used information from them in a RICO-type affidavit," Morris said later. "But [Bulger and Flemmi] did provide information of value, and I wanted to make sure that they received some type of credit for the information that they had provided. Administratively, in the Bureau, an agent and a source receive credit for information if it's used in Title III affidavits or search warrants, and there's actually a statistical count kept. I wanted to make sure that they were given a stat and the agent was given a stat for participating in that Title III.

"I felt that these sources had long-term potential and use, and I was concerned about justifying their continuation. Their statistical accomplishments in terms of information for Title IIIs and search warrants could be relevant in justifying their continued existence. They, in fact, had provided information of value there. It actually wasn't needed in that particular type of Title III, but I wanted to make sure that they were given proper credit."

The Angiulo bugging effort was a huge success. As it progressed it began to consume the squad and eat up a lot of other resources at the Boston FBI office: thirty to forty agents, plus research analysts, clerks, and secretaries. When the wire actually went up in January 1981, four years of intensely difficult investigation culminated in what Morris called "the most chaotic period of time that I have ever been through.

"It was literally a twenty-four-hour a day operation involving large amounts of people, resources, huge scheduling problems," Morris said. "Nothing at all was easy in that case."

The FBI agents weren't the only ones conducting surveillances and getting ready for wiretaps in 1979 and 1980.

There was some surprise among the investigators of the Massachusetts State Police Special Services Unit that Bulger and Flemmi weren't indicted in the race-fixing case. It was no secret that they were an integral part of the Winter Hill Gang. The state troopers also knew all about the FBI's fixation on the Italian Mafia, which they figured was the reason it was apparently up to them to go after the two up-and-coming gangsters.

In a way, they were lucky to be conducting any probe at all, since long-term investigative work hadn't always been a priority with the State Police. The department was traditionally torn between two factions: the detectives and the uniform branch. The uniforms wore their hair in razor-sharp crew cuts underneath navy-blue Smokey-the-Bear-style hats and proudly sported the traditional departmental uniform as they patrolled Route 128 and the Mass Turnpike, a duty they viewed as the department's primary job. The detectives mostly felt ridiculous in the uniform and couldn't wait to get out of their baggy navy-blue riding breeches and knee-high black leather boots. As one side or the other would gain the upper hand in what seemed like a never-ending battle for the soul of the department, resources would be transferred from the highways to the investigative squads and back again.

The early 1980s were good times for the detectives because Jack O'Donovan, the lieutenant colonel in charge of investigative services, beat out a rival from the uniform branch and was named colonel, the equivalent of chief. One of his first acts was to beef up two of the squads that investigated gambling and organized crime, Special Services and Major Crimes.

"O'Donovan wanted guys who would work. He was always looking to make big cases," one investigator who worked on the Major Crimes Squad at the time said.

Special Services was headed by a hard-driving young sergeant named Charles Henderson, who would later become colonel himself, and it was the primary organized crime and gambling unit. The SSU was deeply involved in a big bookmaking case at the time, so it fell to Major Crimes, headed by an equally ambitious young staff sergeant named Robert Long, to go after Bulger and Flemmi.

Informants were telling Long and his troopers that with Howie Winter out of the way, Bulger and Flemmi were re-organizing the gang's bookmaking empire, using old friend George Kaufman as a go-between. They had moved out of Somerville to a new garage on Lancaster Street near the Boston Garden, in a neighborhood called the West End. Long gathered a group of aggressive young troopers to help start building a case. It took just one drive up Lancaster Street for the troopers to see how hard their job would be. They could see why the wiseguys liked Lancaster Street; like the North End, the area had tall buildings on relatively narrow streets, making it easier for the criminals to spot surveillance. The troopers rented an apartment nearby and donned disguises to begin spying on Bulger and Flemmi.

Trooper Rick Fralick, for example, went for the hippie look. He grew a beard, wore a leather coat, and sported a floppy felt top hat with a peace sign button on it. Greg Foley tried to look like a construction worker, sporting a dirty sweatshirt, denim Levi's, and light brown Herman Survivors work boots. The squad had a beat-up brown '78 Dodge van that had been outfitted with small square windows of smoked glass in the back as well as several small cutouts in the side that could open for a camera lens to poke through.

The van was used as part of a small fleet of vehicles that began a three-month intensive surveillance of Bulger and Flemmi. Most days, the troopers would wait outside Flemmi's home in Canton, pick up his tail when he left in the morning, follow him up the Southeast Expressway to the housing projects in South Boston. There, Flemmi would pick up Bulger and they would begin their criminal business, making stops at various locations in the city. Sometimes one trooper would pull the van over and pretend to fuss under the hood to allow the one inside with a camera and a 300-millimeter lens, more time to take photos. The troopers called the surveillance duty "A Day in the Life of Whitey and Stevie."

When the troopers weren't tailing Bulger and Flemmi, they were watching from two fixed sites, a second-story apartment on Lancaster that looked directly down on the garage and an unused office space in the Boston headquarters of the U.S. Coast Guard. The Coast Guard building overlooked Commercial Street, a semicircular roadway that formed the northern, eastern, and southern borders of the North End, and had a convenient view of the north side of Hanover Street and Giro's Restaurant, Patriarca family soldier Nicky Giso's place.

Giso was underboss Jerry Angiulo's primary go-between for the Mafia's dealings with Winter Hill. The job fell to Giso for two reasons: one, he was a funny, affable man who wouldn't exacerbate tensions between the two rival groups, and two, the vain, prickly Angiulo didn't like him very much. The sixty-something Giso, always on thin ice with Angiulo, was essentially drummed out of the Mafia after he took up a liaison with a younger woman—she was fifteen. Giso eventually got the last laugh—he was one of the few members of the Boston Mafia who was never sent to prison. He died peacefully at home.

A couple of times a week Whitey and Stevie double-parked in front of Giro's. The troopers watched as Nicky would come out and get into the backseat. After a few minutes he would get back out, carrying a brown paper bag. He would then walk the bag up Hanover, past the Café Pompei, take a right on Prince Street and enter building number 98, Angiulo's headquarters. From their apartment vantage point across from the Lancaster Street Garage, they also monitored reciprocal visits from the Italian wiseguys. Zannino would pull up in his big Lincoln, get out and kiss his old friend Flemmi on the cheeks. Other visitors came in a steady stream, most of them bookmakers delivering tribute, but others included major suspected drug traffickers such as Michael Caruana and Frank LePere.

Meetings with the Italian mob. Bookmakers paying tribute. Discussions with drug smugglers. The Lancaster Street
bug was shaping up as a potential blockbuster, the troopers
thought. After nearly four months of watching Flemmi and
Bulger get up in the morning, and putting them to bed at
night, they were ready to plant some microphones.

They went to O'Sullivan, whose office was funding and
overseeing the bugging operation. The prosecutor was solicitous and he seemed gung ho, asking Long and his troopers
to bring their surveillance photos and log in for meetings
with his strike force attorneys, who "didn't know the players." O'Sullivan looked intently at the pictures of Bulger and
Flemmi meeting with Zannino and Danny Angiulo—but did
nothing to betray that he was aware that not only were the
two men Top Echelon FBI informants, but also the key to
the biggest case of the prosecutor's life. As William Weld, the
former governor and top Justice Department official later
put it, the Angiulo case "was the crown jewel in Jerry
O'Sullivan's kingdom." Years later there would be some dis-
agreement among the troopers about O'Sullivan's intentions. Some believe the prosecutor acted honorably in a
difficult situation, others took a harder line.

"O'Sullivan duped us," one of the state cops said years
later, after learning about O'Sullivan's role taking Bulger
and Flemmi off the race-fixing indictment. "In reality, it was
all bullshit. The meeting was for us to show them how much
we had. Afterward, he knew how much we had and he knew
what it could do."

In the summer of 1980 the strike force filed a bug application on the State Police's behalf; a federal judge approved
it. From nearly the first moment, the operation phase of the
Lancaster Street bugging case was a disaster.

At first there were technical problems. They planted a van
in the garage with a trooper hidden inside a secret compartment (he nearly suffocated waiting for the gangsters to go
home for the night), but the bug he installed failed to transmit. Then a 400-pound Italian mobster sat on and crushed

another microphone they had hidden in a couch. When they finally did get a microphone working right, it recorded only wisecracks. One gangster warned another to be careful on the roadways. "Those state troopers, they don't miss a trick," he said, laughing. Bulger and Flemmi's movements suddenly became more circumspect. They stopped showing up at Giro's to pay their tribute to Nicky Giso. The day after troopers bugged a bank of pay phones near a Howard Johnson's on Route 93, the two wiseguys stopped using them.

The troopers realized that they had been had. Bulger and Flemmi must have been tipped off. "We had heard about all the leaks, the Boston cops had told us that they had problems with things in the past," one of the investigators said.

There had been whispers on the street about Bulger and Flemmi starting soon after the horse-race-fixing case was announced. That was to be expected. There were always rumors that so-and-so was a rat, that someone who ducked an indictment or got early parole or low bail or who had just dropped out of sight for a while was an informant. Most of the fingers were pointing at the FBI, so Long had asked O'Sullivan to keep the Bureau away from the Lancaster Street probe. When the troopers later told the strike force chief that the wire had been blown, he downplayed their suspicions. "It couldn't be them, I know these guys," he said, referring to Morris and Connolly.

Someone had obviously tipped off their wires, the troopers thought, but who? The more they thought about it, the more the trail seemed to lead back to the FBI—through the Boston Police Department and a detective named Eddie Walsh.

Walsh's beat was the North End. He was there all hours of the day and night. The low-level wiseguys, loansharks, and bookies, dressed in their razor-crease slacks, silk shirts, and gold chains, made sport of Walsh's wardrobe behind his back—he usually wore rumpled pants and shirt, an old, fading fedora, and sometimes a blue windbreaker. Everyone knew his car too, a beat-up hulk of a sedan of a faded, inde-

terminate hue that looked even worse next to the gleaming
Cadillacs and Lincolns perpetually double-parked in front of
underboss Jerry Angiulo's Café Pompei.

Yet the guys on the street gave the Irish detective a reluctant respect. For one thing, he seemed to know everyone
and, for an Irishman, was extremely plugged into the neighborhood rumor mill—even the hard-core gossip that barely
made it outside the unmarked social clubs where the silk-
shirt guys played cards and barbut, a dice game, and drank
espresso all day. Plus, his reputation for being reasonable instead of a hard-ass kept him from being shut out by the locals. If some jewelry disappeared from a Hanover Street
storefront, Walsh could sometimes get it back no-questions-
asked without an arrest. Such acts had two purposes. One,
the parties involved owed him a favor. And two, it showed
that he was in tune with the neighborhood's desire to operate the Sicilian way, keeping disputes in the family instead
of involving government authorities.

The State Police guys all took notice of Walsh as they followed Bulger and Flemmi into the mob's home neighborhood. After all, the rumpled Irishman was hard to miss in a
sea of Italians. The odd thing was that Walsh seemed to be intently noticing them right back. One day, they decided to turn
the tables. After being followed through the neighborhood,
Foley and another trooper circled back and followed Walsh.
He walked up Hanover Street, across Washington, through
Haymarket Square straight to the JFK Building, the FBI's
offices.

"As soon as he would see us, he would go straight to the
FBI building. He was working with the FBI. He was telling
them when we were in the North End. It was a horror show,"
one of the Lancaster Street investigators said, looking back.

Had it not been for John Morris's big mouth, however, the
State Police might never have been gifted with twenty-
twenty hindsight. Morris was several glasses of red wine
into a law enforcement party when he ran into Robert Ryan,
a sergeant in the Boston Police Intelligence Unit.

"You know, if you guys have something going over at Lancaster Street, the bad guys know about it," Morris said.

Ryan, who had been pushing for the Boston Police to install their own bug at Lancaster Street, reported the encounter with Morris to a state prosecutor, who told Colonel O'Donovan. The State Police commander exploded, demanding a meeting with O'Sullivan, the Boston Police, and the FBI. They met in a room at a Ramada Inn, where O'Donovan demanded to know how Morris knew about the investigation. Boston FBI Assistant Special Agent in Charge Weldon Kennedy promised to look into it. When confronted, Morris denied leaking any information about the bug, saying Bulger and Flemmi had simply seen "a lot of new faces" around Lancaster Street and assumed that they were the State Police detectives.

At their next meeting, Weldon Kennedy declared to O'Donovan that the FBI had not compromised the State Police bug. Virtually none of the troopers bought it and the tension in the room was palpable. "It was apparent during the discussions that, although unstated, everyone in the room was aware of the identities of the two informants of this office," Kennedy wrote in a report to Lawrence Sarhatt, the new Special Agent in Charge. "At least on the part of the State Police, there is extreme suspicion on that our relationship with these two sources is questionable."

The incident soured relations between the two agencies for the next twenty years. So who did tip off Lancaster Street? The question has never been fully answered.

Flemmi later said that the initial tip came from a State Police source, a trooper named John Naimovich, and was confirmed by Connolly, who spoke with Morris and O'Sullivan. Naimovich *was* later indicted for leaking information to a mob-connected bookmaker, but he was acquitted at trial and had conveniently died by the time Flemmi made his allegations. Many people, including Judge Mark Wolf, believed that Flemmi was lying about Naimovich to protect his old friends at the FBI.

Morris simply denied being part of the leak. Connolly, meanwhile, blamed a private investigator who helped the State Police with the bug technology, who was later discovered to have ties to Mafia boss Raymond Patriarca. In his Salemme decision, Judge Mark Wolf found that the culprit was Connolly, saying he doubted Flemmi's story "particularly with regard to O'Sullivan." Some investigators, who only learned years later that O'Sullivan knew all along that Bulger and Flemmi were FBI sources, were stunned by O'Sullivan's duplicity and have speculated that O'Sullivan may have been the leak, though O'Sullivan has denied that.

"I really wanted to believe O'Sullivan, I always thought he was a good guy," one of the State Police investigators said years later. "He knew the whole thing. He sandbagged us. He told them. Connolly was his go-between to tell them to shut down right away. We knew in our heart of hearts that it was Connolly, we could just never prove it. But we didn't suspect O'Sullivan. It turns out he lied right to our faces. I always thought Connolly was a punk and a wiseguy, but I thought that O'Sullivan was a good guy. It's very, very, very disheartening."

The final humiliating end to the Lancaster Street episode was a visit from Flemmi himself. A short time after the last bug failed, the troopers gathered at their offices near Boston University for a postmortem. O'Donovan excused himself to take a telephone call. He came back with a look of complete incredulity on his face.

"That was Stevie Flemmi. He's coming in. He said he wants to talk."

The troopers blinked at each other, dumbfounded. Flemmi hadn't said much, O'Donovan said, other than that he wanted to talk "from one kingpin to another" about the ongoing investigation.

Flemmi strolled into the building on a Saturday. O'Donovan and Flemmi went inside his office. O'Donovan emerged a few minutes later.

Flemmi had gone out the back, O'Donovan said. "He wanted to know whether we tried to bug his car. I told him I couldn't confirm it or deny it. He told me: 'I have a good feeling it was you and your guys. That's fine with me, I know what you do, and you know what I do, but I just wanted to know if it's another bad guy coming after me because, if it is, I have to take certain measures.' "

O'Donovan wasn't about to give Flemmi the satisfaction, but the troopers *had* tried to bug his Chevy Caprice in the garage of Flemmi's girlfriend's house in Brookline. They disabled the car's alarm system, but Flemmi had *two* alarms in the car, and the second one went off in an ear-splitting cacophony of horns and sirens. The troopers managed to run from the garage with their gear before being discovered. Flemmi took the car to a junkyard and had it crushed.

The humiliation of Lancaster Street and Flemmi's visit would burn in the collective memories of the State Police for the next two decades. Flemmi was growing more secure that this new generation of FBI agents was going to protect him, but it was the first time he had openly taunted his would-be pursuers.

It wouldn't be the last.

While the troopers stood amid the ashes of their Lancaster Street investigation, the FBI tape machines hummed for four months in the beginning of 1981, greedily recording nearly every word spoken inside Jerry Angiulo's supposedly impregnable stronghold and in the social club where Zannino held court.

The garrulous mobsters held forth on a variety of topics: the joys of "this thing of ours," the people they had killed, and what they were going to do to people who owed them money. At other times the agents, who were sitting in a listening post across the harbor listening to the bugs transmit over a microwave booster signal, just heard the television set as the mobsters watched Boston Celtics games.

The FBI also heard exactly how well-integrated its Top Echelon sources had become into the Mafia—and the treachery and violence they were capable of.

"I'll tell you right now, if I called these guys [Flemmi and Bulger] right now, they'd kill anybody we'd tell them to," Angiulo said at one point.

Another conversation inside Larry Zannino's social club was particularly instructive. Zannino had called in Jerry Matricia, a fringe underworld figure, to lecture him about the dangers of screwing the Winter Hill Gang. Matricia was criminal partners with John Cincotti, one of Zannino's soldiers. He had also done some business with Johnny Martorano and owed money to Winter Hill. Matricia was having ideas that his Mafia ties might enable him to stiff Bulger and Flemmi, who had assumed power in the gang after the old boss, Howie Winter, was sent to prison on the race-fixing case. Zannino quickly disabused him of the notion.

"Now, if you fuck someone that is close to us . . . I'm going to give you a shake now, so that you understand me . . . Do you know that the Hill is us? Maybe you didn't know that. Did you?"

"No I didn't," Matricia said.

Matricia then brought up Johnny Martorano's name, which obviously carried some weight with Zannino, himself a feared killer.

"Johnny's a man," Zannino said.

Zannino, Cincotti, Nicky Giso, and Ralph "Ralphie Chong" Lamattina then sent Matricia out of the room, and discussed among themselves how Bulger and Flemmi were probably getting ready to murder Matricia.

"As far as they were concerned, he owes the money," Zannino said.

"They were going to hit this kid," Lamattina said.

Lamattina asked Cincotti if the Winter Hill guys knew that Matricia was his associate, and thereby somewhat protected.

"How do they realize this kid is around with you? Have they seen him?"

"I have no idea."

"I know if Stevie or Whitey sees him . . ." Lamattina began.

"They're going to hit him," Zannino said, finishing the sentence.

"Well, Jesus. I know I would. Would you?" Lamattina said.

"What I'm trying to do is prevent that," Zannino replied.

The Italian mobsters could see how cleverly Winter Hill was setting up the murder. According to Matricia, Johnny Martorano told him to lie to all his friends, saying he was "even" with the Winter Hill Gang even though he still owed them money. By having Matricia tell everyone that he had paid them off, the Winter Hill guys were insulating themselves from being blamed for his murder.

"If you want to clip someone, tell him: 'Tell everybody you paid it,' " Giso said appreciatively.

"Yeah, and then crack him," Zannino said.

". . . won't get the blame," Giso said.

They brought Matricia back in. Zannino told him that Cincotti would make sure that from now on Bulger and Flemmi got a cut of his criminal proceeds.

"You make a score, I'm going to see Whitey and Steve get the money. You understand?"

"Uh-huh," Matricia replied.

"After all, you fucked them, didn't you? You out and out fucked them. But you don't fuck them because they're with us. Are they with us? Are they with us?" Zannino asked.

"A thousand percent," Cincotti said.

The pattern would repeat itself throughout Flemmi and Bulger's careers as criminals and Top Echelon informants. Thanks to their careful plotting, there would usually be another plausible suspect in the murders they committed—a Jimmy Flynn in the case of Brian Halloran, for example—or another way of covering their tracks.

Between the bug in Zannino's social club and the one in Angiulo's headquarters, the FBI secretly recorded more than five hundred tapes between January and May 1981. Cap-

tured for posterity were more than 850 irrefutable hours of
the Angiulo brothers' deepest criminal secrets, including the
details of four murders.

The preparation for the case and the trial would go on for
another five years, but there was no fighting the FBI's
almighty tapes. Thanks to Title III and the Top Echelon program, for all intents and purposes the Angiulo regime was
history.

Although Jerry Angiulo was blissfully unaware of what was
about to befall him in the early 1980s, Roger Wheeler was
getting downright paranoid.

The numbers out of World Jai Alai had never added up.
More people than ever were choosing South Florida as a vacation spot, and the "handle" (the total amount bet at the jai
alai frontons) was rising, yet World Jai Alai's revenues were
somehow going down. By 1980, Roger Wheeler was having
serious regrets about the original deal that had forced him to
keep Dick Donovan and Paul Rico with the company. He
wanted to sell, only he couldn't seem to get rid of either
Donovan or World Jai Alai. Larry Wheeler said his father
had a handshake deal with the investment banking firm
Drexel Burnham to sell the company for between $47 and
$50 million, which would have netted Roger Wheeler a cool
$25 million profit. The deal died when jai alai revenues took
another sudden dive.

"Whenever he came close to selling, the numbers would
take a dip," said Larry Wheeler, who believes Donovan was
trying to block the sale of WJA because he was putting together a bid to buy the company on his own, highly favorable terms. At one point Donovan offered $16 million, Larry
Wheeler said, an amount completely unacceptable to his father, but Donovan seemed to be the only viable buyer.

The frustrating situation, and some behind-the-scenes
talks with Connecticut investigators over their suspicions
about organized crime influence at the Hartford fronton,
deepened Roger Wheeler's distrust of the whole WJA oper-

ation. He began taping his telephone calls, and installed a voice stress meter on his office line in Tulsa. He sent his secretary to a special school to learn how to work the machine.

"You know for a price I'd get out. Donovan is going around—I mean, he's a pain in the ass, let's put it that way. You know he has resentment toward any suggestion [of selling the company]. He's just difficult to live with and that's made it very uncomfortable," Wheeler said during one taped telephone call with an investigator.

Later on in the conversation, Wheeler suggested he might even try to tap Donovan's telephone.

"Are wiretaps legal?" he asked.

"No. They are illegal," the investigator replied.

"They're illegal?"

"Right."

"You know, I don't know much about this kind of stuff. Just what you read and all that. But what I was going to say was that I would have no hesitance if you guys would want to tap his line down there."

"No, no. It's a federal offense."

"Oh, it is? Well, sorry about that."

"We'd all go to jail."

"Oh," Wheeler said, obviously disappointed.

The war with Donovan continued into early 1981, as Wheeler's suspicions continued to mount. He did manage to get rid of the Hartford fronton, selling it Buddy Berenson. Berenson told Wheeler that he had uncovered a "big skim" out of the company after taking over, according to Connecticut Chief State Attorney Austin McGuigan.

A former catering manager in Hartford, meanwhile, was telling Connecticut investigators that in the late 1970s "pilferage" was a major problem at both the Hartford and Florida frontons and that there seemed to be some fooling around with the company's books. The employee told Connecticut state investigators that "on several occasions, the report [profit and loss statement] that we sent to [WJA headquarters] in Miami would show a profit on our end and it would be deep in the red when it came back from Miami."

Wheeler asked Donovan point-blank if there was any skimming going on at World Jai Alai. Donovan denied it.

By the early spring Wheeler was badly spooked. He believed WJA security chief Paul Rico, the former FBI agent, was taking an inordinate interest in the details of his schedule. On March 2, Wheeler had a near nervous breakdown at Tulsa International Airport, just before boarding his Learjet to fly to Connecticut for a gaming commission hearing. He frantically ordered his pilot, Bill Baggett, to "check the plane for bombs or sabotage." Baggett went through every compartment, equipment panel, and wheel well, but found nothing. Wheeler then ordered Baggett to take the plane in the air to its cruising altitude to make sure there was nothing wrong. Only then did Wheeler board the plane with his wife and their lawyer.

Wheeler had sometimes joked about such matters before on trips to Miami. "Well, I hope they don't bomb my plane today," he would say. Now he was serious. He had never asked that the plane be searched before.

Roger Wheeler sent Larry and David down to WJA headquarters in Miami to do a complete audit of the company. Wheeler had encouraged his middle sons to become involved in the business, and Larry in particular loved hanging out with his father at work in the early 1970s, sitting in the back of the room during Telex board meetings or trying to fix defective tape drives in a workshop space set up just for him.

The two developed a close bond. When Larry scraped together enough money to buy a Kawasaki dirt bike, his father at first protested, then, when he saw the meticulous care his son put into maintaining the motorcycle, he went out and bought his own, a monster-sized Bultaco. They started traveling together on father-son trips to Arizona or to the famous Baja 1000 road rally in Mexico. After graduation from Tulsa's Thomas A. Edison High School, Larry chose Rice

University, his father's alma mater, and earned a degree in accounting.

Larry's job was to check on the company's books. David, a computer expert, was supposed to check the company's bet-processing system, which had been under suspicion since John Callahan had hired a computer consultant five years earlier. The consultant billed the company $50,000, but no one was able to tell the Wheelers what he had actually done.

The family suspected that the skim might be a computer scam—which experts had told them was theoretically possible—or was some sort of purchasing scheme involving kickbacks or overbilling. Larry Wheeler favored the last possibility, based on a disturbing experience during a previous visit to Miami. No one there knew his face, so he was able to move around anonymously. He was shocked by how dark and foreboding the fronton was, and by the general surliness of the help.

He went into the restaurant and ordered a steak and a salad. Growing up in Oklahoma, Larry was used to steaks like the one's at Jamil's, a rustic wooden eatery where visiting celebrities flocked for two-inch-thick slabs of buttery sirloin and tenderloin. He was shocked to see the sickly looking quarter-inch strip of meat in front of him with a disconcerting purplish hue. It was accompanied by a wilted brown salad. Wheeler was equally surprised to look over and see H. Paul Rico dining alone at a table nearby. Wheeler knew Rico from pictures, but they had never met. Larry looked over at Rico's plate and saw a thick, juicy cut of sirloin that would have done Jamil's proud. On the side was a bowl full of crisp greens.

You fucking scumbag, Wheeler thought.

As they were preparing the audit, the two sons took a break and met with their father at the WW Ranch. They rode motorcycles and talked about the business. Roger Wheeler told his son that he was planning to fire Rico and Donovan. He hadn't told the two World Jai Alai executives about his decision, but he believed they knew something was coming, the elder Wheeler said.

Roger Wheeler was back in Tulsa the following Wednesday, May 27, going through his usual routine. Wheeler pulled into the Southern Hills Country Club parking lot just after lunchtime. Back at Telex Corp., Wheeler's girl Friday, Julie Tallent, took an odd telephone call between two and three P.M.

"Is Mr. Wheeler there?" the caller, a man, asked.

"No, he's out of the office."

"Is he playing golf today?"

"Yes."

"Thank you."

The man hung up without leaving a message. Tallent immediately regretted giving out the information because the man sounded suspicious.

Wheeler pulled his navy-blue Cadillac into the Southern Hills parking lot, but someone had parked in his normal spot, so he drove around the side to a spare lot behind the swimming pool. He changed clothes, joined the foursome of members that the pro shop had put together, and teed off. He preferred to walk the lengthy course rather than ride a cart. His fellow golfers noticed that he seemed preoccupied, but managed to shoot an 88, a respectable score for his handicap. He stopped to make three telephone calls at the turn. After the round, his partners said, he seemed in a good mood.

After changing back out of his golf clothes, Roger Wheeler walked out a back door of the clubhouse past a Dumpster to his car. Fourteen people, several of them children atop the pool's ten-foot diving board, saw what happened next. As Wheeler walked toward his Cadillac, a stocky man followed him, carrying a paper bag and a small towel. Witnesses said the man wore dark glasses, was in his mid-forties, about five feet ten inches tall and 200 pounds, with dark gray hair, a salt-and-pepper beard. A few later said he looked "like Kenny Rogers."

Wheeler put his leather gym bag on the front passenger seat and shut his door. As he went to put the key in the ignition, the man following him yanked the driver's door open, pressed a .38 caliber revolver to the bridge of Wheeler's glasses, and fired. The bullet entered between his eye socket and the bridge of his nose, causing a starfish-shaped spatter around the wound and sending one half of Wheeler's glasses onto the dashboard, the other half into the backseat. Wheeler's car keys fell to the floor as he slumped over toward the passenger seat, his head falling into his unzipped gym bag. Police examining the car would later remark on how clean it was. The contents of Wheeler's gym bag, however, several shirts, pairs of socks, and some golf balls, had to be fished out of a couple inches of blood sloshing around at the bottom.

The shooter shut the door back up with his hand and strode quickly over to a copper-colored Ford LTD sedan driven by an accomplice, who was also wearing a beard. They took off fast—but not too fast—out the Sixty-first Street exit, and faded into rush-hour traffic.

Even in the worst year for murders that anyone could remember in Tulsa—twice as many as usual, including an honest-to-goodness ax murder—Roger Wheeler's murder was deemed the biggest homicide case ever. Police found $900 still in his wallet and his Rolex still on his wrist, so the consensus was that Wheeler was the victim of a gangland execution. The story created a brief sensation in the national media.

Michael T. Huff, of the Tulsa Police Homicide Squad, the youngest detective in the history of the department, was one of the detectives who caught the case. Huff and his partners had both cut their teeth working the "whore stroll," the 700 block of North Main Street in Tulsa, a notorious haven for drug dealers, gang members, and prostitutes.

Huff was not imposing-looking; slightly below average height, he had a round, kindly face, wore wire-rim glasses, and had a habit of being unfailingly polite. No one was ever surprised to learn he had graduated from Will Rogers High School, where he lettered in both football and basketball for the Ropers. His unassuming looks and manner usually encouraged people to underestimate him, but his Tulsa Police superiors saw in him a keen investigative mind and a mulish stubbornness remarkable even for an Oklahoman. Still, he had only worked on Homicide for a year, and he hadn't worked many big cases, certainly not a big "whodunit"—the term Tulsa detectives used to refer to cases where a suspect wasn't immediately obvious.

This is the one I've been looking for, Huff thought to himself.

The next morning he strode into the office still charged up about working the Wheeler case. His sergeant, a wise old veteran named Roy Hunt, who bore an uncanny resemblance to General George Armstrong Custer, took one look at the young detective and pulled him into his second-floor office.

"Son."

"Yes sir?"

"You really want to be on this case?"

"Y—"

"Think about it," Hunt interrupted. "Let me tell you, your life is about to change today."

"Why wouldn't I want to be on this case, Sergeant?"

"Because it's going to test you. Every part of your life."

"I'm good to go," Huff replied.

Hunt's words would prove prophetic over the next nineteen years, but at the time Huff was too excited and busy to give them much thought. The investigation was going too many places at once. Several suspects emerged, including alleged "Dixie Mafia" murderer and bomber Patrick H. Early, who was rumored to be in the area. Early was also suspected of murdering the wife of a sheriff in Tennessee named Buford Pusser.[11] The detectives worked hard to find a

---

[11]Pusser's life story was later made into the movie *Walking Tall*.

motive, a bad business deal, perhaps trouble in Wheeler's personal life, but the strongest leads kept pointing back to World Jai Alai—Wheeler's suspicions about the company and his paranoia about former president John Callahan's alleged ties to the Boston underworld.

As weeks of investigation stretched into months, Huff became more and more convinced that the murder had something to do with WJA. He began digging into the company's past and present officers, including Callahan and especially H. Paul Rico. The more he learned about Rico, the more disturbed he became.

A few hundred yards into a wooded section of Joe Barboza's hometown of New Bedford, *Boston Herald Traveler* reporter Jim Southwood's WWI-surplus gas mask was fogging up. The same thought ran through his mind over and over as he nervously fingered the .38 revolver in his pocket and squinted through the misty glass eye holes at the serial killer whose life story he had agreed to write.

What the Hell am I *doing* here?

Barboza, backed by two fierce-looking men Southwood had never seen before, was talking to two emissaries sent by the boss of the New England Mafia, Raymond Patriarca. The gas mask had been Barboza's idea of a disguise, so that the mob guys, who were looking for a way to get at the notorious contract killer turned informant, wouldn't see his face. Southwood didn't want the wiseguys coming through him, book or no book, but the claustrophobia induced by the mask was making him panicky. Then he heard Barboza say something that made his guts seize up.

"I'm going to get them out. All of them. I want a million dollars. I want you to give the million to Jimmy Southwood from the *Herald* . . ."

Oh, shit, Southwood thought. This is bad. He had never signed on as Barboza's bagman with the Mafia, only as his biographer—a job that entailed a mind-numbing level of risk as it was. Now that the mob knew his name, given the fact that Barboza had sent Patriarca and four other wiseguys to prison and tried to do the same to Boston underboss Jerry Angiulo, the assignment was quickly turning into a suicide mission. And it probably wouldn't be a particularly quick death either; the wiseguys would surely torture him to find Barboza's whereabouts.

I've got to get out, he decided. Under his breath he muttered a curse against the two FBI agents who got him into the mess, H. Paul Rico and Dennis Condon.

The two men had approached him about writing a book with Barboza. It was a way for the FBI to reward Barboza for his cooperation without spending any more of the government's money and raising the notoriously cheap Hoover's ire. Barboza was keen on the idea, and with typical braggadocio was convinced that his life story would be a best seller.

Southwood had actually been a third choice. Truman Capote, who had just published *In Cold Blood* in 1966 to great critical acclaim, had been the first. Capote revolutionized the true crime genre by writing about an actual murder in Kansas in the style of a novel, but the deal with Barboza fell through. One evening, the Animal was in a motel room watching Capote being interviewed by Johnny Carson on *The Tonight Show*. Capote told Carson that one of the killers from *In Cold Blood* had the words "love" and "hate" tattooed on his knuckles and that he believed the words were a sign of latent homosexuality. Barboza grabbed a chair in his massive hands—which were adorned with similar tattoos—and destroyed the television set. Barboza believed that some of his sexual exploits were as impressive as his criminal ones, and for the lisping, effeminate writer to suggest that he was gay was too much.

"He said he didn't want a fag writing his book," Southwood recalls.

A second writer turned down the project after his life was threatened, so Paul Rico and Dennis Condon turned to Southwood. He had a good reputation in law enforcement circles and was uncertain about his future. The *Herald Traveler* was on shaky financial footing, and he was looking for a project that would give him a fallback plan in case the paper went belly up. Barboza was just coming off the trials of Patriarca, Anguilo, and the Deegan defendants and was in the national headlines, so Southwood was hoping for a best seller. Particularly since his cut was going to be a measly fifteen percent.

The writer and the killer spent some time getting to know each other. At first Barboza would call from secure locations where the FBI was protecting him. Then they started meeting in person. One of their meetings was at Fort Knox in Kentucky. Another time, Barboza actually came into the *Herald Traveler* building dressed like a fisherman. After the gas-mask incident, Southwood wanted to break their deal, but the Animal wasn't exactly someone you said no to.

Instead Southwood started stalling, making up excuses about why he couldn't do more work on the project. He was driving a sullen Barboza from his home in East Sandwich to New Bedford when he felt the chill of cold metal on his temple. Barboza had put a .38 derringer to the side of his head.

Southwood froze.

"I could kill you right now, James."

"Joe, who are you going to get to write your book?"

Barboza was silent for a moment. He regarded the tiny gun. "Shit, I don't even know how to work this thing."

"Well, take it away from my head. Please."

Southwood dropped Barboza off. It would be the last time the reporter ever saw the legendary thug. Barboza eventually enlisted another writer, Hank Messick, to pen his life story. Barboza told Messick everything he had told Southwood about his exploits, all the women he had screwed, all the men he had killed. He also told the writer that he had become disenchanted and frustrated with the FBI and Rico and Condon, who made some grand promises—relocation to Australia, plastic surgery—but hadn't delivered.

Southwood remembers the two agents as something of an odd couple. Condon tended to dress and talk like an undertaker. Rico was more of a wildman. Southwood knew enough about the FBI to know that Rico was different from those cookie-cutter Hoover drones, who fretted over whether their regulation white shirts had just the right amount of starch. Rico wore plaid jackets and pink shirts and bright red ties. He hung around in bars and drank whiskey with junk pushers, bookmakers, and truck hijackers in an era when coffee was banned from FBI offices and agents could be censured if caught drinking such illicit beverages while on duty even outside the office.

Rico had a confidence that was almost eerie, Southwood said. Told that Barboza was planning to recant, the agent took it surprisingly well. "He can't do anything," Rico replied, as if he had one of Boston's biggest mass murderers firmly in his back pocket.

Barboza went to prominent attorney F. Lee Bailey of Boston in July 1970 to recant his testimony in the Teddy Deegan murder. Barboza wanted to "set the record straight as to certain perjured testimony he had given in state and federal courts," the famous attorney said in an affidavit he later wrote about the incident. Barboza said it was actually himself and three associates—Roy French, Ronald Casseso, and another man (who was not identified)—who killed Deegan in 1965 during the Irish Gang War. FBI documents later showed that the unidentified man was Jimmy "the Bear" Flemmi.

At trial, Barboza had implicated six men: Joe Salvati, Roy French, Ronnie Casseso, Henry Tameleo, Peter Limone, and Louis Greco. He admitted he testified falsely against mobsters Tameleo and Limone because the federal authorities insisted that he implicate "someone of importance." Barboza was leery about the severe legal consequences of recanting and feared going back to prison. "Because he had become a government witness, he would not expect to live more than a day if he were committed to the general population at [the state prison in] Walpole, as he feared," Bailey wrote.

Barboza's fears of being sent to the tough prison at Walpole were well-founded. He was arrested on a gun possession charge in his native New Bedford a short time later and sent there. It didn't take him long to crack.

"Subsequently, he told me that he had been informed by persons in authority, whom he did not name, that federal agents would arrange for his release provided he discharge me and terminated his efforts to recant his testimony," Bailey wrote. Bailey later said he firmly believes that Barboza was telling the truth when he tried to recant—and that federal authorities "coerced" him into changing his mind.

"I am satisfied of that beyond a doubt," Bailey said.

If federal authorities promised to stick by Barboza, Rico and Condon made good on it.

They came to Barboza's rescue in California the next year, when he was charged with the first-degree murder of an associate in Santa Rosa. Barboza claimed self-defense, even though the associate, Clayton Wilson, was shot twice in the head from behind. Rico and Condon, joined by then–Organized Crime Strike Force Chief Edward F. Harrington, flew west to testify on Barboza's behalf. Barboza pleaded guilty to second-degree murder, and thanks to Rico, Condon, and Harrington's intercession, received a sentence of five years to life. He served just four.

Yet Joe Barboza wasn't the only witness of Rico's to later recant.

John J. Kelley, a Boston underworld figure, testified against Maurice "Pro" Lerner in Rhode Island. Lerner was charged with two underworld murders. Kelley, who like Barboza had been flipped by Rico, was the star witness. Kelley later said that he had spiced his testimony in the Lerner trial with lies that served Rico's purposes, including a story that he had personally cut the barrel off the shotgun used in the killings of Rudolph Marfeo and Anthony Melei. The gun had actually been modified by another of Rico's informants whom the FBI agent wanted to protect, Kelley said.

Kelley also admitted lying about meeting Patriarca at a local restaurant to talk about the planned murders. The meeting had never taken place, he said, but Rico and the FBI had invested hundreds of hours into an investigation of the owner of the restaurant and hoped to manufacture evidence against him. Kelley also said he falsely testified that Rico promised him only immunity and protection for his family, when in fact Rico had vowed to give him a new identity, relocation money, and a yearly income from the FBI.

"Agent Rico told me I should tell all of these things because it looked like I was being paid; that I should just do as he said and everything would come out all right," Kelley said.

When he was asked why he had committed perjury, Kelley replied: "My life was in their hands. He said I had no alternative."

The Supreme Court of Rhode Island reversed Lerner's conviction in an extraordinary ruling, finding that both Kelley and Rico had committed perjury during the trial and finding that it was an "easy case that requires automatic reversal."

"We . . . hold that Kelley's perjury, elicited by the FBI, constituted material, exculpatory evidence withheld in violation of the applicant's due-process rights," the ruling said.

Other authorities, meanwhile, suspected Rico of abetting a crime far worse than eliciting a few lies under oath.

In 1964, thirty-three-year-old Ronald Dermady, Whitey Bulger's former bank-robbing partner, was murdered in Watertown, about a mile from Rico's home in neighboring Belmont, a few days after making several calls to the agent's unlisted home phone number and the FBI office, according to police reports.

On parole after serving nine years for the 1955 Rhode Island bank robbery with Bulger, Dermady was shot twice in the head as he sat in a brand new white Austin sedan on School Street in Watertown. Detectives probing his murder found that for the week preceding the killing, he had been holed up in the Commander Hotel (now the Sheraton Commander) near Harvard Square with a notorious gangster moll known as "Dottie from Dorchester."

But that wasn't the only interesting twist detectives discovered at the hotel.

A suspicious hotel detective had ordered the Commander's switchboard operator to make notes of all outgoing calls from Room 104. The day after Dermady and "Dottie" arrived, August 30, the operator heard him call Rico's unlisted home telephone number in Belmont.

"Is the girl dressed? Get her out of there right away," a male voice at the Belmont end of the line said, according to a police report. "Have you got that thing? Bring it to Common."

Detectives surmised that "Common" was a reference to Common Street in Belmont, the major cross street near Rico's home, the report stated. Over the next six hours, the operator logged calls from Dermady to another FBI agent at home and the main number at the Boston FBI office. At the same time, he was also making calls to James "Buddy" McLean of Somerville, the founder of the Winter Hill Gang that Bulger and Flemmi would later lead.

Dermady was on the run. That day, witnesses saw him bust into the Capital Café on Broadway in Somerville and shoot a man who was a dead ringer for Buddy McLean. Unfortunately for Dermady, it wasn't McLean but a petty thief named Charlie Robinson. Police immediately surmised that the Robinson shooting was a botched hit on McLean, who was embroiled in a gang war with the infamous McLaughlin brothers of Charlestown. Underworld rumors circulated the same story. Dermady, meanwhile, made a frantic call to McLean—presumably to deny that the Winter Hill Gang leader was his target and stave off retribution—and another to his lawyer.

Eighteen minutes after calling his attorney, he was shot dead. The medical examiner found powder burns in Dermady's hair, indicating that he was shot at point-blank range.

Police and other sources familiar with the case believe that Dermady, infatuated with Dottie, received permission from the McLaughlins to murder her common-law husband. But it was a package deal—Dermady would first have to kill McLean. After the botched hit, Dermady was killed in retaliation by the Winter Hill Gang.

How did they find him just a day later? And how much did the FBI know about Dermady's plans, especially given the telephone reference to "the girl"? The Watertown Police detectives never found out. Their probe ran into a brick wall when it reached the Boston FBI office. Rico, another agent, and the FBI brass denied everything. The detectives concluded that the FBI was lying.

"[Rico] denied . . . calling the Commander Hotel or knowing anyone at the Commander Hotel," a report states. "We believe this to be false because his unlisted number was called."

Reliable sources indicate that in late 1999 and early 2000, a grand jury investigation ordered by Attorney General Janet Reno was probing allegations that Rico helped Flemmi in a similar manner during the mob war, tipping him off to the location of at least one enemy so that his prized Top Echelon informant would survive. Thirty years later, Massachusetts State Police reopened the Dermady case and were probing its suspicious connections to H. Paul Rico.

The Dermady incident reminded Jim Southwood of something Barboza had told him about Rico. "He [Rico] caused half the murders in the gang war," Barboza said, by creating "cold wars of deceit."

"He would call one group up and say, 'These people are planning to kill you,' " Southwood recalled Barboza saying. "Then of course that group would go out and try to kill the other guys before they did it to them."

"Rico probably could have been the boss of bosses in the mob if he wanted," Jim Southwood said. "I think he knew what the FBI was, and he said fuck it. I think he was having a good time."

After Brian Halloran and his friend Michael Donahue were murdered in May 1982, the FBI had a major problem. The Angiulo bugs had long since been shut down, but agents were still transcribing hundreds of hours of conversations, and the case was still months from any indictment. Despite Halloran's dying declaration blaming Jimmy Flynn, the FBI had no illusions that their T.E. informants were suspects in the crime. Morris, for one, believed that Bulger and Flemmi probably were involved, although he kept his opinion to himself. The Bureau began doing everything it could to keep the two T.E. informants out of the case.

Two weeks after the Northern Avenue shootings, the FBI agents assigned to the Wheeler murder case met at FBI Headquarters in Washington. Bob Fitzpatrick and Jerry Montanari were there from Boston, supervisors Ronald Reese and Anthony Amoroso (the case agent from the AB-SCAM probe) and agent Joseph Rush came from Miami, while agent Bob McKenchney flew in from Oklahoma City. Sean McWeeney, the head of the FBI's Organized Crime Section, hosted the meeting with two other Headquarters types, Jeff Jamar and Randy Prillaman.

Fitzpatrick's memo of the meeting is worded extremely carefully.

> Some of the areas covered in the . . . conference were the coordination of the captioned investigation by Miami, Oklahoma City, and Boston offices, especially in ferreting out new leads and establishing a motive for the victim's murder.

There is no mention in Fitzpatrick's memo of the Halloran murder, World Jai Alai, or former FBI agent H. Paul
Rico. According to Fitzpatrick's account, the agents agreed
that Jerry O'Sullivan and his FBI-friendly strike force
would be brought into the case to coordinate a possible
grand jury investigation with the U.S. Attorney from Oklahoma City.

Bulger and Flemmi were discussed, the memo said, but as
a "separate issue."

```
In a separate issue, informants of the
Boston Division were discussed with
FBIHQ Supervising Agent and OC Informant
Chief from FBIHQ. It was recommended
that informants remain open until sub-
stantiated information is received in-
dictating that they should be closed.
```

Fitzpatrick's true feelings about Bulger and Flemmi's
probable involvement in the murders are well hidden. He
later said that after the SAC made the decision to keep Bulger and Flemmi on as informants despite the Lancaster
Street controversy, their continued status as T.E. informants was a fait accompli and he wasn't going to write any
memos that would embarrass his boss. Instead, Fitzpatrick
said, he decided to back agent Jerry Montanari's investigation the best he could and hope it would develop conclu-
sive proof that Flemmi and Bulger were behind the
killings. Sarhatt, he added, knew the issues in the case anyway and didn't need everything spelled out in an exhaus-
tive memo.

The fate of Montanari's investigation, however, appears to
have been sealed within a week. Montanari and Brunnick
were pushing the FBI brass to treat Bulger and Flemmi as
suspects. Morris and Connolly campaigned against it—and
won. Fitzpatrick, Morris, Mike Hanigan, Montanari, Brunnick, and Connolly huddled back in Boston, where Fitz-

patrick broke the news. All information in the Halloran murder case, he wrote in a memo, would be "coordinated" with Bulger and Flemmi.

```
All present had an opportunity to dis-
cuss all facets of this matter, partic-
ularly any differences of opinion
concerning suspects, subjects and all
peripherals connected with Wheeler's
murder. It was mutually agreed that
agents actively working the Wheeler case
would coordinate information with SA
Connolly's sources so that this matter
can be quickly and effectively resolved.
```

If Brian Halloran had been telling the truth about the Wheeler murder, then his own death left Bulger, Flemmi, and Johnny Martorano with one loose end: former World Jai Alai president John Callahan.

Halloran was the ideal patsy to hire for the Wheeler murder. It is likely that Bulger and Flemmi's plan was to murder Halloran after he assassinated Wheeler. Bulger and Flemmi had made it known that they were on the outs with Halloran. Connolly and O'Sullivan then adopted the story and used it to justify their belief that Bulger and Flemmi weren't involved in either the Wheeler or Halloran slayings. As Johnny Martorano's attempt to set up Jerry Matricia showed, the Winter Hill guys were always thinking beforehand how to cover their tracks. In fact, in another conversation captured on the Angiulo tapes, the North End mafiosi can be heard vetoing the idea of loaning one of their guys to Winter Hill for a hit. They decided it was too dangerous—for the hit man.

The day after Halloran was murdered—at least according to a 209 written by Connolly—the agent met with Flemmi, who suggested that "the wiseguys in Charlestown" knew that Halloran had been cooperating.

On 5/12/82, BS [Flemmi] advised that the
wiseguys in Charlestown supposedly heard
that Brian Halloran and his brother, who
is a Massachusetts State Trooper, had
met with Col. O'Donovan of the Massachusetts State Police and that Halloran was
going to cooperate with the law.

Source has no idea how the Charlestown
people knew this information or how they
learned it.

Halloran's death left Callahan as a direct link left between Bulger, Flemmi, and Martorano, and the Halloran,
Donahue, and Wheeler murders. In other words, he was a liability.

Again, Bulger and Flemmi called on Johnny Martorano.[12]
But first Flemmi had to make sure he and Bulger would
avoid taking the blame. In early July he fed Connolly some
bogus information designed to throw the blame for Callahan's murder on an unnamed "Cuban group."

On 7/7/82, [Flemmi] advised that John
Callahan has supposedly returned from
Ireland within the last week and was over
there for ten days. Callahan gave the
Charlestown crew $500 for the July 9th
fund-raiser for Jimmy Flynn, which is
being held at the Malden Irish American
Club. Source advised that Callahan is
supposed to be trying to avoid going to
Florida too often on business.

Callahan was close to a Cuban group who
he was impressed with as being very bad.
Source added that lately Callahan's re-

---

[12]Martorano confessed to the crime in 1999, saying Bulger and Flemmi told
him to kill Callahan because he knew too much about the Halloran and
Wheeler murders.

lationship with this group has cooled
and Callahan is supposed to be avoiding
them. Source is unaware of any reason
Callahan may have for avoiding them or
any specifics of his business dealings
with them, if any.

On July 28, the fifty-five-year-old Callahan called his
wife Mary Jane in Winchester, a Boston suburb, and told her
he would be going to Miami. He didn't say why. She didn't
find the conversation particularly unusual, he was normally
pretty secretive about his business affairs.

Callahan and a friend stayed up drinking at his office on
Boston's Commercial Wharf until about four A.M. on July
31. At 5:50 P.M. that same day, Callahan boarded Delta Air-
lines Flight 541 for Miami. He was apparently planning a
short trip—he had booked a return flight for 10:55 the following evening. An informant later told the FBI that Callahan was on his way to deliver some cash to Johnny
Martorano, who was living in the Fort Lauderdale area.

On Tuesday, August 3, an eighteen-year-old parking at-
tendant at Miami International Airport noticed that a pool of
blood was collecting on the pavement underneath the trunk
of a silver 1980 Cadillac Fleetwood. A powerful stench was
coming off the car. When Metro-Dade Police and firefighters arrived, they opened a door with a slim jim and tried to
hit the trunk release, but it wouldn't work. Firefighters finally opened it with the jaws of life.

Callahan's body was inside. He had been shot several
times. It didn't look like a robbery—his wallet was missing,
but he was still wearing his gold Rolex and a gold claddagh
ring with an emerald and a diamond set into the crown. The
medical examiner found a dime on his chest—which investigators took to be a warning against "dropping a dime" or
informing.

The underworld hadn't been the only group looking for
John Callahan in the summer of 1982. Mike Huff and his

partner Dick Bishop flew to Hartford to do some background checks on World Jai Alai and meet with Connecticut State Police investigators Dan Toomey and Andy Ocif. They all drove up to Boston during the second week of July, looking to talk to Callahan about the Wheeler murder. Callahan was nowhere to be found. They tried his house in Winchester, but his wife said she had no idea where he was. His office in the North End was closed. Neither was he in any of his favorite haunts.

Striking out on Callahan, the detectives turned their attention to the Halloran shooting two months before. Halloran's name surfaced in the Connecticut State Police surveillances of Callahan during the Hartford jai alai licensing battle, and the Boston newspapers were reporting that Halloran had been talking to the feds before he was murdered. It was a lead, and now more than a year had passed since Wheeler had been murdered and they didn't appear to be getting any closer to solving it, so it had to be followed up. They went to see Greg Foley of the Massachusetts state police, and the five detectives went to see Jeremiah O'Sullivan at the strike force offices in Boston.

They were shocked at what they heard during the ninety-minute meeting. O'Sullivan flat out told them that Halloran wanted to get into the federal Witness Protection Program but that he had rejected him.

"Mr. O'Sullivan would not get him in, because the information given by Mr. Halloran was not corroborated," Toomey wrote in a memo concerning the meeting. "He also said he [Halloran] had also refused to testify against Howie Winter."

The detectives then asked O'Sullivan about Martorano, Bulger, and Flemmi. They're "not brilliant," O'Sullivan said. Bulger had served time in Leavenworth and had been released in "1968 or 1970." The three were just "local hoods," although they had "traveled a lot," and sometimes frequented a private club in Fort Lauderdale, Florida, to which John Callahan had also belonged.

The Winter Hill Gang, O'Sullivan said, was closely associated with "organized crime figures," that is, members of the Italian Mafia, and they carried out "hits" for the Mafia. Their modus operandi included a backup car that followed every hit.

Then O'Sullivan offered some startling news on the Halloran hit, which Toomey included in his report:

```
Mr. O'Sullivan told us he had 3rd hand
information that Halloran was offered
the WHEELER "HIT," and he (HALLORAN)
discussed it with the WINTER HILL GANG
and CALLAHAN. The "HIT" was done by
MATARANO (sic), BULGER, and FLEMMI.
Later in our meeting, Mr. O'Sullivan
said that at the time of the murder of
ROGER WHEELER SR., HALLORAN was not in
the gang's inner circles. He also said
H. PAUL RICO was connected with the WIN-
TER HILL GANG.
    Mr. O'Sullivan said they tried to use
HALLORAN to conduct electronic surveil-
lances of JOHN B.CALLAHAN, but that he
(HALLORAN) would not consent to it.
    Lastly, Mr. O'Sullivan said HALLORAN
talked about a lot of "HITS" and that he
wanted into the Witness Protection Pro-
gram.
```

They were stunned. Halloran had laid out virtually the entire Wheeler homicide for the FBI. Why hadn't they heard any of this before?

A week later the Connecticut troopers met with their Massachusetts counterparts again, this time trooper Rick Fralick and Bill Dunderdale. Fralick said a source had essentially confirmed the story O'Sullivan had told them, that Halloran had been approached by Callahan to do the

Wheeler hit and had refused. Again, Toomey made a report
of the meeting.

```
BRIAN HALLORAN refused because of the
other people involved. Those people are
JAMES BULGER, JOHN MATORANO (sic), STEVE
FLEMMI and PATRICK NEE.
```

The two Massachusetts troopers also drew the Callahan
connection, saying they had confirmed that he and Halloran
appeared to be good friends, that they shared a $1,500 a
month condominium in Plantation, Florida, and that they
had traveled together once to Sweden. They also said that
Halloran apparently had access to a safe in Callahan's office.
The troopers confirmed that the FBI had rejected Halloran's
offer of evidence against Whitey Bulger and Steve Flemmi
and that he left the safe house on the Cape after the FBI told
him to give back the car they had loaned him.

It was amazing. In the space of a week they had gone from
being virtually clueless to possessing a very viable theory for the
Wheeler and Halloran murders. They also had a potential witness—Callahan was obviously the man to see. Charged up by
what they had learned, Huff and Bishop flew back to Oklahoma.

They were planning a return trip to Boston when the news
came—Callahan was dead too.

Even with the Angiulo case still under way, the obvious potential that Flemmi was involved in the Callahan murder
brought too much heat even on the FBI. Morris ordered
Flemmi closed as an informant on September 23, 1982, a little more than a month after the Callahan murder. His teletype to FBI Headquarters on the subject, however, made no
mention of the Wheeler, Halloran, or Callahan murders. Instead, it contained only a lie:

```
FOR INFORMATION OF FBIHQ, CAPTIONED SUBJECT IS
BEING TARGETED FOR POSSIBLE PROSECUTION IN CONNEC-
```

```
TION WITH BOSTON INVESTIGATIONS OPERATION "MAN-
DARIN" AND "BOSTAR." ACCORDINGLY, C-3 ORGANIZED
CRIME SUPERVISOR HAS INSTRUCTED THAT THIS MATTER
BE PLACED IN A CLOSED STATUS PENDING RESOLUTION OF
OUTSTANDING INVESTIGATION REGARDING SOURCE.
```

Morris's assertion that Flemmi—who had drawn a diagram for the FBI of the interior of 98 Prince Street—was being targeted for prosecution as part of the Angiulo and Zannino bugging effort (Operations Bostar and Mandarin) was laughable. It did, however, look better in the FBI files than a memo saying a T.E. informant was suspected of three murders.

It wasn't until seven months later, after some of the furor had died down, that John Connolly wrote a memo for the Boston FBI files that betrayed the true reason Flemmi was being closed.

```
(Flemmi) was placed in a closed status
in that (he) was under active investiga-
tion in two separate investigations: UN-
SUBS(2); ROGER M. WHEELER—VICTIM; JOHN
B. CALLAHAN—VICTIM; RICO—MURDER; OO: Ok-
lahoma City and "BOSTAR."
```

In FBI memospeak, Connolly was saying that Flemmi had been closed due to the investigation of two unknown subjects involved in the murders of Roger Wheeler and John Callahan, although he also continued the fiction that Flemmi was under investigation in the Angiulo case. In the memo, which was written to James Ring's attention, Connolly urged that the FBI weigh the value of Flemmi's information versus his alleged criminal activity—a calculation allowed under the informant guidelines.

```
The captioned subject continues to volun-
tarily furnish sensitive information of
```

```
an extremely high quality. In view of the
above, it is requested that a determina-
tion be made as to whether or not an in-
dictment regarding subject is imminent in
either investigative matter cited above.
   If an indictment is not realistically
imminent, consideration should be given
to re-opening source in view of source's
positive contribution to the [Top Eche-
lon program].
```

Interestingly, Connolly did not close Bulger, who was in the same situation as Flemmi in both the Angiulo, Wheeler, and Callahan matters. Quite possibly it was an indication that Bulger was more deeply involved with Connolly than Flemmi. Or perhaps it was simply good old South Boston loyalty—Connolly couldn't bring himself to close Bulger—thereby casting suspicion on him. It was apparently too much of a betrayal, despite the fact that being "closed" was essentially meaningless. It certainly was for Flemmi, who later swore under oath that he was never told of his closing and that instead he continued to meet with Bulger and the FBI as before, as if nothing was different. Federal prosecutors would later stipulate that the FBI files contained *forty-six* reports of contact with Flemmi during the three years he was supposedly "closed" as an informant.

Pressure within the FBI (but outside the Boston office), meanwhile, began to mount for at least interviews with Bulger and Flemmi about the murders. The FBI office in Oklahoma City sent a memo to Headquarters on April 4, 1983, asking for interviews with the Boston office's informants. Four days later Bob Fitzpatrick wrote a memo to Ring and Mike Hanigan, the supervisors of the two squads, saying that the FBI brass had denied the request.

```
Re: Oklahoma City teletype to director
dated 4/4/83 with copies to Boston and
```

> Miami requesting interview of (Bulger)
> and (Flemmi) concerning information re-
> lated to captioned subjects. This memo
> will record that no interviews of in-
> formants shall take place at the present
> time.
> It should be pointed out that case
> Agent is in continual contact with in-
> formants and reports all positive infor-
> mation from informants with appropriate
> dissemination.

Fitzpatrick, however, also betrayed his discomfort with the decision.

> It is further noted that teletype puts
> Boston Division in a "double bind" sit-
> uation in that, as informants, there is
> confidentiality and, as subjects, there
> is advice of rights.

Essentially, Fitzpatrick was stating something that should have been obvious to everyone in the FBI—it was impossible to treat Bulger and Flemmi both as protected informants and as murder suspects (or "subjects" in FBI-speak) if for no other reason than that their Miranda rights might be violated. Again, though, Fitzpatrick decided not to rock the boat. For the time being, he stated, Bulger and Flemmi would continue to be considered sources of information for the Wheeler and Callahan murders.

Throughout most of 1983 the Bureau continued to straddle the fence as the internal pressures simmered. On November 3, Montanari and Brunnick were finally allowed to meet with Bulger and Flemmi in South Boston. Most of the report of the interview is still secret, but the unsealed portions predictably show Bulger and Flemmi denying everything.

Bulger denied that he or Flemmi ever had any business relationship with Callahan, and certainly no relationship with Callahan or anyone else in World Jai Alai. Bulger said that it is not the style of either Bulger or Flemmi to be involved in any criminal activities that they cannot control completely and they generally feel that they could not exercise sufficient control over things outside their own geographical area.

Bulger suggested several times during the course of the interview that if he (Bulger) or Flemmi ever agreed to do a crime for someone such as Callahan for a sum of money, that it would be easy for them to collect the money and not do the crime; there's nothing the guy can do about it, certainly not go to the police.

Bulger said that it would be nonsense to think that he and Flemmi were getting any "skim" out of World Jai Alai because they have nothing to show for it. He said that after some of the Winter Hill people went to prison a few years ago, he and Stevie Flemmi "inherited" the two hundred and fifty thousand dollar Winter Hill debt to the Mafia that had been incurred seven years ago. He advised that $5,000 was repaid almost right away on the principal, but that since then the remaining toward $245,000 has been "put on the shelf" and that he and Flemmi had been paying only the weekly "juice" which amounts to almost $2,500 per week. Bulger said that if they were getting money out of World Jai Alai, which cer-

> tainly would be large sums, they would
> have repaid the $245,000 to get those
> guys off their backs.

The interview was completely self-serving and contained one key lie. By saying they had "no relationship" with anyone at WJA, Bulger and Flemmi were obviously protecting their former FBI handler H. Paul Rico, who was vice president of the company.

The way the interview was handled also indicates that the FBI was intent on tanking the probe.

First, Bulger and Flemmi were interviewed together, violating one of the most fundamental rules of law enforcement investigation. In a case with multiple suspects, virtually all local, state, and federal law enforcement agencies in the U.S. (including the FBI) require that suspects be interviewed separately. It is a primary method police use to tell whether someone is lying or telling the truth. Investigators pore over the different versions, and the more differences between the two accounts they find, the higher the likelihood that the suspects are lying and, therefore, guilty. Suspects together in the same room, however, can easily get their stories straight.

FBI documents also show that Bulger and Flemmi refused to take polygraph tests—probably the only other way to determine whether their story was true—and there is no evidence of any repercussions from their refusal. Bulger, for example, still wasn't even closed. The lack of lie detector testing in the case is even more remarkable considering that, practically since its invention, the polygraph has been one of the FBI's primary investigative tools. In fact, at about the same time, a class of prospective FBI agents at Quantico was being forced to take lie detector tests on whether they had cheated on exams. Other FBI agents, including Morris and even top-ranking FBI officials, have been required to take polygraphs about whether they had leaked information to the press.

In short, the FBI was treating its Top Echelon informants better than its own employees. The reason was obvious: If Bulger and Flemmi were involved in the Wheeler, Halloran, and Callahan murders, the FBI didn't want to know.

CHAPTER SEVEN

Paying the Devil's Due

••••••••••••••••••••••••••••••

Top Echelon informants as killers

UNDER THE GLARE of mercury-vapor lights, the yellow front-end loader moved toward a shallow culvert in the shadow of Interstate 93 South, passing a line of grim-faced men shivering against the cold. A thirty-knot wind made the temperature feel like fifteen-below and whipped little grains of hard snow across their faces. The investigators from the Massachusetts State Police, the DEA, and the Boston Police had picked the coldest day of the winter of 2000 to dig for three bodies that had been missing for more than fifteen years, and they knew the frozen earth wasn't going to give them up without a struggle. Eventually, tents and portable heaters had to be brought in, both for warmth and to shield the dig site from the curious media. The television news stations had already dubbed the place the "Mob Burying Ground."

Eventually, the forensics team moved in and found the bodies right where Kevin Weeks, Whitey Bulger, and Steve Flemmi's top lieutenant said they would be. Weeks had given up the location as part of his proffer—a sort of legal informational tease designed to entice a favorable plea deal out of the federal prosecutors who had charged him with racketeering. His bosses had been exposed as FBI informants, so any further notion of loyalty to them was absurd. Even before he was indicted, Weeks had shown hints that his loyalty was wavering. All the pressure from law enforcement, he told Flemmi, was giving him "gray hairs." It was literally true—a large splash of gray had appeared in the middle of his normally thick, curly brown hair.

After the ground had sufficiently thawed, the investigators found three skeletons, their limbs intertwined as if they had been buried in a last group hug. The investigators didn't believe this was true—Weeks would later confirm that the killings had happened separately and the bodies were moved—but their intertwining was symbolic. There had been no connection between John McIntyre, Bucky Barrett, and Deborah Hussey in life, but in death they were united by their relationships with two dangerous men—Whitey Bulger and Steve Flemmi.

The linking of the three bodies—who all disappeared under suspicious circumstances in the early 1980s—appears to show that after the FBI let Bulger and Flemmi off the hook on the Wheeler-Halloran-Callahan murder investigation, the two informants were sufficiently emboldened to embark on another, equally vicious killing spree.

Just as they had in the horse-race-fixing case, the two informants learned that their association with the FBI made them virtually bulletproof.

Louis Litif

When *Boston Record-American* reporter Paul Corsetti and a rival from the *Boston Herald* pulled up to the crime scene together, Corsetti knew it was going to be a messy one. He was right. A Boston Police detective laid out what had happened: two drug dealers—good friends, actually—had apparently been sitting in a car arguing. Witnesses said the driver abruptly pulled a sawed-off shotgun from under the seat, put it to his friend's left temple and fired, blowing out the passenger side window and half of the passenger's skull. The driver kicked the corpse out of the car and took off.

As the detective was telling the story, Corsetti and the *Herald* reporter edged closer to the body. Peering around a hulking Irish patrolman who was keeping the crowd at bay, they could see that half the skull was missing and that most of the dealer's brain was sitting on the street near the body. An assistant medical examiner scooped up the brain and put it back in the remaining half of the skull with a wet plopping sound. The big cop turned around and smiled.

"Well, that's not going to make him any smarter."

Corsetti roared with laughter as the *Herald* reporter puked on the curb.

Corsetti was from the old school of urban journalism; he met his sources on the streets and in bars and after-hours joints, often in the predawn hours of the morning over a couple of beers. He was as likely to share a drink with Howie Winter and Jimmy Martorano at Chandler's in the South End as he was to toss a few back with the cops a few blocks away in Park Square, a favorite police hangout. There wasn't much in the gore department he hadn't seen during his two tours of duty in Vietnam with the Marines. The war had interrupted the lanky, six-two Corsetti's career in journalism, which was ordained almost from birth, but it also gave him a leg up on the streets, which were regularly spattered with blood in the late sixties and early 1970s.

Newspapering was a family business for the Corsettis. His father Ed was a longtime reporter for the *Boston Record*. His grandfather had run the *Record*'s composing room. Paul was fifteen when he got his first official job in journalism as an office boy, although he had been around the *Record* practically since birth. He worked fetching coffee, running errands, and ferrying film back and forth from crime scenes for the *Record*'s photographers. There were a lot of crime scenes in the mid-1960s. The McLean-McLaughlin war was in full swing, and the papers were doing a brisk business as they gleefully kept the crimson tally. DEATH TOLL SOARS TO 33: LONGSHOREMAN HUGHES VICTIM the *Record*'s huge head-line shouted on March 26, 1966, after the McLaughlin Gang enforcer Connie Hughes was killed by one of twenty-two bullets fired into his car as he was driving down the ex-pressway in Revere. The eighteen-year-old Corsetti enlisted in the Army the same year.

Corsetti came back from Vietnam in '69, landing first in San Francisco, where the hippies spat on his uniform and called him a baby burner, then back to Boston, where things weren't much more hospitable. He enrolled at Newman Preparatory, a school in the Back Bay where a lot of other Vietnam vets—most of whom had also been spat on, liter-ally or figuratively—were also augmenting their incomplete or unimpressive high school transcripts so they could go on to college on the GI Bill. They found solace at Newman, clinging to each other for support in a hostile America that would not appreciate the physical and psychological sacri-fices they'd made for their country.

Many of his Newman Prep friends joined the Boston Po-lice, the State Police, or other departments, and a good num-ber of those quickly made detective because they were older and more worldwise than the other recruits. "They could swallow the blood and gore because they had seen it all in 'Nam," Corsetti said later. Corsetti, meanwhile, was drawn back into the family business. His school friends became some of his best sources on the night beat at the *Record*, which was renamed the *Herald-American* after a merger.

Corsetti had already won several reporting awards by 1980, when he had an interesting conversation with some of his friends on the State Police. Some investigators were complaining bitterly that the FBI had sabotaged their at-tempts to wiretap a suspected Winter Hill Gang hangout on Lancaster Street in the West End. The troopers were making no bones about the fact that they believed the prime target of the probe, James "Whitey" Bulger, was an FBI informant. Bulger was a dangerous man, his sources said. A major

South Boston bookmaker connected to him, Louis Litif, had recently been murdered, and they suspected that Bulger had a hand in it.

Corsetti was engrossed by the Litif story. A stocky, mustachioed man of Syrian descent, Litif came from the same South End/Roxbury neighborhood that spawned Larry Zannino and Stevie Flemmi, but he had managed to ingratiate himself in mostly Irish South Boston in two areas: bookmaking and handball. Litif made himself a fixture on the handball courts at the L Street Bathhouse, playing all comers for $25 or $50 a game. He was also a talented and prolific bookmaker. His reputation as an earner made him popular with South Boston's criminal elite, and at one point police believed he was essentially running the numbers rackets, taking in as much as $200,000 a week. Litif's boss, his sources said, was Whitey Bulger.

When the bookmaking business started tailing off, Litif began dealing in cocaine. A new product didn't bring any change in the way he conducted his business; if anything, Litif became more violent. He already had one pistol-whipping arrest on his record from 1975, and he still pulled out the .357 Magnum he carried in his waistband whenever he felt the urge. He wore natty monogrammed suede loafers and wasn't above kicking someone bloody with them if they were late with the money they owed. The newspapers reported that he was suspected of shooting a man six times after an argument in the alley outside Hap's Lounge, the barroom he co-owned with another bookmaker, Jimmy Matera. Somehow, the doctors at Boston City Hospital managed to patch Litif's alleged victim together.

Matera wasn't as lucky. A burly, certified tough guy in his own right, who listed his occupation as a business agent for a construction workers' union, his fuse was almost as short as Litif's. When a water bill for the bar came in at an unexpectedly high $500, the two men got in each other's faces and neither would back down. Matera slapped Litif across the face. Litif walked away. The next day, August 30, 1979, appearing much calmer, Litif suggested that he and Matera go down to the cellar, check the meter again and split the bill fifty-fifty.

The day bartender at Hap's later told police that Matera turned to him before going downstairs with Litif and said: "If I don't come up in a reasonable amount of time, then come down and check on me because I might be dead." Matera's words were prophetic. When he got to the foot of the stairs, he found himself staring at a .357. He took five bullets in the face and was dead before he hit the ground.

With a murder rap hanging over his head, Litif knew enough to know that he knew too much. After the Matera murder, fears that he would cut a deal made him persona non grata in the South Boston underworld. Someone scrawled the word "nigger" on his car—a sure sign that Southie, always plagued by racial tensions, had turned on him. He began taking elaborate precautions, fortifying his apartment in Quincy with shotguns and an alarm, and putting the name "Nick Noonan" on his mailbox and "Louis Woodward" on his telephone bill.

It wasn't enough. Seven months later Litif's body was found in the trunk of his Lincoln in the South End, not far from where he grew up.

From the information he was piecing together on Litif, Corsetti knew he had a good story. Right away, his sources were telling him that Whitey Bulger was suspected in the murder. It made sense, because before Litif was killed, the reporter had heard that Bulger had ultimately been the backer and chief beneficiary of Litif's bookmaking operation. Corsetti usually had what he liked to call an "in my pocket" story, something he could write on a Saturday, when the *Record-American* paid guaranteed overtime, so one Friday afternoon in late April 1980, Corsetti walked over to Boston Police Headquarters on Berkeley Street to see if he could get enough information to cobble together a story.

In those days, Boston reporters could walk right into police headquarters and nobody would bat an eyelash. Corsetti bounded up to the second floor offices of the Criminal Investigative Division. The room was empty except for Edward Walsh, the detective from South Boston whose beat was the North End. Corsetti liked Eddie Walsh, who knew a lot about organized crime and generally gave straight answers on Mafia questions.

"Hey, Eddie." Corsetti pulled up a chair and kicked his feet up on Walsh's dented metal desk.

"Hey."

"I need a story for the Sunday paper and I'm working on the Litif thing. What'ya got?"

"There's not much I know there."

"I heard Whitey Bulger might be involved."

"Huh?"

"What's this I hear from the State Police, that the FBI tipped off Whitey to the bug in his garage over on Lancaster Street? I heard the staties are complaining to anyone who will listen. Is it true?"

"No. Nobody got tipped off."

"They say Whitey is an informant for the FBI, is that true?"

"No. No. Jesus. That's ridiculous. That's crazy."

"What's the relationship between Billy and Whitey? I mean, there's something that's never gotten any scrutiny before. Is there something there that we should know about? Something funny? I mean, one brother is the king of the underworld, the other—"

Corsetti saw Walsh's eyes flash serious. The cop leaned forward.

"Listen," he said, sounding almost angry. "The connection there is nil, and I will tell you this story. After the father died, the family had a wake. Did Whitey show up with everyone else? No. He waited until after closing hours and went in a back door to visit his father one last time. He did it so he wouldn't embarrass his brother by being there at the wake in front of all the mourners."

Corsetti was having a drink the next night, after his Saturday overtime shift, in the Dockside, a bar in the popular

Quincy Marketplace shopping area. The place was jammed, as usual, so Corsetti was standing pretty much in the middle of the aisle. He had just taken a drag off a cigarette when a man walked up to him and grabbed one of the lapels of his jacket. The guy wasn't particularly big—Corsetti, at six-two, had at least five inches on him—but he was shockingly strong, and he dragged Corsetti a few feet over toward a corner.

"Do you know who I am?" the man hissed.

"I don't have a clue who you are."

"Well, my name is Whitey Bulger, motherfucker, and I kill people for a living."

"Well, you certainly have my attention," Corsetti said, frantically trying to glance down to see if Bulger's hands contained a gun or a knife.

"I understand you're doing a story about me and my brother."

Corsetti breathed half a sigh of relief. He honestly hadn't been planning to write a story about the Bulger brothers, just the Litif murder, so he had a chance to defuse the confrontation with Bulger without lying.

"No, that's not the case. I checked it out with the Boston PD and they said there's no connection with either of your activities," Corsetti said. "It was just a shot-in-the-dark question."

"Listen to me, motherfucker. I know where you live, I know what kind of car you drive, and I know where your daughter goes to school. You'd be easy."

Bulger released his grip on Corsetti's jacket and snaked his way out through the door. Corsetti put another beer into his still-shaking hand—there was no way he could face the ride home without another drink. He walked to his car and closed his eyes when he turned the key in the ignition, expecting an explosion. The car roared to life. He drove home and looked tearfully into the bedroom where his five-year-old girl lay peacefully sleeping.

He told his editors about the encounter the next morning.

They called the Boston Police, who put Corsetti under twenty-four-hour police guard until he could get a pistol permit. He began carrying a small .22 automatic holstered in the small of his back. After a few days he looked at it and decided he would probably do more damage if he simply threw the gun at Bulger.

To his credit, though, Corsetti never backed down on the Litif story. It ran on the front page of the *Record-American* and won a regional news writing award—with Bulger's name included not as a suspect but as Litif's boss. Before the story ran, though, Corsetti appealed to Jerry Angiulo and Larry Zannino in the North End through a friendly source in the underworld, hoping he could get Bulger to back off.

Sorry, the friend said.

"We can't do anything with the guy, he's uncontrollable," his friend said.

The best the North End could offer, the friend said, was to have an intermediary close to Bulger when he read the story to gauge his reaction. On the afternoon the story came out, Corsetti's friend called and said, "Don't worry about it."

Kevin Curry's first-floor suite at the corner of North and Commercial streets, on the outskirts of the North End, was as much a clubhouse for his clients as it was a working law office. Curry, a tall Irishman with a sonorous voice and a weakness for a good conspiracy theory, represented many of the low-level bookmakers in the North End in the late 1970s. On warm summer nights Curry's garrulous, snappily dressed clients would stop by his office, shoot the breeze, then move to the High Tide, a seedy barroom next door.

Eddie Walsh, the Boston Police detective, was another frequent visitor, though he rarely allowed himself to be seen inside Curry's office—the building's exterior was floor-to-ceiling glass, and it wouldn't do for Curry's clients to see their lawyer as too chummy with the police. But Curry and "Walshie" could help each other once in a while, like the time when some office equipment Curry and his partner purchased from a local dealer turned out to be hot. The lawyers got their money back, no questions asked. When the detective wanted to chat, Curry would either get in Walsh's car for a ride or they would agree to meet somewhere else. On one particular afternoon in March 1980, Curry was so anxious to see Walsh that he dispensed with their usual circumspections and flagged the detective's battered sedan right on the street.

The aggressive, thirty-something lawyer possessed what he thought was the breakthrough of a lifetime. Curry had been contacted by a new witness, who was not only going to get one of his clients off the hook, but would blow the lid off corruption inside the Boston Police Department.

About two years earlier, the Boston Police Drug Control Unit had raided the Hen's Nest, Larry Goldman's luncheonette in downtown Boston. Goldman, who had a prior record of drug offenses, hired Curry as his defense lawyer, insisting that the cocaine found at the restaurant had been planted to frame him. It wasn't exactly an original story. Besides, Goldman was still on parole for a federal drug charge, so even Curry, who was usually willing to believe the police were capable of anything, was skeptical. Yet Goldman also had an intriguing story about a mysterious caller, who identified himself only as "Nick." During their conversation, Goldman said, Nick had recited the chronology and circumstance of the Hen's Nest bust and Goldman's subsequent court appearances to the smallest detail—as if he were reading off a police report.

"We should meet. Alone," Curry told Goldman.

He didn't say why. A worried Goldman called Curry, who reported the overture to Eddie Walsh.[13] Goldman agreed to meet "Nick" at the Last Hurrah, the basement bar in the Parker House Hotel, if Walsh and another detective would be there watching.

---

[13]Walsh, through John Connolly, later denied talking to Curry about Litif.

Goldman was stunned by what "Nick" had to say at their meeting.

"I have friends among certain members of the Drug Control Unit. For ten grand I can straighten your case out for you. And I want some coke too. Maybe eight or ten ounces," Nick said.

"Why should I believe you?" Goldman asked.

"Because we fucking know everything about you. Don't believe me? Wanna know the reason they set you up now? Because you only had twenty days left on your federal parole, that's why," Nick said.

Goldman paled. On the day of the arrest he had been exactly twenty days shy of parole.

"I'll think about it," Goldman said.

"You do that," the man said. "The next guy to contact you is the man that's going to make the deal."

According to court documents, Goldman said he then received a call on his nonpublished telephone number from Boston Police Detective Robert Mack, who had applied for the search warrant for the Hen's Nest. "We should meet," Mack suggested. Goldman agreed. Mack picked up Goldman near the South Station Amtrak terminal and they drove to Santoro's Subs, a sandwich shop on the South Boston waterfront. "Nick" must have been the Bad Cop in the scheme, Goldman thought, because Mack seemed to be playing the Good Cop (although still Corrupt Cop) role.

"We got a gold watch during that search," Mack said in calm, soothing tones. "It looks like a real antique, like it meant something to someone. It wasn't on the [search warrant] return, so ordinarily it would be gone. But I know the guy who's got it and I can get it back for you.

"You should make the deal," Mack said. "It'll all be okay then."

Again Goldman said he would think about it.

Goldman eventually told his story to the State Police. No criminal charges were brought, but Mack retired on September 30, 1978, after only ten years on the force, well short of his pension.

Kevin Curry, meanwhile, learned through his own sources that "Nick" was actually a South Boston bookmaker and hoodlum named Louis Litif. Curry spent the entire summer of 1978 trying to track Litif down—using connections through other wiseguy clients and scouring underworld watering holes—without success. In the meantime, now convinced that Goldman's story was true, Curry tried in vain to sell it to prosecutors. First the U.S. Attorney's office turned him down, then state Attorney General Frank Bellotti's office.

If Goldman thought Mack's retirement was the end of his troubles, he was sadly mistaken. At just about the time that Mack was being cashiered, his old friends in the Drug Control Unit hit Goldman again, pulling over his car in Boston's working-class Dorchester section and placing him under arrest. The police, including detectives Alton Frost and Walter Robinson, found no drugs in the car, but took Goldman home to the nearby basement apartment he shared with his wife and eleven-year-old daughter, to execute a search warrant. The police later said they found a plastic bag containing fourteen ounces of cocaine on top of an electric organ in Goldman's daughter's bedroom. Again Goldman insisted that the cocaine was a plant. Two tickets to the play *Man of La Mancha,* $5,000 worth of jewelry, and $8,000 in cash hidden in the back of a shadow box were gone after the police left. Goldman's sister-in-law said she saw Frost take the money out of the shadow box, roll it into a wad and stick it in his pocket.

Curry got a judge to force the District Attorney's office to turn over the name of the Drug Unit informant who had given the police the information for the search of Goldman's apartment. The informant agreed to swear in an affidavit that he had been coerced into cooperating against Goldman and that Frost's search warrant application contained numerous falsehoods—including that he had seen prior cocaine deals transacted inside the apartment. In fact, the informant said, the first time he met Goldman was on the night of the raid.

Armed with the informant's affidavit, Curry went to Newman Flanagan, the new Suffolk County District Attorney, who referred the case to the Boston Police Internal Affairs Division.

The Internal Affairs probe confirmed that it was Frost who had searched the shadow box. They also confirmed that the missing $8,000 came not from drug proceeds but was a loan from a friend to help pay Goldman's legal expenses from the Hen's Nest case. Frost, meanwhile, had gone out on disability after being being shot in the thigh trying to disarm a drug dealer. The alleged dealer was never found, and some of Frost's colleagues suspected that the wound was self-inflicted.

Frost was indicted for larceny by the Suffolk County District Attorney's office and found guilty by a state judge after a jury waived trial. A quirk in Massachusetts criminal law at the time, though, allowed defendants what amounted to a second bite at the apple—automatic appeal of a judge's verdict to a second trial *with* a jury. Defense attorneys loved the system because it gave them a free preview of the prosecution's case and strategy.

During the second trial, Frost took the stand in his own defense and denied taking the money. He did admit being strapped for cash due to a bad business deal, and to having difficulty paying his mortgage, alimony, child support, and other debts on his police salary. Goldman, meanwhile, took a beating on the witness stand, admitting his role in a burglary where a man was killed[14] and taking the Fifth on numerous questions about his drug dealing. Frost broke down and wept when the jury found him not guilty on all counts.

The Boston Police Department, while denying any widespread corruption, quietly disbanded the narcotics drug unit over the next year, sending sixteen of the seventeen detectives to other assignments, including Walter Robinson, who "found" the cocaine in Goldman's apartment, according to

---

[14]Goldman insisted that his accomplices committed the murder.

the Internal Affairs investigation. Curry filed a civil suit on Goldman's behalf, but it died when Goldman was busted in 1982 as part of a major federal cocaine smuggling sting. Curry finally got a small measure of satisfaction in the mid-1990s when Robinson was forced to admit to a federal judge that he was exactly what Curry said he was—a dirty cop. After pleading guilty to a long string of drug money rip-offs, Robinson went to prison.

In the days following Frost's acquittal, though, Curry was still burning that the police had been able to dispose of the entire Drug Control Unit mess like so much cocaine down the toilet. In early 1980 he caught a break. He got an unexpected call from Louis Litif, the man he had unsuccessfully tried to track down for nearly two years.

"I hear you've been looking for me," Litif said.

"Who is this?"

"Louis Litif."

"I have been looking for you. I wanted to talk to you about what happened to Larry Goldman," Curry said.

"Okay, I want to talk to you too. I'll meet you at Anthony's Pier 4," Litif said, naming a date and a time. "Come alone."

Curry went to the venerable fish house at the appointed time, but no Litif. He sat on a bar stool for nearly an hour nursing a beer, until the barman approached him, telephone in hand.

"You Kevin Curry?"

"Yes."

"It's for you."

Curry picked up the receiver.

"What are you, an idiot?" It was Litif.

"What do you mean? Where the hell are you?"

"You're in the middle of the fucking bar. Anyone can fucking see you. We'd get spotted for sure."

Curry was nonplussed. Litif had chosen the meeting place, so why was *he* the idiot? He was relieved when Litif called again and set another meeting at the Arch Street

Tulsa Police Department Sergeant Michael Huff *(left)* with former Tulsa prosecutor Jerry Truster.

(Photo courtesy of the author)

U.S. Justice Department officials at a press conference announcing that former FBI agent John Connolly had been indicted. *(From left to right):* Connecticut Deputy U.S. Attorney John Durham, U.S. Attorney Donald K. Stern, Boston FBI Special Agent in Charge Barry Mawn, and FBI Inspector Gary Bald.

(Photo courtesy of the author)

Assistant U.S. Attorney Fred Wyshak, a harsh FBI critic and the architect of the Massachusetts State Police DEA-IRS investigation that led to Bulger and Flemmi's 1995 indictment for racketeering.

(Photo courtesy of the author)

FBI Director Louis Freeh appears at an August 5, 1998 press conference in Boston and admits that the Bureau "made significant mistakes and there was probably some wrongdoing by some of our people."

(Photo courtesy of the author)

Detectives stand over the body of William "Billy" Bennett. Flemmi's double cross of his allies, the Bennett brothers, got him in the Mafia's good graces and made him an effective Top Echelon informant.

(Photo courtesy of the *Boston Herald*)

Francis P. "Cadillac Frank" Salemme *(far right)*, who was betrayed for two decades by his best friend, Steve Flemmi, appears in court with attorney Richard Egbert *(center)* and son Frank Jr.

(Photo courtesy of the *Boston Herald*)

Boston FBI Assistant Special Agent in Charge Larry Potts *(far right),* who approved the continued use of Steve Flemmi and Whitey Bulger as Top Echelon informants and later resigned from the Bureau in disgrace over his role in the Ruby Ridge scandal.

(Photo courtesy of the *Boston Herald*)

U.S. Attorney Donald K. Stern, who made the decision to prosecute Bulger and Flemmi.

(Photo courtesy of the *Boston Herald*)

James J. "Whitey" Bulger, South Boston crime boss, alleged killer and protected FBI informant.

(Photo courtesy of FBI)

Stephen "The Rifleman" Flemmi arrives for one of his court appearances escorted by two unidentified investigators in the early 1970s.

(Photo courtesy of the *Boston Herald*)

Patriarca Mafia family soldier and Top Echelon Informant Angelo "Sonny" Mercurio, who set up the assassination of boss Francis P. "Cadillac Frank" Salemme while working for the FBI.

(Photo courtesy of the *Boston Herald*)

FBI surveillance photo of the infamous Mafia induction ceremony at 34 Guild Street. Boss Raymond Patriarca Jr. *(left, in sunglasses)* arrives at the ceremony escorted by one of his soldiers.

(Photo courtesy of FBI)

Tulsa, Oklahoma business tycoon Roger Wheeler Sr., who was murdered by Winter Hill hit man John Martorano, allegedly on orders from Whitey Bulger and Steve Flemmi.

(Photo courtesy of David Wheeler)

Vincent J. "Jimmy the Bear" Flemmi and his prize witness, Joseph "the Animal" Barboza. Many believe Flemmi was spared a murder charge by FBI Special Agent Paul Rico as a favor to his informant brother Steve.

(Photo courtesy of the *Boston Herald*)

Former FBI Agent Dennis Condon, who first approached Whitey Bulger about being an FBI informant.

(Photo courtesy of the *Boston Herald*)

New England Organized Crime Strike Force Chief Jeremiah O'Sullivan, whose decision to keep Bulger and Flemmi out of a 1979 horse race fixing case gave the two gangsters free rein.

(Photo courtesy of the *Boston Herald*)

rine, a church in the middle of downtown Boston. It was
cked with Catholic businesspeople for daytime mass on
uoly days, but quiet and nearly empty most other times. The
building also had several exits, making it a good place to
meet.

A dark, mustachioed man walked up to the pew where
Curry was sitting.

"You Curry?"

"Yeah."

"Louis Litif. Let's go outside and talk."

They walked outside and sat on a bench and talked. Litif
apologized for the Pier 4 meeting, but explained that he had
to make sure Curry wasn't being followed or working with
the police. Litif was in trouble; he was under indictment for
killing his business partner. Litif also said he was afraid because one of the Boston Police Drug Control Unit detectives
had threatened him. He said he had been impressed by what
Curry had done for Goldman, getting Frost indicted and
Goldman's cases dismissed.

I want a deal, Litif said. What have you got? Curry asked.
Litif then told a fantastic story. Not only was Curry right
about the widespread corruption in the drug unit, but some
of the drugs that Litif himself was putting out on the street
had come directly from the DCU evidence locker. He would
testify against cops, his boss in Southie, Whitey Bulger,
everyone he had ever done business with. "I want to go all
the way," he said. "I'll tell them everything."

Curry's wingtips were three feet off the ground walking
back to his office. He said he flagged down his old friend
Eddie Walsh the next time he saw him.

"Eddie, did you hear?" Curry said.

"Hear what?" Walsh replied.

"Litif. Louis Litif. He's going to be a witness, he wants a
deal and he's going all the way."

"No shit."

"I'm finally going to get those bastards, all of them."

"Huh," was all Walsh had to say in reply. Curry looked in

the passenger seat and recognized John Connolly, the FBI agent who he had heard was Walsh's cousin. Connolly sat stone-faced, saying nothing as Walsh excused himself and drove off.

A few weeks later Litif's body was found in a green plastic garbage bag in the trunk of his big Lincoln in the South End.

Two decades later Curry and some investigators are convinced that he unwittingly had a part in Litif's demise. Had he known then what he knows now, Curry said, he would never have told either Walsh or Connolly what he knew about Litif. John Connolly has admitted that Litif was one of his informants and had been for years. Connolly was also a regular on the L Street handball courts, and had recruited Litif there for his sizable stable of sources. As the handler for both Litif and Bulger, Connolly knew exactly how Litif could incriminate Bulger if he switched from behind-the-scenes informant to cooperating witness.

"Do I think Connolly tipped off Bulger? Of course I do," Curry said.

Connolly and the FBI, of course, knew all about Litif's murder. They were told about it by the same informant who gave them the Wheeler homicide, Brian Halloran. In fact, Halloran said he was the last person to see the doomed bookmaker alive.

Halloran told the FBI that he picked up Litif early on the morning of April 12, 1980, and drove him to the front of Triple-O's pub, Bulger's hangout on West Broadway in South Boston. Halloran said he saw Litif go into the bar, and a few minutes later he saw a body wrapped in a green plastic garbage bag being carried out of the bar by Bulger and an associate. Two years later it would be Halloran in Litif's shoes, the potential liability, running scared and futilely trying to make a deal with the government.

Questions of Curry's credibility will undoubtedly be raised as the FBI scandal continues to unfold. He did himself no favors in that department by becoming involved in one of the most bizarre ethical controversies in the history of the Boston bar. In the early 1990s the family of one of the two brothers who founded the $2 billion Demoulas supermarket chain sued their cousins, claiming they had been defrauded out of their share of the company. In the annals of New England legal history, for sheer duration, high-stakes, and acrimony, the case had no peer in civil litigation. One side, on the losing end of two important rulings by a Middlesex Superior Court judge, hired Curry to investigate their belief that the judge was unfairly biased against them. The case appealed to Curry's belief that most aspects of the legal system in Boston were, in one way or another, fixed. So he and a private investigator cooked up a daring—and in retrospect, incredibly stupid—plan to expose the judge's bias. They bamboozled the judge's clerk into thinking they were representatives of a big international law firm looking to hire him. They asked him a lot of questions about the cases he worked on, including the supermarket case, ostensibly to judge his competence—but really in an attempt to find out whether the judge was biased against them.

Curry and two other lawyers, former Assistant U.S. Attorney Gary Crossen and former Nike Corp. chairman Richard Donahue, confronted the law clerk and pressured him to testify against the judge. Unfortunately for Curry, the law clerk ran to the FBI and accused the lawyers of extortion. *He* was wired at the next meeting with Crossen and Donahue and turned the tape over to the FBI. His lawyer held a press conference, alleging that Crossen and Donahue's actions amounted to extortion. The lawyers insisted they had been zealously representing the interests of their client and were trying to root out judicial bias. A team of Justice Department lawyers in Washington probed the case for several years without bringing any charges, but the damage to Crossen and Donahue's reputations—and Curry's— had been done.

Yet other evidence: Corsetti's story, Morris's testimony, etc., appears to overwhelmingly back up Curry's account, pointing toward Connolly as a leak of informant information to Bulger and Flemmi—with fatal results. Indeed, in his monumental *Salemme* decision, Judge Wolf found:

"In an effort to protect Bulger and Flemmi, Morris and Connolly also identified for them at least a dozen other individuals who were either FBI informants or sources for other law enforcement agencies."

Arthur "Bucky" Barrett

After much of the town of Medford had emptied out for Memorial Day weekend of 1980, several men lugging concrete drills and acetylene torches broke into an optometrist's shop next to the Depositor's Trust Co., a popular local bank. They moved slowly, deliberately, making sure they weren't seen or heard.

They moved some furniture away from a preselected spot on the wall and used sledgehammers to break through cinder block into the bank next door. They weren't worried about the bank's alarm, it had been taken care of with a nine-volt battery and a resistor spliced to the wires leading from the bank to a panel in the Medford Police station. Once the hole was big enough, they climbed through, onto the twelve-inch, steel-reinforced concrete ceiling of the Depositor's Trust's vault. Once there, they put the drills and torches to work, cutting another hole big enough to climb through.

For the next three days they took turns drilling and prying open safe deposit boxes and looting the cash from the shelves. They took their time, ignoring a crowd gathered right on the sidewalk outside the bank for the town's annual parade. They had little fear of being caught—three of the six conspirators were current or former police officers, two of them shift commanders, Medford Police Lieutenant Thomas K. Doherty, and Captain Gerald W. Clemente of the Metropolitan Police, a state-run force that also had jurisdiction in the town. In an ironic role reversal, while they were looting the bank over the weekend, the robbers actually called Doherty to report suspicious noise coming from the Brigham's Ice Cream shop next door. A squad car checked out the noise, which turned out to be a night manager working late, and the robbers resumed their work.

By the time they cleared out, they had stolen more than $1.5 million in cash and as much as another $2 million in jewelry, negotiable securities, and other valuables from five hundred safe deposit boxes. It was a far cry from what the original plan had been—a simple burglary at a television store in Somerville dreamed up by Joe Bangs, a part-time drug dealer and full-time Metropolitan Police Department detective. Bangs and a fellow dealer had set up the television store heist and enlisted Arthur "Bucky" Barrett, who was renowned as an expert in bypassing alarm systems. They brought the idea to Clemente, who was thinking bigger—his friend Tom Doherty in Medford actually had the blueprints for a bank with a badly antiquated alarm system.

Lucrative as the heist was, the reality was nothing compared to the rumors and speculation in the newspapers, reporting that the take was upward of $15 million and $20 million, which would have made it the biggest robbery in New England history. Over the next few years, the FBI's investigation into the robbery fizzled, but among Barrett's criminal brethren, word spread that he was the Croesus of the underworld, with millions stashed away from the Depositor's Trust, other burglaries, and drug deals. The stories did not escape the notice of Whitey Bulger and Stevie Flemmi. In reality, Barrett told his friend and marijuana-smuggling partner Joe Murray, his share of the robbery had been just $175,000 plus some "swag" from the safe deposit boxes.

In early 1983, Murray, his brother Michael, Barrett, Joe Bangs, and several other men involved in Murray's marijuana operation were hanging out at Barrett's bar, Rascals, in the Financial District, unaware that a group of DEA and FBI agents had them under surveillance. The rival agencies usually didn't work together, but President Ronald Reagan had declared a national "War on Drugs," and the Justice Department was pushing the agencies together in an awkward shotgun marriage.

In early April the agents spotted Michael Murray's car parked behind a warehouse on D Street in South Boston, so they moved their surveillance operation there. On the afternoon of April 6, they watched as a pickup truck with a camper top drove into the warehouse, then left again twenty minutes later, followed by two pickup trucks. The agents moved in, pulling over the three vehicles loaded with bales of marijuana. The agents arrested the drivers and entered the warehouse, expecting to find the men who had loaded the marijuana onto the trucks. They found only a huge pile of pot, fifteen tons in all.

After throwing together a quickie search warrant, the agents seized the marijuana and began preparing drug indictments against both Murray brothers and Bucky Barrett. One of the FBI agents, Roderick Kennedy, called John Connolly, who dropped a bombshell. Joe Murray, Connolly said, was required "to pay rent to Mr. Bulger and Mr. Flemmi for having used South Boston as a storage warehouse for his drug activity."

"I think there was a payment of $60,000 to $90,000," Kennedy later testified at the *Salemme* hearings. "It was like rent money for having gone into South Boston and using that area for illegal drug activity."

"In fact, Mr. Connolly told you that that was the initial payment?" he was asked.

"Yes, sir."

"You understood from that conversation, did you not, that Mr. Murray was expected to make more payments?"

"That was my understanding."

The new FBI-DEA cooperation was only going so far, though. Kennedy didn't share Connolly's information with his DEA counterparts or with the prosecutor in the warehouse case. It was understood within the FBI office,

Kennedy said, that any information about the two Top Echelon informants was confidential to the Bureau.

Yet just because Bulger and Flemmi were never charged in the warehouse case didn't mean it wasn't a potential problem. The Murrays were Charlestown guys—the neighborhood was famous for its code of silence about criminal activity—and could be reasonably expected to stand up if the law pressured them to cooperate. Barrett was another story. There were rumors that he had already fed some information to the authorities (which family members later vehemently denied), and with both a drug prosecution and the Depositor's Trust case hanging over his head, it didn't take a criminal mastermind to figure he was ripe to become a government witness.

Bulger and Flemmi, the master strategists, figured out a way to head off a potential problem and enrich themselves at the same time, according to FBI reports and information given to investigators by John Morris and Kevin Weeks. The two informants had actually originally been the ones who told the FBI that Barrett was one of the Medford burglars.

Then Bulger suggested that Morris tell Barrett that "Whitey and Stevie may try to shake you down for your cut of the Medford Depositor's Trust burglary."

Later, Morris testified: "I recall a recommendation—I believe it was primarily Mr. Bulger—that we could approach Barrett and use their names, that we had picked up informant information that they were aware that Barrett was involved in the bank burglary, and they would be looking for a piece of the score. It was an effort to gain Barrett's cooperation by approaching Barrett and giving him this information, hoping that he would find that information credible and cooperate in the Depositor's Trust investigation." Morris made the approach, but Barrett turned him down, saying he would take his chances.

Amazingly, Bulger and Flemmi then *did* shake down Barrett, according to Joe Murray, Kevin Weeks, and allegations in court documents.

On the night Bucky Barrett disappeared, Murray said he was down at the Constitution Marina, a boat landing for private yachts near where the historic USS *Constitution* is berthed in the Charlestown Navy Yard. A friend from South Boston told Murray that his brother Michael was looking for him down at the liquor store he owned.

"Bucky called," Mike Murray told his brother. "He's going to call you back, he said it's an emergency."

Joe Murray hung around for a while until the phone rang again. It was Bucky.

"I need money, Joe, a lot of money. Tonight," Barrett said.

"How much?" Murray asked.

"A couple of million."

"What?"

"I'm serious."

"Jesus, it's eight or nine o'clock, where the hell am I supposed to get that kind of cash right now?"

"I *need* it, Joe. I've been *tied up* all day."

"What do you want me to do? I can't get it."

"I could give you up in a minute Joe, you know that—"

Murray slammed down the phone.

The next day, Barrett's partner from Rascals, Jake Rooney, and Bucky's wife Elaine, both obviously worried, pulled Murray aside and told him a foreboding story of the events of the previous night. Elaine Barrett had received a call telling her to take their baby, leave the house in Quincy, and "leave the alarm off." She and the infant spent the night at a friend's house. When she returned the next morning, she found that the inside of the house had been torn apart and a shoe box where her husband sometimes kept bundles of cash was on the floor, empty. She hadn't heard from her husband since and she was worried that something had happened to him.

Rooney said that a cabdriver had come into Rascals that night looking for Bucky's cut of the receipts. Murray nodded. It was another ominous sign—sending a cabdriver to pick up money was an old Winter Hill Gang tactic.

Word on the street later confirmed what Murray suspected—Whitey Bulger and Stevie Flemmi had kidnapped Barrett, forced him to make as many telephone calls as he could, then killed him. There were also rumors that Whitey and Stevie had yanked out Barrett's teeth one by one in an attempt to extract the secret of his supposed riches. When the State Police and the DEA dug up Barrett's body seventeen years later, the skull was missing most of its teeth.

Morris never told his FBI colleagues about Bulger's plan. Again Bulger and Flemmi had insulated themselves. The supervisor of the FBI's Organized Crime Squad had essentially been part of their plan to shake down Barrett. Morris was effectively neutralized.

By the time Barrett disappeared, Whitey Bulger and Stevie Flemmi were masters at using the FBI to shield them from prosecution and get rid of their competition. One of the motives for Barrett's murder may have been his potential to implicate them in a drug case and spoil their carefully crafted image as gangsters who never dealt in drugs.

Part of their longevity as FBI informants was based on the myth—particularly for Bulger in South Boston—that while they might be involved in other crimes, even murder, they frowned on drug dealing. Elderly women, taxi drivers, and junior high students were all schooled in the same fable: Whitey kept the drugs out of Southie. There is evidence that John Connolly was careful to perpetuate the same impression inside the FBI. In a 1980 memo written to SAC Larry Sarhatt, justifying Flemmi's continuation as an informant, Connolly even blamed himself for sullying their reputations by sending the gangster to talk to drug dealers believed to have information about a federal judge's murder.

It should be noted that source's contacts, at my direction, with individuals thought to possess information regarding the Judge's murder may have resulted in

```
the false belief that source is involved
in narcotics.
```

Four years later, when Connolly again had to justify Bulger's informant status when the FBI was deciding whether to join the DEA investigation, he did it again.

```
[Bulger] stated that they find it hard
to believe that Colonel JACK O'DONOVAN
would be part of a drug investigation on
them as they feel he knows better.
```

Connolly's memos were directly contradicted by information in the FBI's own files. Informant reports traced Flemmi's drug connections back into the 1970s, including several memos that outline Flemmi's alleged ties to a drug-related murder.

```
For information, the MDC police, Boston
Massachusetts allege that in 1977,
Daniel Jasie, a narcotics distributor . . .
was shotgunned to death in what was be-
lieved to be a drug-related murder in the
Randolph, Massachusetts area. Jasie's
murder was allegedly ordered by Stevie
Flemmi.
```

As for Bulger, a 1982 memo from another FBI informant said another drug dealer was "making five thousand dollars a week from drugs and . . . paying Whitey Bulger a large percentage for the right to operate South Boston." Of course, that was a relative pittance compared to the $60,000 to $90,000 Murray was paying to Bulger for the privilege of using his warehouse, the fact Rod Kennedy had been told by John Connolly. Connolly was careful, however, to file an informant memorandum the day after the warehouse seizure, suggesting that they *weren't* involved.

> Source advised that the Murray crew are
> concerned that Whitey Bulger is upset
> with them for storing marijuana in
> Southie. Bulger got word through Pat Nee
> to the Charlestown crew that he is upset
> and that cops . . . think that the South
> Boston crew had a piece of the action.

Connolly seemed to be so close to his informants that Rod Kennedy said he warned him that Bulger and Flemmi might someday be his undoing. "Basically . . . I suggested to him that, if and when Mr. Bulger and Mr. Flemmi are arrested and indicted, the first thing they'll do is turn on him and try to hand him up."

Connolly replied that he wasn't worried, he had covered himself. "I'm writing everything down," he said, according to Kennedy. "But Jimmy Bulger and Stevie Flemmi are way too smart for the FBI to ever catch them."

John McIntyre, Marijuana, and the IRA

When the "Mob Burying Ground" was discovered in Dorchester, Bucky Barrett's bones were found mixed in with those of another man, John McIntyre. As it turned out, McIntyre was a neighbor of Barrett's, from a section of Quincy known as Squantum.

McIntyre was the son of a former U.S. Army intelligence officer and a German woman who met right after World War II at an American spy installation in West Germany. They returned to the U.S. to raise their family in the seaside city in the early 1950s. Their eldest boy, John Jr., enlisted in the U.S. Army in 1970, hoping to follow in his father's footsteps. He was court-martialed a year later, after MPs found a bag of marijuana in his footlocker. His family insisted later that it had been planted by one of his Army buddies who feared that John would be sent to Vietnam in the late, bloody stages of the war there. He successfully appealed his conviction and went back into the military, but without any illusions that it would be a career. He was honorably discharged in 1974.

When he returned to his hometown, he took up fish and clam poaching for a while, and after being arrested again, tried to make a living as a legitimate lobsterman. It was on the run-down docks where McIntyre berthed his lobster boat, the *Royal Scam*, that he met Joe Murray. McIntyre was impressed by the charming Murray, who was running marijuana into Boston Harbor and guns over to Ireland as a top local supporter of the Provisional Irish Republican Army.

Murray's support for the cause of freedom in Northern Ireland was infectious. In 1982 John McIntyre pledged his lifelong support for the "provos" in a secret ceremony, and began helping Murray smuggle thousands of plastic-wrapped bales into Boston Harbor on board a small fleet of fishing boats. The plan was sort of a Boston-to-Belfast version of Oliver North's Iran-Contra scheme—Murray was recycling some of the proceeds from the drug sales into gun purchases for the IRA. When McIntyre had a chance to visit Northern Ireland, the poverty and suffering caused by "the Troubles" convinced him that he and Murray were doing the right thing.

The D Street warehouse raid effectively shut down Murray's fishing boat smuggling operation, so he came up with a new plan—he would shift his marijuana smuggling operations to a two-hundred-foot freighter called the *Ramsland*, which had been equipped with a secret compartment in its keel that could hold up to forty tons of dope. His guns, grenades, and ammunition for the IRA would be smuggled into Ireland on a second boat, an old fishing trawler called the *Valhallah*.

Bulger associate Pat Nee, like Murray a diehard IRA backer, was enlisted to compile the arsenal. Nee used the fake name "Patrick Mullen" and the address of a South

Boston yacht club where he was a member to gather up an impressive cache of legal and illegal guns, including 112 assault rifles and shotguns, fifty-one handguns, bulletproof vests, seventy thousand rounds of ammunition, and several rocket warheads, which were ready to go in mid-September. With Kevin Weeks acting as a lookout from a nearby hilltop, the weapons were loaded onto the *Valhallah's* hold and the ship—already laden with 52,000 pounds of crushed ice to maintain the fiction that they were embarking on a swordfishing trip—set out for Ireland from the port of Gloucester.

The eleven-day trip was uneventful, but by the time the American boat reached the Irish coast off the Kerry peninsula for its early morning rendezvous with an Irish trawler, the *Marita Ann,* a bad storm was whipping up. The weapons were transferred in cargo nets over a cable strung precariously between the decks of the two ships, which were pitching heavily in twenty-foot seas. Moments after they were safely stowed aboard on the *Marita Ann,* a Royal Air Force Nimrod reconnaissance jet swooped down and made several passes. One of the IRA men aboard the *Marita Ann* fired a shoulder-fired missile at the plane but missed. If the RAF crew had any doubts about what the two ships were doing, they had just been erased. The chase was on.[15]

Another British reconnaissance jet trailed the *Marita Ann* along the Irish coast for most of the trip to its designated off-loading point, where two Irish Navy vessels, loaded with Uzi-toting members of the Irish national police, the Garda, closed in. After a few warning shots across the big trawler's bow, the weapons from Boston were seized and the crew,

---

[15]Some investigators believed for years that McIntyre had betrayed the *Valhallah* shipment, and that the IRA had killed him in retaliation. In the late 1990s, however, a British informer within the IRA's own ranks admitted that he had betrayed the weapons shipment and the transfer operation.

who refused to speak except to request lawyers, were arrested.

The *Valhallah*, meanwhile, turned west and sped back across the stormy Atlantic. The weather, which had made the offloading operation so difficult, provided good cover for the ship's return voyage home. McIntyre's relatives, who found his logbooks of the trip after his disappearance, said their son wanted to scuttle the ship off the Massachusetts coast and have the crew discreetly paddle back to shore in life rafts and survival suits. The seasick, rattled—and well-armed—IRA men on board, however, insisted on taking the boat all the way into Boston Harbor. McIntyre and the crew managed to get off with most of the incriminating evidence before the boat was located and seized by U.S. Customs agents.

McIntyre saw the entire *Valhallah* incident as a fiasco and a betrayal. The IRA men seemed to have more guns than brains—futilely firing missiles at the British spy plane and bullying him out of his sensible plan to ditch the incriminating boat at sea. Joe Murray, who had flown to Ireland, was supposed to have helped with the weapons transfer but at the last minute begged out and returned to Boston with his wife Suzanne, who was having a difficult pregnancy. McIntyre began looking for a way out.

It came sooner than expected. McIntyre was known to Quincy Police due to his stormy, on-again, off-again relationship with his girlfriend, and one night, after having more than a few drinks, he was arrested while trying to climb over a fence into her yard. Still loaded, he started pouring his heart out about the *Ramsland*, the IRA, and his work with Joe Murray. The nonplussed patrolmen who had arrested him called the head of the Quincy Police Organized Crime Unit, Richard Bergeron, at home and said he better get down there.

Bergeron called in the DEA, who in turn brought U.S. Customs and FBI agent Rod Kennedy into the investigation, since they were still following up on the D Street warehouse bust. "I just sometimes feel like I'm trapped in this whirlpool and I can't get out of it," McIntyre said, according to published accounts. During interviews that took a couple of days at a secret room in a Quincy Hospital building, McIntyre laid out the whole scheme, including a half-dozen marijuana and cocaine smuggling trips made by the *Ramsland*.

He also told how Murray had introduced some new "partners" into the operation in the spring of 1983, Kennedy later testified. It was a startling revelation. Instead of backing off after the Murray warehouse had been seized—contrary to Connolly's memo on the subject—Flemmi and Bulger had become *more* involved in the drug smuggling operation, Kennedy said.

"After April of 1983 he was introduced to individuals from South Boston, and these individuals—he was told by Murray that these individuals were now their partners," Kennedy later testified.

"And the individuals involved were Mr. Flemmi and Mr. Bulger?" Kennedy was asked.

"The individual involved was Pat Nee. [McIntyre] said that Pat Nee advised him that it was Mr. Bulger and Mr. Flemmi. He was their representative."

On October 17, Rod Kennedy filed a detailed memo for the FBI's files about the McIntyre debriefing.

```
Michael Murray would do the financial
work, control the money. Joe Murray
would provide the enforcement and labor
which consisted of approximately 50 in-
dividuals per load. McIntyre stated
prior to the warehouse seizure in 4/83,
Michael Murray, Joe Murray and James
Carter were the main individuals, how-
ever after the seizure, Patrick Nee of
South Boston, Kevin [Weeks] and an indi-
vidual nicknamed Whitey who operates a
```

liquor   store   in   South   Boston   became
partners with Joe Murray.

Despite knowing that Bulger and Flemmi were John Connolly's Top Echelon sources—and having said he knew they expected confidentiality—Kennedy didn't return the favor for McIntyre. Instead of assigning him an informant number or calling him "source" in his report, Kennedy put McIntyre's name in plain sight in his report with just a parenthetical note—"protect identity." Of course there was nothing to protect McIntyre from the danger *inside* the FBI. Kennedy later denied having informed Connolly about McIntyre's identity. There would have been no need to, he said, since it was there in the files for any agent to see. Connolly later denied talking to Bulger and Flemmi about McIntyre—or any other informant—but Judge Wolf seemed to think otherwise in his *Salemme* ruling.

"In an effort to protect Bulger and Flemmi, Morris and Connolly also identified for them at least a dozen other individuals who were either FBI informants or sources for other law enforcement agencies. One of them may have been John McIntyre," the judge wrote.

The *Ramsland* was seized in mid-November coming into Boston with thirty-three tons of marijuana on board. Murray reportedly confronted his confederates, saying "one of you is a rat." U.S. Customs agents, meanwhile, who had been primarily working with McIntyre, were urging him to testify against Murray and Bulger and go into the Witness Protection Program. McIntyre refused and told his family that he had to get out of town.

Two weeks later McIntyre borrowed $3,000 from his father and dragged two survival suits and an inflatable boat out of his cellar. His plan, he said, was to arrange passage out of the country on a freighter and escape by sea. Before he left, he told them, he had to attend one last meeting with Pat Nee. His truck was found, abandoned, a short time later in the parking lot of a Dorchester tavern less than a mile from where his body was eventually dug up. The fact that an uncashed Veterans Administration check was still inside was worrisome—he would have needed the money—but they were still hopeful he had made it to a friendly ship and was on his way to Europe or South America.

Weeks passed, then months, with no word. John McIntyre Sr. was hospitalized and dying by that time, but Emily McIntyre and John's brother Chris started asking his friends what might have happened. They heard conflicting reports: that John had been murdered by the IRA, that he had been killed by an assassination squad sent by British military intelligence, or that maybe his death had something to do with marijuana smuggling aboard the *Ramsland.* Then a mysterious man paid a visit in the hospital to see John Sr., who was too fuzzy on painkillers to describe him well.

"Stick to the story that the IRA murdered John," the man hissed. "Remember you have another son."

A short time later Chris McIntyre was riding his motorcycle in Quincy Square when he felt himself being catapulted through the air straight toward a telephone pole. Had it not been for his wraparound helmet, he would have left half his face on the pavement. He regained consciousness a few seconds later and looked down to see the sole of his own shoe—his ankle had been snapped completely around. He looked up at the car that had struck him, a tan Chevy Impala with a dark brown roof. It was idling a short distance away and a dark-haired man was looking out one of the doors. Later he would say that the man bore a strong resemblance to Steve Flemmi.

Hearing that Kevin Weeks, a Bulger associate, pointed out the grave where their son John, Bucky Barrett, and Flemmi's stepdaughter were all dumped, erased any doubts Emily and Chris McIntyre may have had about who was responsible.

"Flemmi and Bulger killed my brother John in retribution for the *Ramsland,*" he said shortly after the bodies were found.

*   *   *

John McIntyre may have disappeared, but the information he gave the investigators bolstered a probe already under way by the DEA, the Massachusetts State Police, and the Quincy Police into the drug trafficking by Joe Murray, Whitey Bulger, and Steve Flemmi. Like the ill-fated Lancaster Street investigation, Operation Beans became a case study in the difficulties of investigating the FBI's Top Echelon informants.

Albert G. Reilly had been a DEA Special Agent for fourteen years when he began working the Joe Murray marijuana case. Reilly and his partner, thirteen-year-veteran Stephen Boeri, were just coming off a successful case against a major cocaine trafficker and were looking for a new challenge. The same informant who had helped them on the cocaine case confirmed what McIntyre alluded to—Bulger and Flemmi were heavily involved in the drug trade. They opened a new case file under the name "Operation Beans." It made for a pretty good pun, as in getting "baked" in Boston, a marijuana joke.

It wasn't long before the two agents had developed a pretty good idea who the players were, from the lieutenants on down to the street dealers. Their boss, Bob Stutman, the Boston DEA chief, walked into U.S. Attorney Bill Weld's office in the spring of 1984.

"We want to do Whitey Bulger and Stevie Flemmi; will you back us up?" Stutman asked.

The plan, Stutman explained, was to install multiple microphones, the chief one being inside Bulger's condo in Quincy. The DEA believed it could uncover proof of "major narcotics trafficking," Stutman said. Weld said he liked the idea. The big question, though, was whether the FBI was going to participate. Stutman asked Weld, who was close to FBI SAC Jim Greenleaf, to talk to the FBI chief directly, hopefully bypassing the rank-and-file FBI agents who might tip the investigation to Bulger and Flemmi. The FBI was "too close" to Bulger to be on the wire, Stutman said.

Neither man used the word "informant" in the conversation, Weld later recalled, but "it was out there in the air."

Weld, who became U.S. Attorney in 1981, never really believed the rumors that the FBI blew the Lancaster Street wire, but Stutman was wary, he had been burned once already. A few years earlier, the DEA investigated Frank LePere, who had been Joe Murray's predecessor as the city's biggest major marijuana trafficker and was also paying Bulger and Flemmi for permission to operate. Somehow, the DEA's surveillance efforts of LePere had been compromised.

"When we would put up a camera, they would blacken out the camera. When we would put in a bug, twenty-four hours later there were very exculpatory statements made on the bug where it was clear that they knew we were listening," Stutman later said. "We didn't know where it was coming from."

In the end, an Assistant U.S. Attorney named David Toomey, who worked for Jerry O'Sullivan's Organized Crime Strike Force, was prosecuted for leaking information to LePere. The DEA also suspected the FBI, but nothing was ever proven.

"After a while you almost developed a sense of paranoia. You didn't know who to trust and who not to trust," Stutman said.

U.S. Attorneys in other states were often at loggerheads with the FBI SACs in their districts. They got along about as well as you would expect, given the fact that the FBI SAC generally viewed himself as an independent, while the U.S. Attorney viewed him as a subordinate. Not Weld. His view was that the heads of all the various agencies were essentially equals. And he valued cooperation over conflict. Consequently, he never pushed Greenleaf. He was also friendly with FBI Director William Webster, so he put a lot of trust in the Bureau—probably too much, he said later. Not that it would have mattered, certainly, if he had ever asked directly about Bulger's status.

"Had you asked Jim Greenleaf whether or not Bulger was an informant for the FBI, you would have expected a candid answer, would you not?" Weld was later asked.

"I would have expected Jim Greenleaf to tell me the truth so far as he could or tell me nothing. In general, if I, as a political appointee, had gone to the Bureau and said, 'Tell me who your informants are,' I would have expected them to tell me to go pound sand."

It was a weird area, like the crazy uncle in the family that nobody talks about. Anticipating the standard "neither confirm nor deny" FBI party line, few officials pushed the informant issue, but with all the blown wires, it was in the back of a lot of people's minds. Weld's approach was to trust in all the agency heads' integrity and hope for the best. He was friendly with Greenleaf, they had dinner and played tennis on occasion. But he spent even more time with Stutman, since his office worked more closely with the DEA, while the FBI dealt much of the time with the strike force.

Weld promised Stutman that he would talk to the FBI SAC. He met with Greenleaf the next day.

"We're going after Whitey Bulger and Steve Flemmi. We're going to go up on a Title III—do you guys want to be in on it?"

Greenleaf's reply seemed odd.

"I'm going to have to get back to you."

Then it is true, Weld thought, they *are* informants.

A week later Weld was in his office when Greenleaf called him back. Weld was wondering what the hell was going on, but he figured the delay had something to do with Greenleaf going up the food chain at FBI Headquarters in Washington.

"Can I come over and see you?" Greenleaf asked.

"Sure."

Greenleaf walked across City Hall Plaza and up Congress Street to the federal courthouse.

Ever the democrat, Weld came out from behind his impressive desk and sat with Greenleaf on some plush chairs around his coffee table.

Greenleaf leaned forward.

"I am getting back to you on that matter we discussed last week."

"Yes."

"We're just not going to be able to participate."

The one-minute meeting was over.

Between the two conversations, Greenleaf had agonized over what to do. Bulger was still an open informant and, although Flemmi was closed, he was still meeting with Connolly and giving quality information. The SAC called in John Morris (who was then supervising the drug squad) and James Ring to get their opinions.

Ring argued strongly against the FBI being involved in the DEA case, repeating Connolly's assertions that Bulger and Flemmi were keeping drugs *out* of South Boston. Besides, Bulger and Flemmi were too smart to be caught on tape, and too many agencies—DEA, Customs, Quincy, and the State Police—already knew about the probe. Finally, Ring said, given what had happened at Lancaster Street, the FBI would certainly be blamed if the bug went south.

Ring later said he was so concerned that he even warned Connolly, without actually telling him about the DEA probe, to get ready to face more leak allegations or even a polygraph. The DEA was simply in over its head, he said.

"I thought the investigation would collapse and we would get blamed, regardless of what we had done or not done. That's what I was concerned about. Among with the fact that . . . I thought it would collapse because I didn't think it was set up right."

Despite his conversation with Weld, and Ring's urgings, Greenleaf did not end up keeping the FBI totally out of the probe. For reasons never fully explained, he opted for half a loaf. While the FBI would not *officially* participate, it would offer "technical expertise." FBI Special Agent Rod Kennedy would remain on the case as a "liaison," but all information he received would be "compartmentalized" within the DEA probe. "Basically, the information was to be held very tightly, and it was not to be filed with the normal chain of informant files, and the supervisor was to maintain it with a very high level of integrity and security," Kennedy later testified.

Greenleaf later insisted that keeping the FBI involved in the case was "the right thing to do." Some DEA officials, though, believe that the FBI was keeping tabs on their investigation, employing the old wiseguy wisdom of keeping your friends close and your enemies closer. The Boston FBI chief was also probably under moderate to heavy pressure from up the Justice Department chain of command to cooperate with the drug agency.

Whichever, the point was surely moot, because Bulger and Flemmi's friend John Connolly had already known about the probe for months.

At least two months before the official DEA request for FBI assistance, DEA Special Agent Al Reilly sent a routine request to FBI Headquarters in Washington, asking for any information available on Bulger from the FBI's National Crime Information Center (NCIC) computers, a resource used by law enforcement agencies all over the U.S. When an informant's name popped up on an NCIC request, a copy of it was automatically sent to both the informant's handler, in this case Connolly, and his supervisor.

Later, Kennedy said Connolly admitted that he had known about the DEA wiretap plan all along—for different reasons. Sean McWeeney, Section Chief of the Organized Crime Section of the FBI in Washington and the FBI's new liaison with the DEA, called Boston to speak to Ring, who was out of the office. Connolly took the call instead. As part of the Justice Department's new play nice mandate, the drug agency sent McWeeney a copy of a memo from DEA Boston to DEA Headquarters requesting authorization to institute the investigation or wiretap on Flemmi and Bulger. Ring later insisted that Connolly never told him about McWeeney's call.

Judge Wolf, meanwhile, found it most likely that Morris had told Connolly about the DEA probe. He cited "circumstantial evidence" in his decision in *U.S.* v. *Salemme*. "He [Morris] received a second $1,000 payment from them, and a case of wine, about two years later, in the spring of 1984," Wolf wrote. "The timing of this payment suggests that it may have been an expression of Bulger and Flemmi's appreciation for Morris's assistance concerning the DEA investigation." It was no coincidence, Judge Wolf found, that Bulger and Flemmi started "noticing things" in February 1984, just as the DEA-led probe was beginning in earnest. "Based in part on Connolly's previous and future practice, the court infers that he told Bulger and Flemmi about the DEA investigation," the judge wrote.

A bizarre pattern developed through the rest of 1984 and into early 1985. The DEA, Quincy Police, and Massachusetts State Police followed Bulger and Flemmi around and placed pen registers on their telephones to gather enough evidence for a wiretap application. Bulger and Flemmi, meanwhile, watched their watchers watch them, and dutifully reported all their sightings to John Connolly, who recorded them in long, detailed memos. Greenleaf, in turn, shared the information in Connolly's memos with Stutman in what appeared, if anything, to be an effort to convince the DEA that the case was hopeless.

The agents on the street, meanwhile, had no clue that their bosses were talking to each other. All they knew was that Bulger and Flemmi were being more cautious than any criminals they had ever seen before. Things were going so poorly that by late 1984, Stutman knew something had to be done to at least reduce the size of the probe. There was too much pressure from the Justice Department to sever ties with the FBI, so the State Police were chosen as the fall guys. It was decided that the agents would declare the investigation over, cut their ties to the Staties, and then pick up the investigation again in secret.

Connolly appears to have done his best in memos to blame the State Police for tipping off the DEA-Quincy investigation. In one, he said the two informants felt the whole thing was likely a "vendetta" by the Massachusetts State Police stemming from the blown Lancaster Street bug. In another he came right out and said Bulger had an "MSP source."

> [Bulger] advised that his Massachusetts State Police contact is a trooper who was getting his information second-hand from another trooper or troopers who had some direct knowledge of an ongoing investigation pertaining to sources.

Trooper John Naimovich was eventually identified by Flemmi as a source of information on the DEA bugging effort. Naimovich had provided some of the informant information for the electronic surveillance applications, but many of his colleagues still doubt the veracity of the claim—especially since the wiseguy's self-serving disclosure was conveniently made after Naimovich had died. Naimovich may have been too close to some of his sources, they said, but he would never give information to Flemmi. DEA agents said they never suspected that the State Police detectives they worked most closely with, Lancaster Street veteran Richard Fralick and Joseph Saccardo, were anything but arrow-straight. "We had the utmost respect for those guys," Stephen Boeri said later.

Kicking the State Police out of the investigation only created a new problem. Perhaps feeling secure with their agreement with the FBI to conduct loansharking and bookmaking activity with impunity, Bulger and Flemmi were less careful about the way they conducted that side of the business. That allowed Boeri to chart a complex system of telephone messaging between Bulger, Flemmi, and their henchmen. Unfortunately, they had comparatively little evidence on drugs. Without the use of the gambling evidence, there would be no wiretap. The DEA had no jurisdiction over gambling crimes and needed a partner that did—and also had the technical expertise to help with the bugging. With the State Police out, that meant only one agency—the FBI.

Reilly tried to talk Stutman out of asking the FBI to become more involved with the probe. Reilly had heard rumors going back to the early 1980s that Bulger and Flemmi were informants. His friends in the Boston Police, the State Police, and the Quincy Police were all pointing the finger at the FBI. Trooper Rick Fralick told him the Lancaster Street stories. "The minute we got the authority to do it or got it implanted in the place, the guys never showed up again. We were dimed out," Fralick had said. Reilly wanted no part of the FBI.

Stutman, under pressure from the Justice Department, tried to rationalize things. The FBI might be useful, Stutman said, in getting the technology necessary to overcome the car alarms in the Bulger apartment and car. The FBI was in.

The T.E. program put the Bureau in a major bind. At a minimum, Bulger and Flemmi had been authorized to commit gambling and loansharking crimes—in fact they had to commit those crimes to remain credible as Top Echelon informants. If, as the Bureau later argued in court, that was *all* they were authorized to do, then their drug activities with Murray, LePere, and others were unauthorized and therefore fair game.

Under the Attorney General's Guidelines, then, the FBI might have told the DEA that Bulger and Flemmi were informants with permission to commit gambling and loansharking crimes, but that their drug dealing was unauthorized. That would have given the DEA fair warning about possible leaks that could threaten their investigation. The FBI could then have legitimately begged off the probe to avoid the appearance of a conflict and let the chips fall where they may.

There were several reasons, however, why the FBI couldn't fess up—and they had little to do with doing, as Greenleaf put it, "the right thing."

For starters, admitting that Bulger and Flemmi were informants was anathema in the FBI's culture. Secondly, once officials like Weld, Stutman, and others had their suspicions confirmed, the Boston FBI would have been under extreme public pressure to explain why two men who were reputed killers, gang bosses, and major drug traffickers were being used by the Bureau as informants. Greenleaf's next choice would be either for the Boston office to take the fall or to point the finger at Headquarters to the Hoover-era Top Echelon policy, turning a local scandal into a national one.

Neither option could have been particularly attractive. Greenleaf, who had been a top official in Headquarters before coming to Boston, knew as well as anyone the cardinal "never embarrass the Bureau" rule, and exposing the T.E. program could also have hobbled the FBI's Organized Crime Program, the Bureau's top priority.

Finally, there was the problem of the Jerry Angiulo investigation. The Prince Street Title III was being hailed as a national law enforcement triumph over the mob, a major victory in the FBI's war on La Cosa Nostra. The racketeering case itself was still pending, however. It would be a public relations disaster—not to mention a major credibility issue with a jury—if the Boston FBI's great triumph turned out to be built on the backs of two major drug traffickers.

The second time around, Greenleaf agreed to help. He ordered Ring, who was still protesting, to assign more manpower to the case. Rod Kennedy was unceremoniously yanked out and replaced by two agents who were not only new to the Organized Crime Squad, but new to Boston—

Richard Carter and Brian Rossi. As a supposed precaution against leaks, Greenleaf essentially kicked Carter and Rossi out of the office, ordering them not to have any unnecessary contact with other local FBI personnel.

An FBI "tech team" from Washington, meanwhile, was called in to help the DEA with the technical side of the bugging effort. They were equally circumspect, telling Boeri and Reilly that they weren't even checking in with the Boston FBI office, a regular part of FBI protocol. They said they had been instructed not to talk to anyone in Boston except the DEA, just meet, do the job, and then leave.

That should have been reassuring to Reilly and Boeri, but it wasn't. Particularly when the FBI's vaunted technical experts were throwing up their hands, saying the bug couldn't be done. Reilly smelled a tank job. The FBI tech guys had been great in an earlier case, against a major dealer named Bobby Sullivan, but this time they seemed to be dragging their feet. They took a full day making long-distance observations of the condo and Bulger's car and examining the replica vehicle the DEA agents acquired. They listened to the drug agents describe the alarms Bulger and Flemmi had installed, which not only included regular motion and door sensors but pressure switches in various locations that could detect when someone was stepping or sitting.

"Do you have the codes?" one of the FBI agents asked.

No, the DEA agents replied. If we had the codes, why would we need you? Sorry, the FBI agents said then, it can't be done.

Screw them and their informants, Reilly thought. We'll do it ourselves.

The agents finally hit on their own idea. They couldn't get into the car without setting off the alarm; even if they did, the pressure switches were waiting on the inside. The same for the condo, so they wouldn't go in at all. They would just drill from the outside, place the bug in that way, then cover the hole. It was simple, but drilling the hole to the exact spot was going to be tricky. They practiced drilling on the look-alike car for three weeks to find just the right spot. They found a condo building with a similar layout and constructed from similar materials as Bulger's and practiced drilling on that too.

The installation went reasonably well. But just as at Lancaster Street, there was little to listen to. Almost immediately Bulger and Flemmi began turning up their radios in an obvious effort to avoid being recorded. The agents also learned that George Kaufman had started to monitor DEA radio transmissions on a scanner at about the same time. Despite all their care, they believed the wire had been blown. Reilly and Bergeron tried to make an adjustment on the car bug so it would better pick up what little conversation there was and less ambient noise. They crept up on the car at about 2:30 in the morning—a time when Bulger was generally asleep. Suddenly, Bulger stepped out his front door and spotted them. They took off and ran.

Bulger's cohort Kevin Weeks was spotted, a short time later, carrying a small red device that the agents correctly figured was a radio frequency (RF) detector—a device used to find hidden microphones by homing in on their transmissions. The agent had to start turning the bug on and off to avoid detection.

Reilly would flip on the bug via remote control.

"Ooh, look at this," they would hear Weeks telling Bulger. "Over here . . ."

Reilly would quickly turn the bug back off, hoping not to give away the bug's location.

The operation ended on March 11, 1985. Reilly and Boeri had been playing their cat-and-mouse game with Bulger and Weeks and the RF detector, but they knew it was pointless. The car might as well have been radioactive, given the care they were taking in approaching it. There was only one thing to do—try to avoid the humiliation of Bulger losing their equipment.

The agents tailed the car from Silver Street to a garage at

295 Old Colony at about 3:15 in the afternoon. Oh, what the hell, Reilly said to himself, switching on the bug from his portable transceiver. They heard some scuffling around. A voice said: "He's right, they did put a bug in the car."

Reilly and Boeri bolted toward the garage, followed by two other agents who had been in on the surveillance. They opened the door.

"DEA!" Boeri said, flashing his creds. "There's government property in that car and we're going to retrieve it. Could you move away from the vehicle please?"

"Okay, no problem," Bulger said. As the two hoodlums were backing up, the agents saw Weeks stick a red metal box into his pocket. It was the RF detector.

"Wait a minute, can I get something?" Bulger asked as Reilly was just about to remove the panel where the bug had been hidden.

"Sure," Reilly said.

Bulger reached into the driver's side door and picked up a black leather zippered pouch.

"Don't worry," he said, acknowledging the agents' watchful stares. "There's no gun in here, just keys."

With no warrant, the agents had to take Bulger's word for it.

"We need to inform you that this equipment was installed by a court order," Boeri said.

"There's no problem if you don't have it with you," the crime boss said with a smile. "You know, I thought my alarm was pretty good, I'm surprised you guys got that thing in there."

"You were looking for it pretty hard, how'd you know?"

"A few nights ago, at twenty of three, I saw some guys next to my car. I figured I should be careful with it after that."

"Take a guess, how long do you think it was in there?"

"Seven to nine days, something like that."

"No way," Weeks broke in. "It was two months, easy."

"You guys probably bugged my house too, didn't you. The fucking Quincy cops and [Norfolk County District Attorney William] Delahunt have been out to get me. I'm going to get out of that fucking place. I heard what they did—they put a fucking Ryder truck next to the liquor store and used to get on the roof. I know they tried to bug the place before. A friend of mine told me he was in a bar with a Quincy cop, who was drunk, and told my friend that they were trying to bug my house, my car, and the liquor store," Bulger said.

"I'm really surprised that you feds were actually able to get a bug in my car. But I'll tell you one thing. It's the last fucking time. From now on I'm changing cars and houses so fast that once you guys get a paper, I'll already be in a new one."

"How much you want for the liquor store?"

"I—" Bulger began.

"You mean how much do *I* want for the liquor store," Weeks chimed in. He and the crime boss looked at each other and smiled. Boeri had almost tricked Bulger into admitting what everyone believed, that Weeks was just a straw owner.

"How about eight hundred thousand?"

"Hey, if someone legit wants to make an offer, I'll consider it," Weeks said.

"How long *was* the bug in the car?" Bulger asked casually.

Boeri didn't answer.

"Never mind, I'll just get my lawyer to get it from the court."

"The warrant is probably impounded."

"I think I'm entitled to know," Bulger said.

While they were chatting and Reilly worked, Boeri had noticed Bulger's big metal belt buckle, which had "Alcatraz 1934–1963" inscribed on it with a picture of the infamous island prison.

"How long were you in Alcatraz?" Boeri asked.

"You must have the wrong guy. I've never been arrested. Those are just the years the place was open. I know you guys have been watching me all the time. I see those two Quincy detectives around the liquor store all the time."

"I bet you guys bugged my car too," Weeks said. "You want to buy it cheap?"

"You know, now I think I may just hang on to this car for a while now," Bulger said as Reilly finished pulling the bug.

The agents left, but Bulger apparently wasn't done gloating. Two days later Boeri and Bergeron were cruising South Boston again at dusk when they spotted Bulger, standing on the sidewalk and beckoning them over.

"Hey, that panel fell off and I'm getting a draft. Can you show me how to reattach it?"

Only about a thousand guys in South Boston could reattach an interior car panel, and for Whitey Bulger would certainly trample each other for the honor of doing it. Bulger was just busting balls, rubbing their noses in it.

"You know I was going by the Fargo Building earlier in the day and I saw one of your guys' cars out front. I was going to leave a note telling you guys to call me, but I didn't want you to take it the wrong way."

"How'd you know?" Boeri asked.

Bulger laughed. "I was on my way to Boston and there it was," he said. "But I've known for a while that you guys were in the Fargo."

"How'd you know that?" Boeri asked.

"Hey, I gotta have my secrets too," the crime boss said, smiling. Then, to Bergeron, he said, "I know you. You're one of those Quincy cops who's been after me."

"Oh, yeah?" Boeri cut in, wanting to test the gangster's knowledge. "What's my name, then?"

Bulger butchered the pronunciation. But it was close enough. Jesus, the agent thought, I've never met this guy before in my life and he knows my name. Where was his information coming from?

"I'm surprised you knew that," the agent said.

Boeri changed the subject.

"So you going to stay in the condo?"

"Who knows? I know you guys had it bugged for a long time. The Quincy Police told me my alarm went off at least twice. It's been a pain in the ass, I can't say anything, and if I do, I'm whispering with the hi-fi on in the background," the crime boss said. "I think you guys were on my phone too."

"No, we weren't on the phone. All we had were pen registers."

"Bullshit. Oh, please, don't you guys think I know you can listen to those things?" Again Bulger was demonstrating an intimate knowledge of law enforcement techniques. The same machine that captured telephone numbers for a pen register could listen to the same line at the flick of a switch. Some agents and officers had no qualms about doing it, despite the fact that it was illegal.

"What good would that do? You couldn't use any of it in court," Boeri said.

"Yeah, but it would make for some great intelligence," Bulger replied with a grin. "You think I trust you fucking guys in the government? I took LSD in prison for eighteen months so I could get out early. Those motherfucking jailhouse doctors called it important medical research and that it wasn't gonna be harmful. Then it turns out that I was a guinea pig for the fucking CIA the whole time. Bastards. You think I trust you guys?"

"You look pretty healthy to me," Bergeron said.

"Yeah," Boeri agreed.

Bulger puffed up a little.

"I take care of myself. I'm at the gym every day and I've got a humidifier in every room of the house, plus a lot of exercise equipment. I even have a trampoline," he said. "Me and Stevie both stay in good shape. He's been working out ever since he was in the paratroops in Korea. Neither of us drink much either.

"I don't trust anyone who drinks. It's for fucking weaklings, guys who get their courage out of a bottle. You just never can tell when one of them is going to go to the cops. Don't listen to everything anyone says about me. I've heard that I have red hair and I'm over six feet. Most of what you hear about me is bullshit."

Bulger was on a roll.

"Guys are always saying shit about me. Even Brian Halloran, that FBI rat, was talking about me before his ticket got punched."

Bergeron was taken aback. He knew the Halloran murder and the rumors that Halloran had been an informant. Jimmy Flynn had finally been arrested for Halloran's murder two months earlier. Why would Bulger bring him up?

"Do you think Jimmy Flynn did it?" Bergeron asked.

"I don't think so."

"Then how do you explain the dying declaration?"

"I'm not saying Halloran didn't hate Jimmy. They hated each other. Jimmy used to piss on Brian in public. I just don't think Jimmy did it," the crime boss said with a smile.

After the humiliating encounters with Bulger and Flemmi, the DEA agents had several meetings with Assistant U.S. Attorney Gary Crossen, to see if there was any way they could build what little evidence they had gathered into a prosecutable case. The consensus was that there wasn't. Reilly and Boeri wrote a politically correct postmortem guaranteed not to wrinkle any of the suits up at Main Justice. It made no mention of their suspicions that the FBI had compromised the case (their boss had, after all, invited the Bureau into the investigation not once, but twice). Instead the memo suggested that sources in the Boston Police Department, which had been involved in the very early stages of the case, might have tipped off Bulger and Flemmi.

Years later, after Robert Stutman had retired from the DEA and had become CEO of a workplace drug-testing firm in Boca Raton, Florida, he said he was convinced that the FBI had betrayed him and his agents.

"I was fully aware of the talk," he said. "I made the decision that we would bring the FBI into this case. I made the wrong decision. I understood the day I walked in and told the FBI about this case that I was running a risk. I had been told by some of my agents that they thought these guys were informants. I understood that very clearly. I bit that bullet and made that decision. I understood that if the FBI was going to burn me on the case that they could burn me.

"I didn't believe that they would burn me on the case even if these guys were informants, just as when I investigate informants of my own office, agents who control those informants do not burn us. It was based on more than that—my trust that the Bureau would not take information we gave them and just compromise a case even though . . . these guys were informants. I assumed that they would do the professional thing."

In the end, Stutman firmly believed the FBI had burned him. It was the only explanation for Bulger and Flemmi's incomprehensible arrogance in their conversations with his agents.

One of his last conversations with Greenleaf about the subject concerned a certain FBI agent.

"I wouldn't send John Connolly down to our office if I were you," he told his FBI counterpart. "A lot of guys don't like him because they feel he may have burned us on the Whitey case."

Debra Davis and Deborah Hussey

Steve Flemmi always had a thing for younger women, but they got involved with him at their peril. Those who believe that the decision by the FBI and the Organized Crime Strike Force to keep Flemmi on the street was a bad one, that the cost in lives was too high, often point to the story of the "two Debbies."

In the early 1970s, blond, striking, seventeen-year-old Debra Davis so impressed Flemmi when he stepped into the jewelry store where she worked, the story went, that he immediately dumped the woman he had come in to buy a gift for and asked her out. Their nine-year relationship was sometimes stormy—most of Flemmi's women knew, or at least suspected, that they weren't the only one—but he was always ready with an expensive bauble, a diamond watch, a red Mercedes or a blue Jaguar.

When she disappeared in the fall of 1981, members of Davis's family said Flemmi broke down and wept right in front of them, insisting that he didn't know why she would leave without taking the expensive gifts he had showered on her. There were reports that on the night she disappeared, she was going to see him at the Marconi Club, a private club Flemmi owned that was one of his primary hangouts. His story was that she had run off to Mexico with another lover. Many people, though, believed all along that he had killed her after a lover's quarrel and buried her body in the basement of the Marconi.

A DEA memo that surfaced during the *Salemme* hearings, however, suggested that his motive may have been more practical. According to the memo, Debra Davis was the sister of the Davis brothers, who were partners in Flemmi's thriving drug business.

```
Additionally, the MDC police advised that
during 1981, Debbie Davis, sister of the
Davis brothers, disappeared and is be-
lieved to have been murdered. Stevie
Flemmi is also a suspect in that disap-
pearance.
```

Clearly, like McIntyre and Barrett, Davis was in a position, if she had wanted, to inform on Flemmi's forbidden drug dealing.

When the news reports hit that the feds had discovered the "Mob Burying Ground" off Route 93, Debra Davis's family members told reporters that they briefly had hopes of finally recovering her body after nineteen years. Those hopes were quickly extinguished.

It was the wrong Debbie.

The relationship between Steve Flemmi and Deborah Hussey, according to family friends and law enforcement sources, was even more sordid than the one with Davis. Flemmi didn't have to look any further than his own house to find the petite, pretty, brown-haired fourteen-year-old— she was the eldest daughter of his common-law wife, Marion Hussey. At least one family friend blames the relationship with Flemmi for Debbie Hussey's eventual slide into a life of drugs and prostitution. During her increasingly troubled teenage years, the friend said, she started exhibiting telltale signs of molestation—rebellion, alienation, self-hatred, and self-medication with alcohol and drugs. "He just ruined her, he killed her as a person," the friend said.

In her mid-twenties, Hussey reportedly made some attempts to straighten out her life, taking college courses and getting a steady job (arranged by her stepfather) at a café in Dorchester. Law enforcement sources also say, however, that she continued to get in trouble with police over drugs and increasingly began dropping Flemmi's name, attempting to get herself out of trouble. In late 1984, according to law enforcement sources, she began threatening Flemmi that she was going to expose their sexual relationship.

She disappeared just before Thanksgiving. For a while her mother had hopes that she had run off to California, but soon weeks turned into months and then years without a word. The next news the family received was that her skeleton had been found intertwined with the bodies of John McIntyre and Bucky Barrett.

The Davis family was forced to wait another ten months before the State Police and DEA investigators, again using information provided by Kevin Weeks and other former members of Bulger and Flemmi's gang, dug up Debra's body. Struggling with tides and sketchy memories, the investigators found her under the dirty brown sands of Tenean Beach, an urban bathing strip along Boston Harbor in the city's Dorchester section. They also found the bodies of Tommy King and Paul McGonagle, two South Boston gangsters who were one-time rivals of Whitey Bulger.

CHAPTER EIGHT

Fidelity First, Integrity Last

....

The FBI's Informant Program corrupts its own agents

> *It is the business of every American citizen who knows anything about Americanism to resign if given such instructions.*
>
> > Federal judge's reply to Justice Department lawyer J. Edgar Hoover and other officials' claims that they were simply following the Attorney General's orders in falsely arresting hundreds of suspected Communists in the "Red Raids" of 1920

JERRY MONTANARI WAS pissed off.

As the case agent for the Halloran-Wheeler-Callahan murders in the spring of 1983, he was supposed to be conducting a "Priority 1" investigation, one where all necessary resources and attention were focused on the case until it was solved.

Right. Bulger and Flemmi were the suspects, but Montanari felt like *he* was the one under the microscope. Ring, the OC Squad supervisor, had also asked for his opinion about whether Bulger and Flemmi had been involved in the Wheeler murder. What was he supposed to say? With the Angiulo case—only the biggest Mafia case *ever* in Boston— still pending, anyone who accused the office's best Top Echelon sources of anything wasn't exactly going to win any popularity contests around the office.

Now things were even worse. His voluminous case files (they would eventually grow to fill thirty-five fat folders) were a mess—reports were out of order, in the wrong folders, some even appeared to be missing. Someone else besides him and his partner Leo Brunnick had obviously been going through them. Montanari had been suspicious of his fellow agents—particularly John Connolly—for some time. Just after Callahan's murder the previous August, he had told Shelton Merritt, a Metro-Dade Police detective from Miami, that he was "concerned about leaks" within his own office. But this was too much.

The agent walked down the hall to Assistant Special Agent in Charge Bob Fitzpatrick's office.

"Hey, Bob, you got a minute?"

"Sure, Jerry, what's up?"

"Somebody's been rifling my files."

Fitzpatrick had taken Halloran's allegations seriously. Halloran knew that diming Bulger was the kiss of death, Fitzpatrick thought, so it was difficult to believe Halloran would simply make something up, piss off his new FBI friends and risk being cut loose with no friends. Fitzpatrick had agreed to keeping the Halloran-Wheeler murder investigation in the family, so to speak, without involving other law enforcement agencies. But he'd be damned if a couple of slick jerks like Connolly and Bulger were going to make fools out of the Bureau.

He asked Montanari who he thought was responsible.

Montanari didn't hesitate. John Connolly, he said.

"Okay," Fitzpatrick said. "We'll do something about it."

Fitzpatrick took Montanari's files and locked them in a filing cabinet in his own office. Not long afterward, an angry Connolly stomped into his office.

"What the fuck is going on, Bob?"

"What are you talking about John?"

"The files, the fucking Wheeler-Halloran files, where are they?"

"They're locked up here, I thought it would be better for everybody that way."

"That's bullshit. You're making me look bad. There's no fucking reason why those files should be taken away."

"Let me tell you something, John, this *is* the best thing for you—if you don't have access to the files, then no one could possibly say you were tampering with them."

Connolly stormed back out.

The Montanari file incident shows the stresses the Top Echelon Informant Program caused within FBI offices. Some agents were trying to investigate criminals, others were trying to protect them. As T.E.s like Bulger and Flemmi got bolder and more powerful, the more difficult the job of protecting them became, and the more the FBI's core mission— investigating crimes and arresting criminals—was warped to accommodate the fundamentally immoral informant program.

While the T.E. program caused trouble for agents who worked in New York with Greg Scarpa, and Cleveland with Jackie Presser, it appears to have created even more profound moral and professional dilemmas in Boston, affecting virtually every agent who came into contact with Whitey Bulger and Steve Flemmi. Some, who had the most to gain, were badly and criminally compromised, like John Morris and John Connolly. Others, like Ed Quinn, did not get blood on their hands, yet appeared to have supported the corrupt relationships by looking the other way—even as they accepted the promotions, cash bonuses, and media acclaim that always followed big Mafia cases. Still other agents allowed themselves to be cowed into inaction and silence.

In the early 1980s, its reputation tarnished by the Lancaster Street mess, and with the Wheeler, Callahan, and Halloran murder cases still open, the Boston FBI needed to deal with some of the problems created by its Top Echelon Informant Program. In early 1983, John Morris was replaced as John Connolly's boss and chief of the C-3 Organized Crime Squad by James Ring. Though Ring never admitted that he was called upon to fix any specific problems, his actions as the new supervisor speak for themselves.

Ring, who had been supervising the FBI's satellite office in the central Massachusetts city of Worcester, was something of an odd duck. Jowly, aloof, and constantly smoking a pipe, he reminded some colleagues of the hookah-smoking caterpillar from *Alice in Wonderland*. Six months into his tenure as supervisor, Ring imposed a radical reorganization on the Boston FBI Organized Crime Program. The old C-2 Labor Racketeering Squad, a holdover from the McClellan Committee–Kennedy days, was renamed the "Nontraditional Organized Crime Squad" and handed responsibility for all non-Sicilian Mafia cases—Winter Hill, the Hell's Angels, the Asian gangs in Chinatown, etc. That left C-3 free to focus exclusively on the high-profile La Cosa Nostra investigations that were earning such accolades from FBI Headquarters in Washington.

It was also a way—at least on paper—to deal with the vexing problem of Whitey Bulger and Stevie Flemmi. "I reorganized the entire Organized Crime Program so the investigations of Bulger and Flemmi would go to the squad who would have the ability and the access to go investigate them," Ring testified at the *Salemme* case a dozen years later. Where John Morris had embraced Bulger and Flemmi as part of the FBI's power structure—and was corrupted in the process—Ring's approach allowed the Organized Crime Program to still reap the benefits of Bulger and Flemmi's cooperation, while removing the moral responsibility of monitoring their criminal activity. The two T.E. informants, Ring declared, were now "fair game" for the new C-2 squad.

While convenient, Ring's new system had several problems. First, it was completely inconsistent with the Attorney

General's Informant Guidelines he was supposed to be following. Nothing in the guidelines said anything about informants being "fair game" for some other FBI squad. Instead, informant crimes were separated into two categories: those authorized by the FBI and those that weren't. Section E.1 of the guidelines states:

> *Each (informant) shall be advised that his relationship with the FBI will not protect him from arrest or prosecution for any violation of Federal, State or local law, except where the FBI has determined pursuant to these guidelines that his association in a specific activity, which otherwise would be criminal, is justified for law enforcement.*

For unauthorized crimes, the guidelines prescribed a series of actions. In regard to *"less serious"* crimes, they stated, *"it may be necessary to forego any further investigative or enforcement action in order to retain the source of information."*

So-called *"serious crimes"*—a term left vague in the guidelines—had to be reported to a supervisor like Morris or Ring, who would make the call whether the informant was to be reported to another law enforcement agency for prosecution. If not, the supervisor was supposed to notify the Assistant Attorney General in charge of the Criminal Division in Washington of what had happened and of the FBI's desire to keep the informant on its rolls.

Any *"serious acts of violence,"* meanwhile, not only had to be reported to local authorities or the Assistant Attorney General, but a yearly statistical count of them had to be made available by the FBI for Justice Department review.

The problem with the guidelines, of course, was that they didn't work with Top Echelon informants—a problem that Ring said he recognized right away. T.E.'s, by definition, were committing serious crimes all the time. While the FBI might fudge and call loansharking and bookmaking nonserious and nonviolent crimes—a point that many Winter Hill extortion victims would no doubt have disputed—there was no way that murder and drug trafficking could be minimized as "nonserious." Given the way things were going, the FBI would be reporting Bulger and Flemmi to the Assistant Attorney General a lot.

Ring , by his own admission, got around the contradiction between the AG's Guidelines and the T.E. program mandates by "counteracting" the guidelines on his own authority. Under his watch there would essentially be *no* authorized criminal activity, so they didn't need to bother explaining to their informants what crimes they could or could not commit.

"Don't come to me with (an authorization) request for criminal conduct, because I'm not even going to entertain it," Ring told his agents.

"My instruction to the squad was, after discussions, that at the high level of informants that we were dealing with, I wasn't going to get involved in authorizing criminal activity or seeking authorization, that I just—I wasn't going to do it," he said later. "That was a discussion that I had very, very early on with the squad. So, I didn't care what the guidelines might have said we could do. At the level we were dealing with, I thought it was impractical, and I wasn't going to get involved in it."

The new rules and structure Ring set up were completely dysfunctional, almost right from the start. For one thing, Ring admitted that the C-2 squad was never actually told to target Bulger and Flemmi. Apparently that was supposed to be understood. "They had the nontraditional organized crime. I don't have to tell them what to do. They [Bulger and Flemmi] were at the top category in nontraditional organized crime," Ring said. The C-2 supervisor, Mike Hanigan, meanwhile, was no match for either Ring or Connolly in terms of office clout. Hanigan was generally known as a good-hearted guy, but somewhat insecure and a compulsive know-it-all, who would pontificate on a wide range of topics with little or no provocation.

Hanigan's squad occupied the same large room with C-3 in the JFK Building, their desks right near each other. On one side sat a handful of agents who were supposed to be targeting Bulger and Flemmi. On the other was a much larger group, the heroes of the successful Angiulo and Zannino wires, including John Connolly, who many agents believed had the power to make or break their careers. Connolly cultivated friendships with agents on the C-2 squad, and in some cases commanded fierce loyalty. In fact, after the scandal over Bulger and Flemmi broke, John Connolly's most ardent supporters would be the agents on the C-2 squad—John Newton and Rick Carter—not his colleagues on the "traditional" Organized Crime Squad. Testimony and FBI documents show C-2 agents routinely going to Connolly with information they had received about Bulger and Flemmi—a practice of which Ring said he was totally unaware.

Instead of the close supervision by the Justice Department and FBI Headquarters envisioned by Attorney General Levi, Ring's new dictates appeared to drive Connolly and Morris's relationship with Bulger and Flemmi underground. The process was probably accelerated by a dinner party at the home of Flemmi's parents' house. Judge Wolf speculated in his ruling that the dinner was most likely held as a "celebration of the Angiulo indictments." Ring said the dinner aspect caught him completely by surprise, that the purpose of the meeting was to see how Connolly was interacting with his sources.

Connolly picked up Ring in his Bureau car on an autumn evening in 1983.

"Why so early?" Ring asked.

"We're going to go over to Stevie's parents' house and meet with them there tonight."

Connolly caught Ring's concerned look.

"Well, Stevie's mom and dad are fixing dinner."

Ring didn't say anything. They arrived at Flemmi's parents' house on East Third Street in South Boston. Ring was introduced to Flemmi's father, who didn't say much in his broken English. They met over dinner for about forty-five minutes—Flemmi, Flemmi's parents, and Whitey Bulger—dining on Italian food and red wine and making small talk. As they were leaving, Ring said, Bill Bulger walked into the kitchen and gave Whitey some photographs. Ring said Billy Bulger didn't speak to anyone but his brother.[16]

"What the hell is going on?" Ring said he asked Connolly.

Connolly replied that Billy Bulger lived next door to Mr. Flemmi's parents.

Ring later insisted that he hadn't known that Flemmi's parents even lived in South Boston, much less next to Bulger's brother. Ring was later asked if he thought the experience of seeing the State Senate president at a meeting between two underworld kingpins and their FBI handlers was "extraordinary."

"I'd prefer the word 'stupid.' I was not happy about this," he replied.

Ring may have been the subject of one of John Connolly's favorite and most successful tactics—inviting Bulger and Flemmi to collegial dinners while urging fellow agents to treat them like "friends," not "informants." All the best T.E. recruiters, including Roemer and Villano, used the same tactic.

Yet for all his alleged unhappiness, Ring didn't discipline Connolly, or complain to the Special Agent in Charge about the dinner. In fact, a search of the FBI's records by federal prosecutors indicates that neither Ring nor Connolly wrote a memo about the meeting, which would have been required

---

[16]John Connolly later denied that Billy Bulger came over during the dinner meeting at Flemmi's parents'. William Bulger declined comment on the meeting, or on any other aspect of the case, through a spokesman at the University of Massachusetts. Bulger had left the Senate to take a post as president of the university.

by Bureau policy. Instead, he said he ordered Connolly not to meet with the informants at private homes anymore, but in hotels or other more discreet locations. Other agents later testified that Connolly basically ignored Ring and went right on meeting with his informants at agents' houses behind the supervisor's back. When Ring did get word that his order had been violated, Connolly never suffered anything more severe than a good talking-to. The bottom line was that Connolly's informants got results. He didn't need to be disciplined, Ring said, just "managed."

Over the next several years, exactly who was managing who was an open question. According to testimony from other agents, it seemed more like John Connolly was managing Jim Ring, and that Bulger and Flemmi were handling their handlers down at the FBI.

Steve and Julie Rakes, a young South Boston couple, purchased a mothballed service station on Old Colony Avenue in South Boston with plans to start a business that would support their growing family. Friends pitched in to help them renovate the one-story, cinder-block building. It wasn't much to look at, but it occupied a strategic location—not only was it between two housing projects, but it sat right on a traffic rotary that was a major access point into South Boston from neighboring Dorchester and busy Interstate 93. They christened the store "Stippo's," which was Steve Rakes's nickname.

The attractiveness of the location was not lost on Whitey Bulger and Steve Flemmi either. They wanted it, and decided to simply take it. Just after New Year's 1984, the two hoodlums took a bag stuffed with $67,000 in cash and paid a visit to the couple's apartment.

Julie was working at the store, but Steve was home, minding their two young daughters.

"We want to buy your store," Bulger said.

"We don't want to sell," Rakes replied.

Steve Flemmi sat down at the kitchen table and pulled a gun

from his waistband. He put it on the table in front of one of the blond-haired tots, who, not knowing what it was, picked it up and put her mouth on it. Bulger commented on how lovely the little girls were. "It would be a shame not to see them grow up," he said, patting the child on the head, according to court testimony.

The terrified couple was out of the store the next day. Though frightened, however, Julie Rakes wasn't completely ready to give up. She appealed to her uncle, Joe Lundbohm, a Boston Police homicide detective, to intercede.

Lundbohm's first thought was to call John Connolly, the FBI agent from Southie who seemed to know every gangster in town. Lundbohm later testified in court that he was completely unaware that Flemmi and Bulger were Connolly's informants. Connolly said that since the Rakes weren't willing to wear wires on Bulger and Flemmi, there wasn't much he could do. "I'll look into it," the agent said, according to Lundbohm's testimony.

A few days later Steve Rakes told Lundbohm that Bulger had somehow discovered that the couple had gone to the FBI, and told him to "back off" or else. Connolly later denied tipping off Bulger about the couple and said there was no prosecutable case since the Rakes weren't willing to testify. At the very least, however, Judge Wolf found Connolly's actions were "in violation of FBI policy and practice; Connolly did not record the information or disclose it to his supervisor as required by the FBI guidelines."

Kevin Weeks became the paper owner of the store, which was renamed the South Boston Liquor Mart. With its great strategic location near the highway, and its unobstructed view of a large open park area that discouraged surveillance, it quickly became Bulger, Flemmi, and Weeks's primary hangout, as well as the purchase point for alcoholic party favors handed out at the FBI's annual Christmas party.

The Rakes weren't the only South Boston residents to feel the hot grasp of Whitey Bulger's greed, followed by a cold shoulder from the FBI. Four years later it was real estate agent Ray Slinger's turn.

Slinger knew another Bulger associate who was frequently seen around the South Boston Liquor Mart, the hulking 300-pound Kevin O'Neill. The liquor store was just a sidelight for O'Neill, however. His primary business (aside from helping Bulger and Flemmi) was running Triple O's, a South Boston watering hole and hangout for the gang. The bar was located in the same space that had housed the late Transit Café, a tavern owned by the late Donald Killeen, the underworld mentor Bulger had double-crossed. The big former amateur boxer also owned several boardinghouses and apartment buildings in South Boston, and Slinger helped him collect rents.

Slinger said he took a call from O'Neill at his East Broadway real estate office, Century 21 Old Harbor, one day in 1988. Someone wanted to see him down at Triple O's, O'Neill said. Slinger went down West Broadway to the bar. Whitey Bulger was waiting for him in an upstairs function room. Slinger was shocked by what Bulger had to say. "He told me that he had been hired to take me out . . . kill me," he said.

An enemy who Bulger would not identify had paid Bulger and his associates to burst into Slinger's office with shotguns and masks and kill him, Whitey said. The only reason he hadn't already, Bulger told him, was because of his [Slinger's] friendship with O'Neill. For that reason, he was generously offering Slinger two chances to save his life: either Slinger could pay him to kill the other person, or he could pay just to scare them.

"Well, of course, I didn't want to kill anybody," Slinger said, "so I asked him to tell the other people to leave me alone. I asked him how much it would cost me to do this, a thousand or two thousand dollars."

"My fucking boots cost more than that," the gangster replied, according to Slinger. Around $50,000, Bulger said, "would be more like it."

"I don't have that kind of money," Slinger said.

"Well, I think you better find it," Bulger replied.

Slinger said he would try. First he staggered into the nearest bar that *wasn't* Triple O's and had a good stiff drink. Then he went home and made several telephone calls, including to City Councilor James Kelly, figuring his thirty years of living and working in South Boston had to count for something.

Kelly called him back, saying he had "talked with someone," and that Slinger shouldn't have any more problems.[17] If he did, Kelly said, he should talk to "the authorities."

A few weeks later, Slinger got another summons to Triple O's to see "the Man," as O'Neill called Bulger. This time Slinger was scared that he might not leave that upstairs room at O'Neill's bar, so he took a handgun out of his desk drawer and stuck it in his belt. Then he asked a woman friend who worked in the office with him to go with him on an errand across town. As soon as they arrived, Kevin Weeks whisked Slinger's female friend into the bar area of the restaurant while O'Neill pulled him into the stairwell.

O'Neill and Weeks frisked him and ripped open his shirt, looking for a wire. They found the gun instead, and laid into him with their fists and feet. "We told you not to tell anyone," they yelled. They dragged him upstairs and threw him in a chair. Bulger walked up holding Slinger's gun. There was a bullet in the chamber ready to fire, he had loaded it himself. The angry crime boss walked in back of Slinger and pressed the gun against the top of his head.

"You know if I shot you this way, there wouldn't be that much blood." Bulger gestured to Weeks, and said, "Kevin, go get a body bag."

Slinger said a silent prayer. "I thought I was done," he said later.

Suddenly, Bulger pulled the gun away. "You shouldn't have told anyone," he said. "This is serious business. If you

---

[17]Kelly later denied ever talking to Slinger.

want another chance to live, you should get that money quick . . . very quick."

Slinger was in no position to argue. He agreed to pay the $50,000 in installments, $10,000 up front and weekly payments of $2,000 to $3,000. O'Neill made the pickups, Slinger said, driving up and waiting in his car outside the real estate office, but never coming in.

As for the FBI's involvement in the Slinger case, there is little that all the parties agree on, except that two months after Slinger started making the payments, two Boston FBI agents, John Newton and Rod Kennedy, went to see him at his office, and the real estate agent told them everything that had happened to him. From that point on the accounts of what happened next diverge radically, except for one other fact: No FBI investigation was pursued against Whitey Bulger or the two Kevins for the alleged extortion.

Slinger and Bruce Ellavsky, the FBI supervisor over Kennedy and Newton, both said later that he was unwilling to testify against Bulger, fearing for his family's safety. Ellavsky said that, in his mind, Slinger's unwillingness to testify made building a case impossible. Bulger had already frisked Slinger, so a body wire was too dangerous. They might try to get Bulger in a hotel room, which was unlikely, or some other place where they could get a microphone installed. Ellavsky said one of his agents told him a short while later that Bulger and O'Neill had "backed off," and that Slinger didn't want to be relocated out of the South Boston area and was refusing to testify before a grand jury.

Ellavsky said he consulted his boss, ASAC Larry Potts, who agreed there was nothing to be done. "Basically the case died at that point," Ellavsky said.

Newton remembered the incident differently, saying he believed Slinger *would* testify, despite his fears, and that he didn't follow up because Ellavsky never told him to. Newton said he wasn't about to go after a Top Echelon informant on his own authority.

"And the reason you didn't follow up on it is because you

knew as of the date of your interview with Mr. Slinger that Mr. Bulger had a unique relationship to the FBI?" Newton was later asked.

"I knew he was an informant."

"A high level informant?"

"Yes, sir, T.E. To target a T.E. is a very unusual event," he said.

Newton, a close friend of Connolly's, had actually met Bulger and Flemmi on several occasions over the years. After Connolly's dust-up with Ring over the dinner at Flemmi's parents' house, Newton let Connolly use his apartment in South Boston to meet with the informants behind Ring's back. Newton, a former Green Beret, attended several of those meetings with the two crime bosses, sipping wine and trading stories about life in the military.

The other agent involved in the case, Rod Kennedy, drew an almost complete blank when he was asked years later about the Slinger affair. Kennedy's lack of memory might be due to his heavy drinking in the late 1980s, during the time his young son was dying of cancer. At one point he drove his sick son to a concert in Rhode Island, only to have his FBI car stolen out of the parking lot. He filed a false report, saying he had been down in Providence investigating an organized crime case, to cover his tracks. Kennedy's drinking, Ellavsky and Newton later said, could have accounted for the complete lack of any FBI reports about the Slinger interview. Judge Wolf, however, found that Kennedy's problems could not excuse Ellavsky or Potts for their "striking" mishandling of the case.

"Slinger's allegations and willingness to testify provided, under the Attorney General's Guidelines, a quintessential case for either referring Slinger's allegations to state or local law enforcement, or reporting the desire not to do so to FBI Headquarters and the Assistant Attorney General. The guidelines, however, were utterly ignored," Wolf wrote. "Instead Potts and Ellavsky evidently decided that no further investigation would be conducted. The FBI did not speak with

Slinger again. Nor was [Slinger's female friend] ever interviewed by the FBI. Moreover, contrary to both the requirements set forth in the *Manual* and standard FBI practice, no . . . written record was made of the interview of Slinger. This dereliction of duty minimized the risks that Slinger's information would ever be used against Bulger and that those responsible for protecting him would ever be held accountable for arrogating to themselves the decision to do so."

In the end, none of the agents interviewed admitted telling Connolly about the Slinger case. Newton said he would have been informed as Bulger's T.E. handler, but Ellavsky insisted that the affair was again "compartmentalized." Connolly later denied that he was told about it.

As always, though, Bulger appears to have learned that the FBI was investigating him. The day after he was interviewed by the FBI, Slinger said O'Neill approached him for a final time, saying he didn't have to pay the half of the $50,000 he still owed. The matter, O'Neill allegedly said, had been "straightened out."

"The FBI apparently decided to deal with that problem . . . by telling Bulger to 'lay off,'" Judge Wolf found in his *Salemme* order. "The court infers that Bulger was advised by Connolly to desist."

Newton and Kennedy weren't the only agents thrust into the ticklish position of investigating valuable Top Echelon informants. Special Agent James Lavin, a member of the C-1 Public Corruption Squad, also had to choose whether to stare down John Connolly and the Bureau's prized informants. Like the others, he blinked.

Lavin's relationship with *Boston Globe* photographer Joseph C. Runci was fairly standard for an FBI-media friendship, in that each side believed they were using the other. In November 1985, unknown to Runci, Lavin sent a routine teletype to FBI Headquarters seeking permission to "operate" the fifty-eight-year-old Runci as an informant. Runci, a former courthouse reporter, saw the relationship the other way—he considered Lavin to be *his* source inside the FBI.

On August 3, 1984, Runci had a photo assignment downtown, so he eased his car onto Morrissey Boulevard heading north, avoiding the perpetually-clogged Southeast Expressway. Runci's shortcut took him through South Boston into the Old Colony Avenue, where he glanced to his left over at the South Boston Liquor Mart.

Something about Whitey Bulger's liquor store caught his eye. Something is definitely wrong with this picture, he thought.

A Boston Public Works Department dump truck was parked outside the Liquor Mart. Nearby, three laborers—two older men in shorts and sneakers and a boy of about eighteen wearing dark sweatpants and no shirt—had apparently used jackhammers to drill numerous holes in front of the store. The holes had been filled with short sections of steel I-beam cut by an acetylene torch, and the men were now bolting sections of steel highway guardrail to the I-beams.

Everything about the scene was out of place. For one thing, the men were installing a guardrail just inches from the cinder-block front wall of the store, on what was obviously private property. Rather than keeping traffic on the busy rotary from jumping the curb, the guardrails were obviously intended to keep customers from bumping the wall of the liquor store when they pulled in to park. The city truck had no business being on Old Colony Avenue at all—the roadway belonged to the Metropolitan District Commission, a quasistate agency.

Runci parked a short distance away and started snapping off pictures. He got the workers, the front of the store, the signs in the Liquor Mart windows advertising $5.99 bottles of DeKuyper schnapps, and the guardrails, but since the truck had no rear license plate, he had to sneak around behind it, driving his car the wrong way up a one-way side street. When he returned to the *Globe* building, Runci made two sets of eight-by-ten black and white prints from the photos, stamping the date on the back of each one. He kept one set and handed the other to one of the editors.

For some reason, the story fell through the cracks and the photos never made the paper. Determined that they wouldn't go to waste, a week or two later Runci stuck the second set of photos in a manila envelope and called the FBI office. He also put in some letters from a friend of his about another South Boston liquor store that he thought might be relevant. He called Lavin and they met in the marble-tiled lobby of the *Globe* building. When Runci pulled out the photos, Lavin looked extremely interested.

"I was going by and I saw the city truck there," he told Lavin. "There weren't any plates on the back of the truck, so I had to go around the one-way street to get them."

Two weeks later Runci was driving through the rotary again. The guardrails weren't there anymore. He called Lavin.

"They're gone," he said.

"Are you sure?" Lavin asked.

"There's nothing there."

"Gee, I can't believe that."

Something was wrong. How would Bulger have known to have taken the guardrails down so quickly? Yet Lavin didn't ask Runci to take any more photos or look into the matter any further. Well, that's it then, Runci thought.

A week or so later Lavin called again and asked Runci to bring the negatives, which had been filed at the *Globe*, over to the FBI office at the JFK Building. He seemed anxious to get them, the photographer later recalled. Lavin showed Runci a short affidavit, which he said would certify that he had taken the photographs. The affidavit would be shown to a grand jury, Lavin said.

"If I don't sign this, are you going to subpoena me?"

"Yes," the agent said.

"Well, I'll sign it, then," Runci said.

Runci left the negatives with Lavin, figuring that he would get them back after the grand jury investigation was over.

Only there never was any grand jury investigation—or any investigation at all.

Lavin could hardly have missed the fact that the photos showed clearly improper activity taking place in front of the South Boston Liquor Mart, a store he knew was controlled by Bulger. If Boston city employees were using city equipment for Bulger's benefit, Lavin was duty-bound, as a member of the Public Corruption Squad, to investigate. But instead of following procedure and filling out a report, Lavin took the photos straight to Morris and explained where they had come from.

"Run it by John Connolly," Morris said.

Lavin, who had heard talk around the office that Bulger and Flemmi were T.E. informants, found Connolly over by the office gun vault and explained about the photos he had received from Runci. Connolly confirmed Bulger and Flemmi were indeed informants and said that they had been very "valuable" in the past.

"What are you going to do with that?" Connolly asked.

Lavin said later that he didn't remember what his reply was. But what he did, essentially, was nothing. He never filled out a report on the incident, ensuring that no one but he, Morris, and Connolly would learn about it. It should have been put in the FBI's vaunted index files, where the C-2 squad, which was supposed to be investigating Bulger and Flemmi, could access it. Nor did he make an attempt to track down and confront the men who installed the guardrails, who might have become witnesses against Bulger and Flemmi. Instead of doing his job, Lavin stuck the photos in an envelope and put them in his desk. When he moved to the South Shore permanently at the Lakeville Resident Agency, he put the photos in a box, moved them with the rest of his belongings, and stuck them in a drawer of his new desk. The photos only surfaced in 1997 when, fearing that he might be accused of obstruction of justice, Lavin turned them over to the FBI's Office of Professional Responsibility.

Lavin's version of the story differs from Runci's. In a

slightly more mitigating account, Lavin said he received the photographs in December of 1987, not 1984, when he only technically was still on Morris's C-1 Public Corruption Squad, but was actually assigned to cover two counties south of Boston, a posting agents called the "South Shore Road Trip." Lavin's version made the lead a three-year-old one rather than a fresh one. He did not explain why Runci would wait three years before sending him the photos.

Regardless of the timing, when he was under oath at the *Salemme* hearings, Lavin called his actions a "mistake."

"Was it unusual for you to stick documents received from an informant in your desk drawer as opposed to placing it in an informant file or a case file or a substantive file?" Lavin was asked by Flemmi's lawyer, Kenneth Fishman.

"Yes, sir."

"Why did you do that?"

"It was a judgment call at that time. In hindsight, I should have put it in the file."

"Well, having in mind the hindsight, I'm asking you what was going on in your mind at the time. Why didn't you do it at that time?"

"I don't know."

"You have no idea why?"

"No, like I said, I just got the information and I was told to provide it to John Connolly, and that's exactly what I did, sir."

Ultimately, Lavin gave the same excuse that Ed Quinn and Ed Clark used after ignoring Joe Murray's murder allegations: just following orders.

Another Boston FBI agent, a member of the drug squad, soon faced a similar situation. In 1986 an informant was telling Special Agent James Blackburn that a drug dealer named Hobart Willis was paying $4,000 to $6,000 per month to Bulger and Flemmi for the right to sell cocaine in South Boston. Instead of opening a case, Blackburn, like Lavin, went to see John Connolly, who said he believed Willis was lying. His nonsensical explanation was that Willis "would have tried to kill Bulger if a demand like that was ever made." The idea that a ruthless, accomplished killer and extortionist like Bulger would be afraid of a lowly coke dealer was laughable, but Blackburn's response in the matter wasn't very amusing.

"I didn't follow that investigative avenue again," he admitted on the witness stand.

Why would Morris tell Lavin to take his corruption case and "run it by" Connolly? Probably because by that time he himself had been thoroughly corrupted. Like Newton, he was still meeting periodically with Connolly, Bulger, and Flemmi behind Ring's back, and he hadn't stopped taking money after receiving the $1,000 for his secretary's junket to Georgia.

Some ex-FBI agents and lawyers who worked with Morris believe he was done in by a combination of his own personal flaws and a carefully managed campaign by Bulger, Flemmi, and Connolly to neutralize him as a threat. After Morris had been swept aside as supervisor of the C-3 squad and replaced by Jim Ring, and due to the friction over their respective informants and the credit for the Angiulo bug, Bulger, Flemmi, and Connolly were smart enough to know that Morris could potentially be trouble. They appear to have worked on him from all sides, adopting a carrot-and-stick approach.

Inside the FBI office, Connolly let Morris know that his career success was pinned to the state of their relationship. As an incentive to loyalty, Connolly, according to Morris's testimony, held out the hope of a lucrative state job after the FBI, courtesy of Billy Bulger.

"He just seemed to know . . . a lot of the politicians," Morris said later. "At some future date, you know, when I retired from the Bureau, John had talked about that there would be a lot of good opportunities for jobs and so forth once we left the Bureau." For proof, Morris needed to look no further than his friend, original Bulger recruiter Dennis Condon, who left the Bureau to become a top official in the State Department of Public Safety.

But it was clear to Morris that Connolly, if he wanted,

could also seriously damage his future at the Bureau. Connolly was extremely tight with the Bureau's organized crime all-stars like Sean McWeeney, Jules Bonavolonta, and Joseph Pistone, who became famous by going undercover as "Donnie Brasco" and infiltrating New York's Bonnano crime family. Pistone and Bonavolonta, in fact, were invited out to dinner with Bulger and Flemmi and Special Agent Nick Gianturco.

"He was a very connected person inside the Bureau, outside the Bureau, and I did not want to place myself in a position where I was in any strong opposition of him," Morris said. "Originally, I considered him a close friend and, quite frankly, as time went by, Connolly became much more influential than what you would normally think an agent to be."

Morris said Connolly was smart enough not to make any overt threats. Instead, Connolly positioned himself as Morris's patron with the powerful organized crime faction at FBI Headquarters, to the point where, were his support to be withdrawn, it would damage Morris's future at the Bureau. "He was supportive of me with individuals that had influence on me personally and my career," Morris said. "I mean, I was concerned it would absolutely destroy me."

One example was Connolly's relationship with SAC James Ahearn. Ahearn was a bona fide member of the FBI's organized crime fraternity; he was the agent who convinced San Francisco mafioso Jimmy "the Weasel" Frattiano to become an FBI cooperating witness. Morris learned a lesson in just how much loyalty Connolly commanded when he [Morris] declined to recommend Connolly for a supervisor's position, an incident that soured their relationship. After the FBI's Career Board gave Connolly's promotion a thumbs-down, Ahearn flew to Washington and personally lobbied Headquarters on Connolly's behalf. "I have never seen a SAC go to FBI Headquarters and recommend somebody be made a supervisor when the Career Board recommended against it, never," Morris said.

The most effective weapons for neutralizing Morris,

though, were the bribes from Bulger and Flemmi, most of which were facilitated by Connolly. In Judge Wolf's analysis, the payments all seemed to follow major leaks to Bulger and Flemmi. The Glencoe plane ticket bribe, for example, came shortly after Brian Halloran's identity was leaked and he was murdered. Shortly after Connolly was told about the DEA–Quincy Police investigation in the spring of 1984, Connolly delivered a case of wine to Morris, which he said was a gift from the two T.E. informants. When Morris opened the box, he found an envelope containing $1,000 in cash.

The next day, Morris said, Connolly called him and asked, "Did you find what was in the bottom of the box?"

Morris admitted that he had found the money, and immediately regretting saying so after hanging up. Jesus, what if he's taping this? he thought. The second bribe had achieved its twin purposes: dirtying Morris up and making him afraid of being exposed.

The best evidence that the bribes were part of a calculated campaign to neutralize Morris is that, while Connolly happily transferred bribes from Bulger and Flemmi, he apparently never said anything to Morris about taking money himself. Years later, when Morris was testifying under a grant of immunity and had a golden opportunity to destroy his rival, the best he could do was a vague allegation that Connolly looked like he was "living beyond his means."

Connolly also tried to endear his star informants to Nick Gianturco. Bulger and Flemmi had allegedly "saved" Gianturco's life when he was working undercover on "Operation Lobster," a highly successful sting of truck-hijacking gangs from Charlestown. Gianturco, posing as a fence buying swag off the hijacked trucks, was invited to a meeting with some of the hijackers toward the end of the investigation. The meeting felt wrong, so Gianturco decided not to go. Connolly later told him the decision had been the right one, because his informants (Bulger and Flemmi) had said the meeting was an ambush. By the time the story made its way around the office, however, it had evolved to Bulger saving Gianturco's life by warning him not to go. Connolly urged Gianturco to exchange Christmas gifts and other tokens of appreciation—bottles of wine, glassware, books, a Lladro statuette for his wife—with the two informants to help strengthen the bond between them and the FBI. The dinner where Bulger and Flemmi met Joe Pistone and Jules Bonavolonta, in fact, was held at Gianturco's house. Gianturco later admitted that doing so was "a mistake," but insisted he never felt professionally compromised.

In Morris's case, however, the apparent plan to compromise him was a resounding success. During one dinner, Morris said he asked Connolly: "What do these guys want from us?"

"A heads-up," Connolly replied, presumably meaning advance warning if they were to be indicted. Such a warning would clearly be committing a federal crime (obstruction of justice). Morris would later say that the reason he didn't report the "heads-up" conversation, or order Connolly not to provide one, was because he was too intimidated and too corrupted.

"Your job as the supervisor of the Organized Crime Squad of the FBI, I take it, was to prevent crime?" Morris was later asked.

"I should have told Connolly no," he replied.

"That was your job?"

"Yes."

The third bribe Morris admitted to, which he said essentially completed the corruption process, happened in the spring of 1985, during a dinner at Morris's house in Lexington that was also attended by Bulger, Flemmi, Connolly, and old FBI friend Dennis Condon. Flemmi brought champagne, presumably to celebrate the successful dodging of the DEA–Quincy Police bug.

The conversation during the meal later became a key dispute. Flemmi and Bulger, apparently concerned that they had been recorded on the Angiulo tapes, again asked for reassurance that they wouldn't be prosecuted. To hear both

Connolly and Flemmi tell it, a somewhat drunken Morris told them, "You guys can do anything you want as long as you don't clip [kill] anyone."

Morris's alleged words later became a centerpiece of Flemmi's defense to racketeering charges in the *U.S.* v. *Salemme* case in front of Judge Wolf. Flemmi said the statement showed that the FBI had given him de facto "immunity" from prosecution as a Top Echelon informant. Morris denied making the statement, but Wolf found that he had either "forgotten" doing so or was lying, telling the prosecutors what they wanted to hear to cement his deal for immunity. Morris had a long track record as a liar, Wolf wrote.

What is undisputed is that Morris, who was having financial problems due to his family's medical bills, was also given $5,000 at the dinner by Bulger and Flemmi. Morris called it a bribe, Flemmi called it a loan, although he admitted that none of it was repaid. In all, by 1985, Morris had taken $7,000 from the two informants, and he was deeply in their debt.

As the afternoon sun bathed the autumn leaves in rural Wayland, Massachusetts, a gangly, blond-haired nine-year-old named Sarah Pryor put on her Sony Walkman and went exploring. It was something she had often done in her home of Peters Township, a Pittsburgh suburb, so there was nothing particularly unusual about what she was doing that day in October 1985. She was last seen by a local waitress, walking through a cornfield more than a mile from her home, on the postcard-perfect New England day.

When she failed to come home on time, her parents assumed she was simply lost. After all, they had just moved to Massachusetts six weeks before. Hours passed, and they called police as night fell. By the next morning, a full-scale search was under way. It intensified as one day stretched into two, then three. At one point, two thousand volunteers were combing the woods near her home and police were using rescue dogs and helicopters and handing out five thousand "missing girl" flyers at a nearby roadblock.

Nothing.

As it became apparent that the case involved foul play, it became a national media sensation. Sarah Pryor became one of the original milk-carton children. The media crush put tremendous pressure on law enforcement officials to find her, or at least a suspect who might have abducted or killed her. Since after a certain time period child disappearances are presumed to be kidnappings, the Boston FBI office was called into the case.

Remarkably, with all the investigative tools the Bureau had at its disposal, Morris and Connolly turned to Whitey Bulger to help solve the case. The story of Bulger's intervention is strikingly similar to the New York FBI's reported use of Greg Scarpa in the MIBURN case in Mississippi, and, taken together, both stories appear to show how deeply some Top Echelon informants became enmeshed in the FBI's institutional structure.

Bulger's involvement began four months after her disappearance, when a Boston woman came forward and said she knew what had happened to Sarah Pryor. The problem was that Laura Hawkins's story seemed to change with each telling. First it was that the fourth-grader had been abducted and was being held in Rhode Island. Then it was that she had been raped and killed and was dumped in a heating duct of an apartment building in a Dorchester housing project. Hawkins's credibility was obviously highly suspect, but at that point all the investigators were grasping at straws, and so they ran down every lead she gave them.

One of the men Hawkins named was a petty thief from South Boston whom she'd had a falling out with. The investigators went to see him in the Salem jail, where he had been taken after being arrested for larceny at a local mall. He denied being involved in Pryor's disappearance, but his lie detector test came up "inconclusive" and his name was added to the investigator's list of possible suspects.

Word quickly leaked to the newspapers that a South Boston man might have been involved in the Sarah Pryor kidnapping. Bulger, Flemmi, Morris, and Connolly were having one of their many get-togethers at about the same time, and Bulger suggested that he might help because he knew the suspect from South Boston. More important, the suspect knew *him*. Connolly said he thought it was a great idea to see if Bulger could pry loose the location of Pryor's body. Morris didn't object.

With rumors circulating that he was the Pryor killer, meanwhile, the man had been transferred from the relative comfort of Salem to murderer's row at the Lawrence House of Correction. A few days later he got a visitor call. "It's the police," a guard said. Instead, as he was looking out the window of the visiting room into the parking lot, he was startled to see two men he recognized from his South Boston days, Kevin Weeks and Whitey Bulger.

Weeks came in alone.

"Look outside," Weeks said. "You know who that is?"

The man looked out at Bulger, who was staring in the window, arms folded. He nodded.

Sure he knew, he said.

We want to know where that Wayland girl's body is, Weeks said.

The suspect denied having anything to do with the girl's disappearance.

We want to know where she is, Weeks repeated.

"If you don't tell us, first we'll kill your brother," Weeks said. The man's brother still lived in Southie. "Then we're coming after you.

"We'll bail you out of there and then we'll kill you," Weeks told him. "You better do the right thing. Here, this is a friend of ours, call him," he said, handing over a card. It had the FBI's distinctive "Fidelity, Bravery, Integrity" seal on it and the words "John Connolly, Special Agent." Watson took the card.

The suspect never heard from Weeks again. A short time

later he read in the newspaper that his old friend Laura Hawkins had failed a lie detector test of her own and had been indicted for perjury. She later admitted lying to collect the $30,000 reward that had been offered by Andy and Meg Pryor, Sarah's parents. Authorities cleared Watson of any involvement.[18] Just as the FBI had used Scarpa in the Mississippi Burning case, Bulger had become a virtual agent. Only the nice thing about Top Echelon informants was that they didn't have to worry about minor issues like brutality, constitutional rights, or whether the guy might actually be innocent.

After Jerry Angiulo and his brothers were convicted and sent to prison in 1986, John Morris apparently began having a change of heart about Bulger and Flemmi.

Morris went to Larry Potts, the new ASAC, and suggested that Bulger and Flemmi might not be pulling their weight anymore as informants. With the Angiulo case over, and since he was long since gone from investigating organized crime cases, Morris didn't need them. Potts told Ahearn, the new SAC, what Morris had said, and Ahearn agreed that Potts should conduct a "suitability review" to determine whether Bulger and Flemmi should remain a part of the Top Echelon Informant Program.

Under the FBI's guidelines, suitability reviews are essentially a balancing test, with the informant's crimes and misdeeds on one side of the scale and his value to the Bureau on the other. Conducted in the field, the suitability reviews carried a lot of weight at FBI Headquarters. Potts later testified that in all his years in the Bureau, he never once heard about Headquarters reversing a suitability finding made by a supervisor in the field. Unfortunately, the opinions of agents who were consulted in the reviews could hardly be viewed as objective—especially for Top Echelon informants whose

---

[18]Fifteen years later a piece of Pryor's skull was unearthed in some dense woods about four miles from her home. The case wasn't solved, but authorities believe the killer may have been a convicted murderer from Texas.

inside information was so coveted by the Organized Crime squads. Not surprisingly, Connolly leaped to their defense, as did Ring, who, unlike Morris, had yet to reap *his* big benefit from Bulger and Flemmi's cooperation.

The review took several days. Potts flipped through Bulger's informant file and interviewed several agents. Initially, Potts said, he was "alarmed that the amount of information in the file had dropped off dramatically since the early 1980s," prior to the Angiulo case. His interviews with the agents—Ring, Connolly, Nick Gianturco, and Morris, however, carried the day. Gianturco told the story about how Bulger had warned him about the Charlestown crew during Operation Lobster. Connolly suggested to Potts that Bulger and Flemmi might have to be called upon to do the same for Vince Dellamontaine, an undercover agent who was posing as a mob associate in East Boston at the time. Ring not only made a "strong" recommendation that they stay open, but told Potts that the informant files were misleading because Connolly, known around the office for being "bad with paper," had yet to write up some important information that the two informants had provided.

That left Morris alone on the other side of the fence. Eventually he chickened out, telling Potts it was "just as well" that they remain open as informants. Not surprisingly, Potts's conclusion was that Bulger and Flemmi were still "suitable" to be Top Echelon informants.

Potts's decision led directly to an investigation that became, simultaneously, one of the Boston FBI's major triumphs against the Italian-American Mafia, and a shameful example of agents putting career ambitions ahead of the law, public safety, and their own regulations.

It began simply enough, with a bug in the back room of a small Italian deli in the Prudential Center, a popular shopping plaza that wrapped around a huge office, hotel, and high-rise apartment complex in Boston's Back Bay. Vanessa's was named after the daughter of the shop's co-owner, Angelo "Sonny" Mercurio, a short, central-casting-type made guy from the North End who really did say "youse" instead of "you." The shop was popular with the lunchtime business-suit crowd, which was a good thing, because Mercurio needed at least the appearance that he was involved in a legitimate business, being still on parole for a stolen securities conviction. Vanessa's was popular with the FBI too. The Boston agents had their periodic physical checkups in a doctor's office in the office building above it and frequently saw Sonny working the counter, dishing out Italian cold-cut and meatball subs, as they walked by.

Mercurio was part of the next wave of North End wiseguys who were trying to reestablish their dominance of the rackets after Jerry Angiulo and his brothers were sent to prison. By getting Angiulo out of the way, Steve Flemmi and Whitey Bulger had solved one of their problems but also created a new one, Joseph "J.R." Russo, who was now the obvious pretender to the Boston underboss throne. J.R. was a throwback tough-as-nails mobster with none of Angiulo's pragmatic streak. He was a mafioso's mafioso, a granite-cold killer who believed that there was one mob in Boston—his mob. It was no surprise, then, that Bulger and Flemmi were only too happy to help the FBI get rid of him too.

Bulger and Flemmi told the FBI that the real business at Vanessa's was being conducted in the back room. Accessible directly and discreetly by freight elevator from an underground parking garage, it was the perfect place for Mercurio's Patriarca family brethren to conduct their criminal transactions. Since Mercurio had been appointed as a liaison between the Boston Mafia and the Winter Hill Gang, Bulger and Flemmi had intimate access to Vanessa's.

They ended up being two of the three "confidential sources" listed in the affidavits submitted to a federal judge in the electronic surveillance application. Just as he had done in the Angiulo case, Flemmi drew a diagram of the interior of the shop for the FBI, including the location of burglar alarms and circuit boxes.

The bug was a major success. Among other things, in early 1987 it recorded Mercurio's Mafia friends threatening to kill two aging bookmakers, eighty-nine-year-old former dentist Harry "Doc" Saganski and his equally aged partner, Moe Weinstein. For years Saganski and Weinstein had been allowed to operate without paying much to the Angiulo regime. But the capos who were now running Boston in Angiulo's absence, Russo, Robert Carrozza, and Vincent "the Animal" Ferrara, weren't going to continue the largesse—particularly since they were responsible for supporting the families of the Angiulo brothers while they were in prison.

Summoned to Vanessa's by Carrozza and Ferrara, Saganski tried to cry poor-mouth, saying the Massachusetts State Lottery had "destroyed" the illegal numbers business.

Too bad, Ferrara said, "It's *your* business."

One of Ferrara's soldiers, a vicious bantamweight extortionist named Dennis "Champagne" LePore, demanded an immediate $500,000 and another $1,500 a week.

"I'm not going to give you no bankroll," Saganski said.

"You don't have an alternative . . . All those years you made all your fucking money. We want something now. And you're lucky it ain't more. This is a serious request. You understand?" the wiry LePore yelled at the wizened old Jewish bookie. "What are we playing, a fucking game here, pal? You reamed the harvest all those fucking years! This is something you're going to pay now! We want it! We're not asking!"

Finally, the two bookies agreed to pay $250,000 up front and the rest in five monthly installments as the FBI tape recorders caught every word. Soon, the wiseguys got a tip that the deli had been bugged, but it was much too late.

The feds had Sonny Mercurio and his friends dead to rights, and they knew it.

Federal prosecutors began filing court papers signaling that a major Mafia indictment was coming, and both of the city's major newspapers, the *Globe* and the *Herald*, picked up the story. The news could not have come at a worse time for the New England Mafia, because fault lines that had developed in the previous few years were starting to crack perilously wider.

After his powerful father's death in 1984, Raymond Patriarca Jr. received the New York Commission's permission to become boss of the New England family. Like so many other sons of strong Mafia fathers, "Junior" was a pale copy of the original; hesitant where the elder Raymond had been decisive, timid where the old man had been calculatingly bold. Contrasted with his father's intimidating bird-of-prey appearance, Patriarca's doughy face didn't help him much either. Some wiseguys, in fact, called him "Rubberlips" behind his back.

"Junior did not have the brains or the power to lead the family. Had his father not come before him, he wouldn't have got the job. He couldn't lead a Brownie troop," a Rhode Island State Police organized crime expert once said.

There had never been much love lost between Boston and Providence. The elder Patriarca, however, had been strong enough to keep the lid on any overt factionalism, and Jerry Angiulo had been relatively content as an underboss and never made a serious attempt to unseat Raymond. With both powerful men now out of the picture, lingering resentments between the two sides were simmering, but hadn't come to a boil. An indictment of the top members of the Boston faction, however, might be just the thing to tip the balance of power dangerously to one side or the other.

The situation was ideal for the FBI. Times of turmoil and stress always presented opportunities to recruit Top Echelon informants. Thanks to Bulger and Flemmi, the Bureau knew that Mercurio was disenchanted with the Mafia, so the Boston office's top informant recruiter, John Connolly, took advantage. Interestingly, years later Jim Ring actually claimed that he orchestrated Connolly's recruitment of Mercurio.

"I said, all right, what I want you to do is go to Vanessa's, go sit down at an outside table, and have a cup of coffee,"

Ring testified during the *Salemme* hearings. "And I want you to wait and see if Mr. Mercurio approaches you. If he approaches you, I want you to do absolutely nothing other than listen. I don't care what he's got to say, I don't care who he wants to talk about, I don't care if he wants to tell you about every crime in the western world. You say nothing."

Ring said he sent Connolly there a second time with the same instructions. On the third visit, Mercurio was ready to talk.

The OC Squad probably got a hoot out of Ring's version when it made the rounds at the water cooler. Connolly, after all, was the man fellow agent Nick Gianturco called "the best informant recruiter I ever saw," and Ring giving him informant recruiting advice was a little like Minnie Mendoza giving Ted Williams tips on how to hit the curve ball. The way Mercurio tells the story, Connolly, as always, did things his way, seizing on a slip of the lip by the wiseguy and using it to blackmail him into cooperating. Blackmailing potential informants was a common enough method of recruiting. Paul Rico was a master at it, and Morris admitted doing it twice, once with Bucky Barrett and another time with a bookmaker named Eddie Miani. Morris, in fact, went so far as to plant a fake bomb under Miani's car, let the police "discover" it, and then tell the bookie that the FBI believed Bulger and Flemmi wanted him dead.

Mercurio said he bumped into Connolly in the Prudential Center in the fall of 1987, after Vanessa's had been searched. The wiseguy, still smarting from the humiliation of being successfully bugged, accused the FBI of trying to "plant" evidence during their secret forays into the store and bragged that the Mafia had outsmarted them on at least that score.

"You come up with nothing. What did you think, I didn't know youse had the keys to go in and out the back? We have better information than youse guys," Mercurio said.

Mercurio was trying to best Connolly in a battle of insider information. It was a mistake. Connolly calmly rattled off the name of the Mafia's inside source for law enforcement information. He was right on the money, Mercurio said.

"Listen," Connolly continued, "we know who the guy is who was giving you the information, but we want to know who that guy is working for. You help us, and we won't let your friends know that you tipped us off about the source."

It was essentially a death threat. Mercurio had stupidly confirmed that the Mafia had a law enforcement source, and he knew what it meant if the FBI ratted him out. His life was now in Connolly's hands. "I got trapped," he said.[19]

Mercurio's conversion earned Flemmi restored Top Echelon status in November 1987. In less than a year, Mercurio had joined him as a T.E., and was constantly feeding the FBI inside information on his pals in the Mafia. In some ways he even supplanted Bulger and Flemmi in importance—the FBI and the Organized Crime Strike Force were targeting the Boston faction of the Mafia, Carrozza, Russo, and Ferrara, and as member of their inner circle, Mercurio was privy to information that even Flemmi could not obtain. He threw himself into his informant role enthusiastically—even the fact that he'd been the best man at Vinnie Ferrara's wedding didn't stop him from thoroughly ratting out his old friend.

Mercurio's value as an informant made protecting him a priority. One potential problem was his federal parole on the stolen securities case. For one thing, how could he be a T.E. informant if he was forbidden from associating with known felons? The FBI and the strike force set about making it go away. Jerry O'Sullivan, the strike force chief, wrote a letter to the U.S. Parole Commission.

---

[19]Despite a well-established pattern of FBI agents coercing wiseguys into becoming informants, Judge Wolf found Mercurio's testimony on how he was recruited "not credible," and inferred instead that Mercurio was swayed by a promise that he would be given a warning to flee before indictments were handed up. The author and the judge part ways on this point. The two reasons for Mercurio to cooperate are not mutually exclusive, and indeed were probably a more persuasive incentive together as a carrot and stick.

> *It is the very strong desire of the Federal Bureau of Investigation that Mr. Mercurio be rewarded with early termination of his parole because of the extremely valuable information that Mr. Mercurio has provided and continues to provide to the FBI concerning the activities of the leadership element of La Cosa Nostra in the Boston area.*

The Chief of the FBI Informant Unit in Washington, James Summerford, also wrote a note to the parole commission supporting the early termination of Mercurio's parole:

> *The FBI will make a factual presentation to the sentencing judge concerning his cooperation to date. Early termination of Mr. Mercurio's parole will help ensure that he is not sent to jail for violating his parole where his safety could be in danger.*

The Summerford letter was garbage. Sonny Mercurio, Ring, and Diane Kottmyer, the strike force prosecutor on the case, all later testified that there was never any talk of telling a judge about Mercurio's cooperation. "Mr. Mercurio, as I understood it, adamantly stated he wanted no special treatment. He was a man. He would do his time. And he did not want his status brought to the attention of the judge or disclosed to any person," Kottmyer said. Also, since Sonny had insisted that he would be a stand-up guy and do his time, why would the FBI be worried about his safety in jail?

The real reason the FBI wanted the parole terminated, Judge Wolf decided, was that as a parolee, if Mercurio were arrested for any crime, he would automatically be sent back to prison with no shot at bail. FBI officials weren't worried about Mercurio's safety at all, the judge said, they just wanted him to get bail so that if he wanted, he could take off.

* * *

Mercurio was granted early parole in February of 1989, and was finally free to meet with whomever he wanted to in the underworld. Had the FBI paid any attention to its own informant guidelines, Sonny might have been useful in preventing a near-disastrous shooting.

The guidelines state:

> When the FBI learns that persons under investigation intend to commit a violent crime, any informants or confidential sources used in connection with the investigation shall be instructed to try, to the extent practicable, to discourage the violence.

Apparently, nobody read Sonny Mercurio that part, because instead of preventing a disaster, he planned one.

Mercurio and Stevie Flemmi were both telling the FBI about deep tensions within the Patriarca family. It seemed almost as though Raymond Jr. was going out of his way to antagonize the Russo faction. First he snubbed J. R. Russo by naming Billy Grasso, a close ally and tough guy from the Hartford faction, as his underboss. Now Boston wasn't even playing second fiddle anymore. An even more egregious insult was the fact that Junior had quietly "made" Flemmi's old friend Frank Salemme, who had finally been released from state prison after serving sixteen years for blowing off the legs of Joe Barboza's lawyer, John Fitzgerald.

The Barboza connection should have made Salemme and Russo simpatico. It was J.R., after all, who had tracked Barboza down in San Francisco and gunned him down with an assault rifle. But it was no secret that Salemme disliked the North End and looked down on Jerry Angiulo for never having made his bones. The "fucking turd," Salemme once said, "never had a gun in his hand."

"Cadillac" Frank's induction to the family had incensed the Boston faction, which was badly depleted after the Angiulo case. Russo, Carrozza and Ferrara desperately

wanted to make new soldiers before they were arrested, so
someone would be around to run their criminal enterprises
while they were inside. Raymond Jr., however, had said
"the books were closed," meaning no new members were
being made. Salemme's promotion, then, was a shockingly naked power play and a humiliating slap to Russo.
Ferrara, Russo, and Carrozza started believing that
Salemme was lining up a Boston takeover after they were
indicted. J. R. even made an unsuccessful plea to Gambino boss "Teflon Don" John Gotti in New York to medi-
ate the dispute.

The FBI had practically up-to-the-minute information on
what was going on. John Connolly wrote a long memo about
what Flemmi told him on June 5, 1989.

> [Flemmi] advised that the relationship
> between the Boston LCN faction (Joe
> Russo, Bobby Carrozza, "Spucky" Spagn-
> uolo, and Vinny Ferrara) and the Revere,
> Massachusetts, Providence, Rhode Island,
> and Hartford LCN has deteriorated badly
> over the last couple of weeks. The Boston
> LCN, under pressure from imminent fed-
> eral indictments and bitter about the
> treatment they are receiving from LCN
> capo Charlie Quintina and Frankie
> Salemme, are frustrated, paranoid and
> extremely dangerous right now.
>
> It is becoming increasingly apparent to
> the Boston LCN that they are being ig-
> nored, and source believes the situation
> to be extremely volatile in that the
> Boston outfit people believe that they
> are running out of time to resolve their
> concerns before they are "snapped up" by
> the FBI.
>
> Source stated that the Russo faction

blamed their problems on Frankie Salemme
(who stands to take over all of Boston
after the indictments), Charlie Quintina,
who has agreed with Raymond Patriarca
Jr. and Frankie Salemme in every decision which has affected the Boston LCN
adversely, and Billy Grasso, who has no
love for Joe Russo is blamed for insti-
gating the "bind" which the Boston LCN
finds themselves in.

Source believes that the above factors
could lead to a violent confrontation
between the factions.

Source believes that the Frankie
Salemme, Charlie Quintina, Billy Grasso
faction would like to "take out" Vinny
Ferrara if they can send him up. Source
believes that they would not be easy in
that Ferrara already believes that is
their intention.

Source stated further that the Boston
LCN would like to "clip" Frankie
Salemme, Charlie Quintina and anyone
else they perceive as a problem, such as
Frank Salemme Jr., Price Quintina, and
"Sonny Boy" Rizzo.

The guns were being loaded.

Under the guidelines, the FBI was required to have Mercurio, Flemmi, and Bulger do what they could to ease tensions and avoid bloodshed. Instead, Connolly appears to
have done his best to inflame them.

A front-page headline in the June 13 *Boston Herald*
screamed:

EX-CON SEEN AS HUB MOB'S
HEIR APPARENT

A TOUGH ex-con is viewed as the "heir apparent" to many of the Mob's Boston rackets—as federal charges loom against reputed Mafia lieutenant and other mob leaders, sources told the Herald.

Francis P. Salemme, 55, of Sharon, has become "a new emerging power" since his Feb. 13, 1988 release from prison after serving nearly 15 years for trying to murder a lawyer by blowing up his car, sources said.

"He did his time and they owe him," another source said. "He kept his mouth shut for 15 years."

A little later on, the article said law enforcement sources were speculating that "Salemme has Patriarca's 'blessing' to take over lucrative loan-sharking and gambling rackets in the Boston area."

The article "may have inflamed the volatile and potentially violent situation," Judge Wolf later ruled. The judge also identified Connolly as the probable source of the leak, because Ring was on vacation and the article closely matched the wording in another report of a meeting between Connolly and Flemmi. Salemme's lawyer, Anthony Cardinale, was more blunt, calling the combination of the leak and the FBI's failure to warn Salemme about the threats to his life "as evil as it gets." Assistant U.S. Attorney Brian Kelly denied there was an "FBI plot" to kill Salemme. "Mr. Cardinale is becoming the Oliver Stone of the defense bar," Kelly said.[20]

---

[20]There has been much debate on the subject of whether the *Herald* article actually contributed to the Salemme shooting. Both sides are probably correct to a degree—while the tensions that led to the Salemme shooting existed beforehand, the article certainly exacerbated them. There can be no doubt, though, that the *Herald* reporter who wrote the story, Shelley Murphy, was doing her job by accurately reporting factual information about tensions in the underworld.

A few days after the *Herald* story, Mercurio called
Salemme and suggested that the two men meet at an International House of Pancakes restaurant on busy Route 1 in
Saugus, a town just north of Boston. According to Cardinale, Salemme was dressed in sweatpants and a T-shirt, having just come from the gym. Mercurio was late, so Salemme
went out front, thinking there had been a mix-up. A car was
coming toward him and he waved, thinking it was Mercurio.
The windows rolled down and a .45 caliber pistol and an
M-16 rifle emerged.

The big, curly haired hoodlum was hit once in the chest in
the first ear-shattering volley. He ducked inside the vestibule
of the IHOP and hit the floor, but the men in the car kept firing. Salemme looked over at the woman behind the cash
register, who was yelling, "It's gunfire! Everybody down!"
and frantically clutching for the phone to call the police.
Then he saw a chunk of plaster exploded out of the wall,
right above where a little girl was sitting with her parents.
Afraid kids would be hurt, Salemme got back up and ran out
the door toward the gun car. Apparently startled, the gunmen
stopped firing for a moment, and then opened up again, hit-
ting Salemme in the leg. This time he ducked into a Papa
Gino's pizza shop and grabbed a knife from the counter,
crouching low behind the door and waiting for one of the
shooters to follow. The shooting abruptly stopped, and the
assassins were gone in a squeal of burning tires.

Salemme slumped into a booth and pressed a pile of nap-
kins against the gushing wound in his chest.

"Call 911," he said to the gape-mouthed girl behind the
counter.

Later that afternoon, as Salemme was under heavy guard
in North Shore Hospital, two fishermen found underboss
Billy Grasso's body on the banks of the Connecticut River
in Weathersfield, just outside Hartford. He had been shot in
the back of the head.

A front-page story in the *Globe* predicted that the two shootings "could mark the beginning of Mafia violence the likes of

which New England has not seen for more than two decades."
Authorities braced for more bloodshed as they tried to figure
out what had happened. Mercurio, who had fled to New York,
met with Connolly and told him that while his faction was responsible for the Grasso hit and the attempt on Salemme, it
was the capos, not he, who had done the planning.

Several weeks later another FBI informant, who has never
been identified, laid out the truth for the FBI.

```
On 8/2/89 informant advised that capos
Vinny Ferrara, Joe Russo, Bobby Car-
rozza, and soldier Sonny Mercurio, were
responsible for the shooting of Frank
Salemme. This group claims that Salemme
was trying to take over some of their ex-
tortion business and they needed to move
on Salemme to protect their business
after they were unable to get their prob-
lems resolved by Raymond Patriarca Jr.
    Informant stated that after the shoot-
ing, Sonny Mercurio took off because it
was him who set up the meeting with
Salemme when he was shot. Ferrara,
Russo, Carrozza and Mercurio are now
looking to "finish off" what they
started before they are indicted by the
Feds.
```

The same informant, a few days later, essentially told the
FBI that the shooting was over. The two sides were looking
to make peace, the source said, but the only possible problem was Sonny Mercurio.

```
On 8/10/89, informant advised that Ray-
mond Patriarca Jr. wants the problems to
be settled by Joe Russo and Frank Salemme.
But Sonny Mercurio is against any peace
```

settlement, believing it can never work
after what their group has done (referring
to the murder of Grasso and the attempt on
Salemme's life). According to informant,
Mercurio has the most to lose as it was
him that set up the meeting with Frankie
Salemme when he was shot.

A month later the same informant reported that J. R.
Russo and Mercurio were:

. . . still upset with the idea of leaving Salemme alive, as Mercurio set up the
meeting where Salemme shot and Russo was
the brains behind the whole move. Both
Russo and Mercurio feel that Salemme
cannot be trusted to forget the attempt
on his life.

The FBI had met the enemy and it was the Bureau's own
Top Echelon informant.

Then came the most stunning move of all. Instead of closing Mercurio and referring him for prosecution, Ring actually lobbied to *keep* him as a T.E., arguing that the FBI
needed to know what *further* bloodshed might take place.

"I was really concerned about the way that this shooting
had taken place in a very public environment with an M-16
high velocity weapon," Ring said. "If there were another
shooting, the possibility was that some civilian would get
killed. What I decided to do was . . . accept the information
that comes from Sonny Mercurio, but we were going to investigate him and indict him for this activity."

In other words, the FBI's own informants were telling
them that Mercurio was the biggest threat to peace, yet
somehow they were going to keep him as both an informant
and a target at the same time. The logic of Ring's solution
seemed to originate on some other planet.

Once again the Boston FBI was ignoring the Attorney General's Guidelines to protect Top Echelon informants. A murder and an attempted murder were clearly "serious crimes" under the guidelines, but Ring later admitted that he made no attempt to notify the Assistant Attorney General's office about Mercurio's role in planning the assassinations. It might have been put down as an oversight during the chaotic time following the shootings—if Ring hadn't been asked point-blank by strike force prosecutor Diane Kottmyer whether they should have told the AAG.

It's not a problem, Ring said.

The suitability test for FBI informants was essentially whether their value to the FBI was deemed greater than the weight of their crimes. Something, then, made Sonny Mercurio more important than murder.

Since Joe Valachi first described it, the secret rite during which Italian-American men pledged never to betray "this thing of ours" under penalty of death had been a source of fascination for both the public and for the FBI. Cooperating witnesses had described the induction ceremonies, informants had even attended them, but up until 1989 no FBI squad had ever put a bug in one—even the famous anti-Mafia New York units who were grabbing all the national headlines with the "Commission" and "Pizza Connection" cases.

The open warfare in the fractured Patriarca family unlocked the door to just such an opportunity for the Boston FBI.

Jim Ring would later disingenuously insist that the taping of a rare induction (or "making") ceremony was not the "Holy Grail" of the FBI's crusade against the Mafia. Special Agent Joseph Pistone of "Donnie Brasco" fame, however, publicly hailed the induction tapes as "one of the great victories" in the FBI's war on the Mafia and a feat that even the vaunted New York agents "once believed impossible." Judge Wolf, meanwhile, found that "the interception was perceived and later proven to be of vast value to the government in prosecuting members of the LCN and in publicizing the success of that effort."

After the Boston faction failed to kill Salemme, FBI informants said, their plans to kill the other Junior Patriarca supporters on their "hit list"—including Salemme's son Frank Jr., his brother John Salemme, aging North Shore ally Charlie Quintina, and five others—were abandoned. Junior Patriarca was to have been spared out of deference to his father, but the renegades' grand plan had been for a triumphant J. R. Russo to travel to Providence and "put it on Junior" to step aside. Since Russo's power play had not been preapproved by any of the New York families, he had to strike a quick, decisive blow or quickly abandoned the project—to start a messy, unsanctioned war was to risk retaliation from the Commission.

Still, Grasso was dead and Salemme was wounded and in hiding, and Patriarca was badly shaken by the loss of his two tough guys. A couple of FBI agents even made a run at him to see if he wanted to become a T.E., according to a source close to the family. Instead he sued for peace with Russo, offering him the position of consigliere (chief adviser, generally considered to be an equal to underboss), and agreed to open the books and let the Boston faction "make" some new soldiers before they were indicted.

The talk of an impending induction ceremony began reaching the FBI from several sources, including Sonny Mercurio, just after the assassination attempt on Frank Salemme.

In July, Ring assigned a new agent, Walter Steffans, to begin putting together an affidavit for a new type of eavesdropping warrant, a so-called "roving" electronic surveillance.

Criminals were getting smarter. Well-aware of the legal hurdles involved in getting a standard Title III telephone wiretap or bug for any one particular location, wiseguys and drug traffickers started regularly changing their meeting places. By the time the feds identified one spot, they were using another. It was getting tougher for the FBI to simply install a microphone like "Little Al" in Chicago or the Prince Street bug and wait for weeks of incriminating conversations to pour in.

After some intense, behind-the-scenes lobbying by the Justice Department, in 1986 Congress created a new kind of electronic surveillance warrant as part of a broad reworking of federal eavesdropping statutes. Under the new law, as long as investigators could show it was "not practical" to name a specific location where a criminal conversation was going to take place, they could put a bug anywhere they saw fit within the thirty-day life span of the warrant.

Many defense lawyers and civil libertarians say the law gives the FBI too much discretion and violates Fourth Amendment protections against unreasonable searches and seizures. "There was not one word of debate on the constitutionality of the statute before it was passed by Congress. It's staggering," said John Mitchell, a New York defense lawyer and specialist in racketeering and electronic surveillance law who helped represent Frank Salemme. Federal officials defend roving surveillance as a necessary tool against increasingly savvy criminals.

FBI officials also liked the roving wiretap law because it made it easier to hide the identities of informants. The problem with Title III was always that judges demanded detailed descriptions of the location to be bugged. There was always the chance that if information in the application was too "singular"—that is, so specific that it could only come from one person—then the bad guys could figure out who the informant was. In fact, in a speech to a group of prosecutors the same year the roving law passed, strike force chief Jerry O'Sullivan railed against "unscrupulous members of the defense bar" who he believed were scrutinizing wiretap affidavits "to identify informants so they can be murdered." By not requiring specific information about locations, roving wiretaps could be used to hide FBI sources, particularly high-ranking Top Echelon informants, whose information was often, by definition, singular.

Russo, the new consigliere, and capos Ferrara and Carrozza, had indeed learned their lesson from the Angiulo experience, and were constantly moving their meetings around the North End. The FBI's Jim Ring, meanwhile, had studied the new law, and assigned Steffans to start putting together an application for a roving bug. Sonny Mercurio would provide valuable information on that bug, which would be used to obtain one of the most famous Mafia tapes of all time, the induction ceremony. Ring insists that the once-in-a-career chance to bug the Mafia's holiest of holies was *not* the main reason the FBI kept Mercurio on the street after he masterminded a brazen daytime attack that nearly killed innocent women and children. Ring's assertion, however, can be challenged for numerous reasons:

- **The potential for violence.** Ring and others involved in the induction ceremony wiretap said they were still concerned about further outbreaks of violence despite the peace negotiations between the Boston and Providence factions. The claim might have some credibility had Mercurio not testified that although Ring and Connolly "bugged" him "all the time" about the date, time, and especially the location of the ceremony, they never once asked him whether any more violence was possible.

- **The prosecution memo and the criminal complaints.** Government documents confirm that a memo containing a proposed indictment against Ferrara, Carrozza, and Russo had already been submitted for Justice Department approval well before the induction ceremony. A full two weeks before the ceremony, criminal complaints, which gave the FBI authority to arrest the three mafiosi at any time, were filed in federal court. If the FBI was really concerned about violence, the three mafiosi could have been picked up much earlier—although that would have meant missing a chance to bug the ceremony.

- **The ceremony wasn't crucial.** When the arrests were actually made of the Boston faction members, the induction ceremony wasn't even mentioned in the indictment. Strike force chief Diane Kottmyer later confirmed that the ceremony was not crucial to the indictment but rather served mostly to strengthen the somewhat weak case against J. R. Russo. "We were definitely going to indict Russo no matter what," another prosecutor involved in the case later said.

- **Ring's plan to arrest the wiseguys.** Ring's original plan—most likely to make a big publicity splash—was to arrest the principals immediately after the induction ceremony. When it was vetoed by a top FBI official in Washington over fears that it would compromise other ongoing investigations, Ring was so incensed that he never spoke to the man again. SAC Jim Ahearn also wrote a pointed memo backing Ring's plan, saying that if the arrests were delayed after the ceremony, "responsibility for injury or death to any individuals, either LCN members or innocent citizens, rested entirely on the shoulders of FBIHQ." Ahearn did not say who would be responsible for any innocent citizens killed *before* the ceremony.

- **The Walther memo.** Ring denied that the FBI sought a roving electronic surveillance order to hide the identities of Mercurio and Flemmi, who was also an informant for the induction ceremony bug. Yet one day when he was on vacation, his temporary replacement, Special Agent Robert Walther, wrote a memo to FBI Headquarters that told the real story. Walther wrote that a roving application would "help to protect the identity of any confidential sources, who otherwise might be revealed if singular information [in this case, the location of sensitive LCN meeting] provided by the source was incorporated into the affidavit of a traditional Title III application."

- **The Ahearn memo.** Ring may have insisted that the induction ceremony wasn't a "Holy Grail," yet his boss,
  Jim Ahearn, sure made it sound like one, writing in his
  own memo:

> The Bureau had an outstanding opportu-
> nity for the first time ever, of over-
> hearing and recording an LCN induction
> ceremony, which would be invaluable for
> years to come, and other LCN trials and
> congressional hearings. The intercep-
> tions . . . if accomplished, could have
> a major effect on the Bureau's national
> strategy against the LCN.

Mercurio said he told the FBI as early as September or,
at the latest, early October, that four new members were
going to be "made" in a traditional Mafia induction ceremony. His chief job would be chauffeur, transporting members from a busy shopping area in Revere known as
Wellington Circle to the actual location, which was still a
secret. A short time later Mercurio identified the participants. The final compromise had been to "make" three guys
from the Boston faction, Vinny Federico (a protégé of
Vinny Ferrara), Ritchie Floramo, and Carmen Tortora, and
one from the Providence faction, bookmaker and part-time
jeweler Bobby DeLuca.

The hitch was that Federico was in prison, serving time
for attempted murder. Fortunately, at the time, Massachusetts had a generous system where inmates were allowed to
take periodic "furloughs" from prison to see family and
friends. Ferrara didn't want to hold a ceremony without Federico, even though his imprisoned friend was required to list
on his furlough application the address of all the places he
planned to visit. (Surprisingly, Federico did put the address
of the induction ceremony on his application, accurately de-
scribing the occasion as "family business").

"If he gets his furlough, that's when we'll make him," Ferrara told Mercurio.

"How are you making a guy that's in jail?"

"He's my closest friend. I want to do it."

By mid-October the FBI knew that the ceremony was going to take place on Sunday morning, October 29. On Friday the twenty-seventh, when an FBI agent went to the prison and picked up a copy of Federico's furlough application, he saw an address on Guild Street in Medford that was suspiciously close to Wellington Circle—the location where Mercurio had said he was going to be picking up some of the guests. Two agents, Vince Dellamontaine and Joe Hannigan, went out to the neighborhood.

Special Agent Walt Steffans, who had written the application for the bug with Diane Kottmyer, heard a phone ring in the Organized Crime Squad offices and picked it up.

"They're here! They're here!"

It was Dellamontaine, calling from an FBI agent's house on Guild Street two doors down from the home where the ceremony would take place. He had spotted J. R. Russo, Vinny Ferrara, and Sonny Mercurio, who had come out to make some last minute preparations. The car they were driving was registered to Stephen DiStefano, Ferrara's brother in law, who owned the house at 34 Guild Street. The FBI had located the ceremony, and it was practically right next door to an agent's house!

Sonny Mercurio had scouted out the house himself with Ferrara and J. R. Russo. It was located on a narrow street filled mostly with modest-size colonial and Cape-style homes. Thirty-four Guild was a yellow gambrel Colonial with a postage-stamp lawn in front but a nice open layout in the basement room where they planned to have the ceremony. Mercurio saw right away that there weren't enough seats for the twenty-plus wiseguys who would be coming, so he promised Ferrara that he would bring some folding bridge chairs from the deli. He drove back to Vanessa's, closed up at five, and then went to his favorite bank of pay

phones downstairs and dialed one of the three numbers he
had for Connolly.

"Hey."

"Hey."

"The meet is on. It's at Vinny Federico's brother-in-law's
house."

"What's the address?"

"I don't know the address. I just know how to get there."

"That's okay, we had you under surveillance."

"No shit."

"Where are you going to be? I think we want to talk to
you."

"Well, give me a call if you want. Either I'll get a room or
you get one."

Mercurio rented a room under one of his aliases at the
Sheraton Hotel in the Prudential. He met Connolly and Ring
upstairs. "Everything is all set. It should be no problem," he
told them. According to Mercurio's version of the conversation, neither Ring nor Connolly ever asked if there was a
possibility that the ceremony could take place somewhere
else.

Agent Stan Moody's modest two-story Colonial home,
two doors down on Guild Street, was almost the perfect spot
to set up for surveillance. It didn't have a direct line of sight,
the house between Moody's and the DiStefanos' was set on
the apex of the hill, but there was a garage with direct access
into the house so FBI agents could pull in, close the door,
and unload their cargo in secret. Throughout Saturday they
did just that, offloading recording equipment and surveillance agents.

They dressed casually, polo shirts and jeans mostly, and
their number included ASAC Dennis O'Callaghan, Supervisor Jim Ring, Walt Steffans, Mike Buckley, and Brian Rossi
(the agent from the DEA–Quincy Police bug). Even the
SAC, Jim Ahearn, was there, wearing a striped sweatsuit
jacket and a holster for his Bureau pistol. Stan Moody put
them all around his kitchen table and handed his one-year-

old son James to Brian Rossi so he could take a souvenir photo.

The agents watched as DiStefano and his wife left the house carrying small suitcases, apparently leaving for the weekend, prompting Ring to called prosecutor Diane Kottmyer and say that the ceremony was definitely a go. Kottmyer found U.S. District Court Judge David Nelson at a Boston College football game and had him sign the bugging order—although it said nothing about 34 Guild Street or an induction ceremony specifically. She called Ring back and authorized the entry.

Sometime in the dark of late Saturday night and early Sunday morning, a specialized "tech team" of FBI agents somehow installed a hidden microphone inside 34 Guild Street. Mercurio never was able to figure out exactly how. J. R. Russo and Vinny Ferrara were supposed to have stayed at the house from the minute the DiStefanos left until after the ceremony, precisely to guard against the FBI breaking in. "How did you guys bug that joint?" he later asked Buckley.

"There was nobody home," the agent replied.

However it was installed, the bug itself was an ingenious bit of technology. The microphone itself was about the size of a pencil eraser, but that was no big deal—ones that small had been around for years. What was unique was the way it transmitted. Old hard-wired mikes like Bill Roemer's "Little Al" in Chicago had a big drawback—the wire leading back to the FBI listening post was cumbersome to install and relatively easy to find if anyone was looking. Wireless bugs were better, but their transmissions could be ferreted out by RF detectors, which were becoming standard-issue wiseguy equipment. Wireless mikes also had batteries that needed to be replaced every so often, and every reentry into a bugged location increased the chances of discovery.

The newest type of bug actually used the building's existing electrical wiring as both a power source and a piggyback carrier for the signal, without messy wires or radio signals. Using special equipment, the FBI could listen through the existing neighborhood power lines. The same technology had been used successfully in John Gotti's Brooklyn headquarters, the Ravenite Social Club, the year before. According to one agent's account, two such devices were planted in the ceiling above where the ceremony was to take place.

By the time Sonny Mercurio began ferrying wiseguys to the house Sunday morning, the FBI agents were ready. After he picked up the first batch of guys in front of the Howard Johnson's in Wellington Circle, he drove to a parking lot in the North End for the second. Matthew "Matty Gugs" Guglielmetti, a capo from Providence, who was waiting in the parking lot, pointed skyward at a small aircraft.

"That plane followed us from Rhode Island," he said.

"Youse gotta be joking," Mercurio said.

"No. I seen that plane in Rhode Island. It musta followed us all the ways here."

Mercurio made a joke out of it, waving up at the plane—which really *did* contain an FBI pilot and observer.

"What are they going to do? Jump out?" he asked Guglielmetti.

By mid-morning the New England Mafia was assembled in the small house. The largest group was from Greater Boston: consigliere J. R. Russo; capos Vincent Ferrara, Robert Carrozza, Biagio DiGiacomo, and Charlie Quintina; soldiers Sonny Mercurio, Antonio Spagnolo, Vincent Gioacchini, Frederick Chiampa, Alexander "Sonny Boy" Rizzo, Pryce Quintina and the three associates who were being sponsored for membership—Vincent Federico, Richard Floramo, and Carmen Tortora. From Providence there was boss Raymond Patriarca Jr., capo Matty Guglielmetti, soldier Pasquale Galea, and inductee Robert DeLuca. Two other soldiers from Hartford, Dominick Marangelli and Louis Failla were also there, along with Gaetano Milano from western Massachusetts. There were a few notable absences, including Frank Salemme, who had tried in vain to persuade Patriarca not to attend, and Anthony "the Saint" St. Laurent, a Providence soldier who was on the outs with many members of the family. Bobby DeLuca was supposed to have picked up the Saint, but left him standing like an idiot on the street instead.

The inductees took their seats in front of a table laid out with a knife, four holy cards, and a lit candle. The rest of the men sat in strict hierarchical order, Russo and Patriarca and the capos up front, the soldiers behind them. Biagio DiGiacomo, who had been born in Sicily and had the best command of Italian, presided over the ceremony.

"In onore della Famiglia, la Famiglia e abbraccio," he intoned. (In honor of the Family, the Family is open.)

J. R. Russo made sure, in English, that each of the four initiates knew what they were getting into.

"Do you have any brothers, Carmen?" Russo asked Carmen Tortora.

"One," the balding, fierce-looking enforcer replied.

"If I told you your brother was wrong, he's a rat, he's gonna do one of us harm, you'd have to kill him. Would you do that for me, Carmen?"

"Yes."

"Would you do that? This kind of favor, would you do that?" Russo pressed.

"Yes."

"If any one of us here asked for that?"

"Yes."

"You know that. So you know the severity of this thing of ours."

"Yes."

"You want it that badly, that desperately? Your mother's dying in bed and you have to leave her because we called you, it's an emergency. You have to leave. Would you do that, Carmen?"

"Yes."

"All right, this is what you want. We're the best people and I'm gonna make you part of this thing."

"Biag," Russo said, turning to Biagio DiGiacomo, "give him the oath."

All four men eventually repeated the same oath in Sicilian that Tortora did.

"Io, Carmen, voglio entrare in questa organizzazione per proteggere la mia famiglia, e per proteggere tutti i miei amici. Io lo giuro di non svelare questo segreto e di ubbidire di amore ed omerta."

(I, Carmen, want to enter into this organization to protect my family and to protect all my friends. I swear not to divulge this secret and to obey with love and silence.)

Omerta, is the Sicilian word for silence, and a vow never to betray the Mafia, on the penalty of death.

The four initiates each pricked the index finger on their gun hand and smeared the blood on a card bearing the picture of a saint. The card was then burned over the candle.

"As burns this saint, so will burn my soul. I enter alive into this organization and leave it dead," they each repeated in Sicilian.

After the brief ceremony ended, there was collegial back-slapping all around, and the members of the newly expanded family feasted on platters of Italian cold cuts and sweets before heading out into the bright summer day. Two doors down the FBI agents who had captured the whole thing on tape were grinning and shaking hands too. They watched as the mafiosi headed out in small groups. One group had taken out a couple of large bags of trash, which the agents figured was the remnants of the buffet. The last to leave were J. R. Russo and Vinny Ferrara, who were carrying a much smaller trash bag with them. Walt Steffans figured it was probably evidence of the ceremony, so he suggested to Ring that agents follow Russo and Ferrara and see if it could be recovered. No, Ring said, the risk was too great that they would spot the surveillance and take off.

Mercurio, who had taken a Pan Am flight to New York just in case, talked to Connolly the next day.

"Hey, did you guys have an airplane? One of the guys mentioned a plane that was following us around."

"Yeah."

"Gee, that kid was right. He said he thought there was a plane following from Rhode Island. I couldn't believe it. I told him: 'What, are they going to jump out and arrest people?' "

Connolly laughed at the joke.

"Listen," Connolly said. "Who turned down the TV? We almost didn't get anything."

During the ceremony, someone had turned down a television set that had been blaring, threatening to drown out the bugs. The agents thought it might have been an informant.

"I don't have the slightest," Mercurio said.

"Well, I guess you'll get credit for it."

Over the next several weeks, as Kottmyer and the strike force were preparing to indict, Mercurio was officially "closed" as a Top Echelon informant. As usual, it meant nothing and Mercurio helped the FBI keep tabs on Russo, Ferrara, and Carrozza. At one point he said J.R. and Vinny the Animal had gone to a bachelor party at the Trump Castle casino in Atlantic City for the son of a made guy in the Genovese family. The wedding reception two weeks later would be "at the Waldorf Astoria, well-attended by the LCN," the ever dutiful Mercurio reported. A few days later Mercurio also said that the three top Boston mobsters were back in town, but that Ferrara's wife had left him and had taken the car.

Sonny had no plans of staying in town himself, though. He started taking trips to other cities, setting up apartments under false names and stashing cash where he could easily get his hands on it. On November 14, six weeks after the induction ceremony, Mercurio was about to return from one of his trips and called his brother Michael to pick him up. Mercurio testified that his brother told him that Carrozza, Ferrara, and Russo had all been arrested. Mercurio cancelled his flight back to Boston.

Judge Wolf doubted Mercurio's story about being warned
by his brother. There were many reasons for the FBI to want
Sonny Mercurio gone, including payback for his stellar performance as a T.E. and the fact things could get *very* embarrassing if he were ever prosecuted for the Salemme
shooting. "The court concludes that Mercurio was alerted by
the FBI that it was time for him to act on his previously ex-
pressed intention to become a fugitive, and he did so," the
judge said in his ruling. The FBI agents denied tipping off
Mercurio so he could flee.

Reports and testimony about the FBI's efforts to locate
him—or lack thereof—appear to support the judge's conclusion.

The task of finding Mercurio fell to Richard Carter, a
close friend of John Connolly's who had been the other
agent involved in the late stages of the DEA–Quincy Police
probe of Bulger and Flemmi. By Carter's own admission,
the "investigation" of Mercurio's whereabouts had some curious holes in it. Carter put Mercurio's name into the NCIC
computer and interviewed some of Sonny's associates, but
he didn't do much else, like reviewing the telephone records
of Michael Mercurio or of Sonny's mother, a standard FBI
practice. He also never asked Ring or Connolly if they knew
where Mercurio was. He didn't have to, he said.

"If they knew where he was at, we would have arrested
him," Carter said. "They were not going to conceal it from
us."

But conceal it Connolly did. He *was* talking to Mercurio
on a regular basis, without telling Carter or anyone else in
the FBI about it. Mercurio said the calls were all basically
the same. He would phone Connolly and ask what was
going on. Connolly would encourage him to testify against
Ferrara, Carrozza, and Russo and to enter the Witness Protection Program. Mercurio would decline and hang up, then
move to a new city, afraid that the FBI could trace the call.

An incident in 1991, however, shows that if Connolly was
indeed helping Mercurio stay on the run, he wasn't alone.

Jim Ring, who was never going to top the induction ceremony, retired in the summer of 1990, where he joined former strike force chief Jerry O'Sullivan at the Boston law
firm Choate Hall & Stuart as chief of investigations. He was
replaced by Ed Quinn, the onetime Angiulo case agent and
close Connolly friend who, two years earlier, had sabotaged
marijuana trafficker Joe Murray's attempt to cooperate
against Bulger and Flemmi.

In 1991, Quinn was called upon to manage another Top Echelon informant mess—this time involving Sonny Mercurio.

Sonny, perhaps overconfident because of the lack of FBI
interest in finding him, and desperate for cash, had slowly
reestablished contact with his brother and other friends in
the underworld and landed a courier's role in a cross-
country marijuana smuggling ring. One of his new partners
in the scheme was a wired-up cooperating witness for the
DEA, who spotted Sonny at his brother's house during a
Fourth of July barbecue. The DEA snitch told his handlers
about the sighting and said he heard that Mercurio would be
on the Boston waterfront three days later for a party cruise
with his brother and "several girls."

The next day, an FBI agent working with the DEA task
force told Carter and Quinn what the DEA witness had said.
According to Ed Quinn's tale of what happened next, Mercurio was saved from being arrested on the waterfront by
what can only be described as divine intention.

The *same day*, Quinn said he received a different report
about Mercurio from another FBI agent, whom he did not
name. A "reliable informant," the agent said, told him that
Cadillac Frank Salemme and the rest of the Mafia had suddenly begun suspecting that Sonny had tipped off the induction ceremony and were looking to kill him. Only Quinn did
not send squads of agents or a SWAT team to rescue Mercurio. Instead, he later testified, he called John Connolly,
who had already retired from the FBI, and asked him to
"warn" Mercurio of the "threat" on his life. Not surprisingly,
Mercurio disappeared again.

Equally suspicious was Quinn's decision not to tell Rick Carter, the Mercurio fugitive case agent, about the "threat" or his discussion with Connolly. If Salemme and others *were* coming after Mercurio with guns, that was probably something Carter and other agents need to prepare for before confronting Mercurio on a busy wharf filled with tourists and excursion boats. Instead, two days later, Quinn let Carter and several other agents sit around Long Wharf like idiots waiting for Sonny Mercurio and his girlfriends to take their booze cruise. The new Organized Crime Squad supervisor didn't even bother to show up for the harborside charade.

CHAPTER NINE

Coming Undone

••••••••••••••••••••••••••••••

The Boston FBI's Top Echelon program falls apart

JOHN MORRIS'S LIFE was unraveling. He had tried to break
off the affair with Debbie Noseworthy, his secretary, a couple years earlier and make a go of his marriage, but he
couldn't do it. The Morris home had been a mess for a
while. Angina and heart problems sent him to the cardiolo-
gist every six months, and his chronic headaches were becoming more frequent and debilitating. Rebecca hadn't been
happy for years, and the fibromyalgia in her neck and back
gave her constant pain, which John's long hours at the FBI
and his affair had hardly eased.

John sued for divorce just after New Year's of 1988. He
and Rebecca had been full of hope as college sweethearts at
the University of Miami, but now they were throwing bombs
at each other from behind their attorneys. Rebecca's lawyer
subpoenaed all of Debbie's personal financial records to see
what John spent on her (a move Debbie's lawyer fought,
calling it clear "harassment"). John's lawyer accused his in-
laws, who owned a chain of fifty Dairy Queen shops in
Greater Cleveland, of hiding assets to make it appear that
Rebecca was the sole support for her aging mother.

John worried about the strain of it all on Jenifer, his
eighteen-year-old, who had suffered from emotional and

learning disabilities since she'd contracted salmonella as an infant. Back then he'd volunteered for morgue duty in the FBI's New Haven office so he could visit Jenifer more in the hospital. Now he was out of the family home, living in a condo across town with Debbie. Work was no bargain either. It was as if he was living in some bizarro world populated by hypocrites and he was their king.

The "Boston Police Case," as the press dubbed it, was Organized Crime Strike Force chief Jerry O'Sullivan's latest big crusade. "There is an attitude that a certain level of corruption is tolerated in this town," O'Sullivan huffed at one press conference. "Everyone expects an edge. Maybe the inside players think this is all right, but John Q. Citizen doesn't think it's all right. John Q. Citizen is the one who gets screwed over."

In the grand scheme of police corruption, say the Chicago PD during the Capone era, the Boston case was pretty penny-ante stuff. When news of the strike force–FBI investigation hit the papers a few years earlier, fifty cops were supposed to have been targets in a massive corruption probe. In the end, just nine BPD officers and detectives were indicted for shaking down nightclub and restaurant owners for cash, free meals and gifts. Seven of the cops went to trial, where O'Sullivan and Kottmyer alleged they had taken a total of $18,000 over ten years.

That worked out to precisely $257 per year per man, or seventy cents a day—literally a cup of coffee. Some politicians and pundits started calling the case overkill, particularly when Edith Ban, owner of Boston's renowned Café Budapest, refused to testify against her friend, Detective Thomas "Bobo" Connolly, and the strike force lawyers indicted her for obstruction of justice. Ban, who learned to despise informers as a survivor of the Nazi death camp at Auschwitz, was eventually fined $25,000 and given a two-year suspended prison sentence. Her crime—tearing up dinner checks that allegedly showed she had given Bobo Connolly free meals in return for walking her employees to the bank after closing hours.

Perhaps the worst aspect of the case, from the Boston cops' point of view, was the fact that it was charged as a RICO, even though there was little evidence that the cops were working together. The way the indictment was worded, the strike force and the FBI were accusing the entire Boston Police Department, in effect, of being a racketeering enterprise. The case engendered bitter hatred of the feds by the Boston Police—maybe even worse than what the State Police felt after Lancaster Street. The feds, the cops said, used a Howitzer to kill a mosquito. When the cops were convicted and sentenced to prison sentences of two to five years each, one defense lawyer called the whole scene "Kafkaesque."

After the convictions, Boston Police Detectives Association president Daniel Mahoney stood in front of thirty of his stern-faced members outside the U.S. District Courthouse after the convictions and angrily ripped into the strike force and the FBI. "They're letting outrageous crimes and criminals go unpunished in order to achieve carefully crafted convictions against the Boston Police Department," he snapped.

Mahoney didn't know the half of it.·

Jerry O'Sullivan gave racketeers Whitey Bulger and Steve Flemmi a free pass while using RICO to crush a few piggish police officers. The FBI man leading the investigation was none other than Supervisory Special Agent John Morris, the new chief of the Boston FBI Public Corruption Squad, who had already accepted more money than any of the convicted cops.

Actually, the Boston Police Case started out in Ring's C-3 organized crime group, not Morris's squad. Back in 1983, Special Agent Stan Moody, the Guild Street resident, and another agent, Robert Jordan, heard that some Boston Police officers were taking payoffs from bookmakers connected to Stevie Flemmi and Whitey Bulger. It took three years, but Jordan and Moody finally caught a break. They confronted one of the Boston cops, Lieutenant Jimmy Cox, and Cox flipped, agreeing to wear a wire. Moody and Jordan wanted to send Cox at Bulger and Flemmi, to see if they could get them to say anything incriminating. Ring agreed.

With his hidden tape recorder whirring, Cox approached Bulger and Flemmi outside the South Boston Liquor Mart, but, as always, the two informants were ready. As soon as Cox got out a hello, the two crime bosses blew him off. Flemmi later claimed that Ring tipped off Bulger about Cox and his hidden tape recorder, but the judge found that Flemmi was lying to protect John Connolly. The judge sided with Morris, who said Connolly came to him and asked whether Cox was "wired." "The court infers that Connolly is the person who told Bulger and Flemmi that Cox was cooperating with the FBI," Wolf wrote in the *Salemme* decision. Wolf also ruled that Connolly filed a bogus 209 to cover himself a short time later.

Not long after the encounter, Ahearn, the SAC, transferred the case from Ring's squad to Morris's.

"Why?" Ring said he asked his boss.

"Because you have all the good cases on your squad and Morris doesn't have any," Ahearn replied. Ring said he didn't agree with Ahearn, but he didn't protest much either.

In hindsight, the transfer of the case from a squad led by the difficult Ring—he of the "no authorized criminal activity" rule—to one led by the corrupt Morris, who had a track record of protecting Bulger and Flemmi, is highly suspicious.

Morris later testified that Connolly and Ahearn had a "degree of association" as street agent and SAC that was completely unprecedented. "I'd never seen such close relationship," Morris said. One incident in particular stuck out in Morris's memory. At around the same time, Connolly asked Morris if he would support his promotion to supervisory special agent. Morris said yes. Then Morris torpedoed Connolly by recommending to the Boston FBI Career Board that Connolly *not* be made a supervisor. Larry Potts, the ASAC who chaired the career board, agreed with Morris. Potts knew Connolly had a reputation for sloppy and nonexistent paperwork and believed he would be ill-suited for a paper-intensive supervisor's job. Potts convinced the board to turn Connolly down.

Ahearn promptly stepped in on Connolly's behalf, flying to Washington to lobby for Connolly. Ahearn's intervention would both impress and frighten Morris, who realized how powerful Connolly had become inside the Boston FBI. Another high-ranking former FBI official backed up Morris's assessment that Ahearn's intervention was extraordinary.

Robert Fitzpatrick, an ASAC at the time, said he was not consulted on the transfer of the case and believes Connolly engineered it through Ahearn, a friend and fellow member of the FBI's Mafia-fighting clique. "I think Connolly saw that he would have better control of it if it went through Morris," Fitzpatrick said.

Two years later, Moody and Jordan resurrected their investigation, working out a plan to plant bugs and telephone wiretaps against John Bahorian, a bookmaker who was allegedly making payoffs to the police and paying protection money to Flemmi.

Morris told Connolly to warn the two informants about the electronic surveillance on Bahorian.

"And tell them I don't want anymore Hallorans," he added.[21]

Connolly came back and said Bulger and Flemmi wanted to meet with him in person, Morris said later. They all met at his town house in Lexington, where Morris told them he could keep them out of the Bahorian bugging operation, but again warned them to "leave Bahorian alone." The wire lasted three months. When the tapes were later reviewed, Flemmi wasn't on any of them.

---

[21] Years later Morris's "no more Hallorans" admission hit the *Salemme* case like a grenade. Essentially, it was an admission that all along people inside the FBI had been convinced that Bulger and Flemmi killed one of their own cooperating witness.

Morris grew more and more depressed after the Bahorian case. In addition to betraying his own agents, he had just committed a federal crime, obstruction of justice. With everything else in his life going wrong, it was the last straw. "I felt absolutely completely compromised, that I had made a very serious mistake, that I had actually compromised an investigation," Morris said.

"I was the one that did it, and I regretted it, and I made a commitment that that was the end," he said.

Morris now faced a serious problem. He wanted the relationship between Bulger and Flemmi to end, but how to do it? Not through the FBI, Connolly had him boxed in there. The Justice Department and other law enforcement agencies were out too. If Bulger and Flemmi were actually prosecuted, he now believed that their plan had always been to turn him in to save themselves. There was only one avenue left: the press.

Shortly after Ahearn took over as Special Agent in Charge in Boston, the investigative unit at the *Boston Globe*, the Spotlight Team, asked the FBI for permission to tell the inside story on the Angiulo case. The SAC had been praised in print before—"Jim Ahearn's handsome features belied the toughness acquired in those years working the street," author Ovid DeMaris wrote in his book *The Last Mafioso*— and he was eager to let the Boston office crow about the Angiulo triumph. Things went well at first, Ahearn wrote in a memo.

```
I agreed that people of the Spotlight
Team could interview particular Special
Agents of the Boston Division with re-
gard to the Angiulo case, which resulted
in a five-part series of newspaper arti-
cles which were extremely favorable to
the FBI for public image, establishing
an excellent working relationship with
```

the Globe editor and resulting in my
meeting with most of the Spotlight Team
reporters.

One of those agents was John Morris, who was credited
with being the Thomas Edison of the idea to bug Angiulo's
headquarters in the *Globe* Spotlight Series and in a subsequent book written by Spotlight editor Gerard O'Neill and
reporter Dick Lehr.

Understanding that he would be only an unnamed
source, Morris leaked both Bulger and Flemmi's informant
status to O'Neill and the *Globe* early in the summer of
1988. When the Boston FBI learned what the Globe was
working on, the agency did its best to stop the story. When
the *Globe* reporters asked Ahearn, for example, whether
Bulger was getting any special treatment, he didn't bother
with the usual "neither confirm nor deny" crap. He just
lied.

"That is absolutely untrue," he said, according to the published story. "We have not had evidence that would warrant
it, and if we do develop anything of an evidentiary nature,
we will pursue it. We specifically deny that there has been
any favorable treatment of this individual."

Lehr, meanwhile, had written a letter to "Big Tony"
Ciulla, requesting an interview about the race-fixing case.
The letter was sent through official federal channels because
Ciulla was still a protected witness, and it prompted a call by
Tom Daly, the race-fix case agent, to *Globe* reporter Kevin
Cullen, who was considered by many to be one of Boston's
best crime reporters.

According to Cullen's testimony at the *Salemme* hearings,
Daly complained that the *Globe* had breached protocol by
not calling him first before reaching out for Ciulla. "He was
annoyed that we had reached out to his witness," said
Cullen, who went on to become the paper's European Bureau Chief. Daly said he was passing along a warning from
Ciulla that the newspaper should be careful "not to embar-

rass" Bulger, because if falsehoods were printed, "he would think nothing of clipping you."

Then, Cullen said, Daly added his own opinion. "Especially you, Kevin. You live over there. I'm telling you this because I'm your friend."

Cullen felt a chill. He did live in South Boston with his wife. He said he had never considered Daly a friend or even a source, and that he took Daly's words as a threat. "I thought Mr. Daly was trying to intimidate us, not just me, but the Spotlight team. The second emotion was fear. I was afraid."

For his part, Daly has denied threatening Cullen through his attorney, former Assistant U.S. Attorney Paul V. Kelly, saying he never made any call to Cullen. Wolf, in his *Salemme* opinion, sided with the reporter. "Cullen . . . believed that Daly's comments constituted a threat intended to discourage the *Boston Globe* from publishing the story it was planning. Cullen was correct. Daly made no written record of his call to Cullen, as he would have if it had been intended as an official warning by the FBI to a potential victim of violence," Wolf wrote.

Cullen and his wife moved out of South Boston at the *Globe*'s expense for about a week. Undeterred, the newspaper published a series of articles on brothers Billy and Whitey called "The Bulger Mystique," in mid-September. The piece on Whitey didn't use the word "informant," but instead talked about a "special relationship" between the wiseguy and the FBI. No mention was made of Flemmi's relationship with the Bureau. The story quoted unnamed sources from the DEA and other agencies alleging that their investigations had been subverted by the FBI. For the official response, the piece quoted Ahearn's false denial—and a typical display of chutzpah by Jerry O'Sullivan.

"To the people who are whining and complaining, I'd suggest making a case on them. It ain't nuclear physics. It can be done," O'Sullivan said. "What you have is some people taking one shot, then walking away crying that there's been a leak. You've got to keep trying."

Flemmi later testified that Bulger was irate when he read the *Globe* story, and suspected that Morris had been the source of the leak. A few weeks later, though, Bulger said he and Morris had talked and "settled" the matter. Flemmi, who felt both their lives had been endangered by the story, never spoke to Morris again. Morris later insisted that he never intended for Bulger and Flemmi to get hurt.

"I didn't want what had happened to me to happen to anybody else, and that was the only way that I could think to stop it, because I no longer had the decision-making authority to close them," Morris said. "I wanted them closed."

Morris's denial is hard to swallow. Judge Wolf was particularly unsympathetic to it, skewering the agent with his own words by finding that exactly what Morris wanted was to create "another Halloran." Morris was well-aware of the dangers of exposed informants, a fact made clear by an affidavit he wrote about an alleged conversation with a newspaper reporter.

```
I told him that the consequences of in-
dividuals being identified as infor-
mants, regardless of the accuracy of the
information, could be serious. I told
him a human life was a human life, be
that person criminal, informant, or
both.
```

The conversation was highly ironic. Someone involved in the Boston FBI's organized crime effort had finally admitted that even a criminal's life—like, say, Brian Halloran's, Bucky Barrett's, or Louis Litif's—had some human value.

The retribution Flemmi feared never came. Maybe the FBI denials were convincing. Maybe their own fearsome reputations saved them; they were now firmly at the top of Boston's criminal food chain thanks to their FBI friends. Almost certainly, the fundamental immorality of the Top Echelon program was working its old magic—no matter what the *Globe* said, many people still didn't want to believe the FBI would really become involved with someone like Whitey Bulger.

Morris also denied wanting to hurt his FBI enemies, John Connolly and SAC James Ahearn, but that wasn't very credible either. Morris, in fact, suggested to the *Globe* that Connolly might be on the take and was "living beyond his means." Morris also dropped a dime on Ahearn, although exactly what he said was never revealed. The *Globe* apparently could not back up Morris's allegations and did not print them.

The controversy might have died there had it not been for a second leak to the *Globe* about *Billy* Bulger six months later.

Politician Bulger had been implicated in an alleged influence-peddling scandal involving construction of 75 State Street, a large office building in downtown Boston. He was cleared by state and federal law enforcement officials, but the newspaper editorial pages were calling their investigation a whitewash. Responding to the intense criticism, Jeremiah O'Sullivan, who had taken over as interim U.S. Attorney, announced that he would conduct a review of the case.[22] Bulger was still the powerful Senate president, so O'Sullivan ordered that the review be conducted in strictest secrecy. Yet, the day after Billy Bulger sat down for an interview with the FBI agents working on the review, the *Globe* had the story.

> FBI agents questioned Senate President William M. Bulger on Tuesday as part of the reopened investigation of the 75 State Street development, sources said yesterday.
>
> Details of the interview were not available, but Bul-

---

[22]O'Sullivan pledged to return "integrity" to the office after the turmoil of the McNamara years, but given the contribution that Whitey Bulger had made to his prosecutorial career, it was arguably a conflict of interest for him to have pursued a review of State Senator Bulger's influence-peddling case.

ger has been linked to the case because of $246,966 he received in 1985 from attorney Thomas E. Finnerty, his friend and law associate, out of a $500,000 payment that landlord-developer Harold Brown has maintained Finnerty extorted from him.

O'Sullivan would later declare that there wasn't enough evidence to proceed against William Bulger, saying it "was not a close call." But to Robert Popeo, Billy Bulger's lawyer, the damage to his client's reputation was already done. He had promised to raise hell if news of the interview was leaked, and he now called O'Sullivan, demanding an investigation into the leak.

To Popeo's surprise, O'Sullivan actually ordered one, calling Main Justice in Washington and demanding an official inquiry.

An angry Ahearn called Morris into his office.

"Were you the leak to the Globe?"

"No," Morris lied.

Supervisory Special Agent Richard Ramsey from the FBI's Office of Professional Responsibility, and John Ezell, a Justice Department lawyer, flew to Boston a short time later. Ramsey leaned first on Ahearn, who responded by signing a seven-page affidavit that mostly cast suspicion on Morris.

```
I consider SSA Morris to be the most log-
ical source of these information leaks.
I believe he bears hard feelings towards
the fact that Whitey Bulger is being
maintained as a confidential source
rather than being targeted for investi-
gation. There may also be some occupa-
tional jealousy involved given the fact
that SSA Morris maintains a highly pro-
ductive organized crime informant which
has been viewed as not the same quality
as Whitey Bulger.
```

Several knowledgeable sources have identified Morris's "highly productive organized crime informant" as Sammy Berkowitz, the Chelsea bookmaker who got a presidential pardon from Ronald Reagan.

Ahearn's affidavit also contained a vague mea culpa for his bringing the Boston FBI in such close contact with the *Globe* in the first place, stating that *"several Agents in this Division have had the opportunity to come to know the reporters of the* Globe *newspaper."* In other words, the fox was in the henhouse. The FBI's own conceit about its ability to control the press proved to be its undoing, time and again. Starting back with Hoover's close relationship with powerful columnist Walter Winchell, the image-obsessed Bureau shamelessly played favorites, rewarding friendly reporters with planted scoops and access to FBI files, while shutting out ones whose stories were critical of the Bureau.

Once the "friendly" reporters were in, though, there was no guarantee they would stay that friendly, a lesson FBI Director William Sessions learned the hard way. In the early 1990s, Sessions threw the doors of the J. Edgar Hoover Building open to Ronald Kessler, a former *Washington Post* reporter who had written several best-selling books about the CIA. Sessions actually ordered all his field offices to cooperate with Kessler's effort. The result was Sessions's resignation, after the reporter published allegations of misconduct against the FBI director, including that he had used a Justice Department jet for personal visits to family and friends, and that his wife had attempted to steer a no-bid government contract to one of her friends.

Ramsey called Morris in and said the FBI and the Justice Department had decided that they wouldn't pursue a criminal case against him—if he told the truth. Morris lied anyway, filing his own affidavit blaming Ahearn for the leaks. Then he backpedaled a bit, saying he may have accidentally confirmed Bulger's informant to the *Globe*. After Morris refused to take a lie detector test, Ahearn took the gloves off, urging the FBI brass in Washington to fire Morris.

Morris reached out for Potts in Washington.

"They're trying to pin the leaks on me," Morris said. "They're focusing on me as a target, and the interviews are really tough."

"Well, I'm sure the inquiry will be completed, and the truth will come out, and you'll be all right," Potts replied.

Potts wasn't about to stick his neck out to do anything questionable for Morris. When a package of material from the Boston leak investigation found its way to his desk in the Bureau's White Collar Crime Section, he sent it back to OPR without opening it.

Morris's eventual punishment was a letter of censure in his personnel file and a two week unpaid suspension. He was convinced he was a marked man in Boston. He again called Potts, who encouraged him to get out of Boston and onto the FBI's career track, which usually entailed being moved around the country every few years. Morris had always said he would never leave Boston due to family considerations, but he told Potts he'd had a change of heart and was ready to get more involved in advancing his career. Great, Potts said, we have an opening for a mid-level manager in White Collar Crime. Morris eventually chose a spot in the Inspection Division instead and moved to Washington, D.C., with Debbie.

A man who had accepted $7,000 in bribes, endangered the lives of informants by leaking their identities, sabotaged numerous investigations (including ones conducted by his own agents), and lied under oath to his superiors was thusly promoted to a job in Washington judging the work of other FBI agents.

Mess up, move up.

While the FBI was in an uproar about its in-house problems, the DEA had apparently decided to take O'Sullivan's challenge to stop "whining and complaining" to heart. Only this time, the drug agents vowed, there would be no FBI interference.

The new DEA Special Agent in Charge, John Coleman, went to the agency's administrator, Jack Long, for permission to cut the FBI out. Long said he had no problem with it, but that he had to clear the plan with the Assistant Attorney General in Charge of the Justice Department's Criminal Division. Fortunately for Coleman, that was none other than Bill Weld, who had been burned by his attempt to bring the FBI into the DEA–Quincy Police drug probe a few years earlier. Weld happily signed off on Coleman's request.

Despite the blown investigation, the DEA had continued to get plenty of information about alleged cocaine dealing linked to Whitey Bulger. In 1987 the agency interviewed Patrick Perkins, an old Winter Hill hand, who said Bulger was arranging purchases of "multikilos" of cocaine to be shipped from Florida to Boston. Boston Police informants, meanwhile, were identifying leaders of the gang in South Boston. One of their hangouts was said to be Triple O's, the pub where Whitey Bulger threatened to kill real estate agent Ray Slinger. The group, led by a red-haired amateur boxer named John "Red" Shea, kept the housing projects well-supplied with cocaine, the informants said.

In February 1989, Coleman sat down with Ahearn. The DEA had been conducting Title III electronic surveillance for at least seven months, Coleman said, and that information was for Ahearn's ears only. The orders had come straight from Washington that—except for FBI Director William Sessions—Ahearn could breathe a word of the investigation to no one. The tables had completely turned since the Sarhatt-Greenleaf meeting five years prior. Adding to the FBI's humiliation, Coleman also said that U.S. Attorney Frank McNamara had been told that the FBI was being frozen out of the probe. Suddenly, an out-of-the-blue conversation Ahearn had in McNamara's office some months earlier made some sense.

"Hey, is Whitey Bulger a snitch?" McNamara blurted out, completely off the subject of what they had been talking about.

"What?" Ahearn said.

"Whitey Bulger. Is he an informant for you guys?"

"C'mon, Frank. You know I can't answer a question like that. Not about Whitey, not about anyone else."

Ahearn had thought that McNamara, with his flaky reputation, just didn't know the rules. But now he wasn't so sure. Worse, he was hearing that it wasn't just McNamara who knew, but that the IRS Criminal Investigations Division and Boston Police were involved, and that Jerry O'Sullivan and even Newman Flanagan, the Suffolk County District Attorney, had been brought into the loop—virtually everyone *except* the Bureau.

The Boston FBI, which so frequently had excluded other agencies from their investigations, was for the first time humiliatingly on the outside looking in. "Their attitude had always been, 'We're the FBI and you're not,' so this felt pretty good," one DEA investigator on the case later said.

Ahearn wrote an angry letter to Headquarters about the FBI being frozen out of the DEA probe. He even said that the charge that the FBI had sabotaged prior investigations of Bulger and Flemmi had been "investigated by other SACs and found to be groundless." It was all pointless, Headquarters ordered him to do nothing.

In January 1990 a huge force of DEA and IRS agents and Boston Police officers swooped down on South Boston and Quincy, serving search warrants at the homes of Bulger's alleged drug underlings, a warehouse, and a liquor store called the D Street Deli. Court documents showed that the agencies had received court permission to bug Bulger's cellular phone, his car, a convenience store next to the South Boston Liquor Mart, and even the park surrounding historic Fort Independence on Castle Island, where Bulger had taken to meeting some of his criminal cohorts outdoors to avoid being recorded.

Eventually the U.S. Attorney's office returned drug-trafficking indictments against dozens of members of the South Boston ring. Bulger's name was not among them.

Prosecutors found that he was simply too good at avoiding electronic eavesdropping.

The feds asked the drug dealers if any of them wanted to turn state's evidence against Bulger. Many of them knew about the Brian Halloran and John McIntyre killings, so, not surprisingly, there were no takers.

Like the DEA, the State Police hadn't given up either. The memory of Lancaster Street still burned, and while the *Globe* story afforded the satisfaction of watching the FBI squirm, it also deepened the troopers' embarrassment at being had. Their new plan was to attack Bulger and Flemmi through their oldest and most reliable source of income—their bookmakers.

The Jewish bookies had a Tuesday-night tradition, the *schvitz* at the Blue Hill Baths in Boston's Mattapan section. It was an old-fashioned Russian steam bath where the bookmakers and their friends gathered for a steam or a *platza*— a soapy massage administered with a hand broom made of oak leaves by a guy everyone called Naked Joe (nobody actually knew his last name). In between there were breaks for tumblers of scotch, big spreads of takeout Chinese, and war stories back to the thirties about when the city was run by bosses like Frankie Wallace and his Gustin Gang from South Boston, and Joe Lombardo in the North End. They also talked about the relative merits of the jails they had all been in around Greater Boston. Guys like Doc Saganski, Moe Weinstein, and Burton "Chico" Krantz, under the old gaming laws, had been happy to clam up and take a six month bit for contempt or a year or two for a bookmaking conviction—it was better than having your family sit shiva for a week. They still remembered the violence of the early 1970s when the Winter Hill Gang had used Johnny-and-His-Bazooka Martorano to get some of their less fortunate colleagues in line.

It wasn't all chow mein and Chivas Regal, though. The extortion of Doc and Moe by the new crew in the North End was a bad sign of what life in the post-Angiulo era would be like. The state lottery, meanwhile, had killed the once-profitable illegal numbers. Even more ominous were the new federal money-laundering penalties. Congress had enacted them to go after the bankers who were washing drug money for Colombian cocaine cartels and Chinese heroin triads, but investigators soon discovered they could be used against virtually anyone who handled large amounts of illicit cash.

The first big bookmaking/money-laundering case happened practically by accident. A small group of State Police, IRS, and FBI investigators, none of whom where connected with the warring Organized Crime squads at their respective agencies, began looking into allegations of drug dealing at Heller's Café, a seedy barroom in Chelsea. Nobody paid much attention to the investigation at first, even after they discovered that Heller's owner, Michael London, was operating what was essentially a hugely successful underground credit union. Fundamentally, what London did was cash checks, no questions asked—a service that had many uses.

Construction firms, jewelry stores, and even art galleries, for example, used London to cash checks so they could pay their employees under the table and evade payroll taxes. Over a five-year period, prosecutors estimated that as much as $200 million passed through London's dingy barroom.

Mostly, London catered to bookies and their customers. The investigators watched as the elite of Boston's bookmaking crowd came in to meet with their clientele. One stockbroker from Detroit bet $50,000 per week, writing his checks out to "Mickey Mantle," "Muhammad Ali," and "Marvin Hagler," before they were duly cashed by London.

The investigators successfully bugged Heller's, and learned that London was also helping Vinny Ferrara try to recruit bookies who Flemmi and Bulger had snatched up after the Anguilo indictments.[23]

---

[23]Using the FBI to stop Ferrara was obviously another reason why Flemmi and Bulger wanted to continue their Top Echelon status during the late 1980s.

"Whitey can't hold Vinny's jockstrap," London was taped telling one bookmaker.

The Heller's tapes eventually led to a money-laundering prosecution of London, who received an unprecedented fifteen years and $1.3 million in fines and forfeitures. They were also later used against Ferrara in the post–Guild Street arrests by O'Sullivan and the strike force. Yet while the tapes were full of references *to* Bulger and Flemmi, there was little that could be used as evidence against them.

Fortunately, the Heller's tapes provided something just as important—a complete guide to virtually every bookmaker the two crime bosses controlled.

John Connolly struggled to keep his Top Echelon informants in the fold after the *Globe* story ran in the fall of 1988. The new DEA case was more bad news. Had the *Globe* story not forced them to be so careful in the late part of 1988 and early 1989, they might well have been caught. Their FBI protectors, even John Connolly, had been handcuffed by the Justice Department. All three men began making plans to get out.

Flemmi's plan was apparently to remake himself as a legitimate businessman. Using a complex system of trusts in the names of his mother and other family members, he poured money into real estate investments—commercial complexes, apartment buildings in Boston's wealthy Back Bay, and even a Laundromat (which was good for a chuckle when he was later charged with money laundering).

Whitey Bulger's bid for legitimate income was more audacious.

Massachusetts Lottery officials, proud of their national reputation as the country's most profitable and best-run state lottery, saw it all melting away the day Whitey Bulger, Kevin Weeks, and two brothers from South Boston, Michael and Patrick Linskey, showed up at Lottery headquarters in July 1991. The four men had an affidavit stating that they had previously agreed to share the winnings, with half going to Michael Linskey, whose name was on the ticket, and a one-sixth share going to Bulger. The win was front-page news and led every evening television newscast, as perplexed officials yanked Rotary Variety's lottery license and technicians tried to figure out how Bulger rigged their supposedly tamper-proof lottery machine.

Equally horrified were most law enforcement officials, who realized that Bulger now had almost $120,000 in legitimate income a year. (Several years later, U.S. Attorney Donald K. Stern's office seized Bulger's "winnings," charging he had heard that the brother of his associate Pat Linskey had won the lottery and purchased a piece of the ticket after the fact for $700,000.) In retrospect, Bulger claiming the lottery win was probably a rare tactical error. It gave him legitimate income and added to his legend, true, but it was uncharacteristically showy. Rubbing a few DEA noses in a tipped-off bug was one thing, taunting the entire New England law enforcement community was another.

Bulger's real plan was to run, not to risk being imprisoned again—something he vowed would never happen. After it was clear that Connolly and the FBI could no longer protect him, over the next several years he began crisscrossing the country, stashing money and false identification papers. In the Long Island community of Selden, New York, where Kevin Weeks's parents lived, Bulger took out a driver's license under the name "Thomas Baxter." Investigators also believe he stashed secret troves of cash along the Interstate 10 corridor stretching from northern Florida through Louisiana, Mississippi, and Texas.

Yet during all his intense planning, Whitey also took time to smell the roses—he made at least one trip to Graceland—and to take care of a little unfinished business.

When the man in the big Lincoln Continental with the pretty blond friend and the pocket full of $50 and $100 bills drove into tiny Daisy, Oklahoma (population 100), they called him "Naholo," Choctaw Indian slang for "white man." They just didn't know he was *the* White Man. He asked them to call him "James, from Boston," and said he was just a guy there to do a favor for an old friend.

The director of the nearby Atoka Funeral Home, Wayne Embry, got a telephone call from "James" in early 1989. "I'm a friend of Clarence Carnes, he died outside Springfield, Missouri, in a pauper's grave. I want to give him a decent burial and bury him there on Indian land," the man said.

"If you can get him here, I can bury him," Embry replied. Practically the next day, Embry got a call from the son of a funeral director in Ozark, Missouri, who said a guy from Boston had paid to have Carnes exhumed, put in their best casket, and driven to eastern Oklahoma hill country. The Choctaw Kid was coming home.

After Robert Stroud, the famous "Bird Man," Carnes was perhaps the most famous of Alcatraz's inmates. He had been the youngest man ever sent to Alcatraz at eighteen, for kidnapping and murder, and was the sole survivor of the prison's most infamous break, the "1946 Alcatraz Blastout." Carnes and five other prisoners overpowered several guards and stole their keys—only to find that they led only to an interior exercise yard, not freedom. Confused, they used the guard's guns to barricade themselves inside a cell block with their hostages.

Prison officials brought in reinforcements, an elite force of guards from Leavenworth and a borrowed contingent of U.S. Marines on their way home from Okinawa, and finally launched a siege after a tense, three-day standoff. When the smoke cleared, two guards were dead and a dozen more were wounded. Three of the escapees were also killed. Carnes and the other two survivors, Sam Shockley and Miran Thompson, were charged with first-degree murder and convicted. Because he had refused to kill several of the hostages when the other convicts urged him to, Carnes alone was spared execution. He was paroled in 1973, a decade after the Rock was shut down, but spent the next fifteen years in and out of prison for parole violations—most of which had to do with his chronic alcoholism.

When he died at the Medical Center for Federal Prisoners in Springfield in early October 1988, officials, believing he had no next of kin, buried him in an unmarked grave at a local Catholic cemetery. The Associated Press published a brief story about his passing that ran in newspapers across the country.

Embry said the bronze casket Carnes's body arrived in was the nicest he'd ever seen—probably worth about $4,000. The Ozark funeral director's son handed him a crisp $100 bill—a tip from "James"—and said he'd received a similar one himself. Embry invited him to stay. "I'm going to the horse track in Tulsa to spend mine," the young man said.

"Jim" called again.

"I'm coming down. I want a Choctaw funeral for Clarence. I want a Choctaw preacher and some singers and I want to bury him at Billy Cemetery," Bulger said, according to Embry.

The Choctaws were once the largest American Indian tribe in the southern United States and still have tribal councils in Oklahoma, Florida, and four other states. Billy Cemetery is a small burying plot on Choctaw land near Daisy, named after a cousin of the Carnes clan, tribal judge Isaac Billy.

Bulger and his companion—probably Catherine Greig—flew to Dallas, rented the big Lincoln, and drove 120 miles north to Stout's Country Store and U.S. Post Office—Daisy's only commercial concern—arriving a few hours before the funeral. When someone told him one of Carnes's few surviving relatives was in jail in Tulsa, Bulger got back in the car and drove *another* 120 miles north, bailed him out, and brought him back. The Reverend Samuel Parish, a local Choctaw preacher, presided over the ceremony, praying half in English, half in Choctaw. "I think he said something about everyone having some good in them," said Virginia Stout, the owner of the general store and a distant Carnes cousin. The preacher and five local women singers each received a pristine fifty dollar bill in a thank-you card before Bulger and his friend climbed back in the big Lincoln and sped off.

Bulger and Embry stayed in touch for a while afterward.

"If this ever gets back to you, they're going to tell you that I'm the head of the Irish Mafia, but I'm not," Bulger told him once with a laugh.

"What *do* you do for a living?" Embry asked.

"I run a liquor store," Bulger replied.

During their last conversation, Bulger may have been alluding to his upcoming life on the run when he told Embry he was thinking of buying a boat.

"I'm going to take a cruise around the world," he said. "Hey, if you need anything, let me know."

"Maybe I could use a loan someday," Embry said, not realizing what he was saying.

Bulger laughed.

Back in Boston, John Connolly decided it was time to pack it in too. He'd received eight commendations, cash incentive awards, and other accolades for his work with a dozen Top Echelon informants over the years, but nothing was going to top 34 Guild Street.

He and his friend Joe Pistone collaborated on a short paperback book called *The Ceremony*. It was an odd work, a slim 170 pages consisting of a twenty-seven-page introduction by Pistone, a verbatim transcript of the Medford induction ceremony tape, and some photos. Connolly's name was was not listed as an author, but there was a big picture of him and some glowing praise from Pistone.

Pistone wrote about a dinner he and Connolly had shared in Florida at Joe's Stone Crab restaurant in Miami Beach, which, incidentally, had also been one of J. Edgar Hoover's favorite restaurants.

"The reign of the Patriarca Family is virtually ended. A substantial amount of the credit for the demise of that mob family must be given to one man, Special Agent John Connolly," Pistone wrote. "John was justifiably proud of the work of all the people who had a part in obtaining the [Guild Street bug] transcripts. I laughed with him, and then I laughed at the great irony of John Connolly, son of parents born in Galway, Ireland, getting to the heart of the Mafia.

"When I told him what I was thinking, he looked at me and said, 'Joe, you should know better than anyone else, you don't have to be in the Mafia to think like them!' "

The book was not a big seller.

In 1990, Connolly retired from the FBI and took a job as head of security at an electric utility, Boston Edison Co. It was widely rumored that Billy Bulger helped him get the job, but Connolly denied it. After Connolly's retirement, C-3 supervisor Ed Quinn quietly closed Bulger and Flemmi as Top Echelon informants.

Connolly wasn't the only one heading into retirement. O'Sullivan quit his interim post and took a partnership at a big Boston law firm, Choate Hall & Stuart. Maybe it was a coincidence, but his retirement coincided almost exactly with a vote by a committee of federal prosecutors to do away with the concept of independent strike forces and bring the organized crime prosecutors back under control of the U.S. Attorney's offices. Attorney General Dick Thornburg had never liked the strike force concept, and indeed shortly thereafter made them subordinate units of the U.S. Attorney's offices, over the objections of veteran mob prosecutors like U.S. Attorney Rudolph Giuliani in New York. Ring followed O'Sullivan to Choate Hall a year later, becoming head of investigations. He also became a fixture on television and in the newspapers as an "expert" for organized crime stories, developing an image as a pipe-smoking guru who had engineered one of the greatest victories against the Mafia of all time.

"Mr. Ring became the Director of Investigative Services after retiring from the FBI with 25 years experience in both investigative and management responsibilities . . ." the Choate Hall Investigative Group's glossy eight-panel brochure boasted. "He was nationally recognized by the U.S. Attorney General and Director of the FBI for his organized crime investigation that led to the electronic surveillance and tape recording of the secret Mafia induction ceremony." Among other services, the brochure offers help "addressing electronic surveillance and other technical questions."

In the span of little more than a year the architects of the Boston FBI's greatest triumphs against the mob—and the worst abuses tolerated in their name—were gone. Whitey Bulger and Stevie Flemmi were finally on their own.

To anyone else, the contents of the two safe deposit boxes looked like cash—big piles of it, in fact—but to the State Police troopers who had just seized it, it was paydirt. The $2 million they were staring at represented the entire retirement fund of one Burton "Chico" Krantz, who the Heller's Café tapes had revealed as one of Boston's biggest bookmakers.

The black-haired, six-foot-four-inch Krantz was a standout Boston schoolboy athlete in baseball and basketball, but his true love of sports was betting on it, not playing. He had a particular genius for handicapping baseball games—he claimed to have won $1 million on the 1981 World Series alone—and in the 1980s he had become perhaps Boston's biggest bookmaker. But while most bookies were content to live off their commissions and not make bets themselves, Krantz loved being a high roller and a risk-taker.

"If he made $10 million, he wanted to spend $14 million," one friend said. "Chico only wanted to be a bookmaker so he could be a player."

Now the former baseball star was in a bind. Prosecutors had already thrown him a curve by seizing his cash. Now they were coming inside with some serious chin music— they showed him a dummied-up "indictment" with both his and his wife's names on it.

"Leave my wife out of it, I'll play ball with you guys," he said.

Krantz gave the State Police a wealth of information about which wiseguys were shaking down which bookmakers. The Assistant U.S. Attorney they were working with on their investigation of Bulger, Flemmi, and now Flemmi's old friend Francis P. "Cadillac Frank" Salemme later told a judge that, because of the "twenty or so years that he [Krantz] dealt with the defendants, if the Government wanted, we could perhaps charge . . . a hundred different incidents of extortionate conduct."

People sometimes assumed that Fred Wyshak, a tall, prematurely gray, curly-haired Assistant U.S. Attorney, was a New Yorker. He did go to law school there and began his career as a prosecutor in New Jersey, but he also had a natural stubborn, abrasive streak that was pure New York, even though he had actually been raised in Boston's working-class Roslindale section. Wyshak's friends knew he was a good husband and father and that his heart was in the right place, but in terms of being difficult, even they admitted that on a scale of one to ten—when he really had it cranked up—Fred was an eleven. In a sense, it made him the perfect guy to go after Whitey Bulger and Stevie Flemmi—he wasn't the kind of prosecutor who worried that his big shot at a white-shoe law firm partnership would evaporate if he stepped on a few toes. "There are a lot of nice people out there who don't know how to make cases," one friend said.

Wyshak had another qualification that made him the perfect man to go after Bulger and Flemmi. He hated the FBI. The feeling was mutual. John Connolly's friend Nick Gianturco, who emceed the strike force Christmas parties for several years, started giving out the "Most Hated Man in Law Enforcement Award" to the person deemed the biggest pain in the ass by the Bureau. The award was a plaque with a little picture of Fred on it.

His feelings also made Wyshak a soulmate of the new chief of the State Police Special Services Unit, Sergeant Thomas Foley. The white-haired, taciturn Foley also nursed a deep dislike of the Bureau, which dated back to the Lancaster Street era.

Wyshak and Foley eventually added several more members to their team. Baby-faced, affable Assistant U.S. Attorney Brian Kelly had a keen legal mind, but also functioned as a set of elbow pads for Wyshak, playing conciliator to Wyshak's zealot, good cop to his bad. Massachusetts State Police Sergeant Tom Duffy and square-jawed trooper John Tutungian and his cohort Steve Johnson also signed on, as did Dan Doherty, a DEA agent.

U.S. v. *Francis P. Salemme et al.,* the pivotal case that ended up exposing the FBI's T.E. program, actually started as several different cases. While the State Police were pursuing Krantz and the other bookmakers, Wyshak and Kelly were tabbed to prosecute an odd little case against Frank Salemme's son, Frank Jr., and a couple of Teamsters that the FBI code named Dramex. It was short for "Dramatic Exposé," but until a cooperating witness from Boston got involved, it had been neither.

David Rudder Productions was supposed to be an independent film production company in seaside Santa Monica, California. In reality it was an FBI front, and "David Rudder" was actually Special Agent Garland Schweickart, who looked more like a gangly midwestern farmer than a Hollywood producer-type, who was trying to find Teamsters Union officials willing to look the other way on nonunion movie shoots in return for a little payola. But the Bureau had nothing to show for the money it was pouring into the undercover sting—including the cost of renting "Rudder" a Rolls Royce—until Robert Franchi came along.

Franchi was working in L.A., but he was originally from the North End. He was able to connect Schweickart with Dennis "Champagne" LePore—one of the soldiers who had been recorded extorting Doc Saganski and Moe Weinstein at Vanessa's—and Frank Salemme Jr. Later, Frank Jr. brought his father into the scheme.

Nobody cared about the Dramex case in the U.S. Attorney's office, so Wyshak and Kelly picked up, figuring it might be useful in providing evidence against Salemme. It was. The FBI bugged a meeting between Salemme and a mobster from Las Vegas, "Big Chris" Richichi, where

Salemme bragged about his association with Bulger and his old friend Flemmi.

Frank Sr. was now the boss of the Patriarca family, what was left of it anyway. Raymond Patriarca Jr., J. R. Russo, Vinny "the Animal" Ferrara, Bobby Carrozza, and several others had all pleaded guilty to racketeering charges in the case that resulted from the Vanessa's and Guild Street wires. Their lawyers had tried but failed to challenge the induction ceremony wire in court, so the game was over. J. R. Russo, ever the traditionalist, took an extra year in prison in return for not having to admit the existence of the Mafia and violate his vow of *omerta*. The guilty pleas left Frank Salemme Sr. as the boss of a mob with only a handful of soldiers still on the street. He had no choice but to work with Flemmi and Bulger.

The bookmakers told the same story to the grand jury, Salemme and Winter Hill were working closely together. More and more, the case was beginning to take shape. Frank Salemme's Mafia remnants had allied themselves with Bulger and Flemmi, so didn't that make them one big conspiracy? Word began to spread inside the law enforcement community that a major racketeering indictment of all three men was in the works.

The twist was that Wyshak and Kelly had never been told that Bulger and Flemmi were informants. When new FBI SAC Richard Swensen heard about the potential indictment of the Top Echelon sources, he went to U.S. Attorney Donald K. Stern. After a meeting of Stern's top brass, it was decided that the case would go forward, but that a legal "Chinese wall" would be erected between the prosecutors and anyone who knew Bulger and Flemmi's status.

In August 1994, according to Flemmi, he and Bulger received a false alarm from John Connolly that the indictment was coming down.

"It's time to take a vacation," Bulger told his longtime partner.

Flemmi went up to Montreal for a few months, while Bulger took Theresa Stanley down to Memphis to see Graceland. For the next several months, they followed a dizzying itinerary of Dublin, London, Rome, New York, New Orleans, and San Francisco, for a visit to Alcatraz. Finally, at the Grand Canyon, Stanley had had enough and asked Bulger to take her home for Christmas.

Just after New Year's, Flemmi got another call from Bulger. This time it was definite, the indictment was coming down on the tenth. Bulger and Stanley took off again, but Flemmi decided to wait until the last minute and spend a few days helping his son Steven Hussey open a restaurant downtown called Schooners.

On January 5, 1985, he was just leaving the restaurant when he was approached by several large men with guns. "Don't move, Stevie!" one said, pressing a gun to his temple.

"You're under arrest."

CHAPTER TEN

Turnabout

••••••••••••••••••••••••••••••

The Top Echelon program is exposed

BOSTON ATTORNEY TONY CARDINALE was such a big gadget fan, he even bought a Humvee before realizing there was no place in a crowded city like Boston to park it. He always had the latest laptop computers, cell phones, pagers, even highly sophisticated cassette tape players (his clients tended to get taped a *lot*). He was listening intently to one of those tape machines in the summer of 1996, hoping for a break that could help get his clients, Frank Salemme and Bobby DeLuca, off the hook.

The tapes were from a bugged meeting at the Logan Airport Hilton between Salemme, Kenneth Guarino, the pornographer from Rhode Island, and Gambino family capo "Big Chris" Richichi from Las Vegas. Cardinale was almost nodding off listening to Guarino and Richichi chat while waiting for Salemme to arrive.

Mostly, the two zaftig wiseguys were babbling like a couple of coeds.

"How many pounds you weigh now?" Richichi asked.

"Oh, what the fuck," Guarino said. You could almost hear him rolling his eyes.

"You're too fucking heavy," Richichi chided.

"Two eighty," Guarino said.

"You got fuckin' legs, you got. You got two legs as big as my whole body."

"I'm up about two eighty."

"Ah . . ."

"Two seventy-nine."

"I wanna get rid of my fucking stomach, but I'm talking about you, though. You who really . . . you're really too, too much."

"I know."

"I'm only . . . my stomach. I'm two thirty. *I'm* too fuckin' heavy."

"What do you want to drink? Do you want something? Some apple juice? Apple juice?"

"You got the . . . you got a . . . what ya got that's diet?"

"Diet?" Guarino said.

"Ah, Jesus Christ," Richichi said.

"A Diet Coke?"

"Yeah."

Suddenly, something else on one of the tapes caught Cardinale's ear, a faint murmur in the background. Salemme and DeLuca mentioned that there was something funny on the tape, only Cardinale could hear it much better than they could on the cheap little tape player they were allowed to use at the Plymouth County House of Correction. There seemed to be two other people talking, which should have been impossible given that Guarino and Richichi were the only people in the room. Then Cardinale remembered a snippet of news he had heard about the devices the FBI sometimes used to pick up sound from an adjoining room, how they read the vibrations of the walls somehow.

My God, he thought. Those are the agents' voices. Cardinale adjusted the tape player to bring up the background noise.

". . . the Saint to make up a list of questions of shit we could make up and get Kenny to ask him . . . we could, you know, narrow the . . . categories."

"Kenny," Cardinale believed, was obviously Kenneth Guarino, forty-six-year-old Mafia associate and pornographer from Rhode Island, who was in the room. Guarino was paying Richichi millions in protection money. Guarino's publicly traded adult entertainment company, Metro Global Media Inc., grossed millions marketing X-rated magazines, videos, and CD-ROMs with titles like "Zazel, the Scent of Love."[24] Cardinale surmised that "the Saint" was Anthony St. Laurent, a made guy from Providence. Things were starting to make sense.

Guarino had made all the travel arrangements for the Salemme-Richichi meeting—reservations, tickets, even a suite at the Ritz Carlton on Newbury Street. The FBI asked the Ritz for cooperation with the bugging operation, but the hotel had refused, and it had been Kenny who, at the last minute, conveniently changed the location of the meeting to the more Bureau-friendly Airport Hilton.

Guarino had changed the room as well. At one point Big Chris and Bobby DeLuca had been talking in the Hilton coffee shop, waiting for Kenny to come back with the room key.

"We've gotta wait," Guarino said, walking up. "They have to change our room. The room that they gave us had only one bed, and we gotta have a room with two beds." The room they got not only had two double beds, but two FBI agents next door, recording every word they said.

The Saint, meanwhile, had inexplicably been given a ten-month prison sentence on virtually the same gambling charges that had put DeLuca away for five years. Cardinale went to the judge in the case and got an order for digital copies of the original tapes. His audio experts confirmed it—the agents had been talking about "Kenny" and "the Saint"—which meant two things:

1. Kenny Guarino and the Saint were FBI rats.
2. Tony Cardinale had his first big break in the case of *U.S.* v. *Salemme et al.*

---

[24]*Providence Journal-Bulletin,* "R.I. Pornographer Pleads Guilty," January 1, 1997.

Title III requires prosecutors to make a "full and complete" disclosure to the judge approving the wiretap about why a bug or a wiretap, law enforcement's most intrusive tool, was necessary. To show that a bug was necessary, prosecutors had to spell out for a judge why other methods of gathering evidence would not work in the case. It stood to reason that if pornographer Kenny Guarino were working for the FBI, he might have been able to wear a concealed body tape recorder into the meeting with Richichi and Frank Salemme, who showed up later. Legally, body wires were considered less intrusive—if you had an informant willing to wear one, you couldn't get a bug.

It was certainly possible, even probable, that Guarino could have been refused to wear a body wire. The traditional wiseguy *abbraccio* had long since included a quick pat-down to check the other guy for microphones. That's why law enforcement officials had taken to putting the mini-recorders in the underwear of their cooperating witnesses—homophobia in the Mafia usually trumped even self-preservation. An informer who refused a wire was no big deal; you just reported it to the judge and got a court order for a bug instead.

The problem was that Guarino's name was already in Special Agent Walt Steffans's electronic surveillance application as a "target" of the bug. How could you be both an informant for a bug *and* a target? It didn't make sense. Was the FBI really going to use the tapes against and prosecute their own guy? Of course not.

The realization hit Cardinale like a bullet. The Boston FBI, he now believed, was using falsified wiretap applications to hide highly placed informants. By listing the informants as targets with everyone else, they were suddenly above suspicion. Yet at the same time, the affidavits were misleading to the judges issuing the order. It was as if the continental plates that were his basic assumptions on the FBI and its vaunted electronic surveillance capabilities had shifted. If they had done it once, they had probably done it a dozen times. That meant virtually anyone who had been named as a target of a federal bug or wiretap could be an informant.

It also meant he had the break he had been looking for.

While Bulger was still a fugitive, the other defendants were preparing for trial at their new home at the Plymouth County House of Correction. Flemmi, Bobby DeLuca, and Jimmy Martorano arrived first. Johnny Martorano joined them later in January, when he was arrested in Florida by the State Police after sixteen years on the run from the race-fixing case. Frank Salemme joined them in August.

Preparing for trial at Plymouth was difficult—the rules were not designed to accommodate multiple prisoners defending themselves in a massive racketeering case. The wiseguys had hundreds of tapes turned over to them by the FBI and the State Police, but like other inmates, they were restricted to possessing five inches of legal papers and fifteen tapes at a time. The indictment alone was an inch thick, and the guards literally went around enforcing the rules with a tape measure. They were not even allowed to use pens or pencils or legal pads to take notes.

Their attorneys had been trying a variety of strategies since pretrial hearings had started. They attacked the legality of the state wiretaps, argued that the Winter Hill-Patriarca alliance wasn't a true RICO, and charged that Wyshak, Kelly, and their supervisor, James Herbert, had improperly used the grand jury to strengthen their case. The prosecutors, meanwhile, brought revised or "superceding" indictments to fix the problems and add new charges—they even dug up Bobby Daddieco and charged Flemmi and Salemme with the Bennett brothers' murders from the 1960s. Both sides won some and lost some. Wolf upheld the legality of the Busy Bee tapes, but said the Bennett murders would probably be out.

Frank Salemme worked a lot on the tapes. Having gone on the lam, he had little hope of bail. He and his wife,

Donna Wolf, a trim aerobics instructor whom he'd met at a gym in Sharon, had settled in Florida. After the warning from Connolly, Frank and Donna rented a town house in West Palm Beach under assumed names. They brought in a big-screen TV and a weight bench so Frank could work out. Other than dyeing his graying hair brown (it actually came out sort of orange), he didn't do much to disguise himself. Neighbors said they sometimes saw Frank sunning himself on the porch, feeding the ducks that waddled over from a nearby canal or helping the wheelchair-bound woman next door with her groceries. Mostly the couple didn't show themselves much.

South Florida wasn't exactly an original place to hide—it seemed to have a way-above-average share of fugitive mobsters from New England. Johnny Martorano had been picked up in Boca Raton. Nine months before that, Joe Yerardi, the Winter Hill bookmaker and loanshark, was nabbed in Fort Lauderdale. Unfortunately, the region also seemed to have an above average share of Fox TV viewers. Cadillac Frank was profiled on *America's Most Wanted*, and a tipster called to say a man matching his photo was living on Thirty-fourth Way in West Palm Beach.

FBI agents, backed up by local police, surrounded the house at just before midnight. An agent dialed in on a cellular phone.

"Hello?" a groggy voice answered.

"Frank? This is the FBI. We're outside and we have you surrounded. We don't want any trouble. Will you come out peacefully?"

"Okay," he said.

Salemme stepped out the front door in a T-shirt and boxer shorts, looking like he had been asleep. He was placed in handcuffs and driven away. The next day, two groups gathered expectantly in front of the town house. One was a gaggle of reporters from Boston, who interviewed Salemme's neighbors and peered inside the porch windows. The other was a flock of quacking ducks, wondering where their meal ticket had gone.

Johnny Martorano, despite being on the run for sixteen years, took a shot at bail, but he and his lawyer, Martin Weinberg, were pushing a weak hand. He gave Wolf several letters from other parents in Boca Raton commending Martorano's apparent devotion to his son John Jr. Martorano's pregnant daughter Jean pledged the $30,000 equity she had in her home in Plymouth as security for his bail. His in-laws agreed to post $260,000, while a friend of his wife Patty, meanwhile, agreed to put up another $200,000.[25] Even a half-million secured bail wasn't enough to head off some tough questions from Wolf.

"I don't find those letters to be insincere or insignificant. But as I have said in other cases, sometimes genuine affection for one's family coexists with other qualities. Did he have any legitimate employment since 1979?"

"No," Weinberg admitted.

"Shouldn't that cause me concern?"

"I think Your Honor *should* be concerned. I don't think this is going to be an easy decision for Your Honor."

In the end, Wolf decided to keep Martorano in jail pending trial.

"I find that there is no evidence that the defendant has ever engaged in legitimate employment. There is, however, ample evidence that he was able to support himself, in some respects lavishly, including vacations in Hawaii, while he was a fugitive living in Boca Raton, Florida. Thus like the Magistrate, I conclude that the financial resources Mr. Martorano obtained in the past, during the sixteen years he was a fugitive, resulted from illegal activities.

"With regard to the defendant, it seems that he took an arrogant delight in his fugitive status. When he was arrested, he had a Florida license in the name of Vincent Joseph Rancourt as in 'ran from court,' " Wolf wrote.

Stevie Flemmi also lost his desperate bid for release. He had convinced his son Stephen Hussey to sign an affidavit

---

[25]Hearing transcript, *U.S.* v. *Salemme,* June 12, 1996.

saying that his father had no financial interest in the maze of trusts that Flemmi had set up in the family's name. It was foolish. IRS investigators easily uncovered Flemmi's hidden interest in the trusts. Not only was Flemmi's bail denied, but his son was eventually convicted of perjury and obstruction of justice. Increasingly desperate, Flemmi reached out for Kevin Weeks, his and Bulger's trusted lieutenant in South Boston, to ask John Connolly for help. Weeks reported back that Connolly had said he was sorry, that he believed Bulger and Flemmi were getting screwed, but there was nothing he could do.

All Flemmi could do was wait and hope that Whitey Bulger could pull off one more miracle.

Ten months after the indictments, Morris had been promoted again, to Section Chief of the Training Administrative Section at the FBI Academy in Quantico, Virginia. He was in his office when his secretary told him there was a "Mr. White" on the line.

The hairs on the back of his neck stood up. He picked up the receiver.

"John Morris."

He heard a cold voice on the other end, one he'd hoped he would never hear again.

"This is Whitey Bulger, motherfucker."

As he had with reporter Paul Corsetti, Bulger used the fear-inspiring nickname that he personally disliked. Morris didn't need to hear a name, there was no mistaking the voice.

"You ruined my life, you cocksucker. You ruined my family's life. After everything I did for you, you made me a marked man, I could get killed for the shit you told the papers about me," Bulger said. It sounded as if Bulger's teeth were tightly clenched and he was fighting to maintain control.

"Look—" Morris started.

Bulger cut him off.

"Remember Dave Toomey?"

Toomey was the former strike force attorney sent to prison for taking bribes from one of Bulger's pet marijuana smugglers, Frank LePere. Bulger was playing the bribery card.

"The same thing could happen to you. Remember that money you took? If I'm going to jail, you're going with me, you fuck. Don't think that I don't have witnesses—you know I do," Bulger hissed.

"That's an outright lie—" Morris began, suddenly fearing that Bulger was tape-recording the call. Bulger cut him off again.

"Listen, why don't you use that Machiavellian mind of yours to come up with a new story for those newspaper contacts. I want a goddamn story in the *Globe* saying that the other story that said I was a rat was a plot to discredit me, to knock me down," Bulger said.

"Are you taping this?" Morris asked.

"No, and you'd better not be either. You're a hard man to find," Bulger said. "One time I called and I got a voice recording."

Morris, confused and fearful of both Bulger and of being taped, said nothing. There was a moment of silence on the line.

"You still there?" Bulger asked.

"Yes."

"I repeat. You've got one chance to do this. If you don't, I'm going to make damn sure that you go to prison with me."

"I hear you," Morris said.

The line went dead.

Morris was badly shaken. He'd tried to cut the ties to his past in Boston, having virtually no contact with anyone from his old office. He'd only learned about the 1995 racketeering indictment when one of his agents put a newspaper article on his desk.

Morris wrote out a report on the call. He sent a copy to Boston and another to OPR. Surprisingly, none of the investigators who followed up asked him whether Bulger's

bribery allegations were true. Their questions focused instead on where he thought Bulger might be and where the
call might have come from. The answers shook Morris up
even more. The call was traced through the FBI's telephone system. It had been placed directly to Morris's office in Quantico, on a number unavailable to the general
public.

It's hard to imagine a jurist whose career path would better
prepare him to deal with the legal issues raised by the Top
Echelon program than U.S. District Court Judge Mark L.
Wolf. As the case dragged on for more than five years, critics (including some fellow judges) chided Wolf for spinning
off on some personal crusade.

Those who know him well, though, said the *Salemme* case
simply wrapped up many of the issues he cared most deeply
about in one complex and compelling package. Wolf insisted that he was simply following and applying the law,
but by the same token, he frequently quoted his own past
opinions on legal issues in the case and cited his personal
experiences working for the Justice Department and as the
Deputy United States Attorney for Massachusetts. Wolf, for
example, had a great personal interest in both informants
and wiretap law. He had worked in the Justice Department
as a Special Deputy Assistant Attorney General under Levi
and had actually helped draft the stricter DEA guidelines for
the use of informants.

As he passed through the rotunda of the Justice Department building on Pennsylvania Avenue, he would sometimes look up at an inscription etched in the ceiling that said:
"The United States prevails when justice is done its citizens
in the courts." The saying was a reminder to prosecutors that
winning was not synonymous with justice. Friends said
Wolf took it to heart. In the Boston trial, Wolf was generally
viewed as mostly a down-the-middle guy, not too user-
friendly to either defense lawyers or prosecutors—although
like many judges who were former prosecutors, he had a

tendency to lapse into something of a "we did it better in my day" attitude. Socially awkward, fastidious, and a rare Massachusetts Republican, people were often surprised to learn that Wolf also worked tirelessly without fanfare for foundations helping hospitals, refugees, and inner-city children. Under Levi, he also worked on the Attorney General's project to resettle thousands of Vietnamese refugees after the fall of Saigon.

Although not athletic himself, Wolf was a big sports fan who grew up in suburban Newton, the son of a successful accountant for, among others, the Boston Celtics. Through his father he became friendly with legendary coach and general manager Red Auerbach and was later a season ticket holder—although he was more prone to use baseball analogies in court. ("Pitch from the stretch," he once told Cardinale, trying to speed up a cross-examination.) His faults, according to friends, included a certain insecurity, resulting in a tendency to take offense too easily. "But he feels remorseful and will call you back to apologize the next day," one lawyer friend says. He also had a tendency to be overly deferential to powerful men. After the *Ferrara* case, Wolf was criticized in the press for hosting the Mafia defendants in his chambers for Italian pastries.

If the Fates had been picking a judge for *Salemme, Ferrara* was the reason Wolf would have been their man.

Tony Cardinale, who represented Vinny Ferrara, and several other lawyers including Marty Weinberg, who represented Bobby Carrozza, challenged the Ferrara wiretap on the grounds that the FBI and Diane Kottmyer knew in advance that the ceremony would be at 34 Guild Street. Since the government made no mention of it in the application for the bug approved by Judge Nelson, it therefore did not make a "full and complete statement" to the court as required under the law.

During pretrial hearings, Kottmyer had argued that "full and complete statement" did not mean the government had to tell the judge absolutely everything it knew, simply enough to show that ordinary "fixed" electronic surveillance would not work. Wolf ruled against Kottmyer, but said she had made an "honest mistake of law" and that there was no attempt by prosecutors to mislead the court or hide the identities of informants.

Legal experts said Wolf was essentially taking a stand that Congress intended judges to have a real role in determining whether electronic surveillance was proper, and not merely to serve as rubber stamps for prosecutors. Justice Department statistics which showed the fact that ninety-eight percent of all wiretap applications were approved may have played a role in his decision.

Ferrara was a landmark decision, the first ruling on roving wiretap law, and became a precedent cited in numerous other electronic surveillance cases.

Tony Cardinale grew up in a third-floor walkup apartment above a fish store in Manhattan's Hell's Kitchen, but his life as a young man was centered around a restaurant. He spent as much time as he could hanging out at Desomma's, a restaurant that his ex-boxer father Frank and his uncles owned on West Forty-seventh Street, next to the Brooks Atkinson Theatre.

Desomma's, with its crisp white tablecloths and tasteful Tuscan landscapes on the walls, was both a neighborhood institution and a New York melting pot. Broadway types like Jason Robards ate next to fighters like Rocky Graziano, and everybody rubbed elbows with the tourists, businessmen, and the local wiseguys.

Unlike Johnny Martorano, who idolized the Italian wiseguys who frequented his father's Italian restaurant in Boston, Cardinale had no desire for a life in the rackets. Instead, he saw that while his dad was at ease with the fighters, the actors, and the mobsters, he treated the professionals who came in—the doctors and lawyers and bankers—with an old world deference. Their education gave them a higher station in his father's eyes. "I wanted to be the guy who was treated that well," he said.

After the family moved to suburban Totowa, New Jersey, Tony won a full football scholarship at tiny Wilkes College in Pennsylvania. After graduation, he applied to various law schools, and was accepted at Suffolk University on Beacon Hill in Boston. He moved to Massachusetts permanently in 1973, yet friends said that while that you could take Cardinale out of New York, you never could take young Tony out of his father's restaurant. Cardinale loved being around the boxers and wiseguys. He liked their warrior code. While becoming the top lawyer for organized crime cases in Boston, Cardinale also kept his hand in the fight game—opening a gym in Somerville and promoting fighters like John "the Quiet Man" Ruiz.

"The passions he has right now are so clearly derived from his father and that restaurant," said his friend, Ken Fishman, who represented Flemmi.

Fishman and Cardinale met at Suffolk and later worked as young lawyers at F. Lee Bailey's firm. As transplanted New Yorkers, it was only natural that they would gravitate toward each other, and they became close friends. They later discovered that their fathers were born on the same day. George Fishman was a nuclear physicist who worked on the Manhattan project and moved his family from Harlem to Long Island's Oyster Bay after the war. Ken Fishman grew up in a modest, largely Jewish section of the city dubbed "Hanukkah Heights" by locals, and went on to the Wharton School of Finance and Commerce at the University of Pennsylvania.

After their whirlwind apprenticeship under Lee Bailey, they might have become partners had it not been for Cardinale's desire to represent wiseguys. Fishman hadn't even planned on being a criminal lawyer, much less a "mob lawyer," and didn't want to be pigeonholed.

Truthfully, Fishman believed Cardinale was the superior courtroom lawyer between them. He had all the tools: a re-

lentless drive to win, the priceless ability to think on his feet
during cross-examination, and the sort of likable courtroom
personality that let him go after prosecution witnesses full-
throttle without alienating jurors. Yet Fishman also believed
Cardinale's passion for defending mobsters limited his practice.

Cardinale, though, viewed himself as a trial lawyer and
resented even the inference that he was some tainted Mafia
mouthpiece—so much so that he was always calling reporters and editors to chew them out whenever he was identified as a "mob lawyer." He liked to think of himself as a
watchdog against the abuses of power by prosecutors and
police—but particularly the FBI. Growing up, he had believed as much as anyone in the image of the incorruptible
G-man, but was quickly disabused of that notion during one
of his first cases with Bailey.

Peter McDonald, chairman of the Navajo nation in Arizona, hired the famous Boston attorney to defend him in a
conspiracy and corruption case brought by the FBI and the
U.S. Attorney's office in Arizona in the spring of 1977. Bailey had his young associate, who had passed the bar less
than a year earlier, fly out early to do the groundwork for the
trial.

Cardinale quickly discovered that a recent U.S. Supreme
Court case was highly favorable to McDonald's defense. In
U.S. v. *Nixon,* the high court ruled that to convict someone
of conspiracy, the government had to have at least one piece
of direct, not circumstantial, evidence linking the defendant
to the scheme. The government didn't seem to have anything
direct against McDonald, just evidence that one of his underlings had been reimbursed by the tribe for false and in-
flated bills from an aircraft charter company. The theory was
that the money had been passed to McDonald, but there was
no proof, and Cardinale told the judge so at a hearing on the
Friday before the trial was set to begin.

On Monday the federal prosecutor announced that during
a weekend meeting with the FBI, one of his witnesses had

miraculously "remembered" making a cash payment directly to McDonald. A stunned Cardinale told Bailey, who had flown in to start the trial, that there was no way the witness's testimony could be true. To prove it, he flew down to the bank where the witness, a pilot for the charter company, said he had cashed a check before delivering the cash to McDonald. The manager of the bank took a look at the code numbers on the cancelled check and said it could not have been cashed until at least half a day *after* the pilot said he had delivered the bribe.

Armed with Cardinale's information, Bailey unleashed one of his trademark, blistering cross-examinations on the pilot, destroying him as a witness. The judge dismissed the case against McDonald without sending it to the jury. His eyes had been opened, he said, to what the FBI was capable of.

"It was an FBI interview. It was clear that the FBI was part of it," Cardinale said years later. "Before that happened, I really did think that they were the best thing since sliced bread. But that was the end of that."

Wolf's courtroom on the twelfth floor of the J.W. McCormack Post Office and Courthouse was an impressive, if slightly threadbare reminder of what the WPA-era building must have been in its heyday. It had high ceilings, tall windows, dark wood paneling, and a monumental granite and brass wall behind the bench crested with an enormous brass eagle, but peeling paint in numerous places diminished its grandeur.

The first few moments of the case didn't exactly foreshadow the historic events that would follow. Unable to hear well from the first row of the spectator benches, Salemme, Flemmi, DeLuca, and the Martoranos were constantly whispering "What?" and trying to fill each other in on what their lawyers were saying. An exasperated Wolf finally asked the U.S. Marshals to move them to the comfortable, swiveling leather chairs in the jury box on his left. The four defendants would stay for months in the same familiar positions—Salemme on the far left, DeLuca next to him, Flemmi in the middle, Johnny Martorano on Flemmi's right, and his brother Jimmy on the far right—through almost the entire hearing process.

"Your Honor, this jury is acceptable," Cardinale joked after they were all grinning and happily swiveling in their new seats.

The defense team sitting at two long tables behind the prosecutors was one of the best the Boston bar could offer.

In addition to the talented Fishman and Weinberg, Cardinale also called in John Mitchell, a Manhattan attorney who was one of the nation's foremost experts in both RICO and electronic surveillance law. Even the other lawyers on the team admitted their brains sometimes ached when Mitchell waded into his complex legal theories. Jimmy Martorano picked Robert George, a noted Boston criminal lawyer. George, well-known for forsaking exercise in favor of a brutal work schedule, slumped over in his chair during one of the early hearings and fell unconscious to the floor from exhaustion. Michael Borbeau, another well-respected Boston criminal attorney, was brought in as his replacement.

The defense lawyers didn't know that the three prosecutors at the table in front of them were struggling over how to deal with one of their clients. There was simply no precedent for protecting a Top Echelon informant's secret identity while prosecuting him for conspiracy.

The previous August, AUSA James Herbert had gone to a magistrate judge, Lawrence Cohen, and filed a sealed motion to keep Flemmi's informant status a secret, saying there was nothing exculpatory that the other defendants needed to see. Cohen agreed, but ordered the government to at least give Flemmi an affidavit by Paul E. Coffey, a top FBI legal official who, after a 1995 review of Flemmi's FBI informant files, had found that the FBI had "at least tacitly authorized" the gangster's participation in "illegal gambling and LCN policymaking." How, in a conspiracy case, the fact that one of the alleged "conspirators" had been authorized to commit crimes by the government wasn't exculpatory, was anybody's guess. Under the law, a true conspirator must have a so-called *mens rea* or "guilty mind," which didn't apply to the government or its agents working undercover, since they were merely playacting at being criminals.

Indeed, Wolf later found that Cohen's ruling was "simply incorrect" and that the FBI and the U.S. Attorney's office had improperly kept Flemmi's cooperation a secret from him and from the defendants. The prosecutors violated Cohen's order anyway, and didn't disclose Coffey's affidavit until much later.

That might have been the end of it—had it not been for the snippet of tape from the Airport Hilton with the FBI agents' voices on it. Cardinale's mind was running wild with the possibilities of who among the dozens and dozens of wiseguys the FBI had taped over the years might be a rat. Actually, it wasn't even all that hard to make some educated guesses. If the FBI and the strike force had been making their own informants as "targets" of electronic surveillance—then the informant could only be rewarded in one of four ways:

1. A warning in advance to stay clear of the wiretap
2. A walk on the indictment
3. A light or nonexistent sentence
4. A tip to flee before charges were brought

Cardinale began combing through old wiretap affidavits and court dockets for wiseguys who fit the profile. Kenny Guarino? Probably. The Saint? Little doubt. Bulger? At least according to the *Globe*.

Sonny Mercurio? Definitely. Sonny's criminal career had come to a rather pathetic end in 1994. He was wanted on state marijuana trafficking charges in Georgia and was arrested because he had apparently spotted a $500 Shimano fishing reel in a Sandy Springs sporting goods store that he couldn't live without. He put the fishing reel in his pocket and just walked out of the store, giving the manager at the front a "Stop me, I dare you" look. The manager, a marathon runner, gave chase, and Sonny made it about two blocks before collapsing in a breathless heap on the sidewalk.

"He just ran out of gas," the manager told a newspaper reporter. "He was an old guy. He ran until his little legs just buckled."

Sonny was booked for shoplifting but released since the fake name he was using that day wasn't in the FBI's national crime database. A short time later, though, he was pulled over for suspected drunk driving, and this time his bogus driver's license was a match. When word got back to the Boston FBI that Sonny had been arrested, Special Agent Mike Buckley visited him in jail.

Soon afterward, Mercurio pleaded guilty in the *Ferrara* case. The government asked for just nine years. Despite Sonny's obvious role setting up the attempted murder of Frank Salemme, it was significantly less time than Russo, Ferrara, and Carrozza received. Not only that, but federal prosecutors recommended that it be served concurrently with Mercurio's ten-year sentence in Georgia. In effect, Mercurio got no prison time at all.

Buckley approached him again at his sentencing and asked if he wanted a copy of his FBI file.

"You've got to be joking. Burn it," Mercurio told the agent.

"I've got to ask you, what do you want to do with this?" Buckley pressed.

"I don't want nothing. Just burn the whole thing."

Cardinale, Mitchell, and the other lawyers in the case, meanwhile, started working on a brief requesting a hearing under a U.S. Supreme Court decision called *Franks* v. *Delaware*. The *Franks* decision gave defense lawyers the right to a hearing if they could make a strong preliminary showing that a judge was misled or tricked into issuing an order for electronic surveillance.

The motion for a *Franks* hearing laid out their suspicions on Mercurio, Whitey Bulger, Kenny Guarino, Anthony St. Laurent, and Robert Donati, Vinny Ferrara's former driver who had been reportedly murdered a few years before because he was cooperating. The argument was a brilliant bit of pushing Wolf's hot buttons. Not only did it raise the specter that the FBI had not made a "full and complete statement" as required by his *Ferrara* decision, but also that Wolf had been snookered into giving Mercurio his slap-on-the-wrist federal sentence. All the major wiretaps in the *Salemme* case—the DEA–Quincy Police tapes, the induction ceremony, and the Airport Hilton tape—were potentially tainted, the motion stated. The Hilton bug was particularly important because the FBI applied for it six months *after* his seminal decision in *U.S.* v. *Ferrara*. The Bureau might be excused for playing hide-the-informant before *Ferrara,* but not after. The government should be forced to admit whether any or all of the five men were informants, the motion argued.

All the defendants signed onto it except Flemmi. On March 11 the prosecutors and the defense lawyers held a meeting with the judge in his chambers. Cardinale and John Mitchell dropped the Sonny Mercurio bomb. In Mercurio, they said, the FBI had an informant who was not only intimately involved in the planning of the induction ceremony, but was *there*—raising questions about whether he could have worn a wire and made the bug unnecessary. At a minimum, the lawyers argued, the strike force and the FBI had not told Judge Nelson everything they should have.

The way we read *Ferrara*, the defense lawyers said, the decision requires a "full and complete statement" to the court.

That's exactly what it says, Wolf agreed.

After the defense presentation, Wolf finally got the materials that the prosecutors had given to Cohen. He called in

Flemmi and Paul Coffey, the FBI lawyer, for a private conference in his chambers off the courtroom. The judge asked a puzzled Fishman to wait outside for a minute.

Do you want your lawyer to know about your work as an informant? the judge asked. Flemmi said sure. Fishman was invited back in and told the truth about his client.

Fishman, Flemmi, and Coffey huddled for a brief private meeting.

"We want you to cooperate with us. Because of your past, we want to be of some assistance," Coffey said.

"If I was so valuable to you, why am I here being indicted?" Flemmi said, cutting him off.

Wolf held several weeks of closed-door hearings on whether the government should be forced to disclose the informant identities. The U.S. Attorney's office and the FBI vehemently objected, at one point issuing a dire warning that "disclosure would adversely affect law enforcement in general, and the informant program in particular, by undermining the pledge of confidentiality that the FBI makes to informants, by signaling to other informants and potential informants that the United States may not continue to honor its pledge of confidentiality, and by placing current informants in great danger."

Wolf was not swayed. In early April he ordered the Justice Department to say whether the five men were informants. If they didn't, he would hold one of Attorney General Janet Reno's top aides in contempt and order him thrown in jail. The deadline was set for May 29.

The day after the deadline, the new Boston FBI Special Agent in Charge, Barry Mawn, held a press conference to announce a $250,000 reward for information leading to Bulger's capture. Mawn was a veteran of organized crime investigations, but he had also grown up in the suburb of Woburn and had a pronounced Boston accent. (Like a true native, he pronounced the town's name "Woo-bin.")

Mawn impressed other law enforcement officials as not

being particularly slick, which, along with his local roots, may have been the point of his getting the job. His reward announcement smelled to a lot of people like an attempt to preempt the furor over the disclosure that Bulger and Flemmi were FBI informants. The FBI would deny it, but throughout the *Salemme* case, the timing of press conferences always mysteriously coincided with impending major news stories that might embarrass the Bureau.

The FBI was now going public, Mawn said, because its "intensive" search for Bulger had stalled.

"Everybody in this room knows that it hasn't been productive and you might say this is a shift. We are going to put as much out there as we can," he said. Among the tidbits Mawn released were that Bulger was traveling with his longtime girlfriend Catherine Greig, that he was taking heart medication, and that he was carrying a knife "at all times." Mawn said he was "very satisfied" that an "all out effort" was being made to catch Bulger.

Mawn's definition of "all out" was apparently fairly loose, evidence and testimony in the *Salemme* case later showed.

The FBI didn't contact Bulger's other longtime paramour, Theresa Stanley, for nearly fifteen months after he disappeared—even though it was common knowledge in South Boston that she was back in town. "By the time that she was interviewed . . . the information that Stanley could provide was dated and of diminished value," Wolf later wrote. It apparently took another year after that for Special Agent Charlie Gianturco—the brother of Nick Gianturco, who had followed John Connolly to Boston Edison—to get around to seeing Bulger's former handler.

Gianturco took along Walt Steffans, who later testified that Connolly also told the "The Ice Cream Cone Story."

"He said it was going to be the first paragraph of a book he was writing," Steffans said, who added that he was stunned to hear Connolly also say he "hoped Bulger would never be caught." He and Gianturco decided not to put the information in their report of the interview, however, because it had nothing to do with "the fugitive investigation."

About the same time that the $250,000 reward was offered, the investigation was quietly reassigned from Gianturco and the C-3 Organized Crime Squad to the Fugitive Squad, an FBI-led, multiagency squad that included investigators from the Bureau, the Boston Police, and the U.S. Marshals Service.

The Justice Department responded to Wolf's order by stalling. They agreed to turn over the Bulger file, but then filed motion after motion asking him to reconsider the disclosure order for the others. Frustrated, Wolf decided to "cut the Gordian knot," and ordered Mercurio, Guarino, and St. Laurent to appear in his courtroom.

Sonny was wearing a smirk and a white two-piece prison outfit with powder-blue stripes running up the sleeves that made him look like an extra from *Cool Hand Luke*. Salemme and Bobby DeLuca stared at him sternly, and Frank slowly pursed and unpursed his lips. Mercurio avoided their eyes, staring mostly at the floor.

As a last ditch effort, Coffey tried to sway Wolf by invoking the name of another T.E. informant who had been identified in court, Willie Boy Johnson.

"I don't claim it's going to change anybody's mind, but Willie Boy Johnson was called over his objection in that case to testify that he was an informant, and he did, over his objection and over the FBI's objection, and later he was murdered by Tommy Pitera, a contractor from the Gambino family," Coffey said.

Wolf was unimpressed. "All of this is serious. That's why we've had several months of closed proceedings."

Later that afternoon, the government made one last ditch effort to give Wolf some ex-parte papers to forestall Mercurio's testimony. The judge didn't look at them. When they returned to the courtroom the next morning, Mercurio was still wearing the same prison jumpsuit. He avoided eye contact with Salemme, who was decked out for the occasion in a well-tailored, double-breasted, navy-blue suit, a powder-blue shirt, and an understated maroon tie.

"Do you want another lawyer in connection with today?" Wolf asked.

"No. I'm happy with the way things are. You can ask the question," Mercurio said, smiling as the gallery tittered.

"Well, now it's unanimous; everybody wants the question to be asked," Wolf said. "Mr. Mercurio, would you state your full name for the record."

"Angelo Joseph Mercurio."

"Are you also known by any other name?"

"Sonny Mercurio."

"Were you acting in cooperation with any agency, agent, or attorney of the Department of Justice, including, but not only, the Federal Bureau of Investigation, in connection with the meeting held at 34 Guild Street, Medford, Massachusetts, on October 29, 1989, and that includes, but is not limited to, providing any agency, agent, or attorney of the Department of Justice information about that meeting at 34 Guild Street in advance?"

"Yes."

A murmur went up from the gallery as Cardinale asked Wolf to sequester FBI agents from the courtroom. He rattled off the names of the potential witnesses he would call for the *Franks* hearings on the alleged FBI misconduct: Steffans, Ring, John Gamel, Connolly, Buckley, Nick Gianturco, Quinn, Potts, Ahearn, Greenleaf, Sarhatt, O'Callaghan, Morris. His mind was racing so fast he started repeating names, so he finally just said:

"In addition, Your Honor, every member who I off the top of my head cannot recount, every member of the Organized Crime Squad of the Boston office of the FBI during the relevant period of time."

Everyone sat stunned for a moment.

The tables had been turned. The gangsters were putting

the FBI on trial. Frank Salemme looked over at his smiling
wife Donna and winked.

The *Herald* headline the next day screamed RAT POISON.

In the meantime, Cardinale had finally worked it out about
Flemmi. Holy shit, Cardinale thought. Flemmi? The guy
who had been Frank Salemme's best friend all those years
had been working with the FBI? The magnitude of the betrayal blew his mind.

The big blow-up, though, never came. Amazingly, now
that Flemmi's betrayal of Salemme was finally out in the
open, the interests of the two men were converging. Fishman,
with Flemmi's blessing, confirmed for the others that his
client had been a Top Echelon informant since the early
1960s. The scope of his criminal activity was truly awe-
some—and what he was saying about how the FBI had
helped him get away with it was equally impressive. In fact,
Flemmi said, John Morris had once told him and Whitey that
they "could do anything we wanted as long as we didn't clip
anyone."

Mitchell and Cardinale, meanwhile, had heard about the
Greg Scarpa Sr. case in New York, and how the defendants
in the Orena case used government misconduct claims to get
off. They were soon preparing another motion for Wolf—a
claim that the promises made to Flemmi and the actions
taken on his behalf amounted to de facto "immunity" from
prosecution and that the case should be dismissed on the
grounds of "outrageous government misconduct."

In June 1997, Flemmi filed two blockbuster affidavits,
containing his accounts of the chummy dinners with agents,
the $5,000 payment to Morris, the promise to warn him so
he could flee, and more. In response, Wolf ordered his entire
informant file, as well as most of Bulger's, turned over to the
defense.

At the Sonny Mercurio hearing, Wolf invited, but did not
order, Michael DeFeo, Chief of the FBI's Office of Profes-

sional Responsibility, to attend the hearings. DeFeo didn't show, but told an underling to tell Wolf that he would "read a transcript."

When the shocking revelations contained in the Flemmi affidavits made national headlines, however, DeFeo changed his tune. He sent a huge team of OPR agents—thirty in all—up to Boston to investigate. Lawyers on both sides of the case still question whether those agents were sent to uncover the truth or cover it up.

At times they appeared clueless. Cardinale and Mitchell agreed to meet with Joshua Hockberg, deputy chief of the Public Integrity Section, and afterward said that Hockberg didn't seem to know the first thing about the issues in the case. "I don't know what these people have done in order to bring themselves up to speed," Mitchell later complained to Wolf.

Other interviewees said the OPR agents seemed, at best, indifferent and sloppy. Former SAC Sarhatt, a key figure in the relationship between the two informants and the FBI, said he spent only "a few minutes" on the phone with an OPR agent. At least a half dozen other people interviewed by the OPR team said the reports of their interviews either contained omissions or errors. One of the most egregious examples was the handling of Morris's admissions about how he had tried to extort the cooperation of informants: planting the fake bomb under Eddie Miani's car and telling Bucky Barrett that Bulger and Flemmi wanted to kill him. Both were serious violations of FBI policy and the law, but they somehow were missing from the FD-302 report of Morris's interview by the OPR agents.

Flemmi, Connolly, Morris, and Condon, meanwhile, did their best to duck and weave even the seemingly friendly OPR investigation. In his first contact with DeFeo's agents, Paul Rico, for example, tried to claim that Flemmi "provided only limited information that at the time seemed inconsequential." He then said he "remembered" more about Flemmi after he was confronted by his own 209s. For Morris, the news that OPR wanted to talk to him hit like a boot to the stomach. He had been living a semblance of a normal life with Debbie, his former secretary and now second wife, out in Tennessee, working for an insurance company. Morris called a lawyer and refused to be interviewed.

John Connolly and his attorney, Robert Popeo, met with the OPR agents and AUSA Jamie Herbert. Is my client a target? Popeo asked. He'll only talk to you if you can assure us that he is not a target.

He's not, Herbert replied, but only according to the Justice Department definition. "Target," in federal criminal law, is a term of art that refers to someone whom prosecutors believe they have enough evidence against to indict. People who are being investigated at a more preliminary stage are "subjects." A subject letter from an Assistant U.S. Attorney is a cause for concern, a target letter is a red alert.

No, Popeo said, I want to know if he's a target in the literal sense, if they're going after him. We won't clarify his status under your definition, Herbert replied. Fine, Popeo said. No interview.

In July the defendants received a letter from Boston FBI ASAC Michael Rolince, saying they had found precisely *two* instances where FBI agents may have strayed from the Attorney General's Guidelines. The OPR team had found no evidence of crimes that could be prosecuted within the statute of limitations.

Mitchell labeled the probe a "whitewash." Even AUSA Fred Wyshak told Wolf that prosecutors did not believe the conclusion was true—crimes *had* been committed within the statute of limitations, and the government was pursuing them. Later, after the FBI documents and testimony started rolling in, Wolf could see for himself that the first OPR probe was a joke.

In the fall of 1997 the defendants fired their last, and most bombastic, legal broadside. Their motion to dismiss the indictment was more that 150 pages long and laid out allegations of systematic and outrageous government misconduct, including one nearly identical to the charges leveled against agent Lindley DeVecchio in the Scarpa case—that John Connolly had purposefully sparked the assassination attempt of Frank Salemme by leaking to the *Herald*.

The government filed a 99-page response. After several more weeks of arguments, Wolf made his decision: after the New Year, the defendants would get their hearing and he would listen to Flemmi's claim of immunity. In the interest of economy, though, a full hearing on the "outrageous government misconduct" charge would have to wait.

The *Salemme* hearings began in January 1998, almost six months after Wolf issued his discovery order.[26]

Both Ken Fishman and Tony Cardinale looked confident and relaxed, they even wore similar expensive blue pinstripe suits. Kimmi DeLuca, Bobby's wife, looked over at him from the second row of the spectator benches. She held out her hands toward him, letting them shake a bit as if to say, "I'm nervous."

Donna Salemme was in the second row, next to Frank's mother. To her left were Ram Nyberg and Greg Smith, detectives from the Metro-Dade Police Department in Florida who had reopened the investigation of John Callahan's murder. Detective Sergeant Mike Huff from Tulsa sat next to Nyberg, a slightly bemused expression on his face.

The presence of the homicide detectives underscored the fact that, although Flemmi had gotten his hearing, he was walking a legal tightrope. In order to push his de facto immunity defense, he would have to essentially admit that the FBI had allowed him to commit crimes. But that only went

---

[26]Author's Note: The hearings in the *Salemme* case covered forty-five witnesses, hundreds of hours of testimony, and thousands of pages of exhibits and court filings. Most of the factual testimony has already been incorporated into this narrative.

so far. No one, not even the defense side, was arguing that the FBI had the power to immunize Flemmi against murder charges, and a lot of people were hoping that enough evidence would emerge from the hearings that the murders of men like Roger Wheeler and John Callahan could finally be solved.

The way the hearings were set up, however, neither side was tempted to paint a true portrait of the Top Echelon Informant Program and its deadliest excesses. On the government side, it was in Wyshak, Kelly, and Herbert's best interest to paint Flemmi, John Morris, and John Connolly—who was increasingly emerging as a target for criminal prosecution in their eyes, if not FBI OPR's—as rogues operating outside the law and the FBI's informant guidelines. While the defense lawyers were trying to show that the FBI showed Flemmi special treatment as a T.E., they could not argue that he and Bulger were authorized to commit murder.

The picture of the Top Echelon program that emerged from the hearings, therefore, was somewhat skewed, but was nonetheless a vision of a troubled scheme which most rewarded the agents who acted with the least ethics.

Former Boston FBI SAC Larry Sarhatt testified first. He was followed by his successor, Jim Greenleaf, who was the first to talk about the Attorney General's Guidelines. He confirmed that they allowed the FBI to always apply a balancing test to determine whether to keep an informant who was also a killer.

Greenleaf denied knowing that Bulger and Flemmi were suspected by the FBI's Miami office of being involved in the Wheeler-Halloran-Callahan murders.

Wolf asked him what he would have done if he had been told.

"I would have looked at that very carefully and tried to weigh what these individuals were involved in against the quality of the information that they were providing. But my sense was if crimes got serious, we should probably have our own independent investigation," Greenleaf replied.

"Why would you have weighed the competing consideration?" Wolf asked.

"I think that was the policy," Greenleaf said.

Paul Rico was next. A month earlier, a front page *Herald* story had reported that the Metro-Dade Police Department in Miami had reopened their investigation into the World Jai Alai murders of Wheeler, Callahan, and Halloran. If Rico was worried about it, it didn't show. He was neatly dressed in a dark gray suit, a beige shirt and a floral-print tie held in place by a tie clip that said "Metro Dade" on it with the county seal.

Rico confirmed that the FBI knowingly recruited murderers as potential T.E. informants. He was aware that Flemmi "might have been involved in shylocking, and he might have been involved in homicide" when he was recruiting him.

"They had reputations as being pretty serious guys," he said.

"Murderers?" Wolf asked.

"I think that people had speculated over the years that they may have killed people, yes."

"Did you discuss with anybody higher than you in the FBI the propriety of maintaining people with such reputations in the criminal community as informants?"

"We have many that have those type of reputations, and people at all levels of the Bureau recognize that."

Morris and Ring, the two Organized Crime Squad supervisors, were perhaps the most important witnesses, since they were given the most authority under the Top Echelon program.

In one sense, they could not have been more different, Morris throwing himself wholeheartedly into the relationship with Bulger and Flemmi, while Ring adopted his "see no evil" approach. Yet they did manage to agree on several key points.

Both said the guidelines requirement to report informants' "serious" crimes was completely incompatible with the Top Echelon program. They both said they chose, in their own way, to ignore them. Finally, both confirmed that the Boston FBI listed informants as "targets" in wiretap applications, with all the potential problems that caused.

The two most interesting witnesses were perhaps Bill Weld and former FBI Supervisory Special Agent James Darcy, the ex-supervisor of the FBI Organized Crime Squad in Atlantic City.

Weld made it clear that the FBI and the strike forces were playing by a different set of rules than everyone else when it came to informants. "I don't think I would have let any loan-sharking or extortion walk. I might have let a little gaming walk if it was necessary to reel in a big fish down the line a little bit," he said. And there was no way, he said, that as an Assistant Attorney General he would have let a knowingly misleading affidavit be submitted to a judge. "That would undercut the entire process that Congress enacted," he said.

Darcy, called as an expert witness, said that, unlike the supervisors in Boston, he had applied for and received permission from his superiors to authorize crimes by his informants.

"It was just another memo," he said.

The hearings went from January to mid-October with only a couple of breaks. At one point Wolf stopped—when it was discovered he had been mentioned as a possible information leak during his tenure as Deputy U.S. Attorney. The U.S. Attorney's office investigated and found the allegation baseless. Wolf also took his usual month-long vacation on Martha's Vineyard.

The questioning fell into a fairly predictable pattern. Cardinale or Fishman would question a witness, elicit the day's bombshell, then turn the questioning over to Weinberg, who would methodically run through his technical questions, which were designed to show that the FBI gave Flemmi immunity, or at least authorization. Wyshak or Kelly or Herbert would then try and poke whatever holes they could in the defense lawyer's logic or the witness's story, and then establish that the words "immunity" and "authorized" were never explicitly mentioned. With the tide of the facts running against them, the prosecutors were fighting the battle on the law—hoping either that Wolf would rule against the defense's "de facto immunity theory" or that he would be overturned on appeal.

Agents Rod Kennedy, Bruce Ellavsky and John Newton were called to testify about the Slinger extortion and the DEA–Quincy Police drug investigation, as were Reilly, Boeri, Bergeron, prosecutors Crossen and Weld, and DEA chief Stutman. James Lavin and *Globe* photographer Joe Runci testified about the guardrails in front of the South Boston Liquor Mart. Kottmyer and several others testified about the induction ceremony bugs at 34 Guild Street.

The only scheduled witness who did not appear was strike force chief Jeremiah O'Sullivan, who had a heart attack on the day he was supposed to give prosecutors an affidavit. An adverse reaction to medicine he was given at the hospital caused a stroke, and O'Sullivan was declared too ill to testify after being examined by an independent doctor.

John Connolly took the Fifth. Instead of testifying, he kept up a steady stream of denials. He seemed to have a three-part defense strategy: (1) Everyone but me is lying; (2) if they're not, then what I did was justified because we put away forty-two members of the Mafia; and (3) if it wasn't justified, then I was just following orders.

Connolly called the author the day after Morris accused him of telling Bulger and Flemmi about Halloran's cooperation, highly agitated.

"I was no rogue agent, I did my job!" he said.

"I'm not the one saying that, John, it's the prosecutors who are saying that, right in open court."

"You gotta consider the source. They are terrified of me taking the stand and talking. The truth is that they won't give me immunity because of what I have to say. Everything I did I was told to do by Jerry O'Sullivan and the SACs. The files are replete with references to that."

I asked him if he, indeed, had tipped off Bulger and Flemmi about Halloran as Morris had said.

"Absolutely not."

Then why did they kill Halloran?

"They denied having anything to do with it."

He said he had to go and hung up.

As he sat in the leather-covered swivel chair in the jury box next to Bobby DeLuca and the hearings dragged on, John Martorano wore his trademark scowl. Underneath, he was seething. Included in his packet of Flemmi and Bulger materials were numerous FD-209s where Bulger and Flemmi were telling the FBI about his criminal activities and giving information that—if the Bureau had been at all inclined to look—could have led to his arrest.

Weinberg walked Ahearn through one such report, in which Bulger was telling Connolly about a dispute between Winter Hill and Patriarca family soldier Anthony "the Saint" St. Laurent. The report stated:

```
On May 20, 1987, [Bulger] advised that
the Winter Hill people have a layoff guy
in Las Vegas called JOE "NAILS" LNU [Last
Name Unknown]. JOE NAILS was grabbed by
"THE SAINT" from Providence, who advised
that he (JOE NAILS) has to start paying
"rent" to "THE SAINT" in Providence,
Rhode Island. JOE NAILS did not tell "THE
SAINT" who he was "with" but he contacted
BOBBY GALLINARO, AKA "BOBBY G" who con-
tacted JOHNNY MARTORANO. MARTORANO was
supposedly on his way to Rhode Island to
whack out "THE SAINT" when cooler heads
prevailed. Source advised that STEVIE
FLEMMI met with JOE RUSSO and SONNY MER-
CURIO in the Sheraton Hotel Lobby where
JOE RUSSO told FLEMMI that he would get
```

in touch with THE SAINT and straighten
it out. MARTORANO, who is on the lam, was
upset because his crew approached JOE
NAILS' 15-year-old daughter.

"If Mr. Martorano was a fugitive at this time, this would
be valuable information to those pursuing him, correct?"
Weinberg asked Ahearn.

"Yes, sir."

"If Mr. Martorano or Mr. Winter and Mr. Sims and Mr.
McDonald were previous associates and partners of Mr.
Bulger, these 209s represent cooperation to the FBI against
those persons, correct?"

Weinberg didn't even mention the worst part—Bulger's
not-so-subtle suggestion to the FBI that Martorano was the
sort of serious hit man who would "whack out" a made guy
like the Saint.

Not much was going right for Johnny. He had been in
jail the previous year when his mother Bess died. He'd
seen her when she was sick in the nursing home, but
missed her funeral due to a perverse U.S. Marshals' policy
in force that prisoners had to choose between either visiting a dying relative or attending the funeral. He was also
out of money. That same week he had to ask Wolf to have
the government start paying Marty Weinberg and one of
his ex-wives, Carolyn Wood, who was still trying to have a
$200,000 divorce judgment against him settled. She'd even
had all his prison canteen money, $695, seized by the
court.

But the worst thing was seeing Flemmi every day, and
being reminded of how that little rat who he had killed for,
and with, had turned around and informed on him to the
FBI. Martorano asked for a secret meeting with the state
troopers and the DEA agent working the case. He wanted a
deal.

Martorano left the Plymouth County House of Correc-
tions in mid-July 1998 and never went back. When Flemmi

realized he was gone, he reportedly went nuts, screaming
and throwing things around his jail cell.

When Flemmi testified in his own defense a month later, the
confident smile was gone. Fishman, Wolf, and the government had been unable to agree on what kind of immunity he
would get that would allow him to testify. If it were too
broad, he could take a so-called "immunity bath" by testifying to everything he had ever done, knowing it could never
be used against him. It it was too narrow—especially with a
hit man like Johnny Martorano negotiating a deal to rat him
out—he might be talking his way into a lethal injection in
Oklahoma or Florida.

The issue was still unresolved when Flemmi took the
stand for nine days in late August and early September 1998.
It was a letdown for anyone expecting fireworks or drama.
With the scope of his immunity in doubt, Flemmi and Fishman played it safe. He cited his Fifth Amendment right
against self-incrimination 382 times in ten days on the witness stand.

Worse, much of what Flemmi said was totally, completely
incredible. It was as if John Connolly were suddenly blame-
less in the whole episode—Flemmi refused to incriminate
him in any tip-offs. As his testimony wore on, Salemme and
DeLuca looked increasingly angry.

Sources close to the men said they were angered by
Flemmi's testimony, which they believed was not true and
was hurting their chances to win the case. Salemme confronted Flemmi before his last day on the stand, and Flemmi
promised that he would finally give up his old protector.

The moment of truth arrived when Judge Wolf asked
Flemmi who had tipped off the 1995 racketeering indictment.

"John . . ."

The words hung in the air for a moment.

". . . Morris."

Frank Salemme's face turned beet red. Stevie Flemmi had

again betrayed him to the FBI. It would be the last time, he promised himself.

On the day after the last witness testified in the *Salemme* hearings, Flemmi talked to Kevin Weeks again at Plymouth. The newspapers had been saying that Weeks himself was now the target of a grand jury. He had also been catching hell from other gangsters about having two rats for bosses.

The two men indulged in a little wishful thinking.

"If I beat them in this fucking case . . . you know this is going to be the biggest fucking humiliation they've ever went through, right?" Flemmi said hopefully.

"Yeah, but you know, you know what's going to happen," Weeks said, reminding Flemmi that he would still be a target.

"They'll have to frame me," Flemmi said.

"Ah. They're gonna come at you with every fucking thing they got."

"Well, they're going to have to come after me, 'cause I'm going to fucking Australia."

"Yeah, I'm fucking going too," Weeks said.

"They're going to have to come and get me in Australia if they fuckin' want me, or fuckin' someplace in fuckin' South Africa. I am not going to do it here."

Wolf worked on his decision in the case for nearly a year. Rumors circulated that he would release his decision after his annual Martha's Vineyard vacation in July. On August 5, FBI Director Louis Freeh held a press conference at the Boston office that officials said was part of a "routine" inspection visit, but he said he would be glad to answer any questions he could about the Bulger and Flemmi case.

The short, perpetually serious-looking Freeh stepped in front of the microphones and said his visit had given him a chance to meet with many of the 435 agents working out of the Boston office, "and probably more importantly [with] a lot of state and local and federal colleagues.

"We had lunch with a number of representatives of the State Police, the chief of the Boston Police, many of the other state and local entities being represented there. We talked very briefly but I think importantly about some of the law enforcement challenges that are facing not only the FBI but also all of us involved in law enforcement. It was remarked how many of our cases were being worked with our state and local affiliates."

Any questions? Freeh asked. The assembled media cut to the chase.

"How's the search for Whitey Bulger going?" Carl Stevens, a local radio reporter, asked.

"It's a very active investigation, as you know. We have a dedicated task force that is responsible for that."

Was the FBI reviewing its informant policies?

"Over the years we along with other agencies have changed the manner in which we deal with informants and the oversight and the internal controls. In 1996, in my capacity as chairman of the Attorney General's Committee on Investigative Policy, we produced a policy called Resolution Number 18. It was the first attempt to standardize informant policies. We found that different components of the department had different policies. We imposed in that policy a lot of restrictions and a lot of checks and balances and oversight in that particular activity.

"We made significant mistakes and there was probably some wrongdoing by some of our people. Those are issues we take with the utmost seriousness and which we will address with the utmost seriousness," he said. "But they should not be viewed as symptomatic of what our people do on a daily basis with thousands of informants."

Finding out the real truth in the case, Freeh said, was the FBI's "highest priority."

Johnny Martorano finally signed his plea deal about a month later. It had taken fifteen months of wrangling back and forth between investigators and prosecutors in Boston, Oklahoma,

Florida, but all the parties finally agreed to sign off on a sentence of between twelve and a half and fifteen years. The Wheeler and Callahan murders were among the crimes Martorano said he would plead guilty to personally committing.

After the deal was announced, disturbing rumors began to circulate that in addition to the twenty murders Martorano admitted participating in, he had also killed a large number of black people. A newspaper column even quoted a veteran police detective saying that Martorano had used local African Americans as "target practice." The comments were attributed to Ed Walsh, the former Boston Police detective and close friend of John Connolly. At a press conference following Martorano's guilty plea, however, U.S. Attorney Donald K. Stern said investigators could find no evidence that the rumors were true.

On September 16, 1999, Judge Wolf released a 661-page ruling, outlining his findings in the *Salemme* case.

Flemmi, the judge found, had no immunity. Instead, the FBI had given him an "enforceable promise of confidentiality" that his statements would not be used against him, a promise that functioned like immunity. The good news for Flemmi was that it meant that none of the court-ordered bugs or wiretaps he helped the FBI get could be used against him. The bad news was that it would take more hearings to figure out exactly what evidence against him had been derived from the wiretaps.

That included, potentially, Martorano's testimony, according to a footnote that was ominous for the agencies that signed the plea deal.

"It is inevitable that if this case is not dismissed, Flemmi will assert that Martorano should not be permitted to testify against him because Martorano's cooperation was obtained as a result of the government's breach of its agreement to maintain the secrecy of Flemmi's service as an FBI informant, and because the government's questioning of Martorano was impermissibly influenced by information that

Flemmi provided to the FBI," Wolf wrote. "The court will decide the challenging question of whether Martorano should be permitted to testify against Flemmi if and when it becomes necessary to do so."

Wolf also said he was suppressing the DEA–Quincy Police wiretap because the affidavit presented to the judge was misleading. He said he would have done the same for the induction ceremony but for a recent U.S. Supreme Court Decision, *Minnesota* v. *Carter*, which radically tightened the standard for who had legal standing to challenge court-ordered electronic surveillance. Even though he was "made" at the ceremony, Bobby DeLuca had no expectation of privacy under the new ruling, and therefore no standing to challenge it in court.

The overall motion to dismiss the indictment was denied.

Flemmi had lived to fight another day, but his old friend Frank Salemme had lost. It was a final indignity in a thirty-five-year legacy of betrayal. Still angry over Flemmi's refusal to implicate John Connolly on the witness stand, Salemme—who had nearly been murdered in a meeting set up by an FBI informant—did the last thing anyone thought he would do. He decided to cooperate with the government himself.

Shortly after the decision, Salemme received a grand jury subpoena. He knew what the subpoena meant: either violating his code as a member of the Mafia or refusing to testify and serve another eighteen months in jail for contempt to protect Flemmi. With Christmas approaching, he talked it over with his wife. They agreed: He would testify before the grand jury and then cut a deal to plead guilty in the racketeering case. "It was a family decision," Donna Salemme said later.

"He decided to do this rather than sit through three more years of hearings next to Flemmi—hearings that would benefit Flemmi," Cardinale said. "He had had enough."

Inside the grand jury room, Salemme related an accidental meeting between himself and Connolly at the Prudential Center in 1994. Connolly invited him upstairs to his Boston Edison vice president's office and told him he was writing a book, and that he would make Salemme look like a "good guy" in print.

Then Connolly said that he had inside information on an indictment that was coming, but that Salemme "shouldn't worry" because he was going to reach out for his old friend Flemmi to warn him when the time came.

Sure enough, before the indictment came down the next January, Flemmi called him, saying Connolly said it would happen on the ninth or the tenth of January. Unlike Flemmi, Salemme took no chances and left for Florida early. Just a few days after Salemme's testimony, and with less than three weeks before the statute of limitations for an obstruction of justice charge would have expired, a team of FBI agents knocked on John Connolly's door in Lynnfield. Connolly was home from work with the flu.

"Mr. Connolly? FBI. We're here to place you under arrest for racketeering."

Later that day, the fifty-nine-year-old former agent was brought into court in handcuffs. His hair was uncharacteristically mussed and the $1,000 suit was gone too, replaced by a plain gray sweatshirt, black jeans, and black Nike crosstrainers that he tapped nervously on the floor as Assistant U.S. Attorney James Farmer read off the counts: racketeering, racketeering conspiracy, conspiracy to obstruct justice, obstruction of justice.

Connolly's codefendants in the racketeering case, Farmer said, were James, aka "Whitey," Bulger and Stephen Flemmi.

The case—and the Top Echelon program—had come full circle. The betrayers had become the betrayed.

EPILOGUE

Justice in the Balance

The Top Echelon informant scandal—
has the FBI learned anything?

THROUGHOUT THE 1990s, the FBI and the Justice Department made sporadic attempts to tighten and clarify the informant guidelines. The Top Echelon program survived every one.

Assistant Director Floyd Clarke issued a written notice to the FBI's fifty-six field offices in 1990 reminding them that they were supposed to be reporting "serious" crimes committed by T.E. and other criminal informants. Clarke believed field supervisors were erroneously waiting until informants were either indicted or arrested before informing Headquarters, or, in some cases, didn't know exactly which crimes they should be reporting, other FBI officials said.

The chief of the informant program at FBI Headquarters in Washington at the time, James C. Summerford, said Clarke was "quite concerned that it was hard for field divisions to determine what criminal activity to report to Headquarters." Unfortunately, some FBI officials, including Summerford, felt that Clarke's directive (the contents of which have never been divulged) only confused matters further. "In my mind, it was in conflict with other sections of the manual," Summerford said.

The 1993 reform effort FBI Director Louis Freeh mentioned in his Boston press conference, meanwhile, on closer inspection, turned out not to be much of a reform at all, at least as far as the Top Echelon program was concerned. The FBI director was asked at the press conference whether the T.E. program was "still part of FBI policy."

"Not in the manner in which you have identified it," Freeh said. "The informant program that we have now is one which is strictly governed by and adherent to Resolution 18. The program as it existed, or did exist for many years in whatever nomination, is no longer part of our routine or operation."

"Resolution 18" resulted from a November 1993 order from Attorney General Janet Reno calling for more unified standards for handling cooperating witnesses and confidential informants by the various law enforcement agencies. Two and a half years later, Freeh, who was serving both as FBI director and head of the Office of Investigative Agency Policy (a post that rotated among the heads of the various agencies) issued an eight-page statement of policies that all the agency heads had agreed on, including DEA, FBI, Customs, Secret Service, and ATF.

On the surface Resolution 18 seemed to address several issues created by the T.E. program. For one thing, it required federal agencies, including the FBI, to take into account whether a criminal "is reasonably believed to pose a danger to the public or other criminal threat, or is reasonably believed to pose a risk of flight" before they could be used as a confidential informant. It also introduced a caveat about confidentiality, which said that while the government "will strive to protect a Confidential Informant's identity," federal officials "cannot guarantee that it will not be divulged." Resolution 18 also seemed to address the interagency problems and the dilemma surrounding the usually bogus "closing" of informants. It required coordination of informant activities in joint investigations and, when an informant was closed, written documentation "witnessed by at least two law enforcement officials" that the informant had been told of the termination.

A close reading of Resolution 18, however, revealed yet another Holland Tunnel–size loophole which guaranteed that informants who were motivated by something other than money would not be affected by any new, stricter rules. A new category of informants was created, called "Sources of Information," for those who were not paid for their services or who were paid below a specified (and secret) yearly amount. While some T.E.'s, like Greg Scarpa in New York, were paid, many others—like Whitey Bulger, Steve Flemmi, and Sonny Mercurio—were not. They were primarily interested in the FBI's protection for their own moneymaking enterprises.

"Sources of Information are not covered by this policy," Resolution 18 states.[27]

Also, despite Freeh's statement that the T.E. program was "no longer part of our routine and operation," documents released during the *U.S.* v. *Salemme* case show that it was still on the FBI's books in mid-1997—well after Resolution 18 was adopted. Indeed, almost exactly a year before Freeh's press conference, U.S. Attorney Donald K. Stern announced that, at his request, the Justice Department would again be reviewing all informant guidelines, *particularly* the Top Echelon program.

---

[27]The FBI was typically reluctant to part with the text of Resolution 18. Although representatives of the Boston FBI's Public Affairs office attended the 1999 press conference where Freeh stated that it was a public document and available to the press, Boston FBI spokeswoman Gail Marcinkiewicz later refused to provide the author with a copy, saying that the Boston office had, in effect, overruled the director. The author finally obtained a copy of Resolution 18 from the Public Affairs office of the Justice Department in Washington, D.C., who ruled that, as a policy document, it was clearly public.

"Whatever the ultimate outcome of the motions pending before Judge Wolf," Stern said, "there are important lessons regarding the handling of informants which must be and are being addressed. Without doubt, administrative and supervisory controls by the FBI need to be carefully reviewed. Other important changes will no doubt result from a comprehensive review of the existing informant guidelines, a process which has already begun at the FBI and the Department of Justice. The rubber hits the road most often in the T.E. program."

At Stern's request, Janet Reno ordered another, more comprehensive review of the informant guidelines in the summer of 1998, headed by Stern himself and fellow U.S. Attorney Mary Jo White from Manhattan. Over the next eighteen months an ad hoc group of about a dozen lawyers from the Justice Department and various law enforcement agencies held meetings and videoconferences to hammer out proposed changes.

Some of the proposals represented a radical departure from decades of past practice, particularly when it came to the FBI's autonomy to operate its own sources. Perhaps the most controversial idea—at least from a Bureau standpoint—was to give Justice Department prosecutors more oversight of both FBI agents and the informants involved in their cases, a clear challenge to the FBI's traditional independence. The group was also working on "avoiding long-term relationships" between the FBI and informants like Bulger and Flemmi, one official said. One proposed solution was the introduction of a so-called "sunset provision" into the informant relationship, which would ensure that, after a period of, say, two years, contact with an informant would automatically end unless there was a compelling reason to continue using them.

The Stern review appeared to be the best chance for fundamental change in the way the FBI and other agencies handle informants. At least one high-ranking Justice Department official, though, said that after two years without any concrete plan, concern was growing that the urgency created by the Bulger-Flemmi fiasco would be lost with the passing of the Clinton administration and Reno's tenure as Attorney General.

Other aspects of the case were similarly up in the air as the new century began.

The further hearings ordered by Judge Mark Wolf in the *Salemme* case were postponed indefinitely when Assistant U.S. Attorneys James Herbert, Brian Kelly, and Fred Wyshak appealed Wolf's order to the First Circuit Court of Appeals. Wolf was wrong, the prosecutors argued, in finding that Flemmi's promise of confidentiality from the FBI entitled him to "use immunity" rather than more limited "transactional immunity." Transactional immunity meant the government's evidence against Flemmi could not include the wiretaps he helped them obtain. "Use" immunity was much broader—it meant that the government couldn't use any evidence that was in any way connected from the wiretaps, such as Johnny Martorano's testimony. The judge's ruling was too broad, the prosecution said, especially given Flemmi's questionable performance on the witness stand.

"The district court clearly erred in finding that the FBI agents offered defendant use immunity," the prosecutors argued. "The district court's finding rests on belated, inconsistent, and inherently implausible testimony from a lifelong organized criminal concerning events in the distant past. It cannot be sustained."

The prosecutors also argued that the FBI had no power to make an enforceable promise of confidentiality without approval from prosecutors in the Justice Department.

After months of watching his client take it on the chin in the papers, Flemmi's lawyer, Ken Fishman, got a small measure of symbolic satisfaction filing a motion for sanctions against the government. Leaks to the press from the Johnny Martorano and Kevin Weeks cooperation deals, and stories about the Wheeler, Callahan, Halloran, Barrett,

McIntyre, and Hussey murders, Fishman argued, had made it impossible for his client to get a fair trial.

Fishman's motion stated: "This unabashed, premeditated, and highly orchestrated media campaign is clearly designed to irreparably prejudice the defendant Flemmi, and his code-fendant John Connolly, so as to deprive him of any opportunity to ultimately obtain a fair trial by an unbiased jury, or to have pretrial proceedings in this Court and the United States Court of Appeals for the First Circuit heard by judges who have not been exposed to damning but unproven and un-charged allegations of murder, cover-up, obstruction of justice, and even unlawful sexual relations. It is further submitted that the government's media blitz is designed to help persuade other individuals to offer their cooperation against Flemmi."

"Fishman's just trying to distract us so we can't indict his client for murder," prosecutor Brian Kelly snapped during one hearing on the motion. Wolf ultimately ruled that no sanctions were warranted.

Michael Natola, a mustachioed, Harley-Davidson-riding lawyer from the North Shore best known for riding with—and defending—the Hell's Angels, was appointed by the court to represent Flemmi in the racketeering case against Connolly and the two T.E. informants. "You don't need a crystal ball to figure out where their investigation is going. There will be a superseding indictment and it will involve allegations of homicides," Natola told the *Boston Herald* after a pretrial hearing in the case.

The arguments in the government's appeal were ominous for John Connolly. The agreement between the informants and the FBI, the government argued, was not official policy or standard operating procedure under the Top Echelon Informant Program, but a "backroom understanding" between Connolly, Morris, and Flemmi not authorized by the Justice Department. "By the early 1980s, this unorthodox relationship had degenerated into outright corruption," the appeal stated.

Also, for the first time, the federal government finally agreed with the defense lawyers, cops, and other FBI critics who had long believed that Brian Halloran was betrayed by the FBI.

"When informed of [Halloran's] allegations, Morris opined that Halloran was untrustworthy and unstable. Morris then told Connolly about Halloran's allegations, and Connolly passed the information on to Bulger and Flemmi."

Connolly eventually retired from his job at Boston Edison and ended up spending much of his time on spin control. He vowed to take the case to trial and told many of his old FBI organized crime investigator friends that the case was "no big deal" and "a bunch of bullshit."

He also offered a defense on *Dateline NBC*. In an interview taped before his indictment, Connolly called the Guild Street induction ceremony wiretap his "greatest victory" and took credit for imprisoning "forty-two members and associates" of the New England Mafia. He made it clear he was going to take the position that his treatment of Bulger and Flemmi *was* standard procedure under the Top Echelon program.

Connolly wore one of his trademark, impeccably tailored blue suits and his best defiant attitude for the interview, but some of his trademark swagger appeared to have deserted him. He swore that he was just following the priorities set by the Justice Department and the FBI by brokering the alliance with Flemmi and Bulger, who he admitted were "probably more dangerous than the Mafia."

"But they weren't organized. They didn't pose the same threat as the Mafia, that's why the FBI wasn't as interested in them," he told *Dateline* correspondent Dennis Murphy in a segment that aired the day before St. Patrick's Day, 2000. "We won the war. We eviscerated the mob around here. They're in tatters." Connolly denied ever tipping off Bulger and Flemmi to the 1995 indictment, though, and ripped Wolf's opinion as an exercise in speculation and Monday morning quarterbacking.

"The judge has obviously never developed a Top Echelon criminal informant and he's never destroyed a Mafia family, and it's easy for him to sit back and speculate about what the right and wrong is twenty years later. Agents of the FBI had the authority to allow their informants to participate in criminal activity. I did the job that I was told and authorized to do by my superiors. These were priorities that were set on Pennsylvania Avenue by the Department of Justice and the FBI. John Connolly just did his job.

"You have to understand the business that I was in. I was in the murder and mayhem business. When I was developing a Top Echelon informant, by the very definition of the program, I was developing a murderer. Do I know what murders they committed? You suspect. But it was never confirmed, and you never discussed it with those guys."

In a perfunctory, 31-page decision issued September 11, 2000, the U.S. First Circuit Court of Appeals overturned the essence of Wolf's 661-page ruling in the *Salemme* case. A three-justice panel of the Boston-based court held that, no matter what agents may have promised Flemmi, the FBI had no power to grant him anything that resembled immunity from prosecution. The appeals-court strategy employed by Wyshak, Kelly and Herbert during the hearings had paid off—the First Circuit agreed with their argument that only prosecutors had the power to confer immunity.

The ruling was a huge blow for Flemmi and Salemme. There would be no further hearings, and the original racketeering charges would stand. Flemmi and Fishman began mulling whether to appeal to the U.S. Supreme Court.

Frank Salemme decided to get out.

Donna Salemme woke up at five A.M. on a cool, windy New England day and meditated for about an hour to calm her nerves. She had given up teaching aerobics and was nearly through three hundred hours of required studying to be a yoga instructor. A few months earlier an unidentified male caller somehow found her unlisted cellular phone number and had been making vaguely threatening calls. She found solace in her early morning meditation. "At times like these, you have to have something like that," she said, staring out at Boston Harbor through the huge, nine-story glass wall of the new U.S. District Courthouse.

There were a lot of changes going on in the Salemme family. Frank, the Last Stand-up Guy, had already broken his vow of *omerta* and testified before the grand jury about being tipped off by John Connolly. Once a certified true believer in the Mafia's code of honor, he was telling friends that even the thought of the rat-infested underworld made him sick. As he was led into Wolf's oak-paneled courtroom by a team of U.S. Marshals, he was preparing to turn his back on the Mafia for good.

Under the terms of Salemme's plea agreement, Wolf had to impose a sentence between a minimum of ten years and six months and a maximum of twelve years and eight months, and both sides were free to argue for either the high or the low end. Tony Cardinale did something he had never done before in his career as a defense lawyer. Citing the FBI's role in the 1989 attempt on his client's life, he *demanded* that Wolf sentence Salemme to the least number of months possible.

Cadillac Frank, he said, was still suffering the effects of the 1989 attempt on his life. There were bullet fragments still in his body, he suffered poor circulation, a painful lump in the area where he was shot, and recurring swelling in the leg and abdomen. The near assassination, he said, was "carried out by a Top Echelon informant, Sonny Mercurio." The FBI not only knew of the danger and failed to warn him, but had purposefully leaked inflammatory information to the *Herald*.

"That action is about as evil as it gets," the attorney said. "It alleviated the need to go after Mr. Salemme, and it would make them look like heroes to go after the men who shot him. It was as simple as that, as sick as that, and as evil as that."

Brian Kelly called Cardinale's allegations too much.

"Mr. Cardinale is becoming the Oliver Stone of the defense bar," the prosecutor told the judge. "There is no evidence that this was an FBI plot. We don't know if [Salemme's would-be assassins] read the *Herald* or if they even know how to read. Although it may be fashionable to bash the FBI for everything, they are not responsible for this."

Donna Salemme clenched her hands together tightly as her husband, wearing one of his well-tailored dark gray suits, a white shirt, and a maroon tie, stood up and made a short speech to Wolf. His days in the underworld, he said, were over—he had found there was no honor either among thieves or among his FBI adversaries.

"I learned my lesson," he told the judge. "I know now what the government is capable of. And for thirty-five years, my best friend betrayed me. Shame on me if that happens again."

Wolf sentenced Salemme to eleven years and four months in prison. With time he had already served, Salemme would be behind bars for another six years. On the day of his projected release in November 2006, he would be almost seventy-two years old. Wolf said he believed that Salemme was capable of following the rules of society if he put his mind to it, but gave no hint that he was cutting him any slack because of the FBI's misconduct. Wolf, in fact, never mention the FBI in his brief remarks to Salemme at all.

"I would expect you would be sick and tired of your criminal colleagues," the judge said instead. "To get involved with them again would not just be wrong, it would be dumb."

Progress in the murder cases was slow. Even though Kevin Weeks's plea deal represented a breakthrough, two years after Johnny Martorano's dramatic turnaround, none of the murders the two men alleged Bulger and Flemmi ordered or participated in had resulted in charges in Massachusetts, Oklahoma, Florida, or anywhere else. The deliberate, some said glacial, progress shouldn't have been a surprise to anyone familiar with the deal, given the difficulty of getting it off the ground in the first place.

The deal had originally been struck between Martorano and the State Police–DEA team, troopers Tom Foley and Steve Johnson and agent Dan Doherty. When Martorano first started opting out of coming to court for the pretrial hearings, it was ironically his codefendants who readily accepted his explanation that he just "didn't like riding in the van" for nearly an hour every day from the jail in Plymouth. The investigators, though, thought they detected an increasing level of disgust in the bearish hoodlum. They used their mutual disgust of Flemmi and Bulger to first connect with Martorano, then finally convince him to flip.

That was the easy part. The logistics of a twenty-murder, three-state plea deal were daunting; five different prosecutors with vastly different personalities and agendas had to sign off on a deal that looked better in some places than in others. To Suffolk County District Attorney Ralph Martin, it was attractive, a chance to close the books on a big pile of dusty cases that would surely never be solved anyway, finally giving the victims' relatives some measure of peace. To officials in Miami, though, agreeing to short prison time for a man who killed more people than Charles Manson and Richard Speck combined in exchange for one unsolved murder (World Jai Alai's John Callahan) didn't seem like such a hot idea, exposing them as it did to allegations of being soft on crime. After months of talks, though, consensus began to coalesce around a figure of twelve and a half years in prison for Martorano's full cooperation, with the exception of Stern and officials in Miami, who wanted fifteen years. The deal was nearly stillborn, however, thanks to the well-honed animosity between the State Police–DEA team and the FBI.

Justice Department officials, including Janet Reno, had seen the first FBI Office of Professional Responsibility for what it was—at best, superficial and flawed, at worst, a deliberate attempt by the FBI to whitewash over the tip-offs and corruption and murder rampant among them. But Reno's choice of John Durham, the Deputy U.S. Attorney from Hartford, Connecticut, to lead a second investigation struck many as disturbing. After all, the biggest case of Durham's career had been the prosecution of Nicholas Bianco—a prosecution in which he worked closely with the Boston FBI's Organized Crime Squad and which had benefited from Bulger and Flemmi's work as informants. And again, Durham's investigators were FBI agents, this time under the supervision of Inspector Gary Bald, a veteran agent from Washington.

As Durham and Bald's investigation, based out of a nondescript office building two blocks from the Boston FBI office, progressed, their seeming earnestness to actually find the truth actually began to win over even a few die-hard doubters. Stories circulated that Boston agents' bank records were being scrutinized, and that John Connolly's home contractor, even his barber, had been interviewed. Even Cardinale, the ultimate skeptic, came away impressed after a meeting with Bald. "The FBI guys in Boston were a bunch of clowns. This guy Bald is the real deal," he said. Mike Huff and Jerry Truster, the Assistant District Attorney from Tulsa who had taken over the Wheeler case, and also began cautiously putting some faith in Durham's sincerity.

The State Police–DEA team, however, remained vehemently anti-FBI and anti-Durham, and refused to share any information. Unfortunately, this was news to Truster and Huff, who considered former agent H. Paul Rico a suspect in their case and hoped that a bona fide investigation of the Boston FBI office might uncover some evidence that would be useful to corroborate what Martorano was saying. In Boston for a briefing with U.S. Attorney Donald Stern, they brought along Durham and one of Bald's agents, Tim O'Rourke, only to meet with icy stares from the troopers and drug agents. Wyshak told O'Rourke to leave.

Attempts to ease the tension over a few beers at Jimbo's Fish Shanty, a bar just a few yards from the spot where Brian Halloran and Michael Donahue were gunned down, only resulted in things getting worse. Foley and Huff nearly came to blows when an angry Foley accused his counterpart from

Oklahoma—whose attempts to solve the Wheeler murder
had been frustrated by FBI intransigence for eighteen years
and who had once lugged sixty pounds of investigative documents to Boston to share them with the State Police—of
"being in bed" with the Bureau and "fucking up the case."
Even when the case had been at its most frustrating, on some
level Huff had always enjoyed coming to Massachusetts; his
great-grandfather, who owned the only authentic Irish pub in
Tulsa, had emigrated from Ireland through Boston Harbor
before heading west for the Land Rush. Yet when he flew
back to Oklahoma after the meeting, he was ready to turn his
back on Massachusetts for good—the very thought of the
city and anything Irish was making him sick. Only his
friendship to Larry and David Wheeler kept Huff from aban-
doning the case altogether.

With tensions threatening to kill the deal, Truster convened a prosecutors-only meeting in Tulsa a month later,
taking Wyshak, Herbert, and Durham out for lunch at Cot-
ton Eye Joe's, a rustic Tulsa joint where they serve the barbecue on waxed paper. After a semisymbolic visit to the Will
Rogers Memorial, he urged them all to work together. "I
said I always thought that law enforcement needed to be a
team thing, and the good guys should be sharing information. We were the good guys, and the egos need to be removed from the equation." The Martorano plea deal was
back on track, all the parties finally settled on 12½ years.

Finally, the officials in Tulsa had the shooter in the
Wheeler case. Jerry Truster, unfortunately, wouldn't stay
around for the final push to an indictment, thanks to the
same internal politics that he had just kept from derailing the
Martorano deal. After the Tulsa meeting, the last major hur-
dle was to get Miami and have Mary Cagle, the Metro-Dade
prosecutor in charge of the case, sign off on it. Truster and
Huff also scheduled meetings with several potential witnesses in the Martorano case over a long weekend and purchased nonrefundable tickets for the trip. On the Friday
afternoon before they were to leave, a secretary dropped a

memo on his desk—it was from his boss, District Attorney Tim Harris, instructing him to cancel his trip so he could cover the office while Harris was away at a conference. Truster blew up. There were plenty of lawyers in the office who were perfectly capable of covering the one workday, Monday, he planned to be away. With Harris already on a plane out of town and unavailable, Truster just went to Miami anyway, where Cagle signed off on the deal.

When he got back, he learned that Harris's top assistant, Sharon Ashe, had "inventoried" his office while he was away—as if they were getting ready to push him out and were afraid he would steal something. Truster, Harris, and Ashe had never seen things eye-to-eye, but now the situation was clearly untenable, so he decided to leave the office and offered to stay on as a special prosecutor—after all, he had been there for the Martorano debriefings and knew the complex case better than anyone, with the exception of Mike Huff.

Harris simply ignored the Truster's offer. Truster had saved the Wheeler case, but it was assigned to another prosecutor, who had to start learning it from scratch.

The murder investigations finally culminated in September 2000. In a sweeping federal indictment, Wyshak, Kelly and Herbert charged Bulger and Flemmi with eighteen murders that they either ordered or committed themselves. A month later, the prosecutors added new charges to their case against John Connolly, alleging he leaked information to his informants that resulted in the deaths of Brian Halloran, John Callahan and bookmaker Richard Castucci.

Five months later, state prosecutors in Oklahoma and Florida filed murder charges against Flemmi, Bulger and Martorano. Tulsa District Attorney Tim Harris announced he would seek the death penalty against Bulger and Flemmi. That news, however, provided little consolation to Larry and David Wheeler, who critized Harris for overruling Sergeant Mike Huff and the Tulsa Police Department, who had recommended that H. Paul Rico also be charged in the case.

On February 25, 2001, Debra Davis's family sued Bulger, Flemmi, Kevin Weeks and Kevin O'Neill for $30 million and made a move to grab the proceeds of Whitey Bulger's lottery winnings. Within weeks, relatives of Michael Donahue, the luckless friend of Brian Halloran, John McIntyre and Michael Milano, the bartender killed in a case of mistaken identity, followed suit. The $36 million Donahue suit and the $50 million McIntyre suit also named Connolly, Morris and other FBI agents as defendants.

An alarmed Bob Fitzpatrick found his name among the agents listed, despite his attempts to kick Bulger and Flemmi out of the Top Echelon program in the early 1980s. The McIntyre suit, he thought, was a particularly cruel irony. He had resigned from the Bureau in 1986, well short of his full pension, after a controversy over a shooting incident involving several agents under his supervision on Cape Cod. His boss, SAC Jim Greenleaf, filed formal charges with headquarters against Fitzpatrick, claiming that he had botched the internal investigation. Fitzpatrick struck back, charging that the charges were a setup and that he was being punished for pushing the McIntyre leak issue too aggressively.

Fitzpatrick knew he was a marked man. Believing the stress of the internal wars within the FBI and the charges and countercharges had contributed to his wife's miscarriage, he left the FBI to found his own private investigation firm after the Bureau agreed to wipe his file clean of Greenleaf's allegations. Years later, Fitzpatrick filed his own claim with the U.S. Merit Systems Protection Board, charging that he had been railroaded out of the Bureau and demanding to have his pension fully funded.

The Durham probe was still ongoing at the time of this writing. While only John Connolly had been indicted, dozens of current and former agents were interviewed or called in front of Durham's grand jury, including Nick Gianturco, Tom Daly, Mike Buckley, Dennis O'Callaghan, Ed Quinn, Ed Clark, and John Newton. Newton, who prosecutors accused of lying to protect Connolly by saying he was told about Morris's "do anything you want short of clipping anyone" in 1995, was put on notice that the Bureau intended to fire him. He filed an administrative appeal.

Coinciding with Freeh's August 1999 visit and mea culpa press conference, the Boston C-3 Organized Crime Squad was completely revamped. John Gamel, the supervisor, was given other non-Mafia duties, as were most of the agents. Other personnel moves in the wake of the hearings, however, appeared somewhat questionable. Charles Prouty and William Chase, agents from the first "see no evil" FBI OPR team, were promoted to SAC and ASAC, respectively, of the Boston office. During the height of the hearings in the spring of 1998, Chase had pulled the author aside in the hallway of the old federal courthouse. "This case isn't what you think. There's nothing here," he said. In early April 2000, Barry Mawn, the SAC who shepherded the Boston office through the Bulger-Flemmi crisis, was promoted to Assistant Director in Charge of the FBI's New York field office.

The Whitey Bulger fugitive investigation remained in the FBI's hands. With few independent leads, it consisted mostly of finally putting Bulger on the Top Ten Most Wanted list (next to terrorist Usama bin Laden) and feeding the information to *America's Most Wanted* in the hope that one of the show's viewers would spot him or Catherine Grieg, his bottle-blond traveling companion. A segment on Whitey that aired in February 2000 produced numerous tips, including one from a hairdresser in Fountain Valley, California, who said a woman who looked like Grieg had come in for a color touch-up while her "husband" waited in the car. Sources close to the investigation, though, said the local FBI office issued a press release on the sighting before consulting the Boston-based fugitive squad, which probably allowed Bulger and Grieg enough warning to escape yet again.

As one of her last official acts before leaving office, Attorney General Janet Reno authorized sweeping changes in the Justice Department's informant guidelines, including the abolition—in name at least—of the Top Echelon Informant Program.

The changes were proposed by a group of federal prosecutors who worked for two years, studying the existing guidelines, gathering input from various experts on them—including the author, who was honored to participate in the process—and negotiating with representatives of the FBI, the DEA, the U.S. Marshals Service, and the other investigative agencies under the Justice Department. The two chief architects of the changes were Assistant U.S. Attorney James D. Herbert of U.S. Attorney Donald K. Stern's office and Jonathan Schwartz, a Justice Department prosecutor and law enforcement policy expert in Washington. Reno also credited Stern with pushing for the changes before both of them left office in January 2001.

Overall, the fact that any changes were made at all was remarkable—especially given the resistance from the FBI and in some other quarters of the Justice Department—and it showed the deep impact that the Boston FBI scandal had on officials in Washington. Yet two aspects of the new Department of Justice Guidelines Regarding the Use of Confidential Informants were truly extraordinary.

For the first time, the traditional wall that had separated the FBI and its informant programs from scrutiny by Justice Department lawyers was, at least to an extent, knocked down in favor of new checks and balances on the use of high-powered criminals as informants. "There was a historic mindset that there was a bright line in the sand between the Justice Department and the investigative agencies and we broke through that, and that is the most significant difference," Don Stern said in an interview with the author after the new guidelines were made public.

The forty-seven-page document dropped the term "Top Echelon informant" in favor of "High Level Confidential Informant," defined as a criminal who is part of the "senior leadership of an enterprise that has a national or international sphere of influence" or of a regional group that has "high significance" to a particular agency like the DEA or the FBI. High Level informants were also classified as criminals who committed acts of violence, attempted to corrupt public officials, trafficked in large quantities of drugs, stole more than $1.5 million, or helped other criminals do so.

For the first time, the guidelines required the FBI to receive approval in advance from a three-person committee, consisting of one FBI official and two Justice Department lawyers, before accepting a high-level informant. Such informants, in the future, would also receive a review every six years by the same committee, forcing the agency to justify keeping the criminal as an informant rather than targeting them. The idea, Stern said, was to avoid secret, long-term informant relationships like the ones the Boston FBI office had with Whitey Bulger and Steve Flemmi.

That was the other remarkable thing about the new guidelines: the changes closely tracked the problems that surfaced during the Boston FBI scandal, showing that Justice Department officials in Washington also viewed the Bulger-Flemmi affair as the perfect case study for what was wrong with the FBI, the Top Echelon Informant Program and the Levi-Civiletti guidelines. While the authors of the new guidelines said other T.E. informant cases—particularly Gregory Scarpa and Jackie Presser—were taken into account, the Boston case most clearly illustrated the problems and provided prosecutors with the ammunition to fix them.

"It helped that there were a lot of specific examples of the problems with the previous guidelines. I think it is fair to say that when we raised these issues with the agencies and the Attorney General we were not talking in hypotheticals but talking about specific situations that had actually occurred and needed to be avoided in the future," Stern said.

The new guidelines, for example, closed numerous loopholes in the old ones. For one thing, they finally did the obvious and defined mob-connected bookmaking as a crime of violence, eliminating the key excuses that the FBI had used to keep from reporting Bulger and Flemmi's activity to the

Justice Department. Just to be safe, the new rules also imposed a general "duty of candor" on agents, requiring them to be forthright and candid when the guidelines forced them to reveal information about their informants.

Specifically, the new rules expressly forbade agents from sharing information with their sources about investigations—an obvious reference to the tip-offs Bulger, Flemmi, Sonny Mercurio, and others received about investigations and indictments—and about the identities of other informants, à la the Brian Halloran murder. Obviously bearing in mind the dinners and gifts given and accepted by Morris, Connolly, Gianturco, and others, the new guidelines also forbade gratuities and fraternization. The Reno guidelines also expressly prohibited the FBI's practice of disingenuously listing informants as targets of Title III electronic surveillance investigations, which had been used by the Boston FBI office and the New England Organized Crime Strike Force to hide Bulger and Flemmi's identities.

Perhaps most significantly, however, the Reno guidelines for the first time forced the agencies to curb the career and salary incentives, which for so long had encouraged agents to recruit and keep sources at all costs and made unscrupulous informant handlers like John Connolly the power brokers in their field offices. By May 2001 all the investigative agencies under the Justice Department were required to submit an employee-evaluation plan to the Attorney General's office that would reward agents for following the rules, not breaking them.

In the author's estimation, however, the new rules, which the Justice Department authors candidly admitted were a compromise, did not go far enough. Although requiring prior approval for High Level informants, periodic reviews and better oversight from outside FBI and other agencies, the Reno guidelines still kept the same dangerous balancing test. There is still no point at which a criminal's actions are so bad, his crimes so heinous, that it will automatically outweigh any information he might give. It is a dangerous piece of wiggle room that, given the secrecy that will inevitably descend back over the federal informant programs, could pave the way for more abuses in the future.

Many current and former FBI officials, including Freeh, insist that today's FBI is a far different animal than it was even during the 1980s and early 1990s—more open, more accountable, and more willing to admit mistakes in the wake of disasters like Waco and Ruby Ridge. The Top Echelon program, they say, was a necessary part of winning the war on the Mafia, but is now a historic relic. Others, though, caution that with other groups such as the Russian mob moving to fill the void left by a weakened Italian-American Mafia, there will always be an effort by the FBI to develop dangerous informants with top-level information.

"The reality is that you need informants," said Valerie Caproni, the former Assistant U.S. Attorney from Brooklyn who uncovered much of the FBI's wrongdoing in the handling of Top Echelon informant Greg Scarpa. "They make possible all sorts of other crucial law enforcement techniques, like wiretaps and electronic surveillance in places where criminal meetings are taking place. The only way you can do those things is through informants who are highly placed."

Thankfully, new rules are now in place that more tightly govern the FBI's use of dangerous criminals as informants. Those rules, however, still depend on human beings to honestly enforce them. It is the author's hope that the costly lessons of the Top Echelon program will not be soon forgotten by those who are trusted by the public to enforce our country's laws.

Glossary of Key Terms

·····························

Attorney General's Guidelines—a series of safeguards designed to prevent the abuse of informants, adopted by the Justice Department in the mid-1970s.

bug—hidden microphone, sometimes installed with a court order, sometimes illegally, designed to capture incriminating conversations between criminals.

cooperating witness—criminal or civilian who has agreed to work in an undercover capacity with law enforcement officials and prosecutors, often in exchange for leniency on criminal charges and/or entry into Witness Protection Program.

electronic surveillance—catchall term for the use of hidden microphones and telephone monitoring equipment to eavesdrop on conversations.

FD-209—FBI secret report of meetings between agents and informants; most FBI agents had confidence that their "209s" would never be seen outside the Bureau.

informant—FBI term for long-term, secret source of intelligence on street-level criminal activity whose identity is closely protected; often incorrectly used for anyone cooperating with the government. (*See* cooperating witness.)

RICO—acronym for Racketeer Influenced and Corrupt Organizations Act, a 1970 law that for the first time allowed criminal groups to be prosecuted for not just individual crimes, but a "pattern" of racketeering activity.

Title III—federal law legalizing court-ordered electronic surveillance and the use of taped conversations as evidence in criminal court cases; required law enforcement agencies to submit affidavits showing probable cause to believe criminal conversations were likely to take place in a given location or between certain people.

Top Echelon Informant Program—secret FBI plan to recruit high-ranking members of organized crime as informants for the FBI's war on the Italian-American Mafia.

wire—hidden microphone worn by cooperating witnesses or undercover agents (not informants) attached either to a radio transmitter or a small tape recorder hidden on the body.

wiretap—eavesdropping equipment secretly attached to a telephone line enabling law enforcement officials to capture incriminating conversations between criminals.

Partial List of Sources

....

Foreword

Source interviews; FBI reports; court testimony, court documents.

Chapter One

FBI reports; Boston Police reports; source interviews; newspaper accounts; *Hoover's FBI: The Inside Story by Hoover's Trusted Lieutenant,* Cartha D. DeLoach.

Chapter Two

FBI reports; source interviews; court testimony; newspaper accounts; *Manual of Instructions,* Federal Bureau of Investigation; *Manual of Investigative and Operational Guidelines,* Federal Bureau of Investigation; *Intelligence Activities: FBI,* Senate Select Committee to Study Governmental Operations with Respect to Intelligence Activities; *The Enemy Within: The McClellan Committee's Crusade Against Jimmy Hoffa and Corrupt Labor Unions,* Robert F. Kennedy; *With Honor and Purpose: An Ex-FBI Investigator Reports from the Front Lines of Crime,* Phil Kerby; *The FBI: Inside the World's Most Powerful Law Enforcement Agency,* Ronald Kessler; *The Secret Life of J. Edgar Hoover,* Anthony Summers; several books by William F. Roemer Jr.

Chapter Three

FBI reports; source interviews; court testimony; newspaper accounts; *Barboza,* Joseph Barboza and Hank Messick; *The Bureau,* William C. Sullivan.

Chapter Four

FBI reports; numerous source interviews; court testimony; newspaper accounts; *The Boston Irish,* Thomas H. O'Connor; *While the Music Lasts: My Life in Politics,* William M. Bulger; *America's Most Wanted,* Fox Television.

Chapter Five

FBI reports; source interviews; court testimony; newspaper accounts; *Mobbed Up,* James Neff; *Brick Agent,* Anthony Villano; *Hoover's FBI: The Inside Story by Hoover's Trusted Lieutenant,* Cartha D. DeLoach; *The Enemy Within: The McClellan Committee's Crusade Against Jimmy Hoffa and Corrupt Labor Unions,* Robert F. Kennedy; several books by William F. Roemer Jr.

Chapter Six

FBI and DEA reports; Belmont Police report; source interviews; court testimony; newspaper accounts.

Chapter Seven

FBI and DEA reports; Boston Police reports; source interviews; court testimony; federal and state court filings; newspaper accounts; *Valhallah's Wake,* John Loftus and Emily McIntyre.

Chapter Eight

FBI and DEA reports; source interviews; court testimony; court documents; *Manual of Investigative and Operational Guidelines,* Federal Bureau of Investigation; newspaper accounts, including the *Boston Herald; The Ceremony,* Joseph Pistone; *Gangland: How the FBI Broke the Mob,* Howard Blum.

Chapter Nine

FBI reports; state and federal court filings; Middlesex County (Mass.) Probate Court documents; source interviews; court testimony.

Chapter Ten

FBI reports; state and federal court filings; source interviews; court testimony.

Epilogue

Resolution 18, U.S. Department of Justice Office of Investigative Agency Policy; source interviews; court testimony; press conference at the Boston FBI office.

Select Bibliography

••••••••••••••••••••••••••••••

Barboza, Joseph and Messick, Hank, *Barboza* (Dell, 1975).

Behn, Noel, *Big Stick-Up at Brinks!* (Putnam, 1977).

Blum, Howard, *Gangland: How the FBI Broke the Mob* (Pocket Books, 1993).

Blumenthal, Ralph, *Last Days of the Sicilians: The FBI's War Against the Mafia* (Pocket Books, 1988).

Bonavolonta, Jules and Duffy, Brian, *The Good Guys* (Pocket Books, 1996).

Bulger, William M., *While the Music Lasts: My Life in Politics* (Faber and Faber, 1996).

Cox, Donald, *Mafia Wipeout: How the Feds Put Away an Entire Mob Family* (SPI Books, 1992).

DeLoach, Cartha, D., *Hoover's FBI: The Inside Story by Hoover's Trusted Lieutenant* (Regnery Publishing Inc., 1995).

Demaris, Ovid, *The Last Mafioso: "Jimmy the Weasel" Fratianno* (Bantam Books, 1981).

Giancana, Sam and Giancana, Chuck, *Double Cross: The Explosive, Inside Story of the Mobster Who Controlled America* (Warner Books, 1992).

Goddard, Donald, *The Insider: The FBI's Undercover Wiseguy Goes Public* (Pocket Books, 1992).

Goldfarb, Ronald, *Perfect Villains, Imperfect Heroes: Robert F. Kennedy's War Against Organized Crime* (Random House, 1995).

Kelly, John F. and Wearne, Phillip K., *Tainting Evidence: Inside the Scandals at the FBI Crime Lab* (Free Press, 1998).

Kennedy, Robert F., *The Enemy Within: The McClellan Committee's Crusade Against Jimmy Hoffa and Corrupt Labor Unions* (Da Capo Press, 1960).

Kerby, Phil, *With Honor and Purpose: An Ex-FBI Investigator Reports from the Front Lines of Crime* (St. Martin's Press, 1998).

Kessler, Ronald, *The FBI: Inside the World's Most Powerful Law Enforcement Agency* (Pocket Books, 1993).

Loftus, John and McIntyre, Emily, *Valhallah's Wake* (Atlantic Monthly Press, 1989).

Maas, Peter, *Underboss: Sammy the Bull Gravano's Story of Life in the Mafia* (HarperCollins, 1997).

Mangione, Jerre and Morreale, Ben, *La Storia: Five Centuries of the Italian American Experience* (Harper Collins, 1992).

Neff, James, *Mobbed Up: Jackie Presser's High-Wire Life in the Teamsters, the Mafia and the FBI* (Atlantic Monthly Press, 1989).

O'Brien, Joseph F. and Kurins, Andris, *Boss of Bosses: The FBI and Paul Castellano* (Island Books, 1991).

O'Connor, Thomas, *The Boston Irish* (Back Bay Books, 1995).

O'Keefe, Specs and Considine, Bob, *The Men Who Robbed Brinks* (Random House, 1961).

O'Neill, Gerard and Lehr, Dick, *The Underboss* (St. Martin's Press, 1989).

Pistone, Joseph, *Donnie Brasco* (Signet, 1989).

Pistone, Joseph, *The Ceremony* (Dell, 1992).

Roemer, William F. Jr., *Accardo: The Genuine Godfather* (Ivy Books, 1995).

Roemer, William F. Jr., *Roemer: Man Against the Mob* (Ivy Books, 1989).

Roemer, William F. Jr., *The Enforcer* (Ivy Books, 1994).

Roemer, William F. Jr., *War of the Godfathers* (Ivy Books, 1990).

Summers, Anthony, *The Secret Life of J. Edgar Hoover* (Pocket Books, 1994).

Swearingen, M. Wesley, *FBI Secrets: An Agent's Exposé* (South End Press, 1995).

Theresa, Vincent, *My Life in the Mafia* (Doubleday, 1973).

Theoharris, Athan, *From the Secret Files of J. Edgar Hoover* (Elephant Paperbacks, 1993).

Unger, Robert, *The Union Station Massacre: The Original Sin of J. Edgar Hoover's FBI* (Andrews & McMeel, 1997).

U.S. Senate, Committee on the Judiciary *Racketeer Influenced and Corrupt Organizations Act* (U.S. Government Printing Office, 1989).

U.S. Senate, Select Committee to Study Governmental Operations with Respect to Intelligence Activities, volume 6, *Intelligence Activities: FBI* (U.S. Government Printing Office, 1975).

Villano, Anthony, *Brick Agent* (Ballantine Books, 1977).

Volkman, Ernest, *Gangbusters* (Faber and Faber, 1998).

Compelling True Crime Thrillers

PERFECT MURDER, PERFECT TOWN
THE UNCENSORED STORY OF THE JONBENET MURDER
AND THE GRAND JURY'S SEARCH FOR THE TRUTH
by Lawrence Schiller
0-06-109696-2/ $7.99 US/ $10.99 Can

A CALL FOR JUSTICE
A NEW ENGLAND TOWN'S FIGHT
TO KEEP A STONE COLD KILLER IN JAIL
by Denise Lang
0-380-78077-1/ $6.50 US/ $8.99 Can

SECRETS NEVER LIE
THE DEATH OF SARA TOKARS—
A SOUTHERN TRAGEDY OF MONEY, MURDER,
AND INNOCENCE BETRAYED
by Robin McDonald
0-380-77752-5/ $6.99 US/ $8.99 Can

THE SUMMER WIND
THOMAS CAPANO AND THE MURDER
OF ANNE MARIE FAHEY
by George Anastasia
0-06-103100-3/ $6.99 US/ $9.99 Can

A WARRANT TO KILL
A TRUE STORY OF OBSESSION,
LIES AND A KILLER COP
by Kathryn Casey
0-380-78041-0/ $6.99 US/ $9.99 Can

DEADLY SECRETS
FROM HIGH SCHOOL TO HIGH CRIME—
THE TRUE STORY OF TWO TEEN KILLERS
by Reang Putsata
0-380-80087-X/ $6.99 US/ $9.99 Can